NARRATIVE AN
IN THE AI
GREEK N

The Greek romance was for the Roman period what epic was for the archaic period or drama for the classical: the central literary vehicle for articulating ideas about the relationship between self and community. This book offers a fresh reading of the romance both as a distinctive narrative form (using a range of narrative theories) and as a paradigmatic expression of identity (social, sexual and cultural). At the same time, it also emphasises the elasticity of romance narrative, its ability to accommodate both conservative and transformative models of identity. This elasticity manifests itself partly in the variation in practice between different romancers, some of whom are traditionally Hellenocentric and others more challenging; but ultimately, it is argued, it reflects a tension in all romance narrative, which characteristically balances centrifugal against centripetal dynamics. This book will interest classicists, historians of the novel, and students of narrative theory.

TIM WHITMARSH is a leading literary and cultural critic of the Greek world during the time of the Roman empire. A specialist in both ancient texts and modern theories, he has written over fifty articles and five books, including *Greek Literature and the Roman Empire* (2001) and *The Second Sophistic* (2005); he has also edited or co-edited four books, and edits two book series.

GREEK CULTURE IN THE ROMAN WORLD

Editors
SUSAN E. ALCOCK, Brown University
JAŚ ELSNER, Corpus Christi College, Oxford
SIMON GOLDHILL, University of Cambridge

The Greek culture of the Roman empire offers a rich field of study. Extraordinary insights can be gained into processes of multicultural contact and exchange, political and ideological conflict, and the creativity of a changing, polyglot empire. During this period, many fundamental elements of Western society were being set in place: from the rise of Christianity, to an influential system of education, to long-lived artistic canons. This series is the first to focus on the response of Greek culture to its Roman imperial setting as a significant phenomenon in its own right. To this end, it will publish original and innovative research in the art, archaeology, epigraphy, history, philosophy, religion, and literature of the empire, with an emphasis on Greek material.

Titles in series:

Athletics and Literature in the Roman Empire
Jason König

Describing Greece: Landscape and Literature in the Periegesis of Pausanias
William Hutton

Religious Identity in Late Antiquity: Greeks, Jews and Christians in Antioch
Isabella Sandwell

Hellenism in Byzantium: The Transformations of Greek Identity and the Reception of the Classical Tradition
Anthony Kaldellis

The Making of Roman India
Grant Parker

Philostratus
Edited by Ewen Bowie and Jaś Elsner

The Politics of Munificence in the Roman Empire: Citizens, Elites and Benefactors in Asia Minor
Arjan Zuiderhoek

Saints and Church Spaces in the Late Antique Mediterranean: Architecture, Cult, and Community
Ann Marie Yasin

Galen and the World of Knowledge
Edited by Christopher Gill, Tim Whitmarsh and John Wilkins

Local Knowledge and Microidentities in the Imperial Greek World
Edited by Tim Whitmarsh

Homer Between History and Fiction in Imperial Greek Literature
Laurence Kim

Epiphany and Representation in Graeco-Roman Culture: Art, Literature, Religion
Verity Platt

Narrative and Identity in the Ancient Greek Novel
Tim Whitmarsh

NARRATIVE AND IDENTITY IN THE ANCIENT GREEK NOVEL

Returning Romance

BY

TIM WHITMARSH

CAMBRIDGE UNIVERSITY PRESS

CAMBRIDGE
UNIVERSITY PRESS

University Printing House, Cambridge CB2 8BS, United Kingdom

Cambridge University Press is part of the University of Cambridge.

It furthers the University's mission by disseminating knowledge in the pursuit of education, learning and research at the highest international levels of excellence.

www.cambridge.org
Information on this title: www.cambridge.org/9781107491021

© Tim Whitmarsh 2011

This publication is in copyright. Subject to statutory exception and to the provisions of relevant collective licensing agreements, no reproduction of any part may take place without the written permission of Cambridge University Press.

First published 2011
First paperback edition 2015

A catalogue record for this publication is available from the British Library

Library of Congress Cataloguing in Publication data
Whitmarsh, Tim.
Narrative and identity in the ancient Greek novel : returning romance / Tim Whitmarsh.
  p. cm. – (Greek culture in the Roman world)
Includes bibliographical references and index.
ISBN 978-0-521-82391-3 (hardback)
1. Greek fiction – History and criticism.   2. Narration (Rhetoric) – History – To 1500.   I. Title.
PA3267.W55   2011
883′.0109 – dc22   2010052774

ISBN 978-0-521-82391-3 Hardback
ISBN 978-1-107-49102-1 Paperback

Cambridge University Press has no responsibility for the persistence or accuracy of URLs for external or third-party internet websites referred to in this publication, and does not guarantee that any content on such websites is, or will remain, accurate or appropriate.

ὀξεῖς οἱ τῶν ἐρώντων λογισμοὶ καὶ πρόχειροι ὑποπτεῦσαι,
δεινοὶ δὲ εἰκάσαι, ἔνθεοι δὲ μαντεύσασθαι.
Keen are the ratiocinations of lovers, and quick to suspect; clever at guessing, and inspired at predicting.
Iamblichus fr. 60.

Contents

Preface	*page* ix
List of abbreviations	xi
Introduction	1

PART I   RETURNING ROMANCE

1	First romances: Chariton and Xenophon	25
2	Transforming romance: Achilles Tatius and Longus	69
3	Hellenism at the edge: Heliodorus	108

PART II   NARRATIVE AND IDENTITY

4	*Pothos*	139
5	*Telos*	177
6	*Limen*	214
	Conclusion	253

Appendix: The extant romances and the larger fragments	261
References	265
Index	295

Preface

This book marks the end of a long and serpentine journey. Versions of these chapters have been tested on audiences patient and inspirational in Atlanta, Berkeley, Birmingham, Bristol, Cambridge, Dublin, Exeter, Fresno, Geneva, Groningen, Leuven, Ljubljana, Lisbon, Liverpool, Los Angeles, Manchester, Michigan, Milan, Nottingham, Oxford, Paris, Pennsylvania, Princeton, Stanford, St Andrews, Swansea, Uppsala and Utrecht; I have also benefited immeasurably from the Welsh KYKNOS group (particularly meetings at Gregynog), the Cretan RICAN team led by Michael Paschalis, and participants in my own *Romance between Greece and the East* workshops.

I have aimed to transliterate Greek names in their most familiar forms for ease of reading, accepting that no system of transliteration is perfect. Translations are mine, but I acknowledge my debt to other translators, especially those of Reardon (1989). For Achilles Tatius I have modified my own translations from Whitmarsh (2001b). For details of texts used please consult the appendix (divergences are noted throughout, where they occur). Iotas are printed adscript throughout; I have preferred BCE/CE to BC/AD.

I gratefully acknowledge the support of the Arts and Humanities Research Council, which (in its former life as a 'Research Board') awarded me research leave to allow me to complete a first version of this book. The Research Council also funded the *Romance Between Greece and the East* workshops alluded to above. Brill Academic Publishers generously allowed me to rework parts of Whitmarsh (2003) in Chapter 2. Chapter 3 contains material that originated in Whitmarsh (1998): thanks to the Cambridge Philological Society.

Heartfelt thanks too, for multiple reasons, to Cliff Ando, Lucia Athanassaki, Siam Bhayro, Ewen Bowie, Camilla Chorfi, Irene de Jong, Elizabeth Dollins, Konstantin Doulamis, Jaś Elsner, Dana Fields, Chris Gill, Maud Gleason, Simon Goldhill, Stephen Harrison, John Henderson, Owen

Hodkinson, Christopher Jones, Daniel King, Jason König, Rebecca Langlands, Anna Lefteratou, John Ma, Francesca Martelli, Stephen Mitchell, Silvia Montiglio, Helen Morales, John Morgan, Hannah Mossman, Karen ní Mheallaigh, Steve Nimis, Daniel Ogden, Boo Onion, Jim Porter, Ian Repath, Michael Sharp, Estelle Strazdins, Susan Stephens, Edmund Thomas, Stuart Thomson, Gail Trimble, Benet Walsh, and Froma Zeitlin. My gratitude to Francesca Stavrakopoulou, to my parents (Judy and Guy), brother (Ben), sister (Kate), and children (India and Soli) goes beyond words. Here's to happy endings.

Abbreviations

ACM	H. Musurillo, *Acts of the Christian martyrs*. Oxford, 1972.
ANRW	*Aufstieg und Niedergang der römischen Welt*. Berlin, 1972–.
AP	Palatine Anthology.
APM	H. Musurillo, *Acts of the Pagan martyrs*. Oxford, 1954.
CA	J. Powell ed. *Collectanea Alexandrina: reliquiae minores poetarum Graecorum aetatis Ptolemaicae 323–146 A.C. epicorum, elegiacorum, lyricorum, ethicorum*. Oxford, 1925.
DK	H. Diels and W. Kranz eds, *Die Fragmente der Vorsokratiker*, 6th edn Berlin, 1951–2.
FGrH	F. Jacoby *et al.* eds *Die Fragmente der griechischen Historiker*. Berlin/Leiden, 1876–1959; continued Leiden, 1998–.
GCN	*Groningen Colloquia on the Novel*.
HU	T. Hägg and B. Utas, *The virgin and her lover: fragments of an ancient Greek novel*. Leiden, 2003.
IE	*Die Inschriften von Ephesos*, eds Wankel, H. *et al.* = Inschriften griechischer Städte aus Kleinasien 11. Bonn, 1979–.
IG	*Inscriptiones Graecae*, 2nd edn. Berlin, 1924–.
KA	R. Kassel and C. Austin eds, *Poetae comici Graeci*. Berlin, 1983–.
KAI³	H. Donner and W. Rölling eds, *Kanaanäische und Aramäische Inschriften*. Wiesbaden, 1962–4.
LGPN	P.M. Fraser *et al.*, *A lexicon of Greek personal names*. Oxford, 1987–.
LIMC	H. C. Ackermann and J.-R. Gisler eds, *Lexicon iconographicum mythologiae classicae*. Zurich, 1981–99.

LS	A.A. Long and D.N. Sedley, *The Hellenistic philosophers*, 2 vols. Cambridge, 1987.
LSJ	H.G. Liddell and R. Scott *et al., A Greek–English lexicon*, 9th edn. with supplement. Oxford, 1996.
MUSJ	*Mélanges de l'Université Saint Joseph*. Beirut, 1906–.
Pack	R.A. Pack, *The Greek and Latin literary texts from Greco-Roman Egypt*, 2nd edn. Ann Arbor, 1965; updated on the Mertens-Pack³ website http://promethee.philo.ulg.ac.be/cedopal.
Pap. Mil. Vogl.	A. Vogliano *et al.* eds, *Papiri della R. Università di Milano*. Milan, 1937–.
P.Fay.	Grenfell, B.P. *et al.* eds, *Fayum towns and their papyri*. London, 1900.
P.Michael.	D.S. Crawford ed. *Papyri Michaelidae, being a catalogue of Greek and Latin papyri, tablets and ostraca in the Library of Mr G.A. Michailidis of Cairo*. Aberdeen, 1955.
P.Oxy.	*The Oxyrhynchus papyri*. London, 1898–.
P.Tebt.	B.P. Grenfell, A.S. Hunt and J.G. Smyly eds, *The Tebtunis papyri*. London, 1869–1926.
PMG	D. Page ed., *Poetae melici Graeci*. Oxford, 1962.
PSI	*Papiri greci e latini: pubblicazioni della Società Italiana per la ricerca dei papiri greci e latini in Egitto*. Florence, 1912–79.
RG	L. Spengel ed. *Rhetores Graeci*, 3 vols. Leipzig, 1856.
SVF	H. von Arnim ed. *Stoicorum veterum fragmenta*. Leipzig, 1923–4.
SW	S.A. Stephens and J.J. Winkler, *Ancient Greek novels: the fragments*. Princeton, 1994.
TGF	B. Snell *et al.* eds *Tragicorum graecorum fragmenta*. Göttingen, 1971–.
Wehrli	F. Wehrli ed. *Die Schule des Aristoteles: Texte und Kommentar*, 2nd ed, 10 vols. Basel, 1967–9.

Introduction

TRUE ROMANCE

Habrocomes, my child, I am not a settler or a native Sicilian but an elite Spartan, from one of the powerful families there, and very prosperous. When I was a young man and enrolled among the ephebes, I fell in love with a citizen girl by the name of Thelxinoe, and Thelxinoe returned my love. We met at a time when an all-night festival was being held in the city, with a god's guidance, and enjoyed the pleasure that our meeting had promised. For a while we used to meet in secret, and swore repeatedly to each other that our relationship would last till death. But one of the gods must have been spiteful. While I was still classed among the ephebes, Thelxinoe's parents agreed to her marriage to a young man called Androcles, who had by this time also fallen in love with her. At first, the girl had to invent all sorts of excuses to put off the wedding, but in the end she was able to arrange a meeting with me, and she agreed to elope from Sparta with me by night. We both dressed up as young men, and I even cut Thelxinoe's hair, on the very night before her wedding. Escaping from the city we came to Argos, then Corinth, where we boarded a ship and sailed for Sicily. When the Spartans learned of our escape, they condemned us to death. We lived out our days here, short of material comforts, but happy in the belief that we enjoyed every kind of pleasure, because we were with each other. Thelxinoe died here not long ago, but her body remains unburied: I keep it with me, maintaining my loving relations.

(Xenophon of Ephesus 5.1.4–9)

The extraordinary story of Aegialeus the fisherman is one of a number of mini-novellas narrated by minor characters within Xenophon of Ephesus' *Anthia and Habrocomes*, a Greek romance of the first century CE.[1] It is

---

[1] This introduction presumes a certain familiarity with the romances: for orientation, see the Appendix, where issues of dating are also discussed briefly. I use the term 'romance' for the heterosexual erotic narratives of travel and return, on which this book focuses, and 'novel' as a more extended category covering works like the *Alexander Romance* and *The life of Aesop* (both are, in any case, anachronistic).

clearly an experiment with the romance mode. The themes of young, reciprocated, heterosexual love and adventure, fidelity and final happiness resonate with the primary narrative. This story of passion that survives beyond the florescence of youth, despite deprivation, is offered as a lesson in both the power of love and the harsh physiological and material realities of life. Habrocomes, Xenophon's male protagonist and the recipient of this story, responds by drawing a conclusion that he applies to himself too: 'now truly (*alēthōs*) I have learned that true (*alēthinos*) love is not limited by age'.[2] A true lesson about true love.

But this story is also heavily counter-realistic. It is a grotesque parable about the delusions wrought by love. Aegialeus has (we learn) embalmed his wife in the Egyptian fashion, so that he can maintain the illusion that she is still living: 'I speak with her constantly *as if she were alive*, and lie with her, and take my meals with her.'[3] The final sentence of the story cited above (which I have translated 'maintaining my loving relations') could be taken to mean that he kisses and even has sex with the corpse.[4] Aegialeus' account of a life of poverty, exile, old age and death is not simply (as Habrocomes takes it) a story of true love; it is also about the denial of truth, about the concealment of present realities beneath a carapace of past memories. The lovers were, Aegialeus tells us, 'happy in the belief (*dokountes*) that we enjoyed every kind of pleasure, because we were with each other':[5] this belief (*doxa*) that they remain prosperous is a fiction willingly entertained. Similarly, when Aegialeus proceeds to show Habrocomes her corpse, lovingly embalmed in the Egyptian manner, he tells him that 'she does not appear to me as you see her; instead, my child, I imagine her as she was in Sparta, as she was when we escaped. I imagine the all-night festival, the promises we made.'[6] Aegialeus seems neurotically obsessed with replaying his own teen romance, and adopting it as a substitute for reality. But it is not simply a case of false consciousness: he is fully aware that Habrocomes will see things differently, whereas he

---

For titles of the romances I use the girl–boy forms, which I believe to be original and generically definitive (Whitmarsh (2005b)); for convenience I abbreviate in the cases of Xenophon (full title: *The Ephesian affairs of Anthia and Habrocomes*) and Heliodorus (*The Ethiopian affairs of Charicleia and Theagenes*). Morgan (2004c) 491–2 discusses the relationship between Xenophon's embedded narratives and his primary narrative; to his list I would add the story of Eudoxus at 3.4, reported in indirect speech.

[2] νῦν ἀληθῶς μεμάθηκα ὅτι ἔρως ἀληθινὸς ὅρον ἡλικίας οὐκ ἔχει, Xen. Eph. 5.1.12.
[3] ταύτηι... ἀεί τε ὡς ζώσηι λαλῶ καὶ συγκατάκειμαι καὶ συνευωχοῦμαι, Xen. Eph. 5.1.11.
[4] φιλῶ ('love', but also 'kiss') καὶ σύνειμι ('conjoin with'), Xen. Eph. 5.1.9.
[5] ἡδόμενοι... πάντων ἀπολαύειν δοκοῦντες, ὅτι ἦμεν μετ' ἀλλήλων, Xen. Eph. 5.1.8.
[6] οὐ γὰρ οἷα νῦν ὁρᾶται σοὶ τοιαύτη φαίνεται <ἐ>μοί, ἀλλὰ ἐννοῶ, τέκνον, οἷα μὲν ἦν ἐν Λακεδαίμονι, οἷα δὲ ἐν τῆι φυγῆι· τὰς παννυχίδας ἐννοῶ, τὰς συνθήκας ἐννοῶ, Xen. Eph. 5.1.11.

himself lives in a world of 'belief' and 'as-ifs'. As a first-person (strictly, a homodiegetic) narrator, he stands both inside the story, living its fictions, and outside it, exposing them.

Romance is centrally about simple truths: the complementary, yin–yang love of a girl and boy of the same station, comparable beauty and (roughly) equal age; a love tested through ordeals of separation and endurance, and redeemed through reunion and return. But literary narrative seems incapable of sheer simplicity. As we can see in the case of the story of Aegialeus (deliberately chosen from the romance usually reckoned the least artful), story-telling can be complex, self-conscious and metafictive even when it handles what is, at one level, a parable with an obviously universal relevance.

This book is about identity in the Greek romances, and the ways that it is turned and re-turned through narrative. Identity is, of course, a hugely complex topic, spreading into history, philosophy, anthropology, psychology, sociology and cultural studies (particularly of postcolonialism, gender, race and sexuality).[7] What I mean, for the purpose of this book, is primarily the set of categories of selfhood presumed, legitimised or questioned in the romances themselves. We can see immediately that Aegialeus uses a number of markers to identify himself. He is 'not local' to Sicily or a 'settler' (Sicelot, or Greek colonist), but an outsider, specifically a Spartan. He is a member of the elite (the Greek describes him as a 'Spartiate', of the city's politically dominant class) and wealthy. Although the sentence expressing these claims omits the verb by ellipsis, the implication is that Aegialeus perceives this as a present-tense identity, which he still holds even in exile. He also refers, however, to transitory stages through which he has now conclusively passed: 'when I was a young man . . . enrolled among the ephebes . . . classed among the ephebes' ('ephebes' being males on the cusp of (*epi-*) maturity (*hēbē*)). A third mode of identity is the assumed disguise: 'We both dressed up as young men, and I even cut Thelxinoe's hair.' These identities are provisional, strategic and designedly false; they will be shed when their usefulness is outlived. Finally, we have a less specific set of self-descriptors referring to mental and emotional states, principally the happiness generated by the illusory love. Even a brief story like this presents a rich narrative of identity. Aegialeus defines himself in terms of his city of birth, Sparta, but never achieved the secure status of adulthood there: he left while still an ephebe, not yet a man, just as Thelxinoe left

---

[7] Discussion and references at Whitmarsh (2001a) 35–7; see now also du Gay *et al.* (2000), a sample of classic essays from a variety of fields.

before she became a woman (i.e. wife). In place of their real, Spartan identities, they adopt first the false disguises they need for their escape, and second the consoling fictions that they are still the people that they were when they first met. There is a notable self-reflexivity to this narrative of identity: Aegialeus does not simply tell Habrocomes about his past, but also reveals the role that such story-telling plays in sustaining his fabricated world in the present. Narrative creates identities to inhabit in the present, as well as accounting for the past.

That identity is a species of narrative is a truism in certain circles. Inspired by Paul Ricoeur's monumental *Time and narrative*, Alasdair Macintyre's *After virtue*, Charles Taylor's *Sources of the self*,[8] and psychoanalytical critiques of the enlightenment identification of the person with consciousness, certain scholars have claimed that (to quote one) 'the self, or subject [is] a result of discursive praxis rather than a substantial entity having ontological priority over praxis or a self with epistemological priority, as originator of meaning'.[9] Even the social sciences, traditionally hostile to qualitative analysis, have caught the narrative bug.[10] It is not my aim in this book to validate such ideas. My approach is historicist: I aim to show not what identity *is* (in a universal sense), but how it is configured within a particular body of literature. It happens that that body was (as we shall see presently) both durable and culturally central in the period under discussion, but narrative was certainly far from the only medium available to ancients for articulating and exploring identity. Numerous other media presented themselves (to name but a few: inscriptions, monuments, clothing, statues, coinage), which may have a narrative dimension, but are not constituted as narratives in any strong sense. Ancient theories of identity were numerous (principally from philosophers[11] and medical writers, but we should include jurists too), but narrative does not play a central role in them.[12]

---

[8] Ricoeur (1984–1988); Macintyre (1984), esp. 204–25; Taylor (1989), cf. esp. 47–8 ('we grasp our lives as a *narrative*', 47). On problems around the definition of 'narrative', see Ryan (2007).
[9] Kerby (1991) 4.
[10] For the general point, see Somers (1994), who argues that narrative studies offer better prospects for comprehending the perspectives of the dispossessed (see 613–17 on the social sciences' rejection of narrative); also Polkinghorne (1995) and (more leisurely and epideictic) Bruner (1987). For an excellent study along these lines of narratives of motherhood, see Miller (2005). For a critique of the 'psychological narrativity thesis', see Strawson (2004), although his argument founders on the odd claim that episodic experience (which he opposes to diachronic) is not a form of narrativity. In chapters 5 and 6, we shall distinguish between 'paradigmatic' and 'syntagmatic' (roughly the equivalent of Strawson's episodic) narrative.
[11] Gill (2006) focuses on Stoic and Epicurean ideas of selfhood, with plenty of lateral glances towards Galen (as well as Seneca, Vergil and Plutarch).
[12] Gill (2006) 69–73, on the minimal role of memory in ancient definitions of selfhood.

Greek romances are not identity narratives in the sense that modern philosophers understand the term, which is to say articulations of individual selfhood. Certainly, we do find figures (like Xenophon's Aegialeus) telling their own stories, sometimes at great length: one of the romances, Achilles Tatius' *Leucippe and Clitophon*, indeed, is almost entirely narrated by the male protagonist. But, of course, such accounts are always embedded in larger narrative frames, which are themselves fictionalised. *Leucippe and Clitophon* is not an ingenuous attempt to express Clitophon's identity, it is an experiment with a literary mode, building on a tradition of first-person narratives stretching back to Homer's *Odyssey*. Yet, as we have begun to see in the case of Xenophon's Aegialeus story, ancient romances do indeed encode paradigmatic models of identity, and have their own ways of theorising it. To understand what identity is doing in such texts, we need first to explore how narrative works in them, about the formative roles of genre and cultural context.

INVENTING ROMANCE

The Greek romance appears to have emerged in the first century CE, in Asia Minor. In antiquity it survived until at least the fourth century CE (whereafter it continued to influence poets such as Nonnus and Musaeus, as well as martyrologists and historians);[13] it was later revived in mediaeval Persia and Byzantium.[14] There are five texts that survive complete: from the first century, Chariton's *Callirhoe* and Xenophon's *Anthia and Habrocomes*; from the second century, Achilles Tatius' *Leucippe and Clitophon* and, perhaps also, Longus' *Daphnis and Chloe*; and, from the fourth century, Heliodorus' *Charicleia and Theagenes*. Although in many ways different, each deals with a shared stock of narrative themes: the love of a young heterosexual couple, the trials that come between them, and a joyous reunion at the end. All are set in an imaginary, more or less classicising (i.e. Roman-less) world; Chariton's and Heliodorus' works are explicitly located in the classical period. In addition to the extant texts, we have a number of summaries by Photius, the swashbuckling ninth-century bishop of Constantinople, and an ever-increasing corpus of papyrus fragments that seem to share these concerns with young love.[15] Some (like the fragmentary

---

[13] Below, n. 61.
[14] For an up-to-date introduction to the Byzantine novels, see Burton (2008), with further literature. On the Persian version of *Metiochus and Parthenope*, see see n. 16 below.
[15] The most substantial collection of fragments and summaries is SW; all fragmentary romances are cited from there, unless otherwise stated. Five more fragments have been published in the interim: *P.Oxy.* 4760–2, 4811, 4945.

romances of *Sesonchosis*, *Ninus* and *Metiochus and Parthenope*)[16] are based on historical or pseudo-historical figures; others, such as Iamblichus' *Babylonian affairs* and the Panionis fragment (*P. Oxy* 4811), are, like the extant texts,[17] fictional. These romance texts should be seen against the back drop of a larger canvas of diverse novelistic literature of the imperial and even Hellenistic periods,[18] including the *Alexander romance*, the *Wonders beyond Thule* of Antonius Diogenes, the *Life of Aesop*, *Apollonius King of Tyre*, the various *Ass* narratives,[19] Lucian's *True stories*, and the anonymous *Joseph and Aseneth*. Two themes distinguish the romance from other novels. The first is the reciprocated heterosexual love that we have already seen exemplified in Aegialeus' story. The second is that of travel and return. This, I have argued, is conspicuously *absent* for Thelxinoe and Aegialeus: they are compelled to create ersatz identities because they do not return to assume their proper adult roles in Sparta.[20]

Why did the romance, this particular species of the ancient novel, emerge when it did, and why did it achieve such success? This question has occupied scholars since Pierre-Daniel Huet's *Lettre-traité de l'origine des romans*, which argued that the romance was a west-Asian form that spread into Greek during the Hellenistic period.[21] Erwin Rohde's pivotal *Der griechische Roman und seine Vorläufer* (1876), the founding work of modern scholarship in the field, is largely dedicated to retracing the Hellenistic *Greek* sources of the romance.[22] But whereas older scholarship focused on producing narratives of diachronic development, critics since Perry's *The ancient romances* (1967) have tended to emphasise the congruity between the romances and

---

[16] For *Metiochus and Parthenope*, see HU, which includes as well as the Greek fragments and testimony an edition and translation of an eleventh-century Persian translation, 'Unṣurī's *Vāmiq u 'Adhrā*.

[17] Notwithstanding that in Chariton's *Callirhoe*, the historical Hermocrates (Syracusan general at the time of the Athenian invasion) is father of the protagonist.

[18] Modern discussions of Hellenistic prose fiction: Ruiz Montero (2003); Whitmarsh (2010d).

[19] Scholarship has focused primarily on the triangular relationship between the pseudo-Lucianic *Ass*, Apuleius' *Metamorphoses* and the lost *Metamorphoses* of Lucius of Patrae (Phot. *Bibl.* cod. 129): see esp. Perry (1967) 211–18; Van Thiel (1971); Mason (1994). The picture has been changed, however, by the publication of *P. Oxy*. 4762, a different version of the narrative (featuring, intriguingly, a 'third-person' (i.e. what narratologists call 'heterodiegetic') narrator). The implications of this have yet to be fully absorbed by scholars in the field.

[20] Comparably, Montiglio (2007) reads Apuleius' *Metamorphoses* as a rejected return narrative.

[21] Huet (1670) 11: 'l'invention [des Romans] et deuë aux Orientaux: je veux dire aux Egyptiens, aux Arabes, aux Perses, & aux Syriens'. More recent versions of the west-Asian argument, differently nuanced, can be found in Barns (1956), Anderson (1984), and Rutherford (2000); discussion at Stephens (2008). I shall address this issue in a forthcoming book, *The romance between Greece and the East*. 'West-Asian' is intended as a more neutral designation than the Eurocentric 'near-Eastern'.

[22] Other studies searching for literary origins: Lavagnini (1922) (local history); Giangrande (1962) (prose paraphrases); S. West (2003) (women's tales).

the cultural context of imperial Greece.[23] These contextualising readings fall, broadly, into three different camps:

(i) The first, emphasising the role of 'private' emotions and selfhood, sees the romance as the expression of a general reorientation away from the public sphere towards the inner person. Sometimes this is expressed in terms of a supposed transformation in civic culture: Greeks, it is claimed, had lost their sense of collective identity amid the vast territories of the Hellenistic and Roman worlds.[24] A slightly different version of this interpretation, routed through the work of Paul Veyne and Michel Foucault, sees the romance in the context of an increased emphasis upon the 'care of the self': the elites under the empire, it is claimed, turned to self-discipline as a compensation for the political authority they had now lost.[25] Yet another variety reads the romances as religious parables of virtuous suffering and redemption, expressing the world of the mystery cult.[26] The usual assumption is that the texts were composed by and for elite males, but sometimes the emphasis upon emotional vulnerability is explained in terms of a demographically expanded readership, now incorporating the 'bourgeoisie'.[27]

(ii) A number of critics have seen the romance as the product of a supposed reorganisation of sexual protocols in the imperial period. Foucault is influential here too, concluding the third volume of *The care of the self* with a brief chapter claiming the romances as articulations of a 'new erotics' of heterosexual mutuality, contrasting with the hierarchical phallocentrism of the classical period.[28] They have been held to articulate the supposed centrality of marriage to the Greek aristocracies in the imperial period,[29] the new prominence of women,[30] and the identification of the sexual being with the innermost core of selfhood (a theme of Foucault's own work).

---

[23] In fact, Perry's contextual analysis was already preempted by Rohde, who devotes a large section of his book to the 'Second Sophistic'.

[24] Perry (1967), esp. 57–60; Reardon (1969) 293–4, (1991) 28–30; Morgan (1995) 143–7.

[25] Konstan (1994); MacAlister (1996); Toohey (2004).

[26] Kerényi (1927); Merkelbach (1962), (1988) (cf., implicitly, Petri (1963)). This view, which has not found general favour, is critiqued and/or nuanced by Turcan (1963); cf. also 1992), Geyer (1977), Stark (1989). See however Beck (2003) and Zeitlin (2008), who explore religious overtones more subtly.

[27] Hägg (1983); Holzberg (1995). Similar claims have been made for the 'Jewish novels' of the Hebrew Bible: see e.g. Wills (1995) 3–6.

[28] Foucault (1990), followed by Konstan (1994); refinements in Goldhill (1995). This general approach is discussed by Morales (2008). See further below, pp. 159–60.

[29] Cooper (1996); Swain (1996) 101–31.

[30] Johne (1987), (2003); Egger (1988), (1994a), (1994b); Liviabella Furiani (1989); Wiersma (1990); Montague (1992); more circumspectly, Haynes (2003) 1–17.

(iii) The third hypothetical context for the romances is the so-called 'second sophistic'. When this term was (apparently) coined by Philostratus in the third century CE, it referred to a form of epideictic oratory, in which the speaker took on the persona of a figure from myth or history (*VS* 481, 507).[31] When modern critics write of the 'second sophistic', however, they are usually making grander claims, about a supposed trend towards self-conscious Hellenic revivalism underpinned by the reinvention of links with the prestigious classical past. It was, again, the enormously influential Erwin Rohde who revived the phrase, linked it particularly with a supposed concern with the defence of 'national-Hellenic' (*national-hellenisch*) values against supposed eastern infiltration and Roman oppression,[32] and located the romance within this supposed movement. Modern criticism tends to downplay the troubling distaste for 'the East' that Rohde's model seems to both identify and endorse, putting the emphasis instead on anti-Romanism (so that the 'second sophistic' becomes a postcolonial rather than an anti-Semitic allegory).[33] Against this, others have reinvented the second sophistic as a more playful, 'postmodernist' culture, revelling in its secondariness, self-awareness and sophistication. Here too, the romance has been seen as a prime exhibit, for its clever refashioning of traditional themes.[34]

We need to be careful here, since each of these contexts has its problems. As far as (i) goes, we can certainly point to the ability of romance narrative to go behind the scenes and portray emotions, but this kind of zooming technique is, in fact, as old as Homer. More problematic still is the belief that post-classical culture was mired in alienated ennui: this is little more than a modernist fantasy, and in some cases a teleological attempt to create a crisis for Christianity to resolve. There is no evidence for wide-scale anxiety, or for the collapse of *polis* culture.[35] Inscriptions, monuments and literary sources (from Dio Chrysostom to Libanius) testify to the ongoing importance of civic culture, even if political structures were in flux. Conversely, public identity is extremely important to some of the romances, notably those of Chariton and Xenophon. The romances certainly contain expressions of despondency (as we shall see in chapters 5 and 6), but these are directed

---

[31] This paragraph in part summarises the critique at Whitmarsh (2005a) 6–9; cf. also (2001a) 42–5.
[32] Rohde (1914) 319.
[33] See Bowie (1970) 9–10 on Chariton and Heliodorus; also Anderson (1993) 156–70; Whitmarsh (2001a) 78–87.
[34] See esp. Goldhill (1995), with ix on the second sophistic (and xi on their 'wit, verve and outrageousness'); also, less directly, Morgan (1995) 142–3.
[35] Swain (1996) 106 effectively critiques the 'anxiety school'.

against fortune and malign gods rather than faceless world empires; and, what is more, they are almost always proven to be misguided. The romances do not demonstrate a shift from public to private identities, for no such shift had occurred. Instead, we should be focusing upon the question of how individual romances structure the relationship of private to public.

Explanation (ii) – proposing a rise in conjugal ideology – is more helpful, since we can certainly point to an increased emphasis upon the representation of the virtues of marriage in a variety of media (epigraphy, literature and philosophy) from the late first century BCE onwards,[36] and a growing celebration of self-control, endurance and fidelity shared between Jewish, Christian and Greco-Roman cultures.[37] On the other hand, it is once again far too simplistic to speak of a shift from hierarchical to symmetrical models of sexuality. Classical sexual protocols were not exclusively dominated by phallocentrism and power.[38] Narratives of reciprocal heterosexuality redeemed in (the re-establishment of) marriage are in the Greek tradition as old as the *Odyssey*, and lie at the heart of Hellenistic new comedy; marital devotion in the face of oppression is the theme of Xenophon's celebrated narrative of Panthea and Abradates;[39] ideas of sexual symmetry can be found articulated in classical mime.[40] Conversely, there is plenty of evidence for asymmetrical pederastic desire in the imperial period.[41] The picture that emerges is of subtle adjustments in a complex system, rather than of a sudden, decisive break.

Explanation (iii), the 'second sophistic', also has its difficulties. There is no doubt that the romances (with the exception of Xenophon's *Anthia and Habrocomes*) are highly sophisticated products of elite, educated Greek culture.[42] They are also composed in a prose (a hallmark of imperial Greek

---

[36] See van Bremen (1996) on the epigraphic record. Milnor (2005) links the reorientation closely to Augustus; see esp. 239–84 on the centrality of marriage to philosophers such as Musonius Rufus (see also Whitmarsh (2001a) 109–13; Nussbaum (2002)). See also Swain (2007) 146–52 on the intriguing Bryson, who survives only in Arabic translation.

[37] The classic statement of this position is Brown (1990a), summarised at (1990b). Perkins (1995) integrates the romances into her study of the ethics of endurance.

[38] Davidson (2007) is controversial, but on this point (I think) absolutely right.

[39] Xen. *Cyr.* 4.6.11, 5.1.2–18, 6.1.45–51, 6.4.1–11, 7.1.29–32, 7.3.2–16. The importance of this narrative for the romances is well-known: see most recently Capra (2009) on Xenophon. The Panthea story was rewritten (perhaps as a rhetorical novella) in the second century CE by one Celer (Philostr. *VS* 524).

[40] Xen. *Symp.* 9.6: 'the boy and the girl are kissed by each other' (τὸν παῖδα καὶ τὴν παῖδα ὑπ' ἀλλήλων φιλεῖσθαι).

[41] Below, p. 160.

[42] On the evidence for elite readership, see S.A. Stephens (1994); also Bowie (1994). Cavallo (1996), by contrast, argues on papyrological grounds that the reading public for the romances diversified in the second century; but his argument depends heavily upon judgements as to what 'un lettore non abituato a testi di cultura superiore' (35) would expect from a text.

aesthetics)⁴³ with marked Atticising tendencies (in the cases of Achilles, Longus and Heliodorus), and their intertextual reference points are broadly in line with those of other imperial authors.⁴⁴ But whatever it was (and I am increasingly sceptical that it was anything very much), the 'second sophistic' was not a unified, manifesto-led organisation. If the romances share some features with other literary productions of the era, it does not follow that they are entirely of a piece with them. We should be particularly careful about Rohdean claims that the era was dominated by a stridently defensive Hellenism. The disturbing political implications apart, it posits a wholly implausible uniformity across a huge time and space, in an age long before nationalist mechanisms like print media. I shall argue in the course of this book that Chariton and Xenophon do display a Hellenocentrism of a kind, subtle and complex in Chariton's case. Achilles Tatius and Longus, however, configure identity very differently. Iamblichus and Heliodorus, finally, offer direct challenges to the Hellenocentric model.⁴⁵

What is crucial is to get away from the paradigm shift model. Relationships between historical processes and the invention of cultural forms are, as a rule, complex and multiform. In some cases we can certainly point to social or political events that impel new genres: for example, the 'May 4th Movement' of 1917, which created the conditions for the rise of the vernacular Chinese novel.⁴⁶ More typically, however, literary works are shaped by multiple influences, which may include, alongside social, political and cultural shifts, the conservatising effects of canons and traditions as well as the idiosyncratic creative aspirations of individual authors. Scholars of Greek tragedy, for example, have retreated from the dogma that the genre was entirely shaped by Athenian democracy. There are, of course, democratic resonances in the interplay between named individuals and anonymous collectives, the relativisation of authority, and the emphasis upon the fall of royal households. But sceptics are right to point out that such themes are already found in literature predating Athenian democracy,⁴⁷ and indeed that they are 'civic' rather than narrowly democratic.⁴⁸ Democracy may be a necessary cause of the emergence of tragedy, but it is not a sufficient one: a full account would need also to address other genealogies of the genre, for example, in Dionysiac ritual, epic narrative and choral festivals.

---

⁴³ On the prosiness of imperial Greece, see Whitmarsh (2005c).
⁴⁴ For general overviews see Fusillo (1989) 17–109; Morgan and Harrison (2008) 218–27.
⁴⁵ For Heliodorus' 'multiculturalism' see Bowersock (1994) 29–53; Whitmarsh (1998), (1999); Perkins (1999); below, chapter 3.
⁴⁶ Zhao (2006), esp. 83–6.   ⁴⁷ Griffin (1998), esp. 48–9.
⁴⁸ Rhodes (2003), titled 'Nothing to do with democracy'; also Taplin (1999) on tragedy's trans-civic portability.

Introduction

The emergence of romance is even more difficult to relate to particular historical changes, because it was, it appears, composed outside of civic institutions. At least with tragedy we can be sure that the Great Dionysia was sponsored by the Athenian democratic state, even if not all tragedies were composed for that festival exclusively (or, in some cases, at all), and even if the performative context did not fully dictate the form that the texts took. The romancers, by contrast, wrote for readers and environments that they could not predict and would never encounter. Their works were composed in the awareness that they would travel beyond the immediate community in which they were composed, to the literate elite across the empire: hence, for example, the appearance of the Aphrodisian Chariton in rural Egypt some 100–150 years after the text's composition (and, for all we know, even earlier as well).[49] The written word also engenders a greater sense of the *longue durée* of literature. A millennium or so of literate culture creates not only a rich sense of the past (the romances are all richly intertextual[50] and set, whether specifically or not, in a yesteryear), but also the expectation that one writes for posterity too.[51] When Longus claims that he has written a 'pleasurable possession for all humanity',[52] it is more than just an allusion to Thucydides.

Now, of course, this universalism can itself be situated historically, albeit in a rather general sense: it is clearly the product of an expanded Greek worldview (from the Panhellenism of fifth- and fourth-century Athens, through the Hellenistic period, to Roman imperialism), the material opportunities of the *pax Romana*, and the culture of classicism. It is attractive to see the ancient romance as fundamentally shaped by new modes of literate production and transcultural circulation.[53] Walter Benjamin famously claims that the modern novel is born of print technology; its appearance marked the end of face-to-face communities and the birth of the 'solitary individual' of deracinated consumerism.[54] It would be misleading to suggest too close an analogy (even if we were to accept Benjamin's judgemental distaste for the reproduction and circulation of texts), but it is not

---

[49] *P.Oxy.* 1019 and *P.Oxy.* 2948 (from the same papyrus = 241 Pack), *P.Michael.* 1 (242 Pack), *P.Fay.* 1 (243 Pack), all dated to approx. 200 CE. The *codex Thebanus deperditus* (244 Pack) is dated to the sixth to seventh centuries CE.
[50] Above, n. 44.
[51] Estelle Strazdins' forthcoming Oxford DPhil will demonstrate the importance of this motif in imperial Greek culture.
[52] κτῆμα... τερπνὸν πᾶσιν ἀνθρώποις, 1 *pr.* 3. The universalism is formally contrasted, via a *men/de* construction, with the metaphor of an epichoric cult dedication (ἀνάθημα... Ἔρωτι καὶ Νύμφαις καὶ Πανί).
[53] Along these lines, see e.g. Morgan (1995) 137–8.   [54] Benjamin (1970) 87.

far wrong to see the ancient romance as similarly emerging from the literate interconnectivity of the Hellenistic and (particularly) Roman empires. I return to this point in my conclusion.

But if the appearance of (aspirant) 'world empires' created the conditions for the romance to arise and prosper, historical determinism still helps little with the content of heterosexual love, ordeals and travel – themes that are, by contrast, widespread in all periods of Greek culture (see the following section). Nor does it explain the specific thematic inflections of the different authors (for example, Longus' pastoral context or Achilles Tatius' parodic approach). This, of course, is not at all the same thing as saying that the individual romances or their components float free of historical anchorage. It is a central claim of this book that these texts respond, diversely, to sociocultural exigencies. The crucial point, however, is that we should not see the relationship of history to genre as one of cause and effect. Each of the romances is itself a distinctively creative working-through of contemporary identity politics.

RETURNING ROMANCE

What, in fact, do we *mean* by referring to romance as a 'genre'? The romance is, for many, the limit case of generic fluidity.[55] 'The novel becomes the great container in which reified fragments of these genres will take their place alongside others';[56] far from a genre in its own right, it is constitutively 'anti-generic, unable to be specified as a single style of discourse; it is a container of styles rather than itself a homogeneous and distinctive style'.[57] This impression of genrelessness is seemingly reinforced by the absence of any evidence for any institutionalisation of the romances: they were not, so far as we know, performed;[58] nor did they appear in school curricula or the

---

[55] Farrell (2003) 391–3. See Holzberg (2003) 11–16 for a survey of attempts to define the genre of the ancient romance; also Goldhill (2008). In scholarship of post-classical romance, the denial of genre has become routine: see e.g. Parker (1979); Elam (1992) 5–8.
[56] Nimis (1994) 407.
[57] Nimis (1994) 398; for similar points, see e.g. Fusillo (1989) 26; Harrison (2003) 515. For a critique of this kind of reading of Bakhtin, see Whitmarsh (2005d).
[58] There is, however, some evidence for theatrical performance of the stories we know as *Metiochus and Parthenope* (Luc. *De salt.* 2, 54; *Pseud.* 25) and *Ninus* (Luc. *Pseud.* 25), but in the form of mimes rather than recitations of the romance text: this is all but explicit at *De salt.* 2 (see further HU 49–52). The relationship between romance and pantomime may have been bilateral: see Mignogna (1996a) and (1997) for mimic themes in Achilles Tatius, and (1996b) for a proposed identification of a fragmentary papyrus as a Leucippe mime. Among several speculations, Obbink (2006) wonders whether *P. Oxy.* 4762 might be a mime version of the ass story. To re-emphasise, however, there is no evidence that the romances themselves were performed. More generally on romance and mime,

Introduction 13

reading lists of advanced literary criticism.[59] There is not even any ancient word for 'romance': even the most plausible candidate, *dramatikon*, does not appear before the ninth century, and even then seems to refer to the 'dramatic' aspects of the plot (sufferings and reversals of fortune) rather than a genre itself.[60] Nor, finally, is there any explicit theoretical discussion of the Greek romances before Byzantine times (although allusions in other texts[61] indicate that they were certainly being read).[62]

The characterisation of the romance as an anti-genre is, I think, too strident;[63] in fact, it only works if we define genre in an antiquated, essentialist way. Genres are in general, as constructionist scholarship has taught us, fluid things, liable to continuous reinvention; they are structured by

---

see Webb (2008) 27, 96–7, 136; and on mimes and pantomimes as a whole Roueché (1993) 15–30, Lada-Richards (2007), Hall and Wyles (2008) and Webb (2008).

[59] Not that this is a surprise, since imperial Greeks rarely discuss their contemporaries (Bowie (1994) 442). Genette (1992) 69: 'the postclassical (or paraclassical) forms suffer a historical erosion that is less their own doing than that of another historical rhythm'. Philostratus is barely mentioned (Menander Rhetor 2.390 *RG* = Russell and Wilson (1981) 116; and in his homonymous grandson's *Imagines* (pr. 2)), as is Lucian (Strohmaier (1976) for the reference in Galen, transmitted in Arabic; Lactant. *Div. inst.* 1.9; Eunap. *VS* 454).

[60] For *dramatikon* used of romances, see Phot. *Bibl.* cod. 73, 50a = Hld. test. IV Colonna; cod. 87, 66a = Ach. Tat. test. 2 Vilborg; cf. cod. 166, 109a (Antonius Diogenes). But in fact Photius happily uses the term of works that are not romances: see e.g. 95, 78b; 107, 87b. For discussion of this term see Rohde (1914) 376–9; Agapitos (1998) 128–30. Nor does *plasma* ('fiction'), the word used in the colophon of the earliest MS of Achilles Tatius (W, twelfth century) have any secure pre-Byzantine ancestry, despite Jul. *Ep.* 89 = 301b (this does not refer to the romances: see Whitmarsh (2005b) 607–8). In any case, this word, which derives from rhetorical theory (see esp. Barwick (1928)), refers not to the literary form but to the type of scenario described, i.e. invented as opposed to historically or mythologically based. Similarly, *erōtika* ('erotic things'), *erōtikon diēgema* ('erotic narrative') and *erōtikē hypothesis* ('erotic plot') are simply bland descriptions of the contents. The variety of terms is further discussed at Kuch (1989) 13–14. I argue at Whitmarsh (2005b) that the romance's titling conventions (*ta peri/kata* + girl's name) are used to denote genre.

[61] See esp. Kost (1971) 29–32 on Musaeus. Lehmann (1910) contains a useful, if not always convincing, list of 'imitations' of Achilles in Aristaenetus (5–12), Musaeus (12–25), Synesius (25–6), Gregory of Nazianzus (28–30), Himerius (30–6), Themistius (36–9), pseudo-Libanius (39–46), Nonnus (46–7) and Philostratus (51–4).

[62] Julian's 89th letter does not, contrary to what is often claimed, refer to the romances: see n. 60. A number of other references have been claimed: I am unconvinced by Persius 1.134 (*post prandia Callirhoen do*: see Whitmarsh (2005b) 590 n. 14) and, while Philostr. *Ep.* 68 is a more plausible reference, it is too brief and allusive to allow any certainty. The first secure mention of a romance is the famous reference to Heliodorus' supposed bishopric by the fifth-century Socrates Ecclesiasticus (*HE* 5.22 = T I Colonna). The Latin novels (explicitly including Apuleius), however, are discussed as a genre (*hoc... fabularum genus*) by Macrobius in the late fourth or early fifth century (*Somn.* 1.2.8, with Kuch (1989) 13–16). That the Greek romances, to return to them, were read in relatively (though not spectacularly) large numbers is evidenced by papyrus finds (up to forty-two in 1994, depending on what one counts: see S. A. Stephens (1994) 415–16), the influence on authors such as Musaeus and Nonnus, and the mosaics from Roman Syria representing scenes from the narratives (if perhaps the mimes rather than the romances: above, n. 58) we know as *Ninus* and *Metiochus and Parthenope* (HU 57–64).

[63] Whitmarsh (2005b); (2005d) 108–11.

'family resemblance' rather than phylogenetic classification.[64] In the case of the romances, shared themes, topoi, and language make it certain that these writers were self-consciously constructing their own relationship to a tradition.[65] The crucial point is to think of genre not as an ossified 'form'[66] but as a flexible system allowing for reinvention and reorientation. Part I of this book aims to demonstrate this. Three chapters describe three phases in the history of the romance, belonging to the first, second and fourth centuries CE. Broadly speaking, the earliest romances celebrate the regenerative power of the Greek community; their second-century successors are more centrifugal and experimental, emphasising the flexibility and capacity for transformation that experience can supply; while Heliodorus' fourth-century *Charicleia and Theagenes* constitutes a radical reorientation, relocating the idealised marriage-based community from Greece to the edges of the earth.

What this book thus offers is an account of a literary form that was both traditionally rooted and flexible enough to respond to changing circumstances. The defining feature of the romance plot is, I argue, the return narrative. The return (*nostos*) is among the most ancient and fundamental in the Greek world (perhaps with its roots in ancient West Asia). Homer's *Odyssey* is the best-known example of this type to Hellenists, not just for Odysseus' literal return, but also for the counterfactual return narratives contained in the hero's various 'Cretan lies', and the gossip told to Penelope about him;[67] such tales of travel and return were no doubt legion in the ancient Mediterranean (much earlier examples include the Egyptian *Sinuhe* and the *Tale of the shipwrecked sailor*, from the second millennium BCE). Their popularity in Greece can be glimpsed from the remains of the *Nostoi* of Agias of Troezen (which told of the returns of the Achaean warriors at

---

[64] The Wittgensteinian phrase comes from Fowler (1982). See further Heath (2004) 168. 'A genre . . . is not simply a taxonomic class . . . If a theory of genres is to be more than a taxonomy it must attempt to explain what features are constitutive of functional categories which have governed the reading and writing of literature' (Culler (1975) 137). For a thoroughly conventionalist reading of genre, see esp. Genette (1992), a revision of Genette (1977); also Derrida (1980), arguing that genre exists only as a call to an impossible purity. On 'speech genres' see esp. Bakhtin (1986) 132–58, lucidly discussed by Morson and Emerson (1990) 271–305. Seitel (2003) has some stimulating remarks on genre as speech act from an anthropological perspective; see also Pavel (2003).

[65] See esp. Létoublon (1993) on *lieux communs*. One of the results of researching this book has been the realisation of how much intertextuality there is *within* the corpus of romances. I have noted instances where they have arisen, but a systematic study of this phenomenon is a desideratum.

[66] Reardon (1991).

[67] On Odysseus' *nostos* as identity narrative, see esp. Segal (1962) and (1967); also Goldhill (1991) 1–68, emphasising the roles of language and representation. Frame (1978) argues that Odysseus' return embodies a a death/rebirth scheme. On the wider *nostos* tradition, see Alexopoulou (2006), (2009).

Introduction

Troy, and Orestes' vengeance on Aegisthus and Clytaemnestra) and of Stesichorus (*PMG* 209),[68] and various tales in the wider mythic corpus (such as those of the Argonauts and Heracles, as well as the later Attic mythology of Theseus). Return stories are typically optimistic and joyous, figuring the renewal of society, and even life itself: hence their alignment with stories of return from the underworld (Heracles, Odysseus,[69] Theseus)[70] and the joyous restoration of the divine order and hence of fertility (the 'return of Hephaestus' to Olympus, featured on a number of archaic black-figure pots,[71] the *Homeric Hymn to Demeter*,[72] the Mesopotamian *Nergal and Ereshkigal*, and Egyptian accounts of Isis and Osiris – to which Kerényi attributed the origin of the Greek romances).[73] It has been argued that the etymology of the very word *nostos* suggests a 'return to the light', and that early Greek *nostoi* like the *Odyssey* manipulate rebirth symbolism.[74] Crucially, return narratives also operate as parables of identity, normative articulations of relationships between self and society: they imply the destiny of the individual (human or divine) in a particular context. Underlying such stories is often a ritual pattern, which scholars (following Van Gennep) tend to call the 'rite of passage': common to many pre-industrial cultures is the idea that the individual is aggregated into society after a period of marginalisation.[75]

What romance distinctively superimposes onto the common return plot is the narrative of heterosexual desire. Greek romances, without exception, begin with the excitation and conclude with the satisfaction of such desires.[76] This combination is not without precedent in the Greek

---

[68] A *Nostoi* is also ascribed to Eumelus of Corinth (Σ Pind. *Ol.* 13.31a), an ascription that may, however, 'be an isolated error' (M. L. West (2003) 26). The archaic *nostoi* are surveyed by Malkin (1998) 1–10, with a particular emphasis upon their role in the colonial imaginary.

[69] Neoplatonists read the *Odyssey* as an allegory of the soul's return from the phenomenal world to the pure world of forms: Lamberton (1986) 106–7.

[70] Frye (1976) 97–126 observes the proximity between romance and *katabasis/anabasis*.

[71] Hedreen (2004), with literature.

[72] The significance of the *Hymn to Demeter* as a canonical text of yearning, separation and 'rebirth' may suggest that it is more than coincidence that the list of Nereids at *HHomDem* 418–23 contains names that would later belong to three romance heroines (Leucippe, Callirhoe, Melite (already a nymph at Hom. *Il.* 18.42 and Hes. *Th.* 247); Rhode (cf. Rhodeia, *HHomDem* 419) is also the name of a slave in Xen. Eph.). The Europa episode at the beginning of Achilles Tatius seems to allude to this passage (among others).

[73] Kerényi (1927).   [74] Frame (1978).   [75] See below, pp. 43–4.

[76] One possible exception is *Metiochus and Parthenope*, which HU 247–50 claim may have had an unhappy ending. I am unconvinced by their arguments (that Parthenope's name suggests perpetual virginity; that there is no trace of reunion in the fragmentary testimony; and that St Parthenope was martyred), but agree that the case remains open.

tradition, although the parallels are inexact. In Homer's *Odyssey*, the protagonist's yearning for homecoming is merged with his desire for his wife, a desire that blends the sexual and the social.[77] Aristophanes' *Lysistrata* begins with the secession of women from their 'proper' place in the community, and concludes with the reincorporation of the genders, symbolised by the communal dancing of female and male choruses. Many a New Comedy focuses on sexual crises that are finally resolved by integrating the sexes into the married household.[78] Comic sex plots, however, tend to avoid travel, and hence the *nostos*. Romance is different: partly because of the medium in which it is circulated (the prose book), but more pertinently for our purposes because it combines the narrative of desire fulfilled with the rite of passage/return plot. In other words, the protagonists begin the narrative as yearning youths and end as fulfilled adults. Let us recall, in this connection, that Aegialeus' story begins 'when I was a young man and enrolled among the ephebes.' Heterosexual marriage is, in the romances, the primary marker of the achievement of adult identity in the *polis* (or not, in Aegialeus' case).

RE-TURNING ROMANCE

The romances, however, are not simply normative maps of identity. Certainly, they can be read in this way: one reason for the very persistence of the return narrative in general is that it responds to a deeply rooted human need to naturalise the human subject, with all his or her uncertainties and desires, within a community: to engender a powerful sense of home and homeland as the *telos* of existence. But home-coming raises questions too: is the returner the same person as the one who left? As Terence Cave argues in a sparkling reading, scenes where home-comers are recognised always (from the *Odyssey* onwards) seem haunted by the *Martin Guerre* scenario, in which an imposter is falsely acknowledged.[79] The romances respond to this anxiety. As Cave himself observes, Heliodorus' *Charicleia and Theagenes* contains a protracted, forensic analysis of Charicleia's identity, so as to determine that she is the true child of the Ethiopian royal couple, with Hydaspes (her father) particularly sceptical.[80] How can we be sure she is who she says she is, he asks (10.13.5)? Different versions of

---

[77] Below, p. 142. [78] See e.g. Hunter (1985) 83–95; Lape (2003).
[79] Cave (1988). The French peasant Martin Guerre left home in 1548. In 1556 a man claiming to be Guerre returned and was welcomed by his wife; it later transpired that he was an imposter who had campaigned with Guerre.
[80] Cave (1988) 17–21.

this question arise in Lockean form even in cases where the identity of the returner is not explicitly called into doubt. In Chariton's *Callirhoe*, the heroine and Chaereas are welcomed back to Sicily by joyous crowds in the final book. But are they the same as the people who left? Callirhoe has learned that deception is the secret of a happy marriage; Chaereas has learned to redirect his vigour from wife-beating to militarism.[81] Their experience has transformed them.

At the same time, however, the return home always suggests the restoration of a prior state, as though the interlude had changed nothing. Bakhtin claims that there is no 'biographical time' in the Greek romance: 'At the novel's outset the heroes meet each other at a marriageable age, and at the same marriageable age, no less fresh and handsome, they consummate the marriage at the novel's end.'[82] This is (as we have seen) not true in an absolute sense, but it captures an aspect of romantic sameness. The protagonists are not ravaged by age and experience like Odysseus; all the sufferings inflicted upon them during the course of the narrative are always reversible. As Frye observes, the Greek romances' emphasis on the integrity of female virginity works as an allegory for the immutability of the self despite everything.[83] There is also a sense of the dependable eternality of the community, at least in the earlier texts: nothing changes in the *polis* either.

Returning romance enacts a paradox: a text in which the protagonists both are and are not the same at the end. This paradox would, I think, be more familiar (but not necessarily more resoluble) for members of a community with a strong conceptualisation of passage rites. Such rites are often imagined as forms of death and rebirth:[84] so when initiates are welcomed into the community, they are in one sense simply the child now fulfilled, and in another a different person. A late Greek orator describes the experience of mystery cult initiation as 'becoming a stranger to myself',[85] a baffling phrase marking the complex duality of this initiate, both within and without his old self.

---

[81] Balot (1998); Scourfield (2003).   [82] Bakhtin (1981) 90.
[83] Frye (1976) 86. See also below, pp. 144–5.
[84] Already at Plut. fr. 178 Sandbach, esp. lines 6–7: 'the language and the reality of death [*teleutan*] resemble those of initiation [*teleisthai*]' (τὸ ῥῆμα τῶι ῥήματι καὶ τὸ ἔργον τῶι ἔργωι τοῦ τελευτᾶν καὶ τελεῖσθαι προσέοικε); and see e.g. Turner (1967) 96 on the Ndembu. Greek marriage in particular is often linked to death, especially for the *parthenos* (maiden) who will be reborn as a *gunē* (woman). See esp. Rehm (1994), Seaford (1987). In Heliodorus, Charicles' first daughter does actually die on her wedding night (2.29.3–4), a widespread topos mapped out by Szepessy (1972); Knoles (1980–1) traces it beyond antiquity.
[85] ξενιζόμενος ἐπ' ἐμαυτῶι, Sopater 114.26–115.1 Walz; see below, p. 101.

It is this unresolved play between sameness and difference that gives romance narrative its richness, complexity and urgency. Todorov once argued that such issues are the very essence of narrative itself. 'Narrative', he claims, 'is constituted in the tension of two formal categories, difference and resemblance', since the journey between beginning and end must describe both continuity and change:

> transformation represents precisely a synthesis of differences and resemblances, it links two facts without their being able to be identified. Rather than a 'two-sided unit', it is an operation in two directions: it asserts both resemblance and difference; it engages and suspends time in a single movement... in a words, it makes narrative possible and yields us its very definition.[86]

Whatever its merits as a general theory of narrative, this nicely summarises the experience of reading romance.

This doubleness has multiple ramifications, which will be traced throughout this book, particularly in part II. There I explore the problematic, challenging nature of the returning romance. Why is it that the same text can be read as conservative expressions of traditional family values, or as a sexual phantasmagoria; as a closed, teleological form or as an open-ended experimental; as Hellenocentric or as centrifugal; as philosophically serious or as comedic? This is in part a question of which elements we choose to emphasise, for these are compendious texts containing many different kinds of utterance, often contradictory. In Heliodorus, for example, we find the same character (Charicleia) variously referring to the cosmos as chaotically unstructured and providentially ordered.[87] One central aim of part II is to interpret such perspectives *relationally*.

As scholars of post-classical literature have emphasised, romance plays out conflicting desires, particularly in relation to closure. For Patricia Parker, notably, it is 'a form that simultaneously quests for and postpones a particular end'.[88] For David Quint, epic and romance are opposed as teleological linearity to digressive episodicity; but in any given text, the two forces will operate dyadically, the one always implying the other.[89] Following such scholars (and this is part of the reason for my preference for the term 'romance' over the more conventional 'novel'), I read the Greek romances as complex and conflicted, at the level of metanarrative, which is to say a text's self-conscious theorising of its own narrativity. There is much

---

[86] Todorov (1977) 233. [87] Chaotic: 6.8.3–6; providentially ordered: 9.24.4.
[88] Parker (1979) 4. [89] Quint (1993), esp. 31–41.

about narrative in this book, but I am not conceiving of this in the static, definite sense familiar from the formal narratology that has dominated the field (much though I have learned from this).[90] This book treats narrative instead as a space of indeterminacy, for the characters of romance and for the reader alike, at least until the closural resolution (and, to an extent, even then). In this respect, I build on the cognitive approaches of critics like D.A. Miller and Peter Brooks, who treat narrative as a realm of possibility and desire.[91] Narrative, from this perspective, is not simply a synonym for Aristotelian plot – the system that gives events their larger significance through logical or plausible concatenation – but rather an experiment with multiple, sometimes contradictory plot*ting* hypotheses.

It may seem surprising to speak of conflicted desire in the romances, whether at the literal or the metanarrative level. Aegialeus and Thelxinoe are the exceptions: elsewhere, almost all other (sympathetic) characters want to go home and live a stable life of marital happiness with their partners. If these articulations of desire figure or stimulate the reader's own sense of plot, can we not simply conclude that romance is entirely trammelled towards the happy ending? At one level, this is surely right: the point bears repeating, that return stories play to a deep, structural desire to locate the individual in a larger pattern of optimistic renewal of life through communal living. As the Aegialeus story has already demonstrated, however, the Greek romances are not simply reflexes of primal instincts, but also mediated through artful narrative. Even by the early imperial period, Greek writers could call upon some 800 years' worth of sophisticated return narratives, together with critical reflections upon them. To give a full account of the romance, we need to explore also the *turns* of narrative and language, the tropes (*tropai*) that are so fundamental to Greek adventure narrative, from polytropic Odysseus onwards. The book is not just about the return romance as paradigm; it is also about how individual romancers cunningly re-turn the tradition.

Even more than any narrative form,[92] romance needs procrastination, unpredictability and amplification, and for a number of related reasons. The first is obvious, namely that in a return narrative, the plot exists

---

[90] Egregious examples include Hägg (1971), Lowe (2000) 222–58, and Morgan (2004b–e) and (2007b), (2007c), (2007d), (2007e); see also Whitmarsh and Bartsch (2008) 237–45.
[91] Miller (1981); Brooks (1984). See also Sturgess (1992) on narrativity, 'the enabling force of narrative, a force that is present at every point in the narrative' (28); Sturgess too conceives of narrativity as potentially contradictory, capable of sustaining 'double logics' (68–92).
[92] Lowe (2000) 65–8.

primarily as a detour. The limit case of a romance with *no* turns would involve its protagonists staying at home throughout; in other words, it would lack all romance narrativity. The second reason follows from the first: the travels introduce the difference into the identity narrative. If I leave the house to buy a newspaper and return five minutes later, I am substantially the same person when I return. If, on the other hand, I am abducted by slavers and return only after three years, I will be transformed. In romance, the travels are the location for what Derrida would call *différance*: a deviation, both temporal and spatial, from the linearity that constitutes identity (in its root sense of sameness).[93] Finally, it is during the detour that romancers get to express their artistry: not just in the ecphrastic descriptions, imported from sophistic oratory, that intercut and arrest the narrative flow, but also in the very creative exuberance that contrives ever new twists and turns. When Chariton refers to Fortune as 'keen on invention' (*philokainos*, Char. 4.4.2), for example, he is self-reflexively vaunting his own capacity to fashion surprising new episodes.[94]

So even if the principal characters express desire for a speedy return home, there are other desires articulated, albeit more subtly, for centrifugal expansiveness. It is in this sense that romance narrative is conflicted. In the course of this book, I argue that the identity modelled in romance incorporates this conflict. In Chapters 5 and 6, I explain this identity in terms of the Freudian division between ego, superego and id. The ego is the 'realist' level of narrative, experienced as a mimesis of the real world: its consciousness, as it were. The superego is the desire for home-coming, and for all the conservative ideological apparatus thereby implied (marriage, social and familial role playing, hierarchies of gender and class). The id, by contrast, is the realm of emotional turbulence, centrifugality, narrative polytropism, alterity, the transformation of identity.[95] The use of this terminology is an analogy (that is to say, it is not intended to imply the universality of Freudian psychology in a literal sense); but it is a productive one, because it allows us to extrapolate from the complexity of romance narrative a more sophisticated model of identity, one that transcends simple either/or models (conservative/experimental, Hellenocentric/Hellenofugal, public/private and so forth).

It is, finally, this flexible model of narrativity and identity that, I argue, accounts for the success of the romance over a period of three hundred or

---

[93] For *différance* as detour, see esp. Derrida (1974) 85–7.   [94] Below, p. 247.
[95] Fludernik (2007) 264: 'In a literal reading of the romance quest motif... the other is a space of alterity... From a psychoanalytic point of view, these uncanny spaces of alterity symbolize the unconscious or *id*.'

so years (in antiquity alone). It means that individual romancers can offer a satisfyingly rich and multifaceted narrative, capable of accommodating divergent readers with their own perspectives and tastes. But it also means that the form is malleable enough to respond, over time, to new historical and cultural circumstances, as different authors adjust the transformational ratio. It is to this diversity that we turn in part I.

PART I

Returning romance

CHAPTER I

First romances
Chariton and Xenophon

The Greek romance as we know it seems to have achieved its canonical form in the first century of the Roman principate.[1] For sure, Hellenistic precedents may well have existed, particularly in the 'national literature' of the subject peoples of the Greek kingdoms:[2] one particularly important case is *Joseph and Aseneth*, which tells of the mutual love, marriage and tribulations of the biblical patriarch, but the dating remains controversial (estimates vary between the second century BCE and the fourth century CE).[3] But it remains true, on the current consensus, that the ideal, fictional romance as we know it is very much a product of the early imperial era. The two first-century romances that survive in full[4] are Chariton's *Callirhoe* and Xenophon's *Anthia and Habrocomes*. Each offers a broadly similar narrative: young lovers meet, fall in love, are separated abroad, and return to be reunited. Each is set in a major Greek homeland (Syracuse for Chariton, Ephesus for Xenophon); the temporal setting is, implicitly (Xenophon) or explicitly the past (Chariton locates his romance in the aftermath of the failed Athenian invasion of 415–413 BCE; his heroine is the daughter of the historical general Hermocrates).

How can we explain the emergence of this genre at this particular historical juncture? In my introduction, I argued that we should not look to historical determinism alone to explain the emergence of the romance; we should be thinking of how individual authors creatively construct paradigms of identity rather than expecting them to reflect them passively. Over the course of this chapter, we shall see how Chariton and Xenophon exploit

---

[1] It was once thought that Chariton belonged to the first century BCE, and the *Ninus* fragment was pushed back as far as the second; the latest thought, however, locates both in the second half of the first century CE. See appendix, and esp. Bowie (2002) 47–52 attacking the Hellenistic date for *Ninus* (but the positive case for the later date, it must be admitted, is more speculative).
[2] Braun (1934), (1938).   [3] Overview at Humphrey (2000) 28–38.
[4] The hypothesis that *Anthia and Habrocomes* is epitomised (Bürger (1892)) has been, in my view, effectively demolished by Hägg (1966) and O'Sullivan (1995) 100–39. I offer some more thoughts on epitome theory and the romances in a forthcoming paper.

and adapt traditional narrative patterns to articulate ideas of selfhood. Still, a quick sketch of the civic contexts in which Chariton's and Xenophon's romances appeared will help to explain some of the background. This is especially valuable for these two texts, since they are the most 'civic' of the romances, in that (particularly compared to the later romances) considerable emphasis is placed on beginning and ending in the *polis*, and the festivities and rituals that take place there. Given that urbanism is implicitly presented as the precondition for civilised life, it makes sense to consider what his own native city may have meant for each author.

Chariton hailed from the Carian city of Aphrodisias, he tells us, and served as the secretary (*hupographeus*) of the orator Athenagoras (1.1.1). This identification, if it is not fictitious ('Mr Favours, from the city of Aphrodite' is a suspect name for an erotic romancer), is extremely interesting, since Aphrodisias occupied a unique position in Roman political history. As archaeology has demonstrated so dramatically,[5] the city grew rapidly from a village to a major civic centre in the imperial period, thanks largely to the patronage of the emperors Augustus and Tiberius. It helped enormously, no doubt, that Aphrodisias had been uniquely loyal to Rome in general and the Julio-Claudians in particular throughout the turbulence of the first century BCE.[6] An inscription dated to 88 BCE records that 'our whole People, together with our wives and children and all our property [?] is ready [?] to risk all for Quintus and the Roman cause... without the rule of the Romans we do not even choose to live'.[7] Inscriptions are not ingenuous expressions of sentiment, but they are contracts with fate. In this case, the decision was inspired. The city was granted free status by Octavian in 39 BCE, perhaps renewing an earlier gift by Sulla. The Aphrodisians had declared their political hand early on, and reaped the benefits. Their theatre was dedicated by a freedman of Octavian. An extensive portico was built for Tiberius, and baths for Hadrian. Most spectacular of all was the Sebasteion, the centre of the cult of the living emperor, with its now-famous relief work allegorically depicting imperial victories over Armenians, Jews, Britons, Arabs and others, and the emperor's rule over earth and sea.[8] Aphrodisias was thus a monument to the regenerative power of benevolent imperial rule.

---

[5] Up-to-date information and bibliography can be found at http://www.nyu.edu/projects/aphrodisias/home.ti.htm. The inscriptions are usefully, and exceptionally well, catalogued at http://insaph.kcl.ac.uk/index.html. On Chariton and Aphrodisias, see now Tilg (2010) 24–36.

[6] For Aphrodisias' support of Rome during the Mithridatic wars see App. *Bell. civ.* 1.97.455, with Reynolds (1982) D2–3 and p. 4; for loyalty to Caesar despite the invasion of Labienus, see Reynolds (1982) 5, 31.

[7] Reynolds (1982) D2 11–14.   [8] Smith (1988).

First romances

This alignment of regional, panhellenic and imperial interests was embodied in the figure of Aphrodite herself.[9] Aphrodisian representations of Aphrodite weave together three cultural strands. The first is a primeval Anatolian deity, or at least such a deity as imagined from the vantage of Roman times: the staid, unerotic cult figure with her distinctive *ependytēs* (or stiff tunic), recalling other Anatolian types such as the Artemis of Ephesus. The second is the familiar Greek goddess; the famous sculptural 'school of Aphrodisias' was particularly keen on Hellenistic depictions of the goddess. The third is the mother of Aeneas[10] and progenitor of the Julio-Claudian dynasty. A statue group in the Sebasteion, for example, linked together Aphrodite (titled 'the fore-mother (*promētōr*) of the divine Augusti'), Aeneas and 'a wide-ranging selection of Julio-Claudian princes and princesses'.[11] As so often in the imperial Greek world, cult served as the symbolic mediator between regional and panmediterranean interests.

Aphrodite is also the central deity in *Callirhoe*. The egregiously beautiful protagonist is compared to or mistaken for her throughout.[12] Her close connection with the goddess begins with a reference in the first chapter to her beauty, which is 'not a human's but a goddess's; and not a Nereid's or a mountain nymph's, but of Aphrodite herself',[13] and ends in the prayer to the goddess that closes the narrative (8.8.15–16).[14] Heavily influenced by the naturalistic conventions of historiography,[15] Chariton portrays a world that is in general relatively free from divine intervention: aside from Aphrodite (and Eros), there are only passing references to Olympian deities.[16] This is a text so light on deity that even Reinhold Merkelbach had to exclude it from his 'mystery text' theory of the Greek romance.[17] Aphrodite's central role is thus all the more significant. Throughout, she

---

[9] For a comprehensive overview, see Brady (2007).
[10] A connection already made in the late republic: Reynolds (1982) 3–5.
[11] Smith (2006) 44. The base featuring the inscription is Aphrodisias inv. 82–117 in Smith (2006); cf. Reynolds (1986) 111.
[12] Callirhoe compared to or mistaken for Aphrodite: 1.1.2, 1.14.1, 2.2.6, 2.3.6, 2.5.7, 3.2.14, 5.9.1. Comprehensive discussion of Chariton's Aphrodite at Alperowitz (1992) 41–57; useful remarks on Callirhoe as epiphany of Aphrodite also at Hägg (2002) 52–5. See also Edwards (1991) 191–200; (1994); (1996) 20–2 (with index s.v. Chariton) for an Aphrodisian reading of Chariton's Aphrodite.
[13] [ἦν... τὸ κάλλος] οὐκ ἀνθρώπινον ἀλλὰ θεῖον, οὐδὲ Νηρῗδος ἢ Νύμφης τῶν ὀρειῶν ἀλλ' αὐτῆς Ἀφροδίτης, 1.1.2.
[14] The circularity is reinforced by the cross-reference to her initial prayer at 1.1.7–8: cf. esp. τοῖς ποσὶ προσέπεσε καὶ καταφιλοῦσα (1.1.8) ~ λαβομένη... αὐτῆς τῶν πόδων... καταφιλοῦσα (8.8.15). Foot-grabbing also appears at 2.2.7.
[15] Bartsch (1934), Zimmermann (1961), Hunter (1994), Alvares (1997), Manuwald (2000) 102–6. Morgan (1993) argues that the romances generally recur to historiography, to corroborate their craving for realism.
[16] As Weißenberger (1997), in particular, emphasises.
[17] Merkelbach (1962); a similar exemption is made by Merkelbach's student Remi Petri (1963).

(alone of gods) is prayed to in the expectation that she will influence events.[18] Elsewhere she is reproached for her actions.[19] On rare occasions, she is directly credited with 'governing' (*politeuesthai*) the plot, by arranging marriages.[20] At the beginning of the final book, in a passage to which we shall return more than once, she is said to have overruled the plans of Tukhē (here in her guise as 'Fortune' or 'Chance' rather than 'Providence') to engineer another 'gloomy' (*skuthrōpon*) event, since she 'was now beginning to be reconciled (*diallattomai*) with [Chaereas], having previously been furiously angry (*orgistheisa*) with him on account of his inappropriate jealousy'.[21] The spending of divine wrath – an epic motif – betokens the closure of the romance, and the harmonious restitution of order. More than this, Aphrodite reassumes her benign and providential role in the ordering of human affairs. In general terms, then, *Callirhoe* expresses an ultimate confidence in the tutelary beneficence of the established order, as embodied in the figure of Aphrodite, who mediates between local *polis*, transpolitical networks and cosmic order (the role she played, indeed, in Aphrodisian cult and architecture).[22] She embodies what Edwards has called 'the web of power'.[23]

Ephesus, whence Xenophon (whose modern surname 'of Ephesus' serves to distinguish him from his better-known Athenian namesake),[24] was by contrast one of the oldest Ionian cities.[25] Its position, on both the coast and the Maeander, lent it an enduring importance strategically and in terms of trade. Mythically, it laid claim to foundation by Androclus, the son of the legendary Athenian king Codrus; in fact, the city's history had been largely shaped by the sixth-century Lydian king Croesus (who was behind the

---

[18] 1.1.7, 2.2.7–8, 3.2.12–13, 3.8.7–9, 6.2.4, 7.5.2–5, 8.2.8. 8.4.10, 8.8.15–16. [19] 3.10.6, 5.10.1, 7.5.1–5.
[20] 2.2.8 (ἄλλον ἐπολιτεύετο γάμον); 5.1.1 (πολιτευσαμένης... τὸν γάμον). Eros, Aphrodite's son (the relationship is stressed at 2.2.8), is also given this kind of match-making role (1.1.4, 1.1.6 (πολιτευσαμένου), 1.1.12, 2.4.5; cf. also 4.7.5; 6.4.3–4).
[21] ἤδη... αὐτῶι διηλλάτετο, πρότερον ὀργισθεῖσα χαλεπῶς διὰ τὴν ἄκαιρον ζηλοτυπίαν, 8.1.3.
[22] See Edwards (1991), and esp. (1994) on Aphrodite as a figure for the 'web of power' in which Aphrodisias was implicated. Aphrodisians seem to have had a sustained interest in providence, to judge by both the cosmic imagery of the Sebasteion and the tract *On fate* by the Severan philosopher Alexander: Sharples (1983).
[23] Edwards (1994).
[24] The 'surname' has no ancient authority, appearing first at *Suda* Ξ 50 (where of course the need to differentiate between homonyms is paramount). The Ephesian origin has sometimes been doubted – e.g. by Griffiths (1978), claiming that 'our author is most at home in Lower Egypt, and especially Alexandria' (426) – but the evidence is so slender (and the possible explanations for distortions of or accuracy in any particular local knowledge so numerous) that I have opted to stick, tentatively, with the traditional identification.
[25] Bammer (1988) offers an accessible sketch, written by a major expert; see also (1984), narrowly on the Artemision. Knibbe (1998) 59–235 gives a narrative survey; see also the essays in Koester (1995). The Roman context is summarised by Rogers (1991) 2–16.

famous cult of Artemis Ephesia, incorporating both Greek and Anatolian elements), and by Lysimachus in the early third century, whose replanning of the city allowed it to develop into the spectacular environment still visible today. Unlike Aphrodisias, Ephesus had a history of non-compliance: it seceded from the Delian League in c. 412 BCE, refused an offer of cash-injection from Alexander the Great, and – most importantly for our purposes – sided with Mithridates against Rome in the first century BCE, despite forming part of Attalus III's bequest to the Romans in 133. The citizens tore down Roman statues, it is said (App. *Mithr.* 21), and massacred even those who had sought sanctuary with the goddess (*ibid.* 23). For this the Ephesians were punished by a vengeful Sulla, who, not content with fining the city and removing its freedom, reserved a most grievous treatment for this city, one that our sources do not relay (*ibid.* 61). Even so, by Xenophon's time the city's natural advantages, its status as an assize centre and the reorganisation of the provinces under the empire (which limited the opportunities for corruption) meant that it had regained its position of primacy in Asia – particularly in matters of imperial cult, in respect of which the Flavian emperors awarded it the prestigious title of *neokoros* ('minister'), apparently the first time that the term had been applied to a city in this way.[26]

Ephesus is presented in *Anthia and Habrocomes* as the centre of the civilised world, together with Rhodes (another city that benefited from Roman favour, thanks to its loyalty in the Mithridatic wars). The patron deities of the two cities, Artemis and Apollo-Helios, steer the narrative (as we shall see in greater detail below). Unlike Chariton, Xenophon (if the biographical tradition is accurate) set his romance in his own city. According to the *Suda* (Ξ 50), he wrote another work *On the city of Ephesus*; this was perhaps periegetical in nature.[27] In line with the general deprecation of our author, many scholars have uncharitably downplayed Xenophon's awareness of epichoric features.[28] It is true enough that his Artemis is the familiar panhellenic goddess of hunting rather than the protuberant Anatolian hybrid, but this does not mean that Xenophon's image is un-Ephesian. It is misleading to allow our idea of the Ephesian cult to be exclusively dominated by the latter image. We do, in fact, have a snapshot

---

[26] Friesen (1993), esp. 50–74.
[27] Ξενοφῶν Ἐφέσιος, ἱστορικός. Ἐφεσιακά· ἔστι δὲ ἐρωτικὰ βιβλία ἱ περὶ Ἀβροκόμου καὶ Ἀνθίας· καὶ περὶ τῆς πόλεως Ἐφεσίων· καὶ ἄλλα. It is occasionally speculated that the phrase 'and concerning the city of Ephesus' may be a descriptive gloss also referring to the romance (e.g. Kytzler (2003) 346), but this would be an anomalous way for the *Suda* to refer to a romance; and moreover καὶ ἄλλα suggests an itemised list of works.
[28] Gärtner (1967) 2058–9; Griffiths (1978) 426.

of at least one facet of the Ephesian cult of Artemis in the early Roman period, in the form of the celebrated inscription of Gaius Vibius Salutaris, set up in 104 CE (so approximately contemporary with Xenophon, on one dating), which stipulates (among other things) a procession of statues to the famous temple.[29] There are many differences between this procession and the festival near the start of *Anthia and Habrocomes* (1.2) – in particular, the former mixes adulation of the emperor (together with the senate and other Romans), a synoptic history of the *polis*, and self-promotion on its founder's part, whereas the latter is presented as a traditional civic festival[30] – but, crucially for our purposes, the inscription represents the goddess, as Xenophon does, in purely panhellenic guise. Of course, we have no way of knowing what the Artemis statues mentioned in the Salutaris decree looked like – perhaps they did depict the goddess in her epichoric form – but the inscription avoids the opportunity to regionalise her presentation, and arguably even actively panhellenises her. The only iconographic markers mentioned in the decree itself are stags (*elaphoi*, l.159) and torches (*lampades*, ll. 164–5, 168, 173 [restored], 186–7, 194 [restored]),[31] elements that are common to the conventional iconographic repertoire. Both elements are connected with the goddess in Xenophon.[32] In other words, Xenophon's Hellenised version of Artemis may well reflect not the author's ignorance of genuine Ephesian cult, but precisely the opposite: a tendency among contemporary Ephesians to downplay non-Greek elements.

Chariton and Xenophon, then, both originated in Asia Minor, and indeed their romances emerge from the provincial (and also imperial) *polis* culture that is so well attested to epigraphically. Asia Minor, indeed, seems particularly important for the early romance. The fragmentary romance that modern scholars call *Ninus* may well have originated from Aphrodisias, like *Callirhoe*: an early name for the city had been Ninoe, and two panels of the basilica reliefs portray, respectively, Ninus and Semiramis in Hellenised garb.[33] (It is possible, although wholly unprovable, that Chariton even

---

[29] *IE* 1a 27; Rogers (1991) controversially argues that it embodies the people's anxiety over the identity crisis generated by Roman intervention.

[30] Rogers (1991) 81: 'no ritual acts took place during the performance of Salutaris' procession. The procession did not form one of the constituent parts of the major religious festivals in the city.'

[31] Rogers (1991) 111 speculatively connects these with chthonic rites and the cult of Cybele, but they are too common a motif in Greek religion to convey these associations unequivocally.

[32] Anthia, who is dressed as the huntress-goddess, wears a fawn-skin tunic (1.2.6); some in the procession carry torches (*daides*, 1.2.4). A further point of comparison is the significant role given in Salutaris' procession to the ephebes (l. 211 [restored]), who are, along with the *parthenoi*, the focus of Xenophon's procession.

[33] On the significance of the Ninus narrative to Aphrodisias, see Yildirim (2004).

wrote *Ninus*: the dates and styles seem to fit).³⁴ Another 'historical romance' seemingly from the same period, and apparently stylistically similar to *Callirhoe*, is the fragmentary *Metiochus and Parthenope*, set on Samos (just off the Ionian coast).³⁵ The Ionian coast also provided the settings for other erotic narratives, now lost (and hence undatable): the *Cypriaca* of Xenophon of Cyprus (*Suda* Ξ 51: probably a scurrilous local history); and Philip of Amphipolis' *Rhodiaka*, an 'absolutely disgraceful' work, a pious Byzantine encyclopedia tells us (*Suda* Φ 351).

What does this localisation in Asia Minor tell us? The first point is that Ionia had suffered terribly at Roman hands in the late republic, as war and the depredations of governors took their toll. By the mid-first century CE, to which period our earliest romances seem to date, however, the region as a whole, and in particular favoured cities like Ephesus and Aphrodisias, had benefited from provincial centralisation, the prosecution of exploitative officials (e.g. Tac. *Ann.* 3.66–9, 4.15) and investment. The first-century romances, as we shall see, celebrate the capacity of Greek cities for post-crisis rejuvenation under benevolent authority. In this respect, they mimic Julio-Claudian imperial rhetoric, which also emphasised the theme of renewal at the cultural, moral and natural-cosmic levels, often imaged in terms of fecundity and legitimate reproduction.³⁶

The texts are not, however, simply allegorical celebrations of the benevolence of foreign empire. The happy ending is closely tied to return to the specifically Greek *polis*; foreigners and foreign lands, by contrast, represent hostility and threat. Xenophon and Chariton are deeply ambivalent towards power, as we shall see in more detail below. One recurring type-scene involves a lusty barbarian wheedling and making threats towards one of the lovers if she or he does not grant sexual favours; the latter nonetheless remains true to his or her beloved.³⁷ There are close links between these scenes and martyr accounts – including, as well as the Jewish and Christian texts, the fragmentary Gentile 'acts of the pagan martyrs' – where virtuous individuals stand up to thuggish despots, particularly Romans.³⁸ As so often in the literature of the Roman era (and, indeed, in Hellenistic Jewish narrative),³⁹ aggressive power relations, particularly in the sphere of

---

[34] Bowie (2002) 49–51.
[35] Edited, together with a text and translation of the Coptic and Persian *Nachleben*, in HU.
[36] Zanker (1988) 101–66.   [37] Char. 6.5; Xen. Eph. 2.3–6.
[38] For the similarities with the *Acta Alexandrinorum*, see *APM* 252–8; and, on the similarities with Christian martyr acts, Perkins (1995) 41–76.
[39] Braun (1938) 44–102 on Hellenistic Jewish texts, principally the Greek *Testaments* of Joseph and Reuben (though the Hellenistic dating of these is now the matter of some controversy), and more

sexuality and interpersonal ethics, serve as allegories for the relationship between imperial power and subject.

In fact, all forms of hierarchical power are treated with caution in the first-century romances: the safety of the individual is only guaranteed in the context of the Greek city, where festivals and assemblies signal the enfranchisement of the entire populace, under the tutelage of a benign oligarchy. Not until Heliodorus in the fourth century do we encounter in the romances any intimation that happiness is reconcilable with monarchical rule. Ultimately, in these earlier texts it is not emperors and kings who guarantee the social order of Greek polities, but gods.[40] Gods, indeed, are politically ambiguous figures: they can be taken either as figurative of the emperor's power, or contrariwise as emblems of what mortal power is *not*, viz. absolute, uncontested and permanent. (This ambiguity of divinity reflects one of the roles of cult in Greek provincial *poleis*, as we saw above, namely simultaneously to emblematise distinctive regional sacrality and transmediterranean interconnectivity.) It is thus misguided to ask straightforwardly whether the romances promote or attack Roman hegemony. Like much early imperial Greek cultural production, they avoid talking directly about Rome, preferring to allegorise power by translating it into other realms (particularly those of ethics and religion), and then treating it in a complex, multifaceted way.

SOCIAL CRISIS

What is certainly the case, however, is that the first-century romances construct the health of the *polis* as the essential precondition for the happiness of the individual. The commonly expressed view that the romance is constitutively post-political – 'a social and personal myth, of the private individual isolated and insecure in a world too big for him'[41] – could not, thus, be further from the truth. The *polis* is at the heart of Chariton's and Xenophon's conception of civilised life (a fact that emerges even more strikingly through the contrast with the later romances of Longus

---

generally Shaw (1986). Interestingly, a similar scene is found at *Joseph and Aseneth* 23, where the sexual aggression of Pharaoh's son defines by contrast the virtues (vigour and wisdom respectively) of the Jews Simeon and Levi. On the issues around the dating of *Joseph and Aseneth* see above, n. 3.

[40] Perhaps reflecting the central role of the gods in dispute resolution, in contemporary cities: Hellenistic and imperial inscriptions from Asia Minor represent the gods as arbiters of social justice (Chaniotis (2004)).

[41] Reardon (1991) 28–9; see also above, pp. 8–9.

and Achilles).⁴² The egregiously beautiful youths upon whom the narrative centres are iconic for the city. Callirhoe is 'a marvel of a girl, the cult statue of all Sicily';⁴³ Chaereas has 'a youthful beauty surpassing all others', and 'gleams like a star'.⁴⁴ The language suggests the effulgence of a Pindaric victor, in the eyes of his compatriots. In return for the lustre bestowed, the people treat the protagonists with a superhuman reverence. Xenophon's Habrocomes 'was cultivated by all the Ephesians, and even all the inhabitants of Asia... they treated the young man like a god, and some even prostrated themselves and prayed to him when they saw him'.⁴⁵ Habrocomes and Anthia appear at the head of the troupes of young girls and boys in the festival processions (1.2), and again the people take a central interest: 'What a marriage it would be between Habrocomes and Anthia!' they shout.⁴⁶ In Chariton, it is the people, again, who agitate for the marriage between Chaereas and Callirhoe, a marriage that the 'patriotic' (*philopatris*, 1.1.12) Hermocrates, Callirhoe's father, feels unable to refuse; consequently, 'the Syracusans celebrated that day with more joy than the day of their victory over the Athenians'.⁴⁷

The young lovers' effulgence at one level separates them from the masses. As so often in aristocratic Greek culture, physical beauty accompanies (and, ideologically speaking, serves to naturalise) social distinction. Yet it would be a misunderstanding of aristocratic ideology to suggest that the elite are somehow *isolated* from the rest of the city. Rather, what distinguishes them is their ability to distil and embody the city's most sublime qualities. In this

---

⁴² Cooper (1996) 20–44 and Swain (1996) 101–31 both emphasise the role of civic values, but without distinguishing the registers of different romances; Morales (2008) 42–3 suggests a more pluralist approach.

⁴³ θαυμαστόν τι χρῆμα παρθένον καὶ ἄγαλμα τῆς ὅλης Σικελίας, Char. 1.1.1.

⁴⁴ μειράκιον εὔμορφον πάντων ὑπερέχων, Char. 1.1.3; στίλβων ὥσπερ ἀστήρ, Char. 1.1.5. This stellar imagery, which goes back to Homer (*Il* 5.5, 22.26), is particularly common in lyric depictions of egregious individuals: discussion and references at Whitmarsh (2004b) 388–90. It is also found in *Joseph and Aseneth* (2.6).

⁴⁵ ἦν δὲ περισπούδαστος ἅπασιν Ἐφεσίοις, ἀλλὰ καὶ τοῖς τὴν ἄλλην Ἀσίαν οἴκουσι... προσεῖχον δὲ ὡς θεῶι τῶι μειρακίωι, καὶ εἰσὶν ἤδη τινὲς οἳ καὶ προσεκύνησαν καὶ προσηύξαντο ἰδόντες, Xen. Eph. 1.1.3.

⁴⁶ οἷος ἂν γάμος γένοιτο Ἁβροκόμου καὶ Ἀνθίας, Xen. Eph. 1.2.9.

⁴⁷ ἥδιον ταύτην τὴν ἡμέραν ἤγαγον οἱ Συρακόσιοι τῆς τῶν ἐπινικίων, Xen. Eph. 1.1.13. Alvares (1997) 619 notes also the pandemic support for a mission to rescue Callirhoe, once it is realised that she is still alive: 'only in *Chaereas and Callirhoe* does the entire *state* strive to reunite the lovers, as if it were a matter of the highest political import'; 'this corporate mission to regain Callirhoe', he also observes, 'recalls the mythical panhellenic effort to recover Helen'. The analogous episode in Xenophon has 'the entire people' praying and sacrificing for Anthia and Habrocomes prior to their departure, (1.10.5), and the 'entire mass of Ephesians' seeing them off (1.10.6; πλῆθος is Hemsterhuis' supplement, but a plausible one: a neuter noun is clearly needed here).

normative model, there is no class friction: the happiness of the aristocracy is celebrated with just as much joy by the people.

Civic harmony, however, is put at risk by the onset of desire, which creates the narrative energy that stimulates the plot. As Edward Said has argued, the beginnings of literary works establish contracts with the reader, marking the state against which the remainder of the narrative defines itself, by more or less deviant forms of repetition.[48] Chariton and Xenophon exemplify this in a distinctive, beguilingly simple way. The beginning defines a state of social and psychic stability that is compromised by the onset of love. The subsequent narrative becomes an attempt to recapture that state; only at the end is it recaptured, but (as we shall see in the course of this chapter) in a way that suggests renewal as well as return.

Chariton (after his one-sentence prologue) and Xenophon show a remarkable degree of congruence in their handling of their beginnings. Each describes an egregiously beautiful young man and woman, who fall in love at a festival – despite powerful reasons why they should not (in Chariton because their parents are political enemies, in Xenophon because Habrocomes shows a Hippolytus-like distaste for sexuality). The differences will emerge presently, but the similarities are so close that they can be tabulated (see Table 1 below).

I leave aside the unanswerable questions of which author follows which, or whether both follow a common source;[49] what is more important to us here is that both describe a similar process. Each emphasises the disruptive power of desire on the community, a case of what the Russian critic Boris Tomashevksy calls 'the exciting force': 'In order to get the story going, a dynamic motif destroys the initial peaceful situation.'[50] The peaceful situation is expressed at the level of discourse by the use of the imperfect and present to describe them in the sections I have marked as A and C in Table 1.[51] This 'iterative' mode of narration exists in narrative primarily to be interrupted by dynamic events.[52] Sure enough, Eros intervenes, bringing about the transition from stasis to the dynamism of narrative: again, this latter state is marked discursively by the use of past tenses denoting change and rapid action ('singulative action').[53]

---

[48] Said (1975).   [49] See appendix.   [50] Tomashevsky (1965) 72.
[51] The exception is ἐξέβαλεν of Habrocomes at Xen. Eph. 1.1.5, where one would expect an imperfect (this may be a corruption: Hemsterhuis proposes ἐξέβαλλεν).
[52] Genette (1980) 116–17: 'iterative scenes are almost always functionally subordinate to singulative scenes, for which the iterative sections provide a sort of information frame'.
[53] In Chariton, the first aorists of the text (ὁ δὲ Ἔρως ζεῦγος ἴδιον ἠθέλησε συλλέξαι... ἐζήτησε δὲ τοιόνδε τὸν καιρόν, Char. 1.1.3); Xenophon however, uses inceptive imperfects rather than aorists (though NB the aorist participles ἐξοπλίσας... παριβαλόμενος, Xen. Eph. 1.2.1).

Table 1: *Similarities between the texts*

Chariton	Xenophon
A. Description of Callirhoe (1.1.1–2)	A. Description of Habrocomes (1.1.1–6)
B. Eros' desire to create an unusual match (1.1.3)	B. Eros' wrath at his contumely, and search for a plan (*tekhnē*, 1.1.6)
C. Description of Chaereas (1.1.3)	C & E. Local festival (*epikhōrios heortē*) where lovers meet, and description of Anthia (1.2.1–9)
D. Eros' pleasure in paradoxes, and search for an opportunity (*kairos*) (1.1.4)	D. 'Such were the devices of Eros' plan (*tekhnē*)' (1.2.9)
E. Public festival (*heortē dēmotelēs*) of Aphrodite and subsequent meeting of lovers (1.1.4–6)	
F. Erotic sickness (1.1.7–10)	F. Erotic sickness (1.3–5)
G. Diagnosis (1.1.10), followed by cure = marriage (1.1.11–16)	G. Diagnosis (by oracle and interpretation: 1.6–7) followed by cure = marriage (1.8)

Eros is an urgent and vital, but perverse and disruptive, force. In Chariton he is said to want to make 'his own kind of (*idion*) match',[54] the phrasing indicating that he has personal ambition rather than the collective good at heart. For this reason, we are told, he brings together the children of two political rivals; for, the narrator comments apophthegmatically, 'he is competitive (*philoneikos*), and rejoices in successes against the odds' (1.1.4).[55] In Xenophon, he is also described as 'competitive' (1.2.1). This, in Xenophon, leads him to 'rage' (*mēniāi*, 1.2.1) against Habrocomes, an anger that no doubt alludes to the comparable narrative-inceptive role as the 'rage' (*mēnis*) of Achilles, thematically announced in the first line of Homer's *Iliad*. Eros thus embodies the qualities of rivalrous individualism that the Greeks considered so destructive of civic unity.[56] The competitiveness

---

[54] ζεῦγος ἴδιον (context cited in previous note). I have offered the conventional interpretation of this phrase (which, I believe, fits better with the emphasis upon Eros' idiosyncratic behaviour); but ἴδιον might also be taken as 'local' (i.e. in contrast to the suitors from Italy and further afield just mentioned).

[55] For similar characterisations of Eros, see 2.4.5 (ἐφιλονείκει), 6.4.5 (φιλόνικος). Τύχη shares this attribute: see 2.8.3, 5.1.4, 6.8.1. I have retained MS readings *contra* Reardon who prefers to standardise to φιλόνικ-, but the palaeographical and semantic conflation of the two (homophonic) terms is notorious (good discussion at Duff (1999) 83).

[56] Konstan and Rutter eds (2003).

that characterises him metonymically figures his effects upon society. In Chariton, notably, the wedding of Chaereas and Callirhoe is compared to that of Peleus and Thetis, where (the near-namesake of Eros) Eris, the personification of strife, began the chain of events leading to the Trojan War (1.1.16): the frustrated suitors gather and plot (1.2), and deliberately engineer in Chaereas the jealousy (*zēlotupia*, 1.2.5–6) that causes him to attack Callirhoe (and indeed energises numerous later scenes in the narrative).[57] Eros is thus at one level a god, an external force who (like Aphrodite in Euripides' *Hippolytus*) afflicts individuals against their will; at another, however, he serves as a figure for the psychic turbulence – the arrogance, competitiveness, frustration and identity confusion – that comes with adolescence.[58]

Eros thus also plays a metanarrative role: he represents the principle of inventiveness and change necessary for a story to progress. He is a strategic plotter: in both texts he is said to 'search' (*zētein*), respectively for an 'opportunity' (*kairos*, Char. 1.1.4) and a 'plan' (*tekhnē*, Xen. Eph. 1.2.1, 1.2.9). Discussing the modern novel, Peter Brooks comments on the regularity with which desire figures the inception of narrative: 'Desire is always there at the start of a narrative, often in a state of initial arousal, often having reached a state of intensity such that movement must be created, action undertaken, change begun.'[59] The first-century romance alchemically transforms high-level theory into narrative praxis (a phenomenon that we shall see again): Eros figures, and also embodies, the magical process whereby narrative energy is created apparently out of nothing, and stillness suddenly becomes chaos. From now on until closure is reached, life for the protagonists is to be experienced in the liminal phase, with its hyperactive, staccato sequence of 'congealed "suddenlys"'.[60] At the same time, however, Eros also embodies the intention of ultimate closure, of legitimate consummation and the final spending of that sexual-narrative energy. Desire exists, at least for the protagonists of the romance, to be ultimately satisfied. In the first-century

---

[57] For ζηλοτυπία, see also Char. 3.9.4, 4.4.9, 5.1.1, 5.9.9, 6.6.5, 6.6.7, 6.7.11, 8.1.3, 8.1.15, 8.4.4, 8.5.15, 8.7.6; Helms (1966) 32–4. Fantham (1986) posits a fundamental link between ζηλοτυπία and violence between the sexes, beginning from the pun at Arist. *Plut.* 1014–16 (ἐτυπτόμην . . . ζηλοτύπος); she also discusses the stock comic motif of the violently jealous lover. But violence towards *pregnant* women (not that Chaereas is aware of his wife's state) is specifically characteristic of tyrannical figures: see Ameling (1986).

[58] Chariton is particularly fond of this allegorical approach, whereby the subjective emotions stimulated in humans by *erōs* are attributed to the god himself: 'Eros is by nature optimistic (φύσει . . . εὔελπίς ἐστιν ὁ Ἔρως, 2.6.4); 'the love of ornamentation is a characteristic of Eros' (ἔστι . . . ἴδιον ἔρωτος <τὸ> φιλόκοσμον, 6.4.3). Ancient orthography, of course, did not distinguish proper name from abstraction.

[59] Brooks (1984) 38. [60] Bakhtin (1981) 102.

First romances 37

romance, that process will coincide with the healing of differences within the *polis*, the restoration of social concord and psychic wholeness – and also the reader's consummation of her or his desire for narrative *telos*.

In both Chariton and Xenophon, falling in love catalyses a crisis in the community. The love-sickness experienced by the lovers is replicated at the civic level, as negative, destructive emotions surface, threatening the cohesion of the social group. This play between social/psychic wholeness and fragmentation is articulated by ritual practice, particularly in Xenophon. I mean 'articulated' in a double sense. Firstly, ritual is the primary 'language' through which these movements are expressed. Secondly, and relatedly, rituals mark the 'joints' (*articuli*) of the narrative, the junctures where societies either reconstitute themselves or decompose into discord.[61] In Chariton, it is at a 'public festival' (*heortē dēmotelēs*, 1.1.4), in Xenophon at a 'local festival' (*epikhōrios heortē*, 1.2.2), that the lovers meet. This idea that festivals are occasions of sexual possibilities is, of course, a staple of erotic literature,[62] and presumably has a certain basis in the reality of ancient Mediterranean life, where such occasions offered a rare opportunity for women and men to commingle. This cliché is reanimated in the romance, however, as the festival metamorphoses from a topical narrative device into a feature in its own right – again, particularly in Xenophon, where it receives an uncharacteristically lavish ecphrasis (1.2.2–9). This description mobilises all the civic themes of the opening section of the romance, bringing the relationship between individual and community into sharp focus. The central dynamic, for Xenophon, is the dialogue between the masses of spectators (both local and foreign: 1.2.3)[63] and the youthful procession. The spectators figure a community united in the act of viewing. The objects of their gaze, meanwhile, ritually perform the harmony of the occasion. Maidens and ephebes are separated; they process 'in file' (*kata stikhon*, 1.2.4). Marriage is the expected outcome, since 'it was the custom at that festival for grooms to be chosen for maidens, and wives for ephebes'.[64] Marriage figures social concord, as so often in this period:[65] the coming together of women and men, maidens and ephebes at the culminating sacrifice (1.3.1) emblematises

---

[61] Lalanne (2006) 118–22.
[62] Rohde (1914) 155; Trenkner (1958) 110. See e.g. Lys. 1.20 (perhaps a source for Chariton: Porter (2003)); Lycophr. 102–9; Plaut. *Cist.* 89–93 (perhaps ~ Men. fr. 382 Körte); Call. *Aet.* 67.5–8, 80+2 Pfeiffer; Parth. *Am.* 32.2; Jos. *Ant. Jud.* 2.45 (δημοτελοῦς... ἑορτῆς, Chariton's phrase: Whitmarsh (2007b) 88).
[63] Though in fact subsequently only Ephesians are mentioned: 1.2.7.
[64] καὶ γὰρ ἔθος ἦν <ἐν> ἐκείνηι τῆι πανηγύρει καὶ νυμφίους ταῖς παρθένοις εὑρίσκεσθαι καὶ γυναῖκας τοῖς ἐφήβοις, Xen. Eph. 1.2.3.
[65] On the shared vocabulary of political and marital concord in this imperial era see Veyne (1978).

the complementarity of opposed elements. The community, meanwhile, invests its aspirations in the projected marriage of the two most beauteous youths: we have already considered their cry, 'what a marriage it would be between Habrocomes and Anthia!' (1.2.9).

There is, however, an ominous underlying theme. Even during the happy festival, we know that Eros has promised discord: the description is introduced by way of explicating the 'device' (*tekhnē*) that this 'strife-loving' (*philoneikos*) god sought to use against Habrocomes. This discord is figured in Eros' anger (he 'raged', *mēniai*: 1.2.1) and military apparel ('he armed himself, and equipping himself with the entire force of his erotic drugs, began his campaign against Habrocomes').[66] This aggressive, militarist iconography leaks into the description of the parade: horses, dogs and hunting equipment are paraded (we read), are a mixture of the 'warlike' (*polemika*) and the 'peaceful' (*eirēnika*).[67] The community's investment in the pair, moreover, is immediately rewarded not with happy marriage but with agonising sickness, which brings each of them close to death. Even when the two lovers are married, the discordant undertones continue. The marriage itself reprises the theme of pandemic happiness, and harmony itself engulfs the entire community ('the city was full of merrymakers'; 'all-night parties were held and many sacrifices were offered to the goddess').[68] Once again, though, the festal occasion is heavily overshadowed: by the oracle's dark intimations; by the foreknowledge that their parents have decided to send them abroad for a certain time (1.7.2); and by the iconography of the coverlet on the marital bed, which presents the Erotes waiting on Aphrodite on one side, but the adultery of Aphrodite with the warlike Ares on the other (1.8.2–3).

In Chariton, characteristically, these themes of harmony and conflict emerge more naturalistically, motivated by personal and interpersonal psychology. Callirhoe goes to a festival of Aphrodite, but rather than meeting Chaereas there (as the serendipitous episode in Xenophon would lead us to predict), she happens to bump into Chaereas (who is coming back from the gym) on a street corner afterwards (1.1.5). The festival is incidental to the action, and not described in any detail; it exists *sous rature*, as though Chariton were reminding us of the clichés adopted by lesser romancers.

---

[66] ἐξοπλίσας... ἑαυτὸν καὶ πᾶσαν δύναμιν ἐρωτικῶν φαρμάκων περιβαλόμενος ἐστράτευεν ἐφ' Ἁβροκόμην, Xen. Eph. 1.2.1.

[67] †τῷδρὶ† πολεμικά, τὰ δὲ πλεῖστα εἰρηνικά, Xen. Eph. 1.2.4. Despite the irresoluble corruption in the initial part of the sentence, the opposition seems secure.

[68] μεστὴ... ἡ πόλις ἦν τῶν εὐωχουμένων, 1.7.3; παννυχίδες ἤγοντο καὶ ἱερεῖα πολλὰ ἐθύετο τῆι θεῶι, 1.8.1.

The tensions, instead, are played out at the political level, and largely in civic space.[69] Chaereas' and Callirhoe's parents have a 'political hostility' (*politikos phthonos*), which is specifically activated by the children's passion for each other (1.1.3). Hermocrates, Callirhoe's father, only assents to the marriage because a 'legal assembly' is held, and the populace insists upon the wedding; the 'patriotic' (*philopatris*) Hermocrates cannot refuse the will of the people and Eros 'the demagogue' (1.1.11–12).

Sexual awakening in young women and men thus forces them to become pawns, and to an extent players, in the political game of dynastic match-making. This game is a complex one, accommodating the partially conflicting will of parents and family, the community at large, and of course the lovers themselves. The discordant notes are sounded not so much (as in Xenophon) by militaristic imagery at the abstract levels of divinity and ecphrastic description, as at the naturalistic level, through the representation of the vagaries of interpersonal conflict and their psychological consequences. The general joy at the marriage is offset by the grief (*lupē*) and anger (*orgē*, 1.2.1) experienced by the band of frustrated suitors (*mnēstēres*, distantly evoking Penelope's suitors in the *Odyssey*). It is these individuals who directly embody the imagery of militarism and strife that is more abstract in Xenophon.[70] Moreover, whereas Xenophon's Eros, a deity, seeks a 'device' (*tekhnē*, 1.1.6) to use against Habrocomes, it is Chariton's human suitors who perform the analogous scheming function (*tekhnē*, 1.2.4; cf. 1.4.1). In Xenophon, the work of disruption and disordering is part of an inscrutable and (in realist terms) undermotivated metanarrative plan; in Chariton, that same work is done by human agents, whose reasons are motivated 'realistically'.[71]

The beginnings of the first-century romances dramatise societies performing their collectivity through time-honoured ritual and political practice – at the same time as the failure of that collectivity, its capacity for self-destruction under pressure. The narrative of separation from the community can thus be read both as a narrative narrowly about named individuals, and more generally as an allegory for the psychic and social trauma

---

[69] Connors (2008) 164–5; Morales (2008) 42–3.
[70] Military imagery: ἐστρατολόγει... αὐτοὺς ἐπὶ τὸν κατὰ Χαιρέου πόλεμον, Char. 1.2.1; χειροτονήσατέ με τοῦ πρὸς Χαιρέαν πολέμου στρατηγόν / ἐφοπλιῶ / σύμμαχον, Char. 1.2.5. They are also associated with athletic agonistics: ὥσπερ ἐν τοῖς γυμνικοῖς ἀγῶσιν, Char. 1.2.2; βασιλέων ἀγωνισαμένων αὐτὸς ἀκονιτὶ τὸν στέφανον ἤρατο, Char. 1.2.3 (a 'naturalistic' counterpart to Habrocomes' figurative wrestling match with Eros, Xen. Eph. 1.4.1–5); ἆθλον, Char. 1.2.4.
[71] Similarly, whereas Chariton's intercontinental chase is motivated by a chain of naturalistic events, Xenophon's lovers are packed off on their travel simply to 'appease' (παραμυθήσασθαι, Xen. Eph. 1.7.2, 1.10.3) an oracle that is itself undermotivated (all the parents wanted to know was why their children were pining away).

that comes with burgeoning sexuality and the prospect of marriage: the complex networks of obligation and competition, the pain and confusion, the end of the unconditional bond between parents and children.

BEGINNING, MIDDLE, END

How are these beginnings set against the rest of the narrative? As Aristotle famously observed, every story needs a beginning, a middle and an end (even if, as Jean-Luc Godard is said to have opined, 'not necessarily in that order').[72] Although (of course) there are variations at the level of cultural practice, this schema, in its most fundamental form, encodes the stark reality of our existence: we are born, we live, we die. All forms of human cultural expression have been, at some level, attempts to manage this awful truth. If the story of birth, life and death is humanity's primordial tragedy, its narratives of redemption and transcendence are no less important. To be human requires not just acceptance of one's own mortality, but also faith in the survival of humanity beyond the individual's death: the end of one generation is the beginning of another. Sexuality is our glimpse of immortality, our compensation for death. The story of sexual fulfilment is again tripartite – we desire, we pursue, we consummate – but its ending is joyous and celebratory. The story of human sexuality is also the story of human sociality, of how the frail transitoriness of the individual is offset by the permanence of the family and the community. It is also, at a more abstract level, the story of religion: of the benign rationality of the divine order, of the indestructibility of the soul, of reproduction as a metaphor for eternity.

This second kind of tripartition underpins the romance. A girl and boy of marriageable age meet, fall in love, endure numerous obstacles, and then are joyously reunited in enduring matrimony at the end. In Chariton and Xenophon, the marriage occurs at the start, and is then reinstituted at the end; in the later romances, as we shall see in the following chapters, the marriage is shifted to the end. This narrative tripartition of the adventure romance is well-known, but has often been misinterpreted. The first point to make is that it is not a primitive, overschematic attempt to narrate psychological development. In an influential account, Mikhail Bakhtin argues that the disjunction between middle and end serves only the crude purpose of separating the two significant episodes located at the beginning

---

[72] Arist. *Poet.* 1450b 25–7; Godard quoted in Sontag (1969) 157.

First romances 41

and the end, namely the conception and the satisfaction of desire. This 'gap', he continues:

> the pause, the hiatus that appears between these two strictly adjacent biographical moments and in which, as it were, the entire romance is constructed is not contained in the biographical time-sequence, it lies outside biographical time; it changes nothing in the life of the heroes, and introduces nothing into their life. It is, precisely, an extratemporal hiatus between two moments of biographical time.[73]

For Bakhtin, then, the 'hiatus' after the moment of infatuation – the middle of the narrative – serves purely to delay the moment of consummation: there is otherwise no meaningful development during this period, which 'leaves no *trace* in the life of the heroes or their personalities'.[74]

Bakhtin's analysis is in fact entirely negative, sensitive only to what the romances lack, viz. a cogent psychology. John Morgan has rightly observed that no ancient romancer ever composed a *Bildungsroman* – 'Love is not developed qualitatively, nor are new insights into the self achieved'[75] – but this kind of claim expresses precisely the problem behind the formulation of the question. Would we expect any ancient text to deal with psychology in this way? Antiquity is not to be berated for its failure to promote the enlightenment conception of the self as 'subjective': consciousness-centred, entirely internalised, independent of external influences.[76] What the romances narrate is not the protagonists' acquisition of mature selfhood – understood in terms of autonomous subjectivity – but the changing ways in which the individual can be understood as a social and ethical being in relation to communities: an objective-participant conception of the self, to use Christopher Gill's phrase.[77]

Callirhoe and *Anthia and Habrocomes* are, as we have said, fundamentally about social life in one's native *polis*, and the traumas that occur when one

---

[73] Bakhtin (1981) 87–90, at 89–90. For an assessment of Bakhtin's value to criticism on the ancient romance, see especially Branham (2002), and (2005); and for a more critical account, Whitmarsh (2005d).
[74] Bakhtin (1981) 90.
[75] Morgan (1996), at 188. For the claimed lack of character development see also Konstan (1994) 45–6. Laplace (1991) and (2007), however, argues for development in Achilles Tatius.
[76] The bibliography is enormous. Especially useful philosophical studies are Long (1991), Gill (1996), and esp. (2006) xiii-xiv: 'what is innovative and distinctive in Hellenistic-Roman thought about selfhood is *not*, as is sometimes claimed, a shift towards a heightened interest in subjectivity'. The contributors to Pelling ed. (1990) approach the problem from a variety of literary and philosophical perspectives. Duff (1999) 13: 'Ancient conceptions of character were... less centred on the private, inner world of the individual'; they were concerned 'more with actions, and their evaluation'. For the relatively limited role of 'character change' in Plutarch, see Gill (1983), Swain (1989), Pelling (1990), and further below pp. 214–20.
[77] Gill (1996), (2006).

is cut off from that. Xenophon even seems to have granted Ephesus equal billing in the full version of the title, namely *The Ephesian affairs of Anthia and Habrocomes*.[78] Both are built around a mythical structure of centre and periphery:[79] the protagonists begin at home, travel abroad into marginal space before returning home at the end. In the simplest terms, the setting of the majority of the suffering narrative in 'barbarian' spaces is underpinned by a self-other model, reinforcing the cultural and ethical polarity of Greek and barbarian so frequently articulated by the characters.[80] The ending thus represents something more than mere affirmation: it is a powerfully symbolic, redemptory celebration of the Greek *polis* as the figurative and literal centre of a world that can ultimately be recognised to be overseen by deities with the interests of civilised, aristocratic Greeks at heart.

The centre–periphery structure creates powerful resonances. Greek culture contains numerous accounts of young women and men at the critical period of adolescence, separated from their society for a period and then reintegrated as adults. Van Gennep's hugely influential study of 1908, *Les rites de passage*, offers a template for the analysis of initiation in terms of three stages: pre-liminal (rites of separation), liminal (rites of transition, experienced in a state of separation), and post-liminal (rites of reincorporation into the world).[81] The model of ritual marginalisation embodied in myths such as those of Callisto, Io, Orestes, Telemachus, Jason and various young hunters (Odysseus, Meleager, Actaeon, Hippolytus) seems to have been mirrored (although the extent of this remains controversial) in civic institutions such as the *ephebeia* attested in various cities, the *arkteia* at Brauron, and the Spartan *krypteia*.[82] The bulk of scholarly work has

---

[78] Whitmarsh (2005b) 598–9.

[79] For the traditional division of space into centre and periphery, see Vidal-Naquet (1986a) 138–9. It is impossible to determine what structure the fragmentary romances adopted: the evidence is most plentiful for *Metiochus and Parthenope*, but still ambiguous (HU 247–50).

[80] See esp. Bowie (1991) on Chariton, and more generally Kuch (2003).

[81] van Gennep (1960), at 20. van Gennep's work has been importantly expanded by Gluckman (1962); Turner (1967) 93–111; Turner (1969). Since the pioneering work of Gluckman and Turner, there has been an enormous quantity of literature on the subject: particularly significant are Vizedom (1976), Droogers (1980) and the various essays in Bianchi (1986). For Greco-Roman applications, Moreau (1992), with extensive bibliography at II. 297–305; Padilla (1999); Dodd and Faraone (2003). For a critical overview of the applicability of initiation theory to Greek culture, see Versnel (1990) 44–59.

[82] See esp. Brelich (1969); Vidal-Naquet (1986a), (1986b), with Ma (1994); Calame (1997). The widespread existence of these rites is argued for by Vidal-Naquet (1986a) 106–28, 129–56 (1986b) and Calame (1997), esp. 89–206. On the other hand, Graf (2003) 20 argues that distinctive ephebic ritual was confined to Crete and Sparta.

focused upon the archaic and classical periods, but much of the evidence is in fact Hellenistic and imperial.[83]

Rather than seeing the romances as failed *Bildungsromane*, it is preferable to consider them, with Sophie Lalanne and others, as building upon and developing the classic tripartite passage rite.[84] The protagonists are invariably of 'ephebic' age, i.e. on the cusp of adulthood.[85] Bakhtin's two 'biographical moments' – initial infatuation and ultimate union – represent the pre-liminal and post-liminal rites. What Bakhtin calls the hiatus – that is to say, the substance of the narrative of separation and trial – marks the liminal phase, when the subjects endure marginalisation; the final reunion, ritually marked (in the three later romances) with marriage, coincides with the reintegration of the lovers into their communities as adults. Considering romantic narrative as a variety of the spatio-temporal paradigm of the passage rite not only offers a less anachronistic model than the *Bildungsroman*, it also allows us to see more sharply what kind of selfhood is being projected, understood in terms not of inner self-realisation (as in the *Bildungsroman*), but of relationships between individual and community.

Two caveats, however, are called for. First, to claim that romances build on passage rite narratives does not mean that they occupy an identical functional role. Sophie Lalanne has argued that the romances, by *narrating* the socialisation of youths into elite patriarchy within Greek society, simultaneously *perform* this process, idealising and legitimising the established routes to the cultural and sexual hegemony of elite Greek males.[86] This kind of reading, however, pays insufficient attention to the play of narrativity in the 'liminal' phase of the novel: in effect, Lalanne presumes (like Bakhtin) that liminality exists solely to be overcome *en route* to the ending, rather than constituting an experimental space in which the arbitrariness

---

[83] Perrin-Saminadayar (2004) offers a recent survey of findings in relation to the Athenian ephebe lists between the first century BCE and the second century CE.

[84] Cf. Schmeling (1974) 137–9; Burkert (1987) 66–7; Dowden (1999), (2005); Lalanne (1998) and (2006) (esp. 101–28, a thorough discussion of passage-ritual motifs in the romances; Alvares (2007). For individual studies, see Lalanne (1998) on Chariton; Laplace (1994) on Xenophon (cf. also Bierl (2006), esp. 93), and (1991) on Achilles; Winkler (1990) 101–26, Gual (1992) on Longus; Laplace (1992), Whitmarsh (1999) on Heliodorus.

[85] Morgan (1996), 165 n. 7 offers an analysis of the protagonists' ages: Xenophon's Habrocomes is sixteen at the beginning (1.2.2), while Anthia is fourteen (1.2.5); Achilles' Clitophon is nineteen at the outset (1.3.3), Longus' Daphnis and Chloe fifteen and thirteen at the start respectively (Long. 1.7.1; and two years older at the end). Heliodorus' Charicleia is seventeen at the end (10.14.4). There is no way of determining the ages of Chaereas and Callirhoe, but the former is designated an ephebe (1.6.5; 8.6.11); Habrocomes and Anthia similarly take part in a procession of ephebes and virgins (1.2–3), as does Heliodorus' Theagenes (3.3).

[86] Lalanne (2006).

and plasticity of social roles can be explored (as the cultural anthropologists Victor Turner and Clifford Geertz have argued).[87] The wider point, however, is that romances are not simply socially programmatic; they are complex literary narratives, and narratives (as we shall see throughout the course of this book) can model multiple, competing forms of identity.

The second point is that the modern concept of 'passage rites' is ambiguous, rolling together as it does the ideas of both coming of age and religious initiation. As we shall see in the following chapters, the later romances do make use of religious-initiatory language (*erōs* becomes a mystery cult); but there is precious little sign of these motifs in either Chariton or Xenophon, beyond a general resemblance at the thematic level ('[j]ourneys out and back, descents to suffering and disintegration, ascents to joy and reintegration, these are the stuff of mysteries and of romances too').[88] Even Merkelbach, in the course of his eccentric argument that the romances are religiously functional, exempts Chariton.[89] Xenophon, certainly, has a prominent scene of divine intercession, and refers on occasion to the characters' 'salvation' by the gods,[90] but there is (*pace* Merkelbach) no reason to take these features as tokens of a subjacent hermetic religious truth rather than of the general credence in the permeability of the human sphere by divine forces that is almost ubiquitous in the Greco-Roman world. But the use of these religious motifs is also deliberate, reflexive and artful; the romances should be read in terms of 'ritual poetics',[91] of literary strategy rather than of 'serious' religious homiletics.[92] The romances are 'religious' in the sense that they testify to the presence of numinous forces among us, but ancient polytheism lacked the sharp lines that categorically excluded scepticism, sexuality, mockery and play from religion.[93] An excellent exemplification of this comes in the fragmentary *Iolaus* romance. Here, it seems that Iolaus undergoes initiation into the number of the

---

[87] See esp. the position statement by Geertz (1979–80), and below p. 214 on Turner.
[88] Beck (2003) 150; cited with approval by Zeitlin (2008) 97, who also notes the aptness of Northrop Frye's description of romance as 'secular scripture' ((1976) 97–157).
[89] Above, n. 17. Merkelbach's claim is that historically the romance has its 'roots' (*Wurzeln*) in religious aretalogy ((1962) 333–40, esp. 333), and the texts that we have can be read on two levels, by a general readership and by religious initiates ((1988) 138–9; (2001) 56–59). For critiques of this position see above, pp. 193–204.
[90] Below, p. 194.   [91] See the essays in Yatromanolakis and Roilos (2004).
[92] See Dowden (1996), arguing for Heliodorus' 'serious intentions'. Anderson (1982), by contrast, argues for constitutive playfulness.
[93] For mocking and obscenity, the classic example is the Athenian γεφυρισμός (Hsch. Γ 468, *Suda* Γ 212; cf. Plut. *Sull.* 2.1); for discussion and further literature, see Halliwell (2008) 155–214 on obscene ritual generally, with 169–71 on the *gephurismos*. For cross-dressing and play as elements of cult, see e.g. Turcan (1992) 226–7.

Galli (castrated servants of Cybele) and dresses as a woman, in order to 'get a crafty fuck'.[94] The joke turns on the bathetic undercutting of the lofty language of initiation with crudely sexual language.[95] This is certainly not a 'realistic' representation of Cybele's cult,[96] but conversely there is no reason to assume that cross-dressing, role-playing, obscenity, and even sex were thought – whether by initiates or non-initiates – to run against the grain of the cult itself. The *Iolaus* fragment thus exemplifies particularly luridly the general principle that a Greek romance can be 'religious' while also being a sophisticated piece of literary fiction. The crucial point is to distinguish between religious *practice*, which was in the Greek world typically demarcated from regular life by clear boundaries marking sacred time and space, and religious *phenomenology*, which permeated almost every area of culture. It makes no sense, then, to see the romances as 'secularising'[97] (or, worse still, as 'parodying')[98] religiosity, since the intellectual sophistication and play that modern scholars might choose to identify as definitively secular were, in Greek culture, compatible with that religiosity. So, in sum: the claim that passage rites underlie the narrative templates of the early romances commits us neither to the position that the texts therefore mechanistically function to promote established social roles, nor to the position that they therefore exist primarily in order to encode deeper religious truths.

SYMBOLIC GEOGRAPHY I: XENOPHON

In the early romances of Xenophon and Chariton, 'abroad' functions as an absence or negation of 'home'; and, qualitatively speaking, it represents an inversion (geographic, cultural and ethical) of the *patris*. Xenophon's symbolic geography is less nuanced than Chariton's.[99] Ephesus, where the narrative begins and ends, is the centre of the romance, even literally (sited as it is pretty much equidistantly between the easternmost and westernmost

---

[94] δόλωι... βινεῖν, p. 370.30 SW.
[95] Mysteries: [ἀ-]πορρήτων (1), μυστικός (14), μυστικοῦ (35), τέλειός... γάλλος (37); comedy: πέπαιχεν (28), βινεῖν (30). SW 361–2 place *Iolaus* in the same 'criminal-satiric' bracket as Lollianus' *Phoenician affairs*; cf. also 462 on *P.Ant.* 18 (= SW 464–5).
[96] SW 360, who note that elsewhere '[i]nitiates are never said to be castrated or to become *galli*, nor are *galli* said to be initiated'.
[97] E.g. Kerényi (1927), at 230; (1971). Similarly, Rohde (1937) and Chalk (1960) argue that *Daphnis and Chloe* draws freely on elements of mystery religion to create a literary dedication (to Nature, in Rohde; to Eros, in Chalk); Petri (1963) argues much the same of Chariton, though (like his teacher, Merkelbach) he sees the other romances as Mysterientexte.
[98] E.g. Gual (1992) 158.
[99] Hägg (1971) 172–5; Lowe (2000) 230–1; Bierl (2006). I begin with Xenophon since his geography is simpler, even though his text may be later (see appendix).

extremes of the lovers' travels, viz. Syria and Italy/Sicily). Conversely, the places visited during the voyage (including Syria, Cilicia, Cappadocia, Phoenicia, Italy, Sicily) signify primarily in terms of otherness, as not-home.[100] Xenophontic space, as Anton Bierl felicitously puts it, is the externalised manifestation of the sensation of absence.[101] Xenophon offers the best support for Bakhtin's otherwise overstated claim that all 'adventures in the Greek romance are governed by an interchangeability of space; what happens in Babylon could just as well happen in Egypt or Byzantium and *vice versa*'.[102] In this space, the characters experience a nostalgia, in the etymological sense: a painful yearning for return. Thus in Tarsus, for example, Anthia meets a shipwrecked Ephesian doctor and 'enjoyed remembering what it was like at home'.[103] For the reader, meanwhile, to remember the Ephesian beginning (as this passage cues us to do) is also to anticipate an Ephesian ending: analeptic memory is merely the converse of proleptic yearning.

What are the primary markers of the world abroad? It is not that there is any qualitative cultural difference between Ephesus and other cities (notwithstanding the odd barbarian name like Apsyrtus, or the different language spoken in Cappadocia, 3.1.2). Greek-style civic culture certainly exists in these spaces:[104] we read, for example, of an elected official in Cilicia (the 'superintendent of the peace'),[105] and a 'big, fine city' in Cappadocia.[106] The central difference, in fact, lies not in the cities, but in the places of brooding threat just beyond their walls. Here we find the semi-urbanised villages (4.1.1, 5.2.4–7), and the wilder spaces inhabited by brigands, such as woods (2.11.3–11, 2.13.3) and caves (2.14, 3.3.4, 4.3.6–6.4, 5.2.3).[107] It is here that the protagonists are most grievously threatened with murder (2.11.3) and human sacrifice (4.6.4–7).

On the seas, outside of these cities (and sometimes within them), gangs of rootless outlaws roam, only occasionally falling foul of the law (2.13.4).[108] In narrative terms, these pirates and bandits represent a restless, energetic

---

[100] See generally Saïd (1999) 87–8. On the presentation of foreign space as an inversion of Greek see Hartog (1988) on Herodotus, and (2001) more generally; also Malkin (1998) on the *Odyssey*.
[101] Bierl (2006) 75.   [102] Bakhtin (1981) 100.
[103] ἔχαιρεν... ἀναμιμνησκομένη τῶν οἴκοι, Xen. Eph. 3.4.3.   [104] Saïd (1999) 95.
[105] ὁ τῆς εἰρήνης... προεστώς, 2.13.3; cf. 3.9.5, where the voting is mentioned. Scholars have associated these passages with the office of eirenarch, first attested under Trajan, primarily because this is taken to offer some clue as to the dating of the passage; but we 'have no right to suppose that our earliest epigraphic testimony is exactly contemporary with the first institution of such an office' (Bowie (2002) 57).
[106] πόλιν... μεγάλην καὶ καλήν, 5.1.1.   [107] Saïd (1999) 87–8.
[108] Hopwood (1998) addresses the role of bandits as inversions of normative masculinity. See also below, pp. 217–18.

mobility, the embodied agents of adventure time. Bandits can kidnap others, and move with astonishing speed: at one point, from Tarsus to Laodicea (in Syria), to Phoenicia, then to Egypt and up the Nile almost to Ethiopia, within the space of seventeen lines (4.1). These are the enemies of narrative stasis, ever accelerating and renewing the plot in unpredictable ways. Bandits thus occupy an ambiguous position in the narrative: morally and culturally they invert everything that the protagonists hold dear, but they also embody the narrative energy upon which the romance depends.

The major exception to this tendency to code foreign space negatively is Egypt, marked out for special treatment since Herodotus on the grounds of the number of its 'wonders' (Hdt. 2.35.1). Here as elsewhere there are certainly bandits and 'uncivilised' spaces, such as caves and villages, but Xenophon also shows a keen awareness of the local topography and religion of the Delta region,[109] and in particular of Egyptian religion.[110] In one extraordinary Egyptian episode, Habrocomes is miraculously saved, firstly, from crucifixion and, secondly, from crucifixion and burning. What makes this passage exceptional is that in general the Greek romancers tend to avoid direct divine intervention, in line with their general commitment to narrative naturalism.[111] In this case, in the first instance Habrocomes prays to Helios(-Ra), specifically in his Egyptian guise ('who dwell in Egypt', 4.2.4); the god is said to 'pity' him (4.2.6), and produces a freak whirlwind that hurls his cross into the Nile. On the second occasion, the Nile waters miraculously rise to put out the flames.[112] This exception from the realist rule is perhaps partially legitimised by the allusion to Croesus' salvation from the pyre (again by Apollo) in Herodotus (1.87.1–2): what is permissible

---

[109] Griffiths (1978) 425–37 and Sartori (1989), *contra* the more critical claims of Henne (1936) and particularly Schwartz (1985), who claim that the Egyptian landscape is largely traditional. By contrast, Plazenet (1995) 7–9 and Nimis (2004) 46–8 thoughtfully and more plausibly discuss Xenophon's representation of Egypt as an active engagement with earlier literary and cultural tradition (with earlier literature); see also in this vein Brioso Sánchez (1992).

[110] Hence some have claimed that the earliest stratum of Xenophon's text is an Isiac devotional text: Kerényi (1927), e.g. 232–3; Merkelbach (1962) 91–113; Witt (1971) 243–54 adds little; Griffiths (1978). Gärtner (1967) 2074–80, however, effectively rebuts this position, which (for Kerényi and Merkelbach at any rate) depends upon the desperate hypothesis of a later, secondary redaction.

[111] Morgan (1993) underlines the general emphasis upon reality effects in the romances. The romancers' practice is also in line with that of New Comedy, where again gods appear in metanarrative roles (notably in prologues), but not as players in the narrative proper: Vogt-Spira (1992) 4–5. See further below, pp. 193–5. A more complex case is Hld. 8.9.10–15, where Charicleia is saved from the blazing pyre: she initially thinks (8.9.16) she owes her salvation to the gods on whom she called (8.9.12), but it is in fact due to the *pantarbe* stone.

[112] Xenophon leaves it unclear to which god Habrocomes prays on the second occasion, but the implication is that it is Helios again (see further below, p. 194). The miraculous nature of the event is indicated by the prefect's wonder (ἐθαύμασεν, 4.2.10). On the religious motifs in this entire episode, see Zimmermann (1949/50) 273–7; Merkelbach (1962) 104–6, (2001) 599.

to the father of history is implicitly sanctioned for his distant descendants too.[113] (It is not impossible, either, that ancient readers would have thought also of Christ's death on the cross and subsequent resurrection.)[114] The crucial point for our purpose, however, is that it is in Egypt that we see the first direct signs of divine intervention in the narrative since the initial references to Eros' malevolence.

Indeed, as a number of scholars have noted, Xenophon's Egypt is (in line with traditional associations) dense with religious motifs, some explicit (such as the cases above, and the oracle of Apis at 5.4.8–11), some implied (notably Anthia's burial alive with Egyptian dogs, which, however, refuse to attack her (4.6.3–7) – a scene that evokes both a rebirth ritual and the kind of miraculous salvation that a later Christian martyr might experience in the arena). Particularly remarkable is the role of Isis: she is named as the lovers' 'saviour' (*sōteirēi*, 1.6.2) by Colophonian Apollo in the prophecy near the start, and appealed to in this capacity by Anthia when she takes refuge in the goddess's temple: 'Queen of Egypt, save (*sōson*) me again; you have helped me so many times before.'[115] Unsurprisingly, this Isiac emphasis has been seized upon by scholars wishing to see *Anthia and Habrocomes* as a devotional work.[116] Less credulously, we could take Egyptian Isis as a metastasis of Ephesian Artemis (the two are sometimes assimilated),[117] whom the lovers thank with dedications and sacrifices in close association with their 'salvation' in the closing lines of the text (*sōtēria*, 5.15.2). Even as Egypt is described in terms that mark it traditionally as a site of inversion and alterity, then, the Isiac-salvation theme simultaneously portends the

---

[113] Compare Habrocomes' second prayer (σῶσαι αὐτὸν ἐκ τῶν καθεστώτων κακῶν, 4.2.8) with Croesus' (ῥύσασθαί μιν ἐκ του παρέοντος κακοῦ, 1.87.1) – both in indirect speech – and also their outcomes (κατασβέννυσι τὴν φλόγα, 4.2.9 ~ κατασβεσθῆναι... τὴν πυρήν, 1.87.2). Habrocomes' earlier prayer (4.2.5), reported in direct speech, also contains a Herodotean allusion, to the latter's discussion of the sacred status of those who dive into the Nile (2.90; Zimmerman (1949/50) 275). Xenophon may also be looking sideways towards the Christian martyr tradition, which also makes use of pyre narratives: see *ACM* 1.15, 2.3, 10.21, 12.4–5. Full discussion of pre-Herodotean sources for the Croesus story (including Bacch. 3 and Myson's vase) at Asheri *et al.* (2007) 141–2.

[114] Ramelli (2001) 60: 'non si può assolutamente affermare che Senofonte avesse in mente la crocifissione di Gesù'. There are also non-miraculous salvations from crucifixion in Chariton (4.2.7–3.6) and Iamblichus (Photius *Bibl.* 78a = SW 198–9). Chariton's crucifixion scene may show some indication of familiarity with the gospels: Ramelli (2001) 36–7. Bowersock (1994) 99–119 also discusses the possible influence of Christ's resurrection on the romances.

[115] ὦ δέσποινα Αἰγύπτου, πάλιν σῶσον, ᾗ ἐβοήθησας πολλάκις, 5.4.6. On the Isiac details see esp. Griffiths (1978).

[116] Kerényi (1927) 131–3; Merkelbach (1962) 104–6.

[117] For the identification of Isis and Artemis, see Merkelbach (1962) 112–13. The hypothesis of this syncresis (and that of Apollo/Helios/Ra) does make the text more coherent, but cautions against oversystematising Xenophon (e.g. Griffiths (1978) 421–3) are certainly sound.

narrative *telos* in the civilised Greek space of Ephesus, under the nurturing protection of Artemis. In sum, the religiosity of the text plays a self-reflexively metanarrative role,[118] in that the ongoing superintendence of Artemis (~Isis) and Apollo figures the guarantee of a happy ending to the plot – but without reducing the role of these deities to that of 'mere' metaphor for plotting.

Another space that occupies a distinctive role in Xenophon's symbolic geography is Rhodes, where the lovers stop off on both the outward and the return journeys, so that the itinerary becomes chiastic.[119] On the outward leg, the Rhodians hold a public festival (1.12.1–2), and Anthia and Habrocomes dedicate an inscription in the temple of Helios (1.12.2). On their return, Anthia dedicates a lock of hair, together with an inscription, in the same temple (5.11.6), again during a festival to Helios (5.11.2); after the recognition, the Rhodians then, in unison as a *dēmos*, offer praise to Isis for rescuing and reuniting the pair (5.13.2–3); Anthia and Habrocomes also thank Isis (once again) for their 'salvation' (*sōtēria*, 5.13.4). The two Rhodian episodes, then, are mirror images of each other, the festivals serving in effect as ritual markers of separation/reincorporation.[120]

What is more, the second sequence foreshadows the culminating return to Ephesus, where 'the entire city' engages in public sacrifice, and a *graphē* (either a picture or a written account) of their story is dedicated in the temple of Artemis (5.15.2). This is conventionally taken as a *Beglaubigungsapparat*, or device to suggest that the narrative really took place;[121] but it also brands the narrative as a whole (or a near-whole)[122] as a monument to the salvific power of Artemis (/Isis). The linkage between Ephesus and Rhodes thus figures the dyadic but hierarchical relationship between the

---

[118] See esp. Plazenet (1995) 15–16.

[119] Bierl (2006) 83, also noting that dreams of female figures occur during the first stay at Rhodes (1.12.4) and just before the second (5.8.5–7).

[120] Xenophon also uses the language of ritual in a different metaphorical sense. After returning to Ephesus, his lovers 'lived the rest of their life together as a festival' (*heortē*, 5.15.3). This phrase alludes chiastically back to a description of their early married life together, before their parents insisted on sending them away: 'their whole life was a festival (*heortē*), everything was full of good cheer, and at this point they had forgotten about the prophecies' (1.10.2). The festival here, however, serves as not so much an instrument of transition as an image of unchanging abundance and happiness: the expression is a popular one (e.g. Plut. *De tranqu. an.* 477c). The *dualité sémantique* of the word is discussed by Laplace (1994) 444–5, although her account is distorted by her view that the romance as a whole is an anti-tragic panegyric.

[121] See e.g. Morgan (1993) 209; Feeney (1993) 243; Hansen (2003) 308. Sironen (2003) 290–2 offers epigraphic parallels for each of the inscriptions in Xenophon.

[122] Hunter (2008a) 268–9 notes that the narrative is not entirely included in the *graphē*, since two sentences' worth of events remain after the act of dedication.

romance's two principle tutelary deities, (Ephesian/Egyptian) Artemis and (Rhodian/Colophonian) Apollo, the moon and the sun.[123] If the impetuous Eros at the start serves partly as a transcription into divine terms of Habrocomes' own problematic arrogance (see the previous section but one), then the closural Artemis and Apollo serve as more mature, normative models for ephebic behaviour, appropriate to be reintegrated into the community. Shades, then, of the west-Asian/Ptolemaic *hieros gamos*, the sexual union between brother and sister, that links the cosmic power of the sun–moon pair to its earthly manifestation in a royal couple. In this respect, Anthia and Habrocomes are not merely returning to consolidate their identities: they have become transformed by their journeys, not just in the sense that they have matured as humans, but also in that they have become other, touched and transfigured by the power of cosmic deities. For Xenophon, then, the rituals that conclude the text do not just mark the reintegration of the lovers into their community, nor even proclaim the divine power that oversees the entire process of separation, marginalisation and reincorporation; they also emphasise the godlike nature of the returning couple, by assimilating them to a divine pair. Like the returning victors in Pindaric epinician,[124] Xenophon's returning lovers *glow* with the magical, transformative power of narrative.

SYMBOLIC GEOGRAPHY 2: CHARITON

Despite the many similarities both general and phraseological between the two texts, the adventure world of *Callirhoe* is very different. The narrative begins in Sicily; the pirates take her to Ionia, where she is sold to a wealthy Milesian called Dionysius, who becomes her second husband. When Chaereas resurfaces, all the parties travel to Babylon, so that Artaxerxes, the Great King of Persia, can adjudicate the claims. The great king falls for Callirhoe himself; Chaereas is carted off into slavery, before leading a slave revolt in Egypt, and eventually rejoining Callirhoe when he captures a ship with her onboard. Through the snowstorm of different place names (there are, additionally, references to Cilicia, Syria, Armenia, Lycia, Aradus, Cyprus, Crete, Ecbatana, to name but a few), we can identify three principal spatial phases in Callirhoe's narrative,[125] corresponding to her three principal lovers: Sicily (Chaereas), Ionia (Dionysius), Babylon (King

---

[123] On Artemis and Apollo as Xenophon's twin deities, see esp. Zimmermann (1949/50) 267–77.
[124] The classic account is Kurke (1991).   [125] Lowe (2000) 229–30.

Artaxerxes),[126] on a sequential west–east axis. Unlike Xenophon, Chariton (together with his characters) operates with a strong ethical–cultural distinction between Greek and barbarian. The association of Greekness with educated civility (*paideia*) is shared between Callirhoe (2.5.11; also 'humanity', *philanthrōpia*) and the narrator (7.6.5); the narrator also refers to the 'natural servility' of barbarians,[127] and opines sententiously that 'all barbarians are in awe of the king, and consider him a divine manifestation'.[128]

Callirhoe thus suffers from progressive deracination on her journey east. A particularly eloquent articulation of this tripartite cultural division comes as she reaches the Euphrates, the boundary of Persia (5.1.3).[129] (This geophysical boundary also falls at a textual boundary: the beginning of book 5 marks the opening of the second half of the romance.)[130] Full of despair, she reproaches malevolent Fortune, in tragic terms,[131] for taking her further still away from home:

now you no longer banish me to Ionia. The land you gave me, though foreign, was still Greek, and I had there the consolation of living by the sea. But now you cast me forth from my familiar air, and I am separated from my fatherland by an entire world. You have taken Miletus from me in turn, as before you took Syracuse. Carried off beyond the Euphrates, I, an islander, am imprisoned in the recesses of a barbarian land, where no more sea exists.[132]

---

[126] Each is pre-eminent in his own context: Chaereas is 'beyond all' in terms of beauty (1.1.3); Dionysius is repeatedly marked out as the top Ionian, in station, culture and wealth (2.1.5, 2.4.4, 2.5.4, 2.11.2, 3.6.5, 4.4.3, 8.7.9); Artaxerxes is of course feted for his wealth and power (cf. esp. 6.5.2–5). According to Alvares (2001–2), '*Chaereas and Callirhoe* can be read as a narrative within which three different lovers . . . fail to measure up to what is appropriate to their respective stages, are punished, and, to some extent, are compelled to play their proper erotic roles' (115).

[127] τὴν ἔμφυτον θρησκείαν, Char. 7.6.6.

[128] καταπεπλήγασι γὰρ πάντες οἱ βάρβαροι καὶ θεὸν φανερὸν νομίζουσι τὸν βασιλέα, Char. 6.7.12. See the fuller discussion at Bowie (1991) 188–92, with the additional nuance that the Persians also are said to mistrust the Greeks; also Alvares (2001–2) and Smith (2007) for the themes of Greek liberty vs barbarian oppression.

[129] For the Euphrates as a significant boundary between East and West, see also 6.8.6, 7.1.10, 7.2.1, 7.4.11, 7.4.13; and further Lalanne (1998) 546–7.

[130] This juncture is marked by a recapitulation of what has been narrated 'in the earlier part of the story' (ἐν τῶι πρόσθεν λόγωι), and a promise that 'now I shall narrate what happened next' (τὰ δὲ ἑξῆς νῦν διηγήσομαι, 5.1.2). On book divisions and narrative segmentation in Chariton and other Greek romances see Whitmarsh (2009b).

[131] Compare e.g. Ajax' yearning for the 'holy soil of my native Salamis' (ἱερὸν οἰκείας πέδον / Σαλαμῖνος, Soph. *Aj.* 859–60).

[132] οὐκέτι γὰρ εἰς Ἰωνίαν με φυγαδεύεις. ξένην μέν, πλὴν Ἑλληνικὴν ἐδίδους γῆν, ὅπου μεγάλην εἶχον παραμυθίαν, ὅτι θαλάσσηι παρακάθημαι· νῦν δὲ ἔξω με τοῦ συνήθους ῥίπτεις ἀέρος καὶ τῆς πατρίδος ὅλωι διορίζομαι κόσμωι. Μίλητον ἀφείλω μου πάλιν, ὡς πρότερον Συρακούσας· ὑπὲρ τὸν Εὐφράτην ἀπάγομαι καὶ βαρβάροις ἐγκλείομαι μυχοῖς ἡ νησιῶτις, ὅπου μηκέτι θάλασσα, Char. 5.1.5–6. This passage is perceptively discussed by Daude (1990) 86–8, who notes the resemblance to the Acheron (only to be crossed once), the symbolic status of the Euphrates

Callirhoe's tripartition of the world is highly visible here, with Ionia as the hybrid centre, 'foreign, but Greek': a paradox she expresses through a polarising jingle, *xenēn men, plēn Hellēnikēn*. She also expresses the division in terms of her affection for the Mediterranean/Aegean, the 'Greek sea' as she has earlier put it,[133] reversing the usual model of sea as terrifying and land as comforting: Sicily is preferred as an island. Ionia is next best, as a coastal mainland. Persia is worst of all, (imagined as) land*locked*, an English metaphor that captures her own phrasing: 'imprisoned in the recesses' images Persia as a jail where she will be constrained, or perhaps more mythopoetically the Cyclops' cave,[134] or even the infernal regions.[135] Even though there is no explicit allusion here, Callirhoe surely has in mind the famous cry of relief 'the sea, the sea', uttered by (Athenian) Xenophon's Greek mercenaries who have felt themselves trapped in Asia.[136] The metaphors she uses of this inland imprisonment suggest suffocation, perhaps even (an aggressive paradox) drowning: she imagines herself deprived of 'air' down in the 'depths' of the Asian continent.[137]

Ionia, as we have noted, is presented as a liminal space, a meeting-point between Orient and Occident. On the one hand, we do find the traditional references to Ionian luxury and the corruptive influence of the East (1.11.7, 5.10.7–8); but this is also where Callirhoe meets Dionysius, nonpareil in the cardinally Greek values of civilised education (*paideia*: 1.12.6, 2.1.5, 2.4.1, 2.5.11, 3.2.6, 4.7.6, 5.5.1, 5.9.8, 8.5.10) and humanity (*philanthrōpia*: 2.2.1, 2.5.3–4, 2.5.11, 2.7.2; in another life, in another romance, he might have been quite a catch). Ionia is Janus-faced, looking both inland to the Persian East (as the pirate Theron comments, 'royal riches flow in from all over Asia', 1.11.7) and out to the Greek-dominated cultural world of the Mediterranean. This is what makes it a site of cultural fluidity and dynamic action, and hence so central to romantic action. For the romancer, the liminality of Ionia, equipoised between East and West, makes it a place of opportunity, brimming with narrativity: it is here that the complex moral questions begin to pose themselves, for Callirhoe and Dionysius alike. That Chariton has chosen this role for Ionia, of all places, is surely no coincidence. Miletus, Dionysius' homeland and the location of most of the Ionian narrative, is the city closest to Aphrodisias, Chariton's own

---

as the boundary of the Roman empire during Chariton's time, and its status within Chariton's romance as an axiological boundary between barbarian and Greek, slave and free.

[133] θαλάσσης Ἑλληνικῆς, 4.7.8 (the narrator speaks here, but apparently focalising Callirhoe's thoughts). Bowie (1991) 189 n. 17 notes the use of this phrase at Hdt. 5.54.2, Thuc. 1.4.1, and Arr. *Anab.* 2.25.1, 5.1.5.
[134] Which also has a μυχός: Hom. *Od.* 9.236.   [135] Cf. Hes. *Th.* 119 (μυχῶι γῆς).
[136] Xen. *Anab.* 4.7.24.   [137] Seas can be imaged in terms of μύχοι: see e.g. [Aesch.] *PV* 839.

(which, of course, did not exist at the time when the narrative is set, at least not as a Greek *polis*): the former lies on the edge of Caria, at the mouth of the Great Maeander, the vital inland trade route in the basin of which Aphrodisias lies.[138] Chariton's Miletus, with its active cult of Aphrodite, seems to serve as an ancient metastasis of the modern city of Aphrodisias.[139] The crucial symbolic role of Ionia in the romance, then, as a place of transition and confluence, figures Chariton's own identification of this romance, and perhaps the romance in general, as an Ionian form.

Callirhoe's symbolic geography is also (as a number of scholars have argued) an allegorical response to the experience of empire, mapping out a secondary story of both benign and malign political hegemony in the background of the primary, erotic narrative.[140] This is underlined by the narrative setting, which focuses upon the victorious Syracusans in Sicily in the aftermath of the attempted Athenian invasion of 416 (the tragic centrepiece of Thucydides' narrative of Athenian decline into deluded arrogance). From the very start – Callirhoe is programmatically identified as the daughter of 'the man who defeated the Athenians' (1.1.1)[141] – there is an air of overweening menace from alien powers abroad. Even the non-Syracusan (?) brigand Theron characterises Athens in negative terms, for the 'inquisitiveness' (*polupragmosunē*) of the people, who are 'gossipy and litigious' (*lalos kai philodikos*); 'sycophants' abound at the harbour, and 'vile suspicion will overtake those wretches' if his crew land there.[142] Chariton's presentation of Athens as a place of malevolence and iniquity, rather than the hub of Greek civility, is all the more striking for its variance from the usual picture painted by early imperial writers.[143]

Like alienation, imperialism intensifies along the West–East axis: Persia is to Athens what Athens is to Syracuse. Callirhoe tells the eunuch Artaxates that the latter is a 'city that not even the Athenians conquered – the Athenians who conquered your "great king" at Marathon and Salamis'.[144]

---

[138] On the importance of the Maeander valley to Aphrodisias, see Reynolds (1982) 3, 31, 81. In late Roman times, it seems, seats were reserved in the theatre of Aphrodisias for Milesian spectators (Roueché (1993) 90).

[139] Ruiz Montero (1989) 126; Jones (1992) 162–3; Alvares (2001–2) 126–7.

[140] Alvares (2001–2); Connors (2002), (2008); Schwartz (2003); Smith (2007).

[141] Other allusions to the campaign at 6.7.10, 8.6.10.

[142] ὑποψία καταλήψεται πονηρὰ τοὺς κακοήθεις, Char. 1.11.6. Theron also refers to the threat posed by the Areopagus court, and its 'archons more severe than tyrants' (ἄρχοντες τυράννων βαρύτεροι, Char. 1.11.7).

[143] On Chariton's representation of Athens, see Oudot (1992) 101–3; Alvares (2001–2) 119–20; Smith (2007), esp. 50–98; for the generally positive view of Athens in the imperial period, see Bowie (1970) 195–7; Smith (2007) 23–49.

[144] πόλεως ... ἣν οὐκ ἐνίκησαν οὐδὲ Ἀθηναῖοι οἱ ἐν Μαραθῶνι καὶ Σαλαμῖνι νικήσαντες τὸν μέγαν σου βασιλέα, Char. 6.7.10.

Syracuse, Athens and Persia form a rising tricolon of (ineffective) militarism.[145] The might and extraordinary efficiency of Persia's army is expressed in the narrator's description of the aftermath of the Egyptian rebellion. 'Everyone agreed on speed, and not to delay even for one day if necessary',[146] but in any case 'the mobilisation of forces is very swift for the Persians'.[147] The following description catches itself savouring the awesome spectacle of empire in action, and invites the reader to do the same. 'It had been decreed since the time of Cyrus', we are told, 'which tribes should provide cavalry and how much, which infantry and how much, how many archers each should provide and how many regular and scythe-bearing chariots, where the elephants should come from and in what numbers, from whom the money should come, in what form and what quantities'.[148] The narrator's emphasis upon precise naming, calibration and quantification temporarily aligns literary with military strategy (as in the passage's distant ancestor, the Iliadic catalogue of ships), performing on the king's behalf the rhetoric of empire. This is romance sloping into epic, which 'loves a parade'.[149]

The tricolon, however, rises in both directions simultaneously: the states become mightier towards the East, but more heroically resistant towards the West. The Sicilians Chaereas and Polycharmus join the rebellion against Persia and its 'tyrant' to demonstrate 'that two wronged Greeks aggrieved the Great King in return, and died like men'.[150] The rebellion becomes a testing-ground for manly virtue.[151] Chaereas 'duplicates the naval victory at Salamis, Xenophon's retreat with the Ten Thousand, and Alexander the Great's conquest of Tyre'.[152] As with the Syracusan defeat of Athens, as with the Athenian defeat of Persia, so the rebellion against the imperial order is successful: military history in Chariton is distilled into a series of dramatisations of the simple ethical truth that the noble and free fight better. Conversely, Chariton's portrait of Persia, as scholars have been quick to recognise, is traditional in its orientalising portrayal of a luxurious but

---

[145] For similar tricola, see 2.6.3, 5.8.8, 7.5.7–8; Smith (2007) 92–3.
[146] πᾶσι... ἤρεσκε τὸ σπεύδειν καὶ μηδὲ μίαν ἡμέραν, εἰ δυνατόν, ἀναβαλέσθαι, Char. 6.8.5.
[147] ῥᾴστη δ' ἐστι Πέρσαις ἡ παρασκευὴ τῆς δυνάμεως, Char. 6.8.7.
[148] συντέτακται... ἀπὸ Κύρου... ποῖα μὲν τῶν ἐθνῶν εἰς πόλεμον ἱππείαν καὶ πόσην, τίνας δὲ τοξότας καὶ πόσα ἑκάστους ἅρματα ψιλά τε καὶ δρεπανηφόρα, καὶ ἐλέφαντας ὁπόθεν καὶ πόσους, καὶ χρήματα παρ' ὡντινων, ποῖα καὶ πόσα, Char. 6.8.7.
[149] Quint (1993) 31.
[150] δύο Ἕλληνες ἀδικηθέντες ἀντελύπησαν τὸν μέγαν βασιλέα καὶ ἀπέθανον ὡς ἄνδρες, Char. 7.1.8.
[151] The rebellion has been connected with both the revolt against Persia in 360 BCE (Salmon (1961)) and events in the Roman era (Alvares (2001)).
[152] Alvares (2007) 13; cf. Lalanne (2006) 91–2, noting the language of *andreia* in books 7–8; also 156–9.

despotic state (even though he may draw on an unexpectedly wide range of sources).[153] As one scholar puts it, 'Chariton deploys all the standard elements of the Persian mirage: luxury, prostration, harem life, eunuchs, satraps, court intrigue, hunts, *magi*, the *paradeisos*'.[154] It is in particular the steepling power, with its vertiginous allure, that overhangs Chariton's Persia. There is in Persia none of the honourable competition between equals that characterises Greek states like Syracuse, only the master–slave paradigm. At the apex sits the king, 'to whom' (opines his favoured eunuch) 'all fine things are enslaved: gold, silver, clothing, horses, cities, nations'.[155] This pattern is reproduced further down the pyramid, so that (for example) the satrap Mithridates is the slave of the king (5.2.2), and Dionysius, the pre-eminent citizen of Miletus, is the slave of Mithridates (6.7.9). This model of human relationships, of course, demands to be set against the norms of Greek society, with its supposed freedom and civic unity. The othering of Persia is compounded by numerous echoes of, allusions to and quotations from the *Iliad*, in particular the explicit comparisons of Callirhoe with Helen, and the implicit associations of the Egyptian revolt with the Greek mission: all of these serve to assimilate Persia to Troy, the enemy that must be defeated.[156]

The stereotyping of Persia, as the model of a state in which interpersonal relationships are warped by vast differentials of power, gains new urgency when considered in relation to the Roman imperial context for which Chariton was writing. As we have seen, the author's home town of Aphrodisias benefited immensely during the early first century from the patronage of the Julio-Claudian emperors, who in commemorating its patron goddess were also honouring their own ancestor. Aphrodite is also the presiding deity of *Callirhoe*, and given a decisive role in the management of the harmonious ending.[157] At one level, then, Chariton's celebration of Aphrodite as a benevolent power reuniting the lovers despite their trials and suffering offers itself as an analogy at the divine level to the Roman emperor's governing of the empire at the political. The imperial resonances are strengthened thanks to the choice of Syracuse as the lovers' homeland. Centring the world in Sicily involves decentring

---

[153] Bowie (1991) 188–95; Baslez (1992) emphasises the range of sources.   [154] Schwartz (2003) 378.
[155] ᾧ τὰ καλὰ πάντα δουλεύει, χρυσός, ἄργυρος, ἐσθής, ἵπποι, πόλεις, ἔθνη, Char. 6.3.4. See, however, below on the ambiguous presentation of the eunuch Artaxates.
[156] Callirhoe as Helen: 2.6.1, 5.2.8, 5.5.9. Persian sexual ethics are assimilated to Trojan when the narrator describes these barbarian nature as 'woman-mad' (γυναικομανές, 5.2.6), invoking the phrase Hector uses of Paris (γυναιμανές, Hom. *Il.* 3.39). On the Iliadic resonances of the Egyptian uprising see De Temmerman (2009a) 255–7.
[157] Above, n. 12.

the Greek mainland, shifting it further towards the barbarian East – a symbolic construction of the world that arguably reflects the Italocentric imperial mapping of Rome more than traditional Greek ideas. Moreover, as Catherine Connors has noted, Rome's relationships with the Greek world had long been played out through its treatment of Syracuse (particularly since the sack by Marcellus in 211 BCE); in Chariton's own day, there was reason to see it as flourishing thanks to Julio-Claudian repression of piracy.[158] If these features emblematise the positive aspects of empire, then conversely Achaemenid Persia represents the inverse: and, via an obvious *décalage*, also the Parthian kingdom that was seen as such a threat to Rome in Chariton's own day (when his hometown of Aphrodisias was still remembered for its resistance to Parthian overtures during the Triumviral period).[159]

It is, however, impossible to insulate Persia from Roman associations. Greeks of the imperial era like to create fleeting, suggestive parallels between Persia and Rome: hence the occasional use of the Persian word *satrap* to denote Roman provincial governors,[160] and Plutarch's famous suggestion to Menemachus of Sardis that orators should avoid inflammatory references to 'Marathon, Eurymedon and Plataea' (*Political advice* 814c), which suggests that analogies could be and were drawn in rhetorical contexts.[161] As one scholar has observed, Chariton's court scene, with its combination of petition and documents, is remarkably evocative of practice at the imperial court at Rome.[162] In fact, despite the othering described above, there is plenty in Persia that seems uncannily resonant to a reader familiar with Roman imperialism.[163] At the level of empire, Persia is ruled politically, militarily and juridically by one man, who mandates the rule of provinces to individual governors – just like Rome. At the religious level too, no attempt has been made to differentiate Persian religious practices from Greco-Roman: the pantheon is identical, as is the use of festival (with the Greek features of garlanding, incense and wind instruments) and sacrifice as the primary means of mediation between the two.[164]

Even more disturbing to any comfortably compartmentalising reading in terms of alterity is the often positive representation of the Great King.

---

[158] Connors (2002).   [159] On Parthian features in *Callirhoe*'s Persia, see Baslez (1992) 203–4.
[160] Dio Chr. 7.66, 7.93, 47.9, 49.6, 50.6; Philostr. *VS* 524.
[161] See further Jones (1971) 113–14 and Whitmarsh (2005a) 66–7.
[162] Schwartz (2003) 382–5; also Alvares (2001–2) 120–3.
[163] Cf. esp. Alvares (2001–2) 120–3, noting particularly Mithridates' Roman-style plantation (4.2.2), the crucifixion of slaves and the presence of freedmen (5.4.6).
[164] Pantheon: Helios (6.1.10), Eros (6.2.4, 6.3.2), Aphrodite (6.2.4), Zeus (6.3.2). Festival: 6.2.3–4. Sacrifice: 6.2.2, 6.2.4.

First romances 57

Like Dionysius, he is a strikingly sympathetic figure, whose struggles with his passion for Callirhoe are offset by a strong awareness of his social and ethical obligations. Particularly telling is his resistance to the allures of power. There are, certainly, suggestions of divinisation: the people 'consider the king a god manifest',[165] and his eunuch Artaxates presents him, albeit problematically, as superhuman: 'you alone, master, can overpower even a god' (i.e. Eros).[166] The king himself, however, resists this: despite some hints (he claims Helios as his ancestor (6.1.10), and refers mysteriously to 'the royal gods' (6.2.2)), he acknowledges the superior power of Eros (6.3.2), elsewhere enjoining a submissive 'piety' before deities in general (*eusebeia*, 6.2.2). Given that living Roman emperors were worshipped as gods in the eastern empire,[167] and that this was a phenomenon that some educated Greeks of the early imperial period found awkward to reconcile with the traditional resistance to the superelevation of mortals,[168] the representation of Artaxerxes as moderate in the face of temptation looks like an intervention on Chariton's part in a contemporary debate on the divinity of the emperor.[169]

More generally, Chariton's king insists on abiding by the law and the 'justice that I practise in all things'[170] – again, in the context of his eunuch's encouragement to break the law (by raping Callirhoe). Here too, he seems to embody one aspect at least of Greco-Roman kingship ideals, here the principle that the king should be 'law incarnate' (*nomos empsykhos*).[171] These debates between king and eunuch serve as a softened, eroticised version of the 'constitutional debate' of Herodotus 3.80–2, conducted (appropriately) by three Persians.[172] Unlike Herodotus, however, Chariton here represents kingship as the only political option; the only question is good or bad. The eunuch's vision of kingship as limitless power represents the alternative road that Chariton has not taken, the extreme othering of Persian kingship that the text represses. The near-homonym Artaxates can be seen as Artaxerxes' shadowy double, onto whom all monarchy's negative potential for abuse and arrogance has been shunted. In the final analysis, the king embodies

---

[165] θεὸν φανερὸν νομίζουσι τὸν βασιλέα, Char. 6.7.12.
[166] δύνασαι... ὦ δέσποτα, σὺ μόνος κρατεῖν καὶ θεοῦ, Char. 6.3.8.
[167] Price (1984) is the classic account, emphasising continuity with Hellenistic practice.
[168] See Bowersock (1973) on Greek intellectuals' awkwardness in relation to imperial cult.
[169] Comparable is Plutarch's (extraordinary!) claim that Alexander adopted divinisation 'moderately and sparingly' (μετρίως καὶ ὑποφειδομένως) before the Greeks (*Alex.* 28.1): Whitmarsh (2002a) 191.
[170] δικαιοσύνης ἣν ἐν ἅπασιν ἀσκῶ, Char. 6.3.8.   [171] Gigante (1993).
[172] Also imitated at Philostr. *VA* 5.27–38: see Whitmarsh (2001a) 230–8, with further literature on both Philostratus and Herodotus (and Pelling (2002)).

not so much the pathological despotism of the East as the kind of benign imperialism that Greeks can do business with.[173]

There is thus a paradox underlying Chariton's geography. At one level, the text rests upon and consolidates a simple opposition between self and other. This opposition offers itself to quick decipherment, as a political allegory opposing Rome's benevolent rule (symbolised by Aphrodite) and the threat of Parthia, corrupt and oppressive. This simple reading, however, is offset by another, whereby the further we get from Italy, the closer we get to Rome, or rather 'Rome' – the idea of absolute power concentrated in one man, of absolute dominion over imperial provinces, and of benign imperialism. *Callirhoe* models the neat Hellenocentrism that underlies *Anthia and Habrocomes*, as warped by Aphrodisian complicity with Roman providentialism. From those like Chariton's compatriots who attempt to shape their own cultural patterns to its ideology, empire demands an impossible feat of intellectual contortion: an accommodation must be found between the face-to-face community's traditional sense of its moral superiority over imperialist threat (epitomised not only by Persia but also by Athens) and a recognition that, by Chariton's time, benign despotism is the best one can hope for.

HEALING THE RIFT

The end of the romance marks the reintegration of the lovers into the home community. Xenophon, as we have seen above, articulates this transition ritually: both on Rhodes and in Ephesus, the lovers are welcomed back with pandemic festivals, in thanks for their salvation. In Chariton, typically, the articulation is by contrast political. The lovers are acclaimed by the Syracusan populace both on the shore (8.6.7–8) and in the theatre (8.7.1–2); the civic spaces are repeatedly claimed to be 'full', the superabundance marking the people's zeal and concord.[174] The people's investment

---

[173] 'In defeating Artaxerxes' forces but returning his Queen, Chaireas, like Hermocrates before him, has reached a *modus vivendi* with a dominant power, as Callirhoe also does in her own way' (Alvares (2007) 14). In particular, the Persians and the Sicilians are united by their common enemy Athens: 2.6.3, 5.8.8, and Smith (2007) 98.

[174] 'The entire harbour *was filled* with people' (πᾶς ὁ λιμὴν ἀνθρώπων ἐνεπλήσθη, 8.6.5); 'The harbour *was full*' (ὁ λιμὴν ἐπληροῦτο, 8.6.10); 'The people shouted in unison' (ἁθρόον... τὸ πλῆθος ἀνεβόησεν, 8.7.1); 'The theatre *was full* of the talk of women and men' (λόγου... ἐπληρώθη τὸ θέατρον ἀνδρῶν τε καὶ γυναικῶν, 8.7.1); 'Prayers from everyone followed' (εὐχαὶ παρὰ πάντων... ἐπηκολούθησαν, 8.8.12); 'The people approved... the people shouted ...' (ἐπευφήμησαν ὁ δῆμος... ὁ δῆμος ἐπεβόησεν, 8.8.13). Incidentally, Chariton's theatre is conceived of as a political rather than a religious space: cf. 8.7.1 (ἐκκλησίαν), 8.8.14 (ψήφισμα ἐγράφη).

First romances 59

in this narrative is also underlined by the claim that they were happier than after the defeat of the Athenians (8.7.2; cf. 8.6.2, 8.6.10, 8.6.12). The reunion of Chaereas and Callirhoe reunifies the city, an analogy that Chariton underlines by explicitly gendering the populace: 'then they [the people] were sometimes split, the men exalting Chaereas, the women Callirhoe – and sometimes then they jointly (*koinē*) exalted them both again, which was more pleasurable'.[175] The harmonious alignment of women and men (distantly invoking the joyous gender reintegration at the conclusion of Aristophanes' *Lysistrata*) points up the positive contrast with Babylon, where (we are told) before the trial 'the barbarian populace was split' along lines not only of gender but also of class.[176] The reference to 'pleasure' also directly links the union of the genders at the civic level to the personal relationship between Chaereas and Callirhoe, recalling the authorial recapitulation at the start of this book (8), promising that this one will be 'the most pleasurable to readers' in that it offers 'legitimate love and marriage in the eyes of the law'.[177] The reunion of Chaereas and Callirhoe figures the unity of the *dēmos*.

Book 8 of Chariton, indeed, is strongly closural.[178] It begins, as we have noted, with a major recapitulation, the second of the romance.[179] The first comes at the beginning of book 5, the half-way point in terms of the book structure, and also the point in the narrative where Callirhoe crosses the boundary between East and West, the Euphrates. The recapitulation serves as a narrative pivot, waymarking the text: it both summarises events 'that have been shown in the story so far'[180] and looks forward, promising that 'I shall now narrate what happened next.'[181] This second recapitulation also serves to segment the text, by explicitly hiving off the eighth book as closural: it distinguishes between the 'gloomy events of the foregoing story'[182] and what will happen in 'this, the final book',[183] which he promises

---

[175] εἶτα ποτὲ μὲν ἐσχίζοντο, καὶ οἱ μὲν ἄνδρες ἐπήινουν Χαιρέαν, αἱ δὲ γυναῖκες Καλλιρόην, ποτὲ δ' αὖ πάλιν ἀμφοτέρους κοινῆι· καὶ τοῦτο ἐκείνοις ἥδιον ἦν, Char. 8.7.2.
[176] ἐσχίσθη ... τὸ πλῆθος τῶν βαρβάρων, Char. 5.4.1–4, at 5.4.1.
[177] τοῖς ἀναγινώσκουσιν ἥδιστον / ἔρωτες δίκαιοι ... <καὶ> νόμιμοι γάμοι, Char. 8.1.4.
[178] Fusillo (1997) 215–16; see further below, pp. 182–4.
[179] For fuller discussion of the recapitulations and their relation to the book divisions see Whitmarsh (2009b), with literature.
[180] ἐν τῶι πρόσθεν λόγωι δεδηλῶται, Char. 5.1.2. The phrase is borrowed from the tags that Xenophon of Athens (or an editor) positions at the start of books 2–5 and 7 of the *Anabasis* (Perry (1967) 358 n. 16). In Xenophon, ὁ πρόσθεν λόγος means 'the previous book', while in Chariton it means 'the story so far'.
[181] τὰ δὲ ἑξῆς νῦν διηγήσομαι, 5.1.2.
[182] τῶν ἐν τοῖς πρώτοις σκυθρπῶν, 8.1.4; cf. ἐν τῶι πρόσθεν λόγωι, 8.1.1, σκυθρωπόν, 8.1.2.
[183] τὸ τελευταῖον τοῦτο σύγγραμμα, 8.1.4.

to be the most pleasurable (*hēdiston*) for his readers.[184] Unlike the parallel passage in book 5, where readers are left to guess 'what happened next', Chariton here leaves his reader in no doubt about the events to follow, explicitly pre-empting the 'pleasurable' ending: 'legitimate passions and marriage in the eyes of the law'.[185] This disclosure is itself a closural device, signalling that suspense no longer has a role to play.

The metanarrative description of the movement from the liminal to the closural phase is reinforced within the narrative at three levels. Cosmically, the president deity (as we shall see in greater detail later in this book) changes from malevolent Fortune to benign Aphrodite. Socially, 'reconciliation' betokens (again as in Aristophanes' *Lysistrata*, where *Diallagē* is personified) the beginning of the closing phase of the narrative, as rifts are mended and anger is healed – under the tutelage of the patron goddess of Chariton's home-city of Aphrodisias, and the ancestor of the imperial dynasty of the day.[186] Psychically, finally, the passing of Aphrodite's anger betokens the maturation of the lovers, as they set aside socially destructive emotions (particularly Chaereas, whose 'jealousy'[187] is recalled here). Indeed, all three levels are interrelated: the lovers, the city and Aphrodite, all master their passions. This technique, whereby gods serve as external manifestations of internal passion, we have already seen in *Anthia and Habrocomes*: the changing identity of the key gods (haughty Eros > serene Apollo/Artemis) also indicates growing up. Again as in Xenophon, anger is the dominant divine motif: Xenophon's Eros 'rages' and 'grows angry',[188] and that the narrative ahead is conceived of by Eros as a 'great penalty' for Habrocomes' arrogance.[189] This discourse of divine anger (transferred, as we have already observed, from epic) serves to construct the forthcoming narrative as a deviation from anticipated equilibrium at the levels of divine and social order. It also looks towards a happier end: anger cannot sustain itself indefinitely in narrative, it exists to be spent. Divine wrath, thus, portends a circumscribed period of punishment, but thereafter a restitution of the normal psychological and social order.

CLOSING THE CASE

This sense of restitution of order is an integral part of the return narrative. The Greek romance is fundamentally preoccupied with closure:

---

[184] On the segmentary role of the recapitulations, see also Reitzenstein (1906) 95–6 and esp. Hägg (1971) 246–52, noting phraseological parallels between the two passages (246–7).
[185] Text at n. 177.   [186] On Charitonian anger management, see Scourfield (2003).
[187] Reemphasised in a passage focalised by Callirhoe, at 8.4.1.
[188] μηνιᾶι, Xen. Eph. 1.2.1; ὠργίζετο, 1.4.5.
[189] μεγάλην τῆς ὑπεροψίας... τιμωρίαν, Xen. Eph. 1.4.5.

narratologically, aesthetically, psychologically, ideologically. We shall return to this point more fully in Chapters 5 and 6, but for now it will be important to make two general points about the first-century romances.

The first is that closure can never, no matter how hard one tries, be total. Closure it not simply the resolution of issues, but the *imposition* of resolution; and when, as readers, we perceive this imposition to be forcible or contrived we protest all the more (as, for example, Aristotle did with the Euripidean *deus ex machina*).[190] What is more, the pleasure of the 'happy ending' – the *hēdonē* predicted by Chariton's narrator – is for the reader deeply ambivalent, since we will be aware how much guilty pleasure we have found in the yearnings and moral cruces enacted in the main narrative. In D.A. Miller's ascetic account, the very precondition for narrative – 'the narratable' – lies in the uncertainties and emotional cruces that are precisely erased by closure. In other words, closure is not part of the narrative, only a device to indicate its absence: 'The closural settlement accommodates the narratable only by changing its status, that is, by putting it in a past perfect tense and declaring it "over". Closure can *never* include, then, the narratable in its essential dimension: all suspense and indecision.'[191] Closure, on this reading, does not resolve the meaning of a narrative, because the meaning of narrative lies in its very indeterminacy; what closure actually does is cancel narrative by transubstantiating it. Even if this is a wilfully restricted definition of what narrative 'is', it nonetheless effectively captures the paradox of closure, which stands both within and without the narrative, simultaneously completing and liquidating it.

These issues matter, because (as, again, we shall see in greater detail in Chapters 5 and 6) they determine whether we see the romances as fundamentally conservative expressions of civic ideology or as ludic experiments with narrative and social possibilities. The best answer to this question comes from Stanley Fish, who emphasises that the meaning of a literary work is not realised in a single cognitive act, but gradually composed over time:

Everything depends on the temporal dimension... In a sequence where a reader first structures the field he [*sic*] inhabits and then is asked to restructure it... there is no question of priority among his structurings; no one of them, even if it is the last, has privilege; each is equally legitimate, each properly the object of analysis, because each is equally an event in his experience.[192]

---

[190] Arist. *Poet.* 1453a37–1454b6; Lowe (2000) 58. [191] Miller (1981) 98. [192] Fish (1976) 474.

If we see meaning-making in this way as a *process*, then closure, for all that it does suggest a final resting point, does not erase the memory of all the steps that led there:

in the end we settle on the more optimistic reading – it feels better – but even so the other has been a part of our experience, it *means*. What it means is that while we may be able to extract from the poem [or narrative] a statement affirming God's justice, we are not allowed to forget the evidence (of things seen) that makes the extraction so difficult.[193]

Closure, then, is not a state but a process. This is crucial. In Xenophon, and particularly in Chariton, considerable attention is given to the ways in which life as experience (open, unresolved) is translated into life as narrative (closed, shaped, heavy with meaning): to the transition from *Erlebnis* to *Erzählung* (to use the terms popularised by Walter Benjamin). The first 'readers' of the narrative are the characters who live through it, and it is their attempts to give shape to their experiences to which we now turn. In Xenophon, the act of narrative control comes in the form of a '*graphē* of all that they had endured and all that they had done', deposited in the temple of Artemis.[194] *Graphē* can mean either a 'written record' or a 'painted depiction', but the sentence obviously advertises its availability to a self-reflexive interpretation, whereby the dedication actually constitutes the book we are reading now.[195] Xenophon's is a 'self-begetting' text.[196] Anton Bierl notes additionally that Anthia and Habrocomes effectively translate their story generically too, so that it becomes an aretalogy: events that were experienced phenomenologically as painful are now metamorphosed into a testimony to the goddess's benevolence.[197] Jason König notes one further translation, from oral into written narrative. The story is now congealed and consigned to the past, and hedged with images of death: 'The closing paragraphs of the work offer a fantasy of fulfilment, but they also have overtones of finality, for example in the atmosphere of death in the final lines, where we hear that the main characters lived out "the rest

---

[193] Fish (1976) 470.
[194] τὴν γραφὴν... πάντων ὅσα τε ἔπαθον καὶ ὅσα ἔδρασαν, Xen. Eph. 5.15.2. Ephesian Artemis' temple seems to have been the final resting place for numerous artistic creations, including Heraclitus' *On nature* (Diog. Laert. 9.6) and the 'psaltery' of Alexander of Cythera (*FGrH* 275 F 83 = Ath. *Deipn.* 183c); see also the following note, on *Apollonius, King of Tyre*.
[195] Hansen (2003) 309 notes the 'light pseudo-documentarism'. See esp. Hunter (2008a) 267–9, emphasising the parallels not only with Longus, but also with Apuleius' *Metamorphoses* (where the afterlife of the narrative as a text is frequently envisaged); and with *Apollonius, King of Tyre*, the B and C redactions of which have copies of the story deposited in the king's own library and in the temple of Diana at Ephesus.
[196] Kellman (1980).   [197] Bierl (2006) 80–1.

of their lives" in Ephesos, with mention also of the building of tombs and memorials.'[198] In metamorphosing narrative into something bounded, with a fixed meaning – the city's patron goddess will save us in times of adversity – Anthia and Habrocomes also neutralise the energy that sustained that narrative, and in a sense destroy their own vitality: all that remains now is to die.

Anthia and Habrocomes is 'finally' about the salvific power of civic religion. In Chariton, characteristically, the emphasis is partly upon community, but partly also on stable psychology and harmonised social relations. When Chaereas and Callirhoe recognise each other, the two lovers recount their stories to each other (8.1.14–17). This reinforces the sense of movement towards narrative resolution, partly in that it echoes the narrator's explicitly closural recapitulation at the start of the book (discussed above), partly in that it reworks the reunion of Odysseus and Penelope (*Od.* 23.310–41 – just after the point (296) where Aristophanes and Aristarchus located the end of the text), but mostly in that it marks the conciliation of the two lovers. Whereas the narrator's recapitulation has 'no organic function in the action itself',[199] Callirhoe's story of her remarriage to Dionysius is a tense moment, threatening as it does to destabilise her relationship with Chaereas: when she comes to Miletus in the story, 'she fell silent, in embarrassment'.[200] Chaereas, however, is all contrition; he exhorts her to tell the story and apologises for his earlier anger. The tension inherent in this act of recapitulation is thus defused (even though both Callirhoe and the narrator recall his 'innate jealousy' (*emphutou zēlotupias*)).[201] Callirhoe finds a speaking cure to her trauma: she overpowers her *aidōs* through narrative recapitulation, by becoming a narrator of her story in her own right. The reliving of narrative, as Freudian critics emphasise, can engender a sense of mastery over traumatic events.[202]

In a parallel scene, Chaereas recounts his story to the Syracusan public in the theatre (8.7.9–8.11) – again, a performance that retraces, and in a sense (to be discussed below) reconstitutes, the narrative that it caps. The different audiences are significant: whereas Callirhoe's primary human relationship is with her husband, the now-mature Chaereas needs to claim

---

[198] König (2007) 18.   [199] Hägg (1971) 251.
[200] ἐσιώπησεν αἰδουμένη, Char. 8.1.15, echoing her reluctance to tell her story to Dionysius at 2.5.6–7. In that context, a brief recapitulation is wrung out of her against her will, testimony not to her mastery of the situation but to her powerlessness (2.5.10–11). Callirhoe's narrative to Chaereas is also parallelled by Stateira's to Artaxerxes (8.5.7–8).
[201] Callirhoe presently writes to Dionysius without her husband's knowledge, 'knowing his innate jealousy' (εἰδυῖα... αὐτοῦ τὴν ἔμφυτον ζηλοτυπίαν, Char. 8.4.4).
[202] Brooks (1984) 99–100, influentially reworked for the *Aeneid* by Quint (1993) 50–96.

his identity as a citizen before the populace. (Callirhoe, in fact, has been led away from the theatre: 8.7.3). Chaereas' account, which lays particular emphasis upon his martial exploits, dramatises his newfound manhood on the public stage (literally so, in the city's theatre).[203] If this self-aggrandising tale of exploits casts him as the Odysseus of the Phaeacian *apologoi*, then the first appearance before the city also evokes Telemachus' maiden speech in the Ithacan assembly, an event that marks the latter's emergence into manhood.[204] The coming-of-age theme is, indeed, emphatic. Chaereas' initial reluctance to relate his whole story is presented as resulting from the shyness of youth: 'Chaereas hesitated, embarrassed (*aidoumenos*) as you would expect by the many events that had occurred against his will.'[205] Hermocrates' subsequent advice to him – 'do not be at all embarrassed (*aidestheis*), my child'[206] – invites him to transcend the very immaturity it acknowledges. His shyness subdued, Chaereas now serves to enact his adulthood through narrative. Hermocrates helpfully fills in the initial part of the story, allowing the young man to focus upon his own exploits: sailing, enslavement, crucifixion and, finally, the rebellion that proves his manhood – a story that, as recent scholarship has noted, does not fully match up with the primary narrator's account.[207] The story culminates in a series of sentences featuring first-person verbs expressing his decisiveness, vigour and (above all) power: 'I achieved great deeds... I personally subdued Tyre, hard to capture though it is... I was chosen as captain, fought a naval battle against the Great King, and became master (*kurios*) of Aradus... I had it in my power (*edunamēn*) to make the Egyptian the lord of all Asia'.[208] The empowered actor of this narrative is, of course, also its newly empowered author.

These narrative acts, then, serve to fix the meaning of the stories, in particular as expressions of the social identity of their actors/authors. In

---

[203] Smith (2007) 220–5, 231–2.
[204] Hom. *Od.* 2.40–79. The Odyssean colouring of Chariton's scene is enhanced by the distinctive Homeric phrase 'starting from the point where' (ἔνθεν ἑλών, 8.7.9 ~ Hom. *Od.* 8.500, 14.74). Chariton also uses this phrase at 1.7.6, 5.7.10.
[205] ὤκνει Χαιρέας, ὡς ἂν ἐπὶ πολλοῖς τῶν οὐ κατὰ γνώμην συμβάντων αἰδούμενος, Char. 8.7.4.
[206] μηδὲν αἰδεσθῇς, ὦ τέκνον, Char. 8.7.4.   [207] de Temmerman (2009a) 258–60.
[208] ἔργα μεγάλα διεπραξάμην [cf. ἔργον... μέγα of the capture of Tyre at 7.2.6]... Τύρον δυσάλωτον οὖσαν ἐχειρωσάμην αὐτός καὶ ναύαρχος ἀποδειχθεὶς κατεναυμάχησα τὸν μέγαν βασιλέα καὶ Ἀράδου κύριος ἐγενόμην... ἐδυνάμην... καὶ τὸν Αἰγύπτιον ἀποδεῖξαι πάσης τῆς Ἀσίας δεσπότην, Char. 8.8.9–10. Chaereas magnifies his account with not only Herodotean echoes (the repeated use of ἀποδείκνυμι and the reference to ἔργα μεγάλα alludes to the preface of the *Histories*, no doubt also underlining the theme of military conflict between East and West), but also tactical assimilations of his own triumphs with those of Hermocrates, his primary addressee (compare κατεναυμάχησα with Hermocrates' defeat of the Athenians: κατεναυμάχησας, 1.11.2).

each case, after an initial *aporia* generated by embarrassment (*aidōs*, the Greek superego), the speaker takes control of the story and fashions it into a statement of identity: Callirhoe's as a faithful wife, Chaereas' as a citizen–warrior worthy of the hand of Hermocrates' daughter. We can see, then, the Fishy temporality inherent in meaning-making: for narratives to signify they need to be worked through, shaped and mastered.

Yet for all that these character-bound narrations attempt to impose a final and total meaning on and control over the narrative, Chariton also dramatises the limitations of that process. Chaereas does not have total control over his narration, at least not at the start: Chariton goes out of his way to emphasise the crowd's role in shaping the story that is told. Initially, Chaereas 'began at the end, not wishing to upset the people with the initial (*prōtois*), gloomy (*skuthrōpois*) events'.[209] This inversion of narrative order is at one level an amusing rewriting of Odysseus' words when he begins *his* account of suffering and manly endurance ('what shall I say first, what last?').[210] It also picks up the narrator's metadiegetic comments at the beginning of book 8, which we have already considered, to the effect that this final book will be 'most pleasurable', and will serve as a 'cleansing of the gloomy (*skuthrōpōn*) events in the initial (*prōtois*) books'.[211] With this echo of both Odysseus and Chariton's primary narrator, Chaereas is at one level transformed into a narrator. At another level, however, this shows his immaturity in this role. A narrative consists not just in the happy ending, but in the totality of the account. 'We beg you', counter the people, 'start from the beginning, tell us everything, leave nothing out'.[212] The shy Chaereas is being coerced into publicly coming to terms with the entirety of his story, even the parts that shame him. As so often in imperial culture,[213] oral performance is rerouted and, finally, determined, by audience response. The act of narration, then, is a dynamic, evolving process, not simply an instantaneous and unilateral imposition of the narrator's fully formed will.

This act of narration, this dramatisation of the creation of the 'meaning' of Chariton's story, is irrevocably linked to closure. Chaereas should, Hermocrates replies, cast aside his embarrassment, 'even if you tell us something very grievous or very bitter; for the luminous ending that has taken

---

[209] ἀπὸ τῶν τελευταίων ἤρξατο, λυπεῖν οὐ θέλων τοῖς πρώτοις καὶ σκυθρωποῖς τὸν λαόν, Char. 8.7.3. This passage is discussed more fully in chapter 5, below.
[210] τί πρῶτόν τοι ἔπειτα, τί δ' ὑστάτιον καταλέξω; Hom. *Od.* 9.14.
[211] καθάρσιον... τῶν ἐν τοῖς πρώτοις σκυθρωπῶν, Char. 8.1.4. On the Aristotelian echo, see Rijksbaron (1984), correcting Müller (1976) (who believes that Chariton has failed to understand Aristotle).
[212] ἐρωτῶμεν, ἄνωθεν ἄρξαι, πάντα ἡμῖν λέγε, μηδὲν παραλίπῃς, 8.7.3.
[213] Korenjak (2000).

place throws all the earlier events into the shade'.²¹⁴ Two points call for particular emphasis. First, Hermocrates asserts that the story is over, its completeness boundary-marked by the 'ending (*telos*) that has taken place'. Narrativisation marks the finalisation of narrativity, as the narrative catches up with its self-begetting. Second, awareness of the end radically changes the entire perception of the story, converting a narrative of dark suffering into one of light. This is perhaps the most profoundly self-reflexive moment in *Callirhoe*, signalling as it does a feature so constant in romantic narrative as to be practically constitutive of it: the tension between the characters' miserable experience of events mid-plot, as the narrative unfurls, and the revisionist sublimation of that experience in the happy ending. In a weak sense, this is true of any narrative, which will *both* naturalistically mimic the indeterminacy of life as it is lived *and* play on the 'preplottedness' of the authorial plan. 'The function of a work of art as a finite model of a "speech text" of real facts which is by nature infinite makes the factor of *delimitation*, of finiteness, the necessary condition of any artistic text in its primary forms.'²¹⁵ The Greek adventure romance, however, exploits this property of all narrative to the full, widening the gap between the (actorial) experience of infinity and the (narratorial) awareness of delimitation to an unparalleled degree.

The final fly in the closural ointment is the way in which, in both Xenophon and Chariton, the romantic narrative overspills the final act of narration. This is subtler in Xenophon, where the narrative continues for three sentences after the lovers' dedication in the temple of the '*graphē* [painting/story] of all that they had endured and all that they had done'. What is interesting about this narrative overspill is that it focuses upon characters other than Anthia and Habrocomes: their parents (who have died of grief), the slaves Leucon and Rhode, and the erstwhile bandit and bereaved pederast Hippothous. This subversive tactic reminds us insistently that narrative is always presented from a certain point of view: the 'official' story of Anthia and Habrocomes in the temple does not capture the variety of experiences undergone by all the figures. Their stories have different rhythms and temporalities, and not everyone gets their happy ending (a point that we shall pick up in chapter 4).

In *Callirhoe*, similarly, the sanctioned, official version of events is offset by an alternative one. While Chaereas is orating in the theatre, Callirhoe

---

²¹⁴ κἂν λέγῃς τι λυπηρότερον ἢ πικρότερον ἡμῖν· τὸ γὰρ τέλος λαμπρὸν γενόμενον ἐπισκοτεῖ τοῖς προτέροις ἅπασι, Char. 8.7.4. Note that Hermocrates' τὸ ... τέλος ... γενόμενον picks up the narrator's initial πάθος ἐρωτικὸν ... γενόμενον, 1.1.1, an elegant circularity.
²¹⁵ Lotman (1976) 10.

visits Aphrodite's temple, gives thanks for her and Chaereas' safe return home, and prays for a happy future (8.8.15–16). This final act of private reverence contrasts visibly with Chaereas' public performance, reminding us that this is not, in fact, his story. The narratorial *sphragis* that closes the text insists as much: 'this is the extent of my story about Callirhoe'. This sentence, harking back to the title,[216] reminds us that despite Chaereas' public monopolisation of the narration, the narrative actually belongs to Callirhoe. What is more, *we* know that Chaereas does not know everything: Callirhoe has secretly written to Dionysius: 'this is the only thing she did unbeknown to Chaereas; she took every effort to keep it secret, knowing of his innate jealousy'.[217] (And the reference at this point to her son may well remind us of another deception she has practised, namely telling Dionysius that he is the father.) Her entrusting of her and Chaereas' son to Dionysius to rear is a significant loose end, an unarticulated narrative 'aftermath' that problematises the romance's closural cadence.[218]

The romantic ending, then, certainly does enshrine the identity of its protagonists as newly matured, ideal agents within the polity. But it does more than this. Identity is here encoded in narrative, and narrative is a slippery thing: the first-century romancers show great awareness of the constructedness, the partiality, the limitations of narrative, and hence also of the identities that they create. The first-century romances are products of a time of cautious hope in the Greek cities of Asia Minor, a tentative belief that communities can be reborn after struggles and sufferings. This is particularly visible in Chariton, where the theme of post-conflict renaissance is strong. But compromises need to be made, accommodations need to be reached, particularly with foreign powers: here represented in the guise of Persia (but readable as a figure for Rome), transmuted from its traditional status as entirely hostile other. Persia can now be dealt with. Underlying all the idealism of the first-century romance is an awareness of the pragmatism that sustains the myth of a happy community.

At the deepest level, then, Chariton and Xenophon both, ultimately, represent optimistic visions of the renewability of the urban community.

---

[216] Whitmarsh (2005b) 590.
[217] τοῦτο μόνον ἐποίησε δίχα Χαιρέου· εἰδυῖα γὰρ αὐτοῦ τὴν ἔμφυτον ζηλοτυπίαν ἐσπούδαζε λαθεῖν, Char. 8.4.4. On such narrative *aporiai* in Chariton's last book, see esp. Brethes (2007a) 179–82.
[218] There may even be more to the text than *we* can know. In history, Hermocrates (the father of the romantic Callirhoe) was succeeded by a famous Syracusan tyrant, Dionysius I; and ancient sources tell us that he married a daughter of Hermocrates, whom he brutally mistreated (Plut. *Dio* 3; Diod. Sic. 13.112). See further Naber (1901) 98; Perry (1967) 138–9; Hunter (1994) 1056–7. On narrative 'aftermaths' see Roberts (1997).

They are best understood as textualised transcriptions of the civic festivals and communal activities that they both describe: these romances seek to capture the sense of joyous celebration of the permanence of the city that festival culture enacts ritually. But this textualisation is itself significant. The first-century romances are *not* functionally equivalent to ritual practice; they are artful, self-conscious narratives, and with narrative comes the depth, richness and complexity that we have traced in this chapter. In the following chapters, we shall see how this sophistication and artistry is exploited in later generations.

CHAPTER 2

Transforming romance
Achilles Tatius and Longus

The first-century romances of Chariton and Xenophon mimic the Hellenocentric model of the classic passage-rite myth, whereby the urban, aristocratic Hellenic 'home' is offset against the barbarian 'abroad'. From the second century, romance patterns shift radically. Of the later romances, at least judging by the extant texts, none is centrist in this way. Achilles Tatius' *Leucippe and Clitophon* and Longus' *Daphnis and Chloe*, the second-century[1] subjects of this chapter, focus on the Syrian littoral and rural Lesbos respectively, while Heliodorus' fourth-century *Charicleia and Theagenes* (the subject of the next) ends in Ethiopian Meroe. Fragmentary texts are, in the nature of things, harder to interpret (and indeed date) with confidence, but the two remaining romances for which the plot is relatively clear fit this trend away from first-century urban Hellenocentrism. The first-century *Metiochus and Parthenope*, which survives in Greek fragments and a Persian version, is centred on the court of the tyrant Polycrates of Samos, while the second-century *Babylonian affairs* of Iamblichus is the only known romance entirely to avoid Greek figures and Greek settings.

It looks very much, then, as if the romance form shifted radically at the end of the first century, claiming as its own the margins of the world rather than its centres. It is possible, of course, that this pattern is nothing more than a coincidence, the result of nothing more than the aleatory processes of transmission. The texts that we call *Ninus* and *Sesonchosis*, the papyrus fragments of which probably date to the first century, were certainly set in non-Greek environs and among non-Greek communities, and may have incorporated return narratives. But it is just as likely that they did not, and that they belong to the broader family of ancient novels written in Greek (a family that includes, for example, *Joseph and Aseneth*, Antonius Diogenes' *Wonders beyond Thule* (which survives in fragments

[1] Longus' date is hypothetical, but likely to be second- or early third-century. See appendix on dates.

and summary)² and the *Journal* of 'Dictys of Crete' (the Latin form of which survives complete, the Greek only in fragments)).³

What is more – and this is crucial – the trajectory away from urban Hellenocentrism is only one of a series of interrelated tendencies in the later romances. The first is the relocation of the marriage from the beginning to the end of the narrative. As a result, the return is seen not simply to restore a prior state of affairs, but to transform the identities of the couple. This, I argue, is the most obvious token of a general amplification of the transformative power of romance narrative. We saw in the previous chapter that romance always supplies a centrifugal, transformative push, tensed against a centripetal pull back towards the re-establishment of pre-existent norms. The later romances place considerably more emphasis on the transformative vector.

The second phenomenon is the increased emphasis on the textualisation of narrative. The first-century romances already (as we have also seen) show considerable awareness of the constructedness of narrative, of the fundamental difference between the plots that human authors shape (*Erzählung*) and the experience of life as it is lived (*Erlebnis*). In the later romances, this play between artifice and nature is exploited much more heavily. For example, the *graphē* (painting/narrative) describing the experiences of Anthia and Habrocomes at the end of Xenophon's romance becomes, in both Achilles and Longus, an elaborate ecphrasis and a pretext for the very narrative itself. Chaereas' oral summary of his feats at the end of Chariton is transformed, in Achilles Tatius, into a first-person narrative that occupies almost the entirety of the text. The effect of these processes is to drive a firm wedge between narration and experience, levering open a large space for irony and play, and also focusing even more attention on narrative as plastic, constructed *form*. At a time when literature and the plastic arts were placing ever more emphasis upon the non-natural, fictive power of artistic mimesis, romance narrative was itself shifting the attention from the message to the medium, from the *choses* to the *mots*.⁴ As Edward Said

---

² Since the publication of SW, *P.Oxy*. 4760–1 have been published: 4760 is almost certainly from Antonius, 4761 probably. I am not convinced by suggestions that he may be first century (e.g. Bowie (2007)), and *faute de mieux* prefer a second-century date; but the evidence is too slight to allow any definite conclusion. See also Morgan (1985) 487–9 against Photius' suggestion (*Bibl.* cod. 166 111b–12a) that Antonius is likely to have been the earliest of the novels, which is probably based on a naively literal reading of the pseudo-documentarist device.
³ The long-recognised fragments of the Greek text (*P.Tebt.* 268; *P.Oxy* 2539) will soon be supplemented by the publication of further Oxyrhynchus papyri (Dirk Obbink reports).
⁴ For mimesis in imperial Greek culture see Whitmarsh (2001a) 41–89. The final allusion is to Foucault (1970), of which the French title was *Les mots et les choses*: the final section posits a shift in the understanding of discourse during the period of the enlightenment, when language was (he claims) held to have lost its claim to transparency.

has argued, such eras will see a greater emphasis on narrative as process, as vehicle or as material substance, rather than as a pellucid window onto the world.[5]

CONTEXTS

How can we explain these changes in historical terms? Here, as elsewhere in this book, I wish to avoid historical determinism, but, even so, there are phenomena that help to contextualise these trends. The most significant is the emergent interest in the malleability and transferability of identity.[6] The steady trickle of elite Greeks attaining Roman citizenship and entering the Roman senate that began in the late republic became much more substantial,[7] until, finally, in 212 CE Caracalla's *Constitutio Antoniniana* Romanised the entire free population of the empire. Conversely, we see a greater focus on the Hellenisation of non-Greeks. Although Roman semiotic Hellenism stretched back to at least the second century BCE (and arguably well beyond that),[8] the second century CE saw a step change, in that emperors were now explicitly self-fashioning as Greek. Nero and Domitian, like Antony before them, had adopted some markers of Hellenic stylisation, but it was Hadrian (117–38) in particular who cultivated an image of himself in unmistakeably Greek terms: accompanying the famous beard,[9] boyfriend and poetry, concrete symbols of his affiliation, were a series of practical policies supporting Greece: the patronising of Greek literary talents,[10] the renewal of urban landscapes and the foundation of new cities,[11] and the creation of the famous, if still partially mysterious, institution called the Panhellenion, a league (based on the Delphic Amphictiony) of cities who could prove their Greekness genealogically, centred in Athens and built around the cult of the emperor.[12] From here on until the so-called 'crisis' of the mid-third century, all emperors would present themselves in Greek guise.

Even more important for the romancers is the emphasis in the literature upon the Hellenisation of easterners, which, while of course in reality it reflects a process that was as old as archaic colonisation, achieves in this

---

[5] Said (1983) 101, on Conrad. [6] See more fully Whitmarsh (2001a).
[7] See esp. Halfmann (1979) on eastern senators, and further literature cited at Whitmarsh (2001a) 18.
[8] Whitmarsh (2010a), with further literature.
[9] Vout (2006) emphasises the iconographic polysemy of the beard. [10] Fein (1994).
[11] On Hadrian's provincial building, see Boatwright (2000), emphasising that Hadrian's civic munificence also extended to central Italy and Africa.
[12] Discussion and further literature at Romeo (2002).

era an unparalleled visibility and salience:[13] well-known examples include Philostratus' Ninevan Damis who articulates his desire to 'become Greek' by associating with the great philosopher Apollonius,[14] the Syrian Lucian's self-fashioning as a Hellenised barbarian, and the Gaul Favorinus' deconstruction of the opposition between true and self-made Greeks.[15] Greek identity thus became both significantly more attractive and significantly more attainable in the second century.

This privileging of Greekness, however, also made it a target. The early imperial period saw numerous claims (in Greek) to the effect that Greek ideas had been pre-empted by Babylonians, Jews, Egyptians and others. Again, the proto-Bernalian claim itself is not new: it can be glimpsed already in the fourth century (Plato's Egyptian priest teases the Greeks as 'children' at *Timaeus* 21b), and is widespread in Hellenistic historiography: for example, in the Jewish historian Eupolemus claimed that Moses was the 'first' wise man, the inventor of the alphabet, which passed to the Greeks via the Phoenicians (*FGrH* 723 F1); or in Hecataeus of Abdera, who makes Egypt the origin of geometry, astronomy and arithmetic (264 F1). For all the deep roots of this tradition, the imperial period saw an intensification of such claims, notably in Josephus' *Jewish antiquities* and *Against Apion* (late first century CE), and continuing forcibly in the second-century Christian tradition: Justin Martyr, Tatian, Clement and Origen represent a strong collective statement that Mosaic law precedes, influences, and morally trumps Greek philosophy.[16] It is, perhaps, particularly this contemporary pressure from Christians (more directly than the non-Christian Hellenistic precursors whom he explicitly identifies) that inspires Diogenes Laertius, in (probably) the early third century CE, to begin his *Lives of the eminent philosophers* with an attack on those who claim that the philosophy is a barbarian invention (1.3).[17] The crucial point, however, is that this entire debate is conducted in Greek itself. Hellenism might be opposed, but it is inescapable.

The second-century romance reflects this fluid world, transforming the Hellenocentric paradigms encoded in the first-century texts by placing

---

[13] Whitmarsh (2001a) 90–130. The idea that barbarians can become Greek through education is, assuredly, as old as Isocrates (esp. *Panegyr.* 50). More generally on *paideia* in the imperial period see Swain (1996) 17–100; Schmitz (1997).

[14] Ἕλλην γενόμενος, 3.43.

[15] Gleason (1995) 16–17 and Whitmarsh (2001a) 119–21, 169–78 on Favorinus, with further literature (adding König (2001) more generally on the context of the speech; Amato (2005) offers an excellent new edition). On Lucian's Hellenism see Swain (1996) 298–329 and Whitmarsh (2001a) 247–94.

[16] The tradition (with its Hellenistic background) is economically surveyed by Droge (1989); for interpretation, see esp. Stroumsa (1999) 57–84.

[17] As suggested at Whitmarsh (2007a) 38–9.

greater emphasis upon alterity and the mutability of identity, and by focusing attention self-reflexively upon the very *narrative* processes of self-construction.

HELLENISM DECENTRED

Whereas Chariton and Xenophon construct the Greek city as the *sine qua non* of civilised living, second-century romances place much less emphasis upon civic identity. In *Leucippe and Clitophon*, the narrator Clitophon announces that his 'homeland (*patris*) is Tyre' (1.3.1), but describes nothing of its people, architecture, religion or institutions. It is not that the romance shows no awareness of institutional structures – the cult temple of Astarte at Sidon (1.1.2), the public buildings of Alexandria (5.1–2) and the courtroom (7.7–13) and temple of Artemis (7.16.2–8.) at Ephesus are all sketched – but the separation–reincorporation narrative is *domestic* rather than civic.[18] The setting for the first two books is Clitophon's family home (described in lavish detail), and it is their relationships with their father and mother respectively that Clitophon's and Leucippe's love for each other compromises (1.11.3, 2.30; cf. 5.18.4).

In *Daphnis and Chloe*, meanwhile, we are certainly told that the protagonists begin life in the *polis* and end up there, but the narrative shows no interest in their life there. After the proem, the narrative opens with an ecphrasis of Mitylene, and indeed the first word is *polis*; but the scene immediately shifts 200 stades away, as if programmatically to emphasise the romance's shift from a civic to a rural focus (1.1). Like Dio Chrysostom's *Euboean oration* and Philostratus' *Heroicus*, *Daphnis and Chloe* challenges its readers' sense that civic living is more civilised, by presenting nature as generally benign and urban wealth as generally corrupt and oppressive.[19] The countryside is where they live from early childhood, and is the formative influence upon them, to the extent that, even after the recognition, they continue to live a pastoral existence. They insist on marrying in the countryside, 'since they could not stand spending time in the city';[20] and afterwards, 'they led their lives in the pastoral way most of the time', cultivating the rustic deities, and suckling their child on a goat and a ewe.[21]

---

[18] See Whitmarsh (2010b).
[19] Discussion and bibliography at Whitmarsh (2001a) 100–8; see further below, pp. 96–9.
[20] μὴ φέροντες τὴν ἐν ἄστει διατριβήν, 4.37.1.
[21] τὸν πλεῖστον χρόνον <βίον> ποιμενικὸν εἶχον, 4.39.1.

The devaluation of the *polis* signals in part a greater concentration upon the complex psychology already latent in the first-century romances. But it also marks a cultural repositioning. The second-century texts no longer seek to naturalise a view of the world centred on traditional Greek values; rather, their tendency is to disrupt received constructions of the world, and multiply the cultural perspectives. Iamblichus' *Babylonian affairs* takes place entirely in Mesopotamia, and seemingly includes not a single Greek figure. *Leucippe and Clitophon* begins and ends on the Phoenician littoral. Heliodorus' *Charicleia and Theagenes*, the subject of the following chapter, takes us to Ethiopia, for Greeks one of the edges of the earth. Fragmentary narratives also used non-Greek locations, such as Lollianus' *Phoenician affairs* (the setting for the surviving fragments is unspecified, but the title is secure) and the story that we call *Calligone* (set in southern Russia).[22]

Non-Greek settings per se, for sure, do not begin in the second century, as we noted at the outset of the chapter. As Martin Braun already argued in the 1930s,[23] the earliest novels were variants of the 'national romances' of the peoples subjected to Greek and then Roman hegemony. Prior to the second century, however, romances on non-Greek themes seem to have focused on iconic individuals of history, particularly rulers. These novels may have incorporated romantic elements (like the *Alexander romance*'s erotic interlude involving Candace, queen of Meroe: 3.18–23). The second-century romance, by contrast, takes the adventure romance format of Chariton and Xenophon – the marriage theme, the centre–periphery structure, the emphasis on maturation and the role of marriage, and the use of (wholly or largely) invented figures – and introduces into it a much greater sense of cultural plurality. Given the ethnocentrism inherent in the first-century centre–periphery paradigm, this in itself constitutes an implicit challenge to Hellenocentric ways of thinking.

This shift in emphasis seems to reflect a diversification of origins among the romancers themselves, although (as ever) our biographical information is sparse. Achilles Tatius is associated with Alexandria by the manuscript tradition and by the *Suda*.[24] It is possible that the association derives simply from the lavish praise of Alexandria found at the outset of book 5,

---

[22] At a greater distance from the erotic romance, we could also point to Antonius Diogenes' *Wonders beyond Thule* and Lucian's *True stories*, although Hellenistic precedents certainly existed for this kind of fantastic travel narrative (e.g. Euhemerus, Iambulus, Eudoxus, Pytheas).

[23] Braun (1934), (1938).

[24] *Suda* s.v. Ἀχιλλεὺς Στάτιος (*sic*), and the MSS titles cited at e.g. Vilborg (1955) 1.

but, in general, scholars have found enough convincing evidence of (apparently) first-hand knowledge of Egypt.[25] Some have claimed that the surname 'Tatius' (Τάτιος) derives from the Egyptian god Thoth (~ Greek *Tat*),[26] which would be an excellent sobriquet for an author, given that Thoth was in some traditions the inventor of writing or 'father of letters'.[27] Others, however, have seen it simply as a form of the Roman name Tatius, common enough in the Greek world.[28] On balance, it is likely (albeit far from certain) that Achilles was Alexandrian. Perhaps he considered himself culturally Greek but 'Egyptian by race', like his own, equally Iliadically named, character Menelaus.[29] Meanwhile Iamblichus was (according to a scholion on Photius, which seems to derive from the romance itself) a native Syrian for whom Greek was the third language, learned after Babylonian.[30] His name is a Hellenised form of the Semitic YMLK 'ĒL (='El rules', or alternatively 'El makes him king'), relatively common in the areas of Syrian Emesa and Palmyra.[31] Heliodorus, as we shall see in the following chapter, also seems to have hailed from Emesa (10.41.4). (As to Longus, all is speculation: even the name, in Greek *Loggos*, may simply be a corruption for *logos*, 'story').[32]

These later romances display a much greater interest in, and narrative exploitation of, cultural heterogeneity. In Chariton and Xenophon, as we saw in the previous chapter, non-Greeks unproblematically speak Greek, recognise Greek institutions, and worship Greek gods. *Leucippe and Clitophon*, by contrast, thematises difference from the start. The romance begins with a brief geophysical description of Sidon:

---

[25] Rommel (1923) 78–81. [26] E.g. Vilborg (1962) 7.
[27] πατὴρ γραμμάτων, Pl. *Phaedr.* 275a. [28] E.g. Plepelits (1980) 2.
[29] τὸ... γένος Αἰγύπτιος, 2.33.2; cf. 3.19.1, with n. 54 below, and ἐμοὶ Φοινίκη γένος at 1.3.1 (Clitophon).
[30] This passage is cited at Habrich (1960) 2 and translated at SW 181. It conflicts in points of detail with Photius' own summary (at *Bibl.* 75b 27–41, cited Habrich (1960) 32–4; translated SW 194), notably in that it makes the author a Syrian rather than a Babylonian. The scholarly consensus, that the scholion is correcting Photius' misreading, is probably right: see esp. Millar (1993) 489–92, SW 181–2. Iamblichus is also called 'Syrian' at Theodorus Priscianus *Eupor.* 133.5–12 (Rose). It is worth noting that elsewhere (*Bibl.* cod. 181 = 125b) Photius claims that an Iamblichus (perhaps ours, but not necessarily) was from Emesa (Heliodorus' homeland: see the following chapter), and descended from an ancient dynasty.
[31] Chad (1972) 143–4.
[32] Scholars have made much of the fact that the name is attested epigraphically for Lesbos; this, coupled with an apparently accurate knowledge of the island (Mason (1979), (1995); Green (1982)), makes a Lesbian origin possible. But the name is common enough: found once on Crete and four times in Cyrenaica (*LGPN* 1:289); four times in Athens (*LGPN* 2: 285); and twice in Thrace (*LGPN* 4: 211).

Sidon is a city on the sea. The sea belongs to the Assyrians, the city is the Phoenicians' mother-city, and its people fathered the Thebans. In the folds of a bay lies a twin harbour, broad and gently enclosing the sea: where the bay bellies out down the flank of the coast on the right, another mouth has been carved out, where the water flows back in. Thus a second harbour is born from the first, so that trading vessels can winter there in the calm, while they can pass the summer in the outer part of the bay.[33]

The first three proper names are exotic: Sidon, the Assyrians, the Phoenicians. The Thebans, meanwhile, play a double role. On the one hand, the allusion to a familiar Greek people implies a Greek framework of reference, controlling and taming the Phoenician otherness (rather as Philostratus' narrator in *Apollonius* describes the Indian landscape by comparing it to canonical Greek sights such as the Athenian acropolis: *VA* 2.20, 2.23, 2.27, 3.13). Intercultural description, as Edward Said stresses, creates cultural subjectivity: it positions 'us' as the controllers of knowledge, and the other as its object.[34] On the other hand, the description of Thebes as a colony of Sidon implicitly places the Greek *polis* in a relationship of dependence and secondariness – especially in the wider context of the 'culture wars' of Achilles' time, when cultural priority was such an issue. The effect is disorientating and confusing.[35]

This sense of disorientation is exacerbated by the bizarre syntax of the Greek: there are no verbs or connective particles at all until we reach the geophysical description, and even there we are thirty-three words into the romance before we reach a main verb (*koilainetai*, 'bellies out'). The phrasing, moreover, seems calculated to confuse, particularly in the third and fourth sentences, which literally read: 'mother of Phoenicians the city; of Thebans the people father'. Each sentence consists of three elements – an unarticulated nominative noun denoting a parent, an unarticulated genitive plural noun denoting a people, and a nominative articulated noun ('the city', 'the people') – but these elements occupy different positions. The rendering given above[36] is the result of much labouring. In fact, a more natural way to construe the Greek syntax is: 'the mother of the Phoenicians

---

[33] Σιδὼν ἐπὶ θαλάττηι πόλις· Ἀσσυρίων ἡ θάλασσα· μήτηρ Φοινίκων ἡ πόλις· Θηβαίων ὁ δῆμος πατήρ. δίδυμος λιμὴν ἐν κόλπῳ πλατύς, ἠρέμα κλείων τὸ πέλαγος. ᾗ γὰρ ὁ κόλπος κατὰ πλευρὰν ἐπὶ δεξιὰ κοιλαίνεται, στόμα δεύτερον ὀρώρυκται, καὶ τὸ ὕδωρ αὖθις εἰσρεῖ, καὶ γίνεται τοῦ λιμένος ἄλλος λιμήν, ὡς χειμάζειν μὲν ταύτῃ τὰς ὁλκάδας ἐν γαλήνῃ, θερίζειν δὲ τοῦ λιμένος εἰς τὸ προκόλπιον, 1.1.

[34] Said (1978).

[35] Even more so when we consider that Cadmus is elsewhere said to come from Tyre, not Sidon (Vilborg (1962) 18). Has Achilles, or Clitophon, made a mistake? Or is this deliberate? If so, to what end? Again, Achilles' primary aim seems to be discombobulation.

[36] Adapted from Whitmarsh (2001b).

is the city; of the Thebans, the people is the father' – albeit this makes less good sense. A further challenge is presented by the play between 'mother' and 'father' here? What is at stake in the gender differentiation? At one level, the answer lies in a play upon Greek grammar, since 'city' is feminine and 'people' is masculine. But that answer just raises another question: why is it that the *city* is the parent of the Phoenicians, and the *people* that of the Thebans? What is more, referring to a city as a 'mother' seems to imply a colonial mother-city (*mētropolis*), and that description would seem to be more appropriate to the relationship between Sidon and Thebes.

Readers of the first-century romance would have been bamboozled. Both Chariton and Xenophon begin with unproblematic descriptions of their central figures and their homelands (Chariton having introduced himself beforehand): 'Hermocrates the general of the Syracusans, the victor over the Athenians, had a daughter called Callirhoe'; 'there once was a citizen of Ephesus called Lycomedes, one of the most powerful men in the city.'[37] Achilles' perplexing beginning, relative to his predecessors, does not simply problematise interpretation; it also highlights the issue of subjectivity, of the vantage from which the scene is being observed: we are struggling to construe the scene not just because the text is challenging and experimental, but also because what is being described is alien to our experience. Description loses its easy naturalism, its pretensions to pellucidity, and becomes instead an object lesson in the perils, and the politics, of intercultural interpretation.

CULTURALLY SPEAKING

Another factor that militates against transparency is the characteristic emphasis upon the ways in which narrative is *mediated*. I have been writing as though the cultural distance we are considering were the space between the reader and Sidon. But interposed between the two, of course, stands the narrator's own interpretation: we readers interpret the narrator interpretating Sidon. After the passage quoted and discussed above, we encounter the figure of this mediator: 'It was there that I arrived, a survivor of a severe storm, and made my thank-offerings for my rescue to the

---

[37] Ἑρμοκράτης ὁ Συρακοσίων στρατηγός, οὗτος ὁ νικήσας Ἀθηναίους, εἶχε θυγατέρα Καλλιρόην, Char. 1.1.1; ἦν ἐν Ἐφέσωι ἀνὴρ τῶν τὰ πρῶτα ἐκεῖ δυναμένων, Λυκομήδης ὄνομα..., Xen. Eph. 1.1.1. Longus and Achilles supply contextualising material both in their external frames and in the secondary narration that thereafter becomes the principle focus: cf. Long. 1 *praef.* 1 (ἐν Λέσβωι θηρῶν ἐν ἄλσει Νυμφῶν θέαμα εἶδον κάλλιστον ὧν εἶδον), 1.1.1 (πόλις ἐστὶ τῆς Λέσβου Μιτυλήνη...); Ach. Tat. 1.1.1 (Σιδὼν ἐπὶ θαλάττηι πόλις), 1.3.1 (ἐμοὶ Φοινίκη γένος, Τύρος ἡ πατρίς, κτλ.). Prefatory strategies are discussed by Morgan (2001).

Phoenicians' goddess, whom the Sidonians call Astarte.'[38] Who is this 'I'? Scholars conventionally refer to an 'unnamed narrator'; I suspect, however, readers without the benefit of Genettian narratological categories[39] would have been more disposed to identify a narrative 'I' more or less directly with the author. I do not mean that the shipwreck story asks to be taken as autobiographically true, but that ancient readers were likely to have associated the claim (however fictitious they may have seen it as) with the author's own voice – as, for example, Augustine famously reads the 'I' of Apuleius' *Metamorphoses* as an autobiography of Apuleius himself, 'whether he recorded it or invented it'.[40] I shall argue presently that the link between the narrator and Achilles enriches the romance. My point for now, however, is simply that the use of this technique lays heavy emphasis upon the question of who is speaking: not the diaphanous, authoritative narrator of Chariton and Xenophon, rather a personalised but mysterious individual, frail enough to be shipwrecked; someone with his own story, his own identity, and (by implication) his own particular set of narrative filters.

Indeed, we can perhaps see these filters at work in the opening passage cited above. The one thing that we do learn about the narrator's background, presently, is that he is *erōtikos* (1.2.1): 'in love', or perhaps 'of amorous disposition', or even 'an erotic expert'.[41] Perhaps this

---

[38] ἐνταῦθα ἥκων ἐκ πολλοῦ χειμῶνος, σῶστρα ἔθυον ἐμαυτοῦ τῆι τῶν Φοινίκων θεᾶι· Ἀστάρτην αὐτὴν καλοῦσιν οἱ Σιδώνιοι, 1.1.2. Most MSS omit θεᾶι, which appears only in F, described by Vilborg as deriving from a scribe who 'used his own judgement in interpreting and emending the text' ((1955) lxx). Vilborg himself prints θεᾶι, despite suggesting that it is an interpolation. Part of the reason for suspecting θεᾶι is the claim that elsewhere Achilles uses θεός of goddesses ((1962) 19). This is not true: θεά is in fact attested by V, G and F at 2.36.2, a reading that Vilborg himself, like all modern editors, adopts. The erroneous claim is repeated by Diggle (1972), who wants to read τῆι τῶν Φοινίκων Ἀφροδίτηι – unjustifiably interventionist, in my view. I have maintained the order of VGE (followed by Vilborg, but not Garnaud) for the second sentence quoted here.

[39] 'That it is essential not to confuse author and narrator has become a commonplace of literary theory' (Chatman (1978) 147).

[40] *aut indicavit aut finxit, Civ.* 18.18 – a confusion that is of course already seeded in Apuleius' *Metamorphoses* itself, where Lucius claims to hail from Madaurus, Apuleius' hometown (11.27; and see, among the many studies on this phenomenon, esp. Laird (1990) on what I shall later in this chapter call the *metaleptic* quality of such passages). 'Augustine clearly takes it as an autobiography, whether real or fictitious: for although he denies the possibility of metamorphosis and doubts the sincerity of Apuleius' account, he assumes without question that Apuleius is claiming to relate his own experience – that he is the Lucius of his novel. The assumption continued to be unquestioned for at least a thousand years, and the identity of Apuleius and Lucius was to play a major role in the interpretation of the *Golden ass*' (Gaisser (2008) 33). Similarly, Photius conflates narrator and author in the *Metamorphoses* of Lucius of Patrae: *Bibl.* cod. 129, with Whitmarsh (2010c). Such confusion is not really straightforward naivety – neither Augustine nor Photius believes that the events described actually happened to the author – but rather the result of a different intellectual mindset, in which first-person statements are attached much more closely to their speakers.

[41] This last interpretation I owe to Ian Repath, whose rich and suggestive book *Playing with Plato* will argue (among many other things) that the unnamed narrator is a Socratic figure.

disclosure retrospectively explains the superabundance in the opening passage of terms for parenthood ('mother', 'father'; also perhaps 'twin', *didymos*, and 'is born', *ginetai*), the corporeal topography (*kolpos* (twice; also *prokolpion*) is not only 'bay' but also 'bosom' or 'lap'; *pleura*, 'flank', can also mean the human flank; *koilanetai*, 'bellies out', literally implies hollowness, suggesting the body's cavities; *stoma* usually refers to the human 'mouth'), and the emphasis upon fluidity: an *erōtikos* might find much to conjure with in the phrase 'another mouth... where the liquid flows back in'.[42]

How culturally inflected is this mediation? Although it is not stated where the narrator comes from, or where he is going to (all that we can say is that he seems to be at Sidon by accident, and apparently as an outsider), the narrator seems to engaged in *interpretatio Graeca*, the translation of foreign elements into a Greek register: this is strongly implied by the reference to 'the Phoenicians' goddess, whom the Sidonians call Astarte'. In an influential discussion, Daniel Selden has argued that the narrator misperceives Sidonian cult from his Greek perspective, whereas Achilles also makes available (to those in the know) a different, Sidonian interpretation; the text thus embodies the rhetorical figure that he names 'syllepsis', i.e. an availability to be read in two opposing ways.[43] Selden's argument focuses primarily upon the lengthy ecphrasis of a painting of Zeus' rape of Europa (1.1.2–13); readers familiar with west-Asian mythology would, he claims, have interpreted this differently, as representing the dominance of Astarte (i.e. the semitic cosmic deity Ištar, sometimes identified with the moon) over the sea: 'The text strategically accommodates both possibilities, so that depending on the reader's frame of reference, Hellenic or Phoenician, the image can be decoded in two opposing ways.'[44]

Despite its attractions, there are a number of problems with the argument as formulated. First, the temple of Ištar may be Sidon's most iconic landmark,[45] and we might assume that the narrator's dedication of his thank-offerings takes place there, but the painting is not located (as Selden claims)[46] within it: what the text actually says is 'when I had made my

---

[42] στόμα δεύτερον... καὶ τὸ ὕδωρ αὖθις εἰσρεῖ.
[43] Selden (1994) 50–1, supported with qualifications by Morales (2004) 38–48.
[44] Selden (1994) 51. The two opposing modes of interpretation are: (i) the Hellenic, which sees Europa as abducted by the bull; and (ii) the West Semitic, wherein the goddess is in control, leading her mate out to sea. Generally, on Phoenicians in the romances, see Briquel-Chatonnet (1992).
[45] Cf. Luc. *DDS* 4 (ἱρὸν... μέγα). On the evidence for the temple see further Lightfoot (2003) 297–301.
[46] Selden (1994) 50; Morales (2004) 37. Lightfoot (2003) 299 recognises the problem.

thank-offerings... I undertook a tour *of the rest of the city*',[47] and it is there that he saw the 'votive picture', while browsing 'the sacred dedications'. It is possible that the text is corrupt – 'sacred dedications' are more likely to be found in a temple than in urban space[48] – but as it stands the text does not connect the painting directly with Astarte. Second, Selden wants to set the narrator's identification of the figure as Europa against what he takes as Clitophon's subsequent correction, when in his later narrative he describes Leucippe as 'like Selene I once (*pote*) saw drawn on a bull'.[49] For Selden, Clitophon is referring back to the painting seen at the outset, and supplying Selene (=Astarte) as the subject. However, even if we discount the textual difficulties here too,[50] it is far from self-evident that he is actually referring to the picture described at the beginning of the text: 'a picture I once saw' is not 'the picture that you and I saw just now'.[51] Finally, the parallel Selden draws with the Lucianic *On the Syrian goddess* (4) actually works against his reading: in the Lucianic text it is the Sidonian priests who identify Astarte with Europa, while the narrator (a non-Sidonian Phoenician) offers Selene. In the Lucianic passage, Europa is the *local* reading, and Selene the external one – the exact inverse of the configuration Selden wants.[52]

Selden is broadly right about the unnamed narrator. Although he is not explicitly marked as 'Greek', this is implicit: his role (as we have seen) certainly seems to be to translate local, Phoenician phenomena into a register accessible to a panhellenic audience. Clitophon, however, is more problematic for his argument, since – despite what Selden claims – he shows no signs of Semitic awareness. Though 'Phoenicia provides my ancestry',[53]

---

[47] σῶστρα ἔθυον ἐμαυτοῦ... περιϊὼν οὖν καὶ τὴν ἄλλην πόλιν, 1.1.2: see below for my proposed emendation.

[48] My proposed emendation is τὴν αὐλὴν περίβολον ('the temple precinct') for τὴν ἄλλην πόλιν ('the rest of the city'). The phrase is not directly paralleled, but for αὐλῆς περίβολος cf. Ael. Ar. *Rom.* 29 (where emendation to αὐλός (so Oliver (1953); Klein (1983)) is misguided: Pernot (1997) 74 n. 61); Hsch. x 653. It could be, then, that Achilles wrote τὸν αὐλῆς περίβολον, although that is palaeographically more difficult. I read this episode as an allusion to ps.-Cebes' *Tabula*, where again the painting stands in the precinct (περιϊὼν οὖν καὶ τὴν αὐλὴν περίβολον καὶ περισκοπῶν τὰ ἀναθήματα ὁρῶ γραφὴν ἀνακειμένην..., Ach. Tat. 1.1.2 ~ πολλὰ μὲν καὶ ἄλλα ἀναθήματα ἐθεωροῦμεν· ἀνέκειτο δὲ καὶ πίναξ τις ἔμπροσθεν τοῦ νεώ..., ps.-Ceb. 1.1.1); cf. also Luc. *Tox.* 6. Vilborg (1962) 19 notes the high concentration of textual uncertainties in the first page of Achilles.

[49] τοιαύτην εἶδον ἐγώ ποτε ἐπὶ ταύρωι γεγραμμένην Σελήνην, 1.4.3.

[50] Σελήνην (WMD); Εὐρώπην (VGE). It has been claimed, reasonably, that Selene is the *lectio difficilior*, since Europa may be a scribal attempt to force the link back to the opening picture (so Vilborg (1962) 21–2).

[51] That *pote* cannot mean 'just now' is noted by Vilborg (1962) 20; Lightfoot (2003) 301; Morales (2004) 40. Note also that after beginning his narrative, Clitophon never elsewhere engages the unnamed narrator or refers to the external narratorial circumstances: Hägg (1971) 125; Morgan (2004d) 495.

[52] Lightfoot (2003) 299.   [53] ἐμοὶ Φοινίκη γένος, 1.3.1.

his name and cultural vocabulary are entirely Greek.⁵⁴ The word 'barbarian' in his mouth always carries negative associations.⁵⁵ At one point, notably, he tells Leucippe the familiar story of Philomela, laying particular emphasis upon the ethical superiority of Greeks over barbarians (5.5.2–3, at 2). His reference points, like those of his cousin Clinias, are entirely drawn from the mainstream Greek tradition; indeed, it is particularly awkward for Selden's argument that Clitophon never mentions Astarte or any local Phoenician deity. At 1.4.3, the passage discussed in the previous paragraph, he refers to Selene, not Astarte, and indeed elsewhere alludes to Europa on the bull (2.15.4) – precisely the story that (in Selden's reading) he is supposed to repress. The one exception is the aetiology of the vine at 2.2, where Clitophon supplies a version of the Icarius story, marked as Tyrian in explicit contradistinction to the Athenian: 'The Tyrians consider that Dionysus is a local god, since they too sing the myth of Cadmus.'⁵⁶ Even here, however, Clitophon distances himself personally from this story, bookending his account in the Herodotean ethnographic fashion with the phrase 'so the Tyrians' story goes',⁵⁷ and proceeding to link it to the festival that 'they' (third person) hold (2.3.1). Clitophon, then, seems (although we shall qualify this below) ambiguously poised in relation to Tyre: although happy to describe himself as Phoenician by ancestry, he presents himself as aloof from local custom.

Now it might be possible to argue that this Hellenised perspective results from the overlaying of the primary narrator's subjectivity onto an originally Phoenician tale, but this raises a related but arguably greater problem. The text as we have it is multiply embedded: it represents (perhaps) Achilles' own Alexandrian version of the panhellenic(?) narrator's version of Clitophon's Greco-(?)Phoenician version of events. (This narrative Chinese-boxing is borrowed from Plato, particularly the *Symposium*, a vital intertext for Achilles.)⁵⁸ But, of course, in a work of fiction it is impossible to tease apart these layers, as a historical *Quellenforscher* might. Neither Clitophon nor the primary narrator exists independently of the text: any account of

---

⁵⁴ A comparable case is his acquaintance Menelaus, 'an Egyptian by birth' (τὸ... γένος Αἰγύπτιος, 2.33.2; cf. 3.19.1; also above, n. 29), but onomastically Greek, and seemingly differentiated from the 'Egyptians' who receive Clitophon's scorn for their cowardice (4.14.9).
⁵⁵ See esp. the dismissive or fearful references at 3.9.2. 3.24.3, 4.17.1, 5.5.2, 8.2.3. Kuch (2003) discusses the Greek–barbarian antithesis in the romances.
⁵⁶ τὸν γὰρ Διόνυσον Τύριοι νομίζουσι ἑαυτῶν, ἐπεὶ καὶ τὸν Κάδμου μῦθον ᾄδουσι, 2.2.1.
⁵⁷ ὡς ὁ Τυρίων λόγος, 2.2.6.
⁵⁸ First noted by Winkler in Reardon ed. (1989) 284 n. 72; more detailed discussion in the forthcoming book of Ian Repath. The general significance of the *Symposium* for Achilles has been discussed by Morales (2004) 51–3; Laplace (2007), esp. 463–532.

the play of voices has to focus solely upon the textual process, and not rely on hypothecations of 'original' subjectivities, whether Phoenician, Greek or any other. There are two issues here. The first is the historical question of what Phoenician cultural consciousness might actually have consisted in by Achilles' time: impossible to answer, given the limited and intractable evidence, but it is highly problematic to use Ugaritic texts from the second millennium as a guide to the thought patterns of Sidonians of the second century CE, who had been creatively hybridising their culture for at least four centuries. The Europa narrative represented a particularly complex case of hybridity: from the third century BCE, Phoenicians had appropriated this myth from Greeks and used it as *their own* narrative.[59] Achilles' Europa story, then, is not a case of Greek misreading of an 'authentic' Canaanite myth, but reflects a genuinely Phoenician process of narrative recycling, arguably even a counterhegemonic case of 'colonial mimicry' that disturbs and subverts Hellenocentrism by emphasising the Phoenician origin of Greek culture.[60]

The second issue relates to reading strategies. There is no possibility of neatly separating Achilles' voices into cultural categories. The *play* of voices is precisely the point.[61] How, then, can we gauge the extent to which Clitophon's words have been re-encoded as Greek by the primary narrator? At the beginning of Philostratus' *Apollonius*, the narrator claims to have 'rewritten' (*metagrapsai*) the crude memoir of Damis, the 'man of Nineveh', polishing the style and combining it with other sources. Has a similar process taken place in *Leucippe and Clitophon*? And if the story has been redacted, to what extent have elements (e.g. Phoenician features) of the 'original' been censored out? Has Clitophon been Hellenised by the narrator's acts of cultural translation? These questions are of course unanswerable: the important point is not to root out demonstrable truths in this fictional text, but to allow these unsettling questions to resonate. *Leucippe and Clitophon* is a subversive text, and one of the many things that it subverts is a reader's anticipated confidence in narratorial veracity: in this story, we never quite know whose voice (or voices) we are listening to.[62]

---

[59] Lightfoot (2003) 297–9. Millar (1983) 48–9 reads Achilles' account as consistent with this process of hybridisation.
[60] For 'colonial mimicry' see Bhabha (1994) 85–92, and further below n. 63.
[61] Whitmarsh (2003), Morgan (2007a), Marinčič (2007); see further below.
[62] Even if from a strictly narratological perspective there is rarely any ambiguity as to the identity of the narrator: Morgan (2004d) 502–6.

Transforming romance

Let us return to the story of Tyrian Icarius, discussed earlier. There, I offered the preliminary claim that Clitophon speaks phrases such as 'so the Tyrians' story goes' (2.2.6). It is true enough that there is no reason to suspect a change of speaker here, even if there is certainly a change of narrative register in this little ethno-mythographic excursus. But might we not attribute this passage instead to Achilles and/or the unnamed narrator, i.e. those narrators concerned with the mediation of discourse between the local and the panhellenic? Or is it perhaps Clitophon himself aping the panhellenising discourse of his Greek interlocutor? Is he engaging in what Homi Bhabha calls colonial mimicry, the 'ironic compromise' between the 'synchronic, panoptical vision of domination' produced by panhellenic ethnography and the specificity of the local?[63] These questions are real in that they are part of the intriguing pleasure of the text; but they are false in that they are irresoluble. In multiply embedded narrative, all voices but the uppermost are evanescent, spectral.

The play of voices becomes even more deliciously complex at the beginning of the fifth book of *Leucippe and Clitophon*, where Clitophon and Leucippe arrive in Alexandria.[64] As Stephen Nimis has noted, this episode 'has the earmarks of a new beginning'.[65] The connections with the opening of the romance, indeed, are striking. Book 1 begins with an unnamed narrator arriving by sea at Sidon; in book 5 Leucippe and Clitophon come to Alexandria by boat. Clitophon's tour of the city (*periagōn... emauton*, 5.1.5) and its spectacles mirrors the narrator's initial tour of Sidon (*periiōn*, 1.1.2); both figures drink in the lavish sights before them, describing them in erotic terms. What is more, both visit the temple of and pray to a culturally problematic god: Clitophon that of 'the great god, whom the Greeks call Zeus, the Egyptians Sarapis';[66] the unnamed narrator that of 'the Phoenicians' goddess; the Sidonians call her Astarte';[67] and, in both cases, the visit is swiftly followed by the viewing of a painting. More specifically, Clitophon's eroticised[68] description of the city looks back to his first encounters with Leucippe.[69] When he comments that 'the lightning-like beauty of the city immediately confronted me, and weighed down

---

[63] Bhabha (1994) 85, paraphrasing Said (1978) 240.
[64] This abbreviates the fuller discussion at Whitmarsh (2009b) 44–7.   [65] Nimis (1998) 110.
[66] τοῦ μεγάλου θεοῦ, ὃν Δία μὲν Ἕλληνες, Σέραπιν δὲ καλοῦσιν Αἰγύπτιοι, 5.2.1.
[67] τῆι τῶν Φοινίκων <θεᾶι F>· Ἀστάρτην αὐτὴν καλοῦσιν οἱ Σιδώνιοι, 1.1.2. On the textual issues here see above, n. 38.
[68] Morales (2004) 100–6.   [69] Γιατρομανωλάκης (1990) 661–2.

(*egemisen*) my eyes with pleasure (*hēdonēs*)',[70] this combines the effect of Leucippe's arrival (she 'struck my eyes like lightning')[71] with the aftermath of the first symposium: the others (we are told) measured their 'pleasure' (*hēdonēn*) with their bellies, whereas Clitophon was 'weighed down with' (*gemistheis*) the sight of the girl's face (1.6.1).[72] All of these echoes serve to cast book 5 as a rerun of book 1, with Alexandria replacing Sidon/Tyre.

That the description is of Alexandria, of all cities, is especially significant, in that it is (probably) the author's own homeland.[73] If it is right, as I have suggested above, that ancient readers would probably have associated the unnamed narrator of the romance with the author himself, then this passage is truly extraordinary: at the halfway point in the romance, Clitophon visits Achilles' homeland, just as 'Achilles' visits Sidon at the start of the narrative (the two passages, as we have noted, powerfully echoing each other).[74] Each is abroad in the other's home. This makes even more intriguing Clitophon's curious sentence 'Many a road criss-crossed this part: *you could be a tourist at home.*'[75] The second, underlined part renders the verbless Greek phrase *endēmos apodēmia*, which is impossible to translate literally: *endēmos* is an adjective meaning 'in the polity', *apodēmia* a noun meaning 'being away from the polity'. The most obvious way of taking the phrase, followed in all translations of which I know (including my own), is as given above: Clitophon is claiming that the city is so large that those in their own polity might feel abroad. But there is a problem here. Clitophon is *not* at home, *endēmos*, indeed quite the opposite: elsewhere, he refers to his time abroad as an *apodēmia* (2.27.2, 2.33.3, 5.10.3, 8.5.7).[76] The person who is at home is, of course, Achilles himself. *endēmos apodēmia* brings together, in a single,

---

[70] συνηντᾶτο εὐθὺς τῆς πόλεως ἀστράπτον τὸ κάλλος, καὶ μου τοὺς ὀφθαλμοὺς ἐγέμισεν ἡδονῆς, 5.1.1. Morales comments that 'It is a fine comic touch that Clitophon is dazzled when he walks through the gates of the Sun' ((2004) 104).
[71] καταστράπτει μου τοὺς ὀφθαλμούς, 1.4.2.
[72] οἱ μὲν δὴ ἄλλοι τῆι γαστρὶ μετρήσαντες τὴν ἡδονήν, ἐγὼ δὲ... τῶν τῆς κόρης προσώπων γεμισθείς, 1.6.1 (alluding, as commentators all note, to Dem. 18.296). Subtler echoes: the gates of Selene (5.1.2) look back to the comparison of Leucippe to a picture of Selene (1.4.3); the 'row of columns' (κιόνων ὅρχατος, 5.1.4) picks up the 'chorus of columns' (χόρωι κιόνων) in Hippias' garden (1.15.1).
[73] See further Whitmarsh (2009b) 44–7.
[74] Clitophon is, for sure, Tyrian not Sidonian, but the two cities are always closely associated.
[75] ὁδὸς δὲ διὰ τοῦ πεδίου πολλὴ καὶ ἔνδημος ἀποδημία, 5.1.3.
[76] See, however, 5.15.1, where Clitophon describes his journey from Alexandria to Ephesus as an ἀποδημία. O'Sullivan 1980 39 classes this as a solitary case referring to a voyage 'from a place that is not one's homeland'; we might, however, put this down to the subjective assimilation between author and narrator discussed above (i.e. this journey would have been a conventional ἀποδημία for Achilles).

giddyingly paradoxical phrase, both Clitophon's and Achilles' perspectives. In this narrative, no one ever quite feels at home.

The dominant figure for cultural reading in *Leucippe and Clitophon* is not Selden's syllepsis, which implies the availability of two equally weighted, alternative perspectives. It is, rather, *metalepsis*. This term, which I take from Gérard Genette, refers to the interpenetration of different narrative levels – as, for example, in the movie *Stranger than fiction*, where a man persuades his author not to kill him off.[77] There is nothing so flagrantly transgressive in ancient fiction: what I have in mind is a softer metalepsis, whereby the 'sacred frontier' that separates primary from embedded narrative becomes permeable.[78] Achilles' romance does not, as Selden suggests, identify and compartmentalise discrete cultural perspectives; rather, it conflates and confuses them.

PROBLEMATISING NARRATION

Leucippe and Clitophon is, indeed, a text in which narratorial reportage is always difficult to assess. We learn to suspect every narrator, and therefore every stage of narrative transmission. In this respect, it has much in common with other contemporary or near-contemporary fictional texts, where narrators are subjected to scrutiny. A prime example is Lucian's *True stories*, which is in form an eyewitness account of the author's travels, but the prologue insists that it deals with 'of things that I have neither seen nor experienced nor heard from anyone else, in fact things that do not exist at all, nor could they in the first place'.[79] A tradition of Homeric revisionism emerges (rooted, to be sure, in Hellenistic writers like Hegesanax, Euhemerus and Dionysius Scytobrachion; and before that in the revisionist tradition of Stesichorus, Herodotus and Euripides) that ironically questions the veracity of the Homeric narrator: examples include Dio Chrysostom's eleventh oration (claiming that Troy really was captured), the *Journal* of 'Dictys of Crete' (supposedly an eye-witness account of the war), and Philostratus' *Heroic tale* (in which Homer is said to have been persuaded by Odysseus to whitewash him, in return for information

---

[77] Genette (1980) 234–7, and esp. Genette (2004), which nuances the figure as *la métalepse de l'auteur*. Excellent discussion at Fludernik (2003); for classical applications see de Jong (2009).
[78] Fludernik (2003) in particular emphasises the pre-postmodern heritage of metalepsis; De Temmerman (2009b) interestingly explores a case of metalepsis in Achilles Tatius, arguing that the ecphrasis at 1.19.1–2 is interfered with by the description of the initial painting. The phrase 'sacred frontier' is Genette's ((1980) 236).
[79] περὶ ὧν μήτε εἶδον μήτε ἔπαθον μήτε παρ' ἄλλων ἐπυθόμην, ἔτι δὲ μήτε ὅλως ὄντων μήτε τὴν ἀρχὴν γενέσθαι δυναμένων, *VH* 1.4.

on the war).[80] Texts like these rely on the premise that Homer is not an authoritative, muse-inspired source, but a human narrator, both partial and corruptible.[81]

Related is the trend towards pseudo-documentarism, the invention of fictional sources:[82] in revisionist accounts, the authority of Homeric narration is undercut by documents such as the Phoenician text that supposedly underlies 'Dictys of Crete'; or the Egyptian pillar inscription that (according to the priests Dio claims to have consulted, 11.38) gives the true story of the Trojan War; or the vintner's consultation of the epiphanic hero Protesilaus in Philostratus' *Heroic tale*. At the same time as it purports to authenticate the narrative it buttresses, however, pseudo-documentarism also ironises it:[83] it is unlikely that all ancient readers really believed that Dictys represented a transcription of a discovered manuscript, any more than modern readers of *The name of the rose* do; or that Dio really saw an Egyptian pillar (particularly when the device so clearly recalls the literary precedents of Herodotus and Euhemerus);[84] or that Philostratus' vintner did literally encounter Protesilaus. Pseudo-documentarism does not simply validate texts, although it may do in the eyes of the naive; for other readers, it simply multiplies and relativises the sources of narrative authority, and thus militates against the possibility of any final truth. It is the product of a culture in which narrative authority is not arrogated to a single 'master of truth', but competed for by multiple masters of persuasion. This is particularly evident in the case of Dio 11, which emphatically shifts the question from 'what is the truth of the Trojan War?' to 'what is a *plausible* account of it?' (11.16, 20, 55, 59, 67, 69, 70, 92, 130, 137, 139). The request to trust

---

[80] Dio 11 is discussed by Kindstrand (1973) 141–62; Seeck (1990); Anderson (2000) 152–3; Saïd (2000) 176–86; Gangloff (2006) 118–36. On Dictys, and the revisionist tradition in general, see Merkle (1994). For Philostratus' *Heroicus*, see the essays in Aitken and Maclean (2004), esp. Mestre (2004) on Homeric revisionism; also Whitmarsh (2009a). There have been a number of recent translations and commentaries on the *Heroic tale*, of which the most comprehensive is Grossardt (2006), who discusses Homeric revisionism at 96–120. On the cultural context of Homeric revisionism see esp. Zeitlin (2001). I have not included Dares in this list, as I am not convinced that (despite the claim in the prologue) a Greek original lies behind the extant Latin. On the Greek Dictys, see above, n. 15.

[81] Imperial texts are distinctive for their attacks on the personal authority of Homer: see Kim (2010), a magisterial discussion.

[82] Speyer (1970) 43–124; Hansen (2003); ní Mheallaigh (2008). Pseudo-documentarism of this kind is, however, not new to the imperial period: earlier instances include Hegesianax' forged account of Cepahl(i)on of Gergitha, and the inscribed gold columns alluded to by Euhemerus (Diod. Sic. 6.1.7–10).

[83] ní Mheallaigh (2008) 404: 'In increasingly self-conscious fiction, such *Beglaubigungstratagien* are converted also into signals to the knowing reader, playfully advertising the fictionality of the text'.

[84] Herodotus hears the 'true' story of Helen from Egyptian priests (2.112–17); for Euhemerus' columns see n. 82.

Dio rather than Homer harms narrative authority in general more than it promotes Dio's in particular.

Homeric pseudo-documentarism is a rich example of what Jacques Derrida calls 'supplementarity'.[85] The supplement occupies an ambiguous role in relation to the original: it can be seen either as a necessary addition, required for completion, or as something that supplants and displaces it. Dictys, Dio 11 and Philostratus' *Heroic tale* all claim to complete the original truth of the Trojan war, by reaching back earlier than the established narrative tradition to sources contemporaneous with the events themselves; but at the same time, they also represent merely the chronologically newest additions to the huge cluster of Homeric interpretations, and in that respect represent, rather than a return to the original, an accretion that obscures it further.

It is in this context that we should locate the most extraordinary example of second-century narratorial problematisation, namely Antonius Diogenes' *Wonders beyond Thule* (which now survives only in fragments and Photius' ninth-century summary). According to Photius, this enormous work (twenty-four books) contained up to eight levels of embedded narration.[86] It also employed a romance twist on the pseudo-documentarism, offering two non-complementary accounts of the genesis of the text. In a prefatory letter to Faustinus, the author claims (so Photius tells us) that 'even if he invents implausible lies, he does have testimony from the ancients for most of his fictions'.[87] In a second letter, however, addressed to his sister Isidora, he claims that the text was discovered, when Alexander sacked Tyre, on cypress-wood tablets that had been laid in a tomb: these represented the autobiography of one of the principle characters, Deinias. The story was then 'transcribed', or perhaps 'translated', by one Balagros.[88] Antonius seems to have blended the kind of strategy found at the outset of Lucian's *True stories* (admitting fantastic lies, but following literary precedent) with that of Dictys (chance discovery of an ancient text). This competing set of epistolary authentications points to an astonishing level of self-consciousness, an awareness of the text as both a physical and an intellectual construction.[89] It also reinforces, once again, the central role of 'soft' metalepsis in second-century fiction: readers of

---

[85] Derrida (1974) 269–316. [86] Discussed at Stephens and Winkler (1995) 114–16.
[87] εἰ καὶ ἄπιστα καὶ ψευδῆ πλάττοι, ἀλλ' οὖν ἔχει περὶ τῶν πλείστων αὐτῷ μυθολογηθέντων ἀρχαιοτέρων μαρτυρίας, *Bibl.* cod. 166 111a.
[88] μεταγραψάμενος (*Bibl.* cod. 166 111b), an ambiguous verb (LSJ s.v. 1–2, appositely citing Luc. *Hist. conscr.* 21: μεταγράψαι [from Latin] ἐς τὸ Ἑλληνικόν).
[89] An awareness paralleled, what is more, within the narrative proper: see SW 149 on *PSI* 1177.

this text will have been encouraged to read it simultaneously as a series of first-person accounts of personal experience (what Genette would call homodiegetic, intradiegetic narration) and as a work of fiction on the part of the author.

If we are to think of the main narrative of the *Wonders* as 'translated' from the Phoenician, then the connection with 'Dictys' is closer still: the preface to the *Journal* claims that the work is a translation into Greek from the Phoenician undertaken in the time of Nero. The Greek text (which survives only in fragments) is thus translated once;[90] whereas the Latin text, the only complete version, also features an initial letter by one 'Septimius' explaining that he has translated the Greek translation.[91] Both the Dictys author and Antonius are presumably picking up on the idea of Phoenician as an originary language, older and more authoritative than Greek – an idea promulgated by historians like Menander of Ephesus (who claimed to have learned the language)[92] and Philo of Byblos, whose claim to have translated the work of one Sanchunyaton (who lived at the time of the Trojan War) itself looks suspiciously pseudo-documentarist.[93] Much as the Phoenician ur-text represents a claim to authenticity, however, it might also have connotations of scurrility and deceit: an ambience of lowlife crookedness surrounds literary Phoenicians from Homer onwards (*Od.* 14.288–9, 15.415–16, 419),[94] a reputation still active in the imperial period,[95] and no doubt mobilised in Lollianus' now-fragmentary *Phoenician affairs*.[96] Translation is the supplementary gesture par excellence, a return to original sources that represents at the same time a total transformation of them; and it seems that specifically Phoenician translation amplifies the supplementarity, connoting both primeval truth and deceitful sharp practice.

The second century, then, sees a generally intensified questioning of narrative authority, and correspondingly an increasing emphasis upon the

---

[90] Above, n. 3.
[91] The epistolary preface to the Latin Dares also claims that the text is translated from the Greek (by Nepos!).
[92] Menander's Phoenician learning: *FGrH* 783 T 3(a)–(c);
[93] Although there is also historiographical precedent, in the not implausible claims of Ctesias, Manetho and Berossus, to have used source material in Persian, Egyptian and Akkadian respectively.
[94] On Homer's presentation of Phoenicians see Winter (1995) esp. 247–9, noting that the negative image is counterbalanced by an appreciation of their craftsmanship. As she proceeds to argue, the portrayal of Phoenician craft and craftiness may be calqued on the image of Odysseus himself (256–8).
[95] Cf. Philostr. *Her.* 1.3, an allusion (διαβέβλησθε) to Homer (*Od.* 15.416; cf. 14.289) via Plato (*Rep.* 436a).
[96] Morales (2004) 50, who links *Leucippe and Clitophon* to this tradition of Phoenician scurrility.

limitations of individual narrators. To be clear, we are speaking here of a general shift of emphasis, rather than a sudden, sharp break. The devices noted above can (as I have made clear) all be found in texts that predate the second century; what is distinctive about our period, however, is the distillation and concentration of these techniques in specific texts like Antonius Diogenes, Lucian's *True stories* and (presumably) the Greek Dictys.

CORRUPT NARRATION

In Achilles Tatius too, the Phoenician context is significant: for reasons given above, second-century readers are likely to have approached a Phoenician story with anticipations of both sacred antiquity and deceptive depravity. More specifically, *Leucippe and Clitophon* is also a multiply embedded tale: there may be no pseudo-documentarism, but there is a chain of transmission, a narrative audit trail. We have already mentioned the primary narrator, whose distinctive perspective colours his ways of seeing. As an *erōtikos*, he translates all that he sees into a collage of innuendo and reminiscences drawn from the Greek tradition of literary erotica. Let us briefly consider three further ways in which his perspective shapes the narrative. First, his ecphrasis of the Europa painting again emphasises the erotic aspects of the scene,[97] and overlays motifs borrowed from the Greek tradition (particularly Moschus' *Europa*).[98] Second, the very decision to begin

---

[97] Europa's navel, belly, hips, genitalia and breasts are emphasised (1.1.11), and even the foliage is said to 'mingle' and 'embrace' (ἀνεμέμικτο... συνῆπτον... συμπλοκή, 1.1.3). Talk of 'meadows', 'horns' and 'foam' is provocative, too. See Henderson (1991) 136, 127 respectively for λειμών = female pubes and κέρας = erect penis; ἀφρός = semen is common (LSJ s.v. 2, and esp. West (1966) 213); Aphrodite's name is sometimes so etymologised (Corn. *ND* 45; Nonn. *D.* 13.439–40). The eroticisation of flora and fauna also looks forward to the garden scene beginning at 1.15 (De Temmerman (2009b)). On the eroticism of the (description of the) painting, see further Bartsch (1989) 48–51. von Möllendorff (2009) 157–8 rightly links the eroticised pleasure in viewing to an aesthetic dimension, noting the multiple references to the language of construction and creation (τέχνη, γραφ-). On the wider role of the Europa narrative, and particularly its connection to the plot, see Reeves (2007) and von Möllendorff (2009).

[98] Moschus' flower catalogue (narcissi, hyacinths, violets, herpylli, roses: *Eur.* 65–71) is subtly transformed in Achilles' description (narcissi, roses, myrtle: 1.1.5): Campbell (1991) 71 (too contemptuous of Achilles' 'half-hearted effort'). The similarities have been often asserted (e.g. Mignogna (1993) 180–1), but not systematically discussed, to my knowledge. Verbal echoes: 'She was seated on the ox's back' (ἐπεκάθητο τοῖς νώτοις τοῦ βοός, Ach. Tat. 1.1.10) ~ 'she sat on the ox's back' (ἐφεζομένη... βοέοις ἐπὶ νώτοις, *Eur.* 125); 'holding onto the horn with her left hand' (τῆι λαιᾶι τοῦ κέρως ἐχομένη, Ach. Tat. 1.1.10) ~ 'with the one hand she held onto the bull's long horn' (τῆι μὲν ἔχεν ταύρου δολιχὸν κέρας, *Eur.* 126, where (a) the phrasing ultimately derives from Hom. *Il.* 23.780 ([Ajax] κέρας μετὰ χερσὶν ἔχων βοός ἀγραύλοιο; horn-seizing with a *single* hand is, however, a widespread motif in Hellenistic poetic accounts of bull-wrestling, perhaps impelled by Call. *Hec.* fr. 258 Pf. = 67 Hollis: cf. Ap. Rh. 3.1306–7, [Theocr.] 25.145–6, *AP* 16.105), and (b) δολιχόν implies the ship simile that Achilles will further develop (Campbell (1991) 110); 'the folds of her robe were stretched out, swollen at every point' (ὁ δὲ κόλπος τοῦ πέπλου πάντοθεν

a tale of East–West interaction with a story of female abduction story is traditionally Greek: the obvious examples are the Trojan War (and, relatedly, the wrath of Achilles, motivated by Agamemnon's theft of Briseis) and Herodotus' *Histories*, where the Persian and Phoenician explanations for the origins of Greco-barbarian hostilities are directly linked to reciprocal thefts of women (among them Europa).[99] Finally, his description of the landscape where he meets Clitophon borrows heavily from Plato's *Phaedrus*, the most clichéd setting for erotic narrative possible.[100] The initial narrator, then, certainly does seem to colour the narrative with his own kaleidoscopic reminiscences of the Greek[101] erotic tradition: this encourages us to suspect that the narrative has been filtered.

Then we turn to Clitophon himself, the most unreliable of narrators. How can we trust someone who starts with the claim that 'my story resembles fiction (*muthois*)?'[102] Clitophon is repeatedly shown up as a frustratingly flittish reporter.[103] At 1.6.6, he tells how he walks around the house pretending to read a book and peeking up at Leucippe. Readers, of course, would love to know what this book is: the temptation to take this passage as a self-referential commentary upon the reading of erotic literature is almost unbearable.[104] But the point is that the book is precisely what Clitophon is not interested in, and we are left frustrated.[105] Similarly later in this book, the transition from the mention of the burial of Clinias' boyfriend to Clitophon's resumption of his pursuit of Leucippe is so abrupt

ἐτέτατο κυρτούμενος, Ach. Tat. 1.1.12) ~ 'the folds of the deep robe of Europa above her shoulders were filled' (κολπώθη δ' ὤμοισι πέπλος βαθὺς Εὐρωπείης, *Eur.* 129); 'she used her robe like a sail' (ὥσπερ ἱστίωι τῶι πέπλωι χρωμένη, Ach. Tat. 1.1.12) ~ '[the robe is used] like the sail of a ship' (ἱστίον οἷά τε νηός, *Eur.* 130).

[99] Hdt. 1.1–4. On the motif of woman-stealing as an aetiology for war, and the celebrated parody (?) at Ar. *Ach.* 528–9, see Lang (1972) and now Wright (2007) 414–7.

[100] Pl. *Phaedr.* 229a–30c (particularly beloved of Achilles: Trapp (1990) 155). The cliché is already acknowledged at Plut. *Am.* 749a; Clitophon's reference to the location as a τόπος ἡδύς (1.2.3) implicitly plays upon the idea of a literary *topos* (LSJ s.v. 4).

[101] And possibly Latin? Like Achilles' unnamed narrator, Vergil's Aeneas survives a shipwreck. Coming ashore, he finds a temple for a goddess, covered with artworks, which the narrator describes as Aeneas surveys them (Verg. *Aen.* 1.441–93). Most suggestive of a direct link is the figure of 'Sidonian Dido' (as Vergil styles her: 1.446) herself. There is, indeed, something eminently Europa-like about the westward flight from Phoenicia of this descendant of Agenor (1.338), with her Astarte-like features (Hexter (1992) 348–9). It is not, in my view, impossible that Achilles read Latin (a separate study of this is needed); but in any case, Greek translations of the *Aeneid* did exist, albeit our papyri are late-antique (Fisher (1982) 183–9).

[102] τὰ... ἐμὰ μύθοις ἔοικε, 1.2.2. Morales (2004) 53–5 emphasises the ambiguous use of the Platonic *logos-mythos* distinction: 'my story is true but resembles fiction' or 'my story has the properties of fiction'?

[103] Whitmarsh (2003); Morgan (2007a). On Clitophon's 'blindness to himself and others', see Morgan (1997) 182–5, at 182.

[104] See e.g. Goldhill (1995) 70–1; Morales (2004) 79.   [105] See further Whitmarsh (2003) 199.

and hasty ('After the burial, I *immediately* set off *hurriedly* to find the girl',[106] my emphasis) that one critic has suspected a textual lacuna;[107] but the point is that Clitophon is once again proving himself a brutally self-interested narrator, with no concern for pederasty or the suffering of others.[108] The effect of reading *Leucippe and Clitophon*, distinguished among the extant romances for its character-bound, homodiegetic narrative presentation,[109] is like watching a secret camera film for a viewer used to Hollywood widescreen panoramas: we see only what the focaliser, Clitophon, wants us to see, and we are left more or less guessing what is happening in the penumbra.

What is more, Clitophon is evidently capable of refashioning a narrative to suit his own agenda. Towards the end of the text, Leucippe's father Sostratus asks him to recap the story for him (8.4–5). This episode is modelled on the analogous episode, towards the end of Chariton's *Callirhoe*, where Chaereas is encouraged by his own father-in-law, Hermocrates, to retell the story in the Syracusan theatre (8.7.3–8.8.11). As we saw in the previous chapter, Chaereas' narrative there is presented as an act of mastery over the trauma induced by his sufferings, and signifies his public acquisition of a mature identity. Achilles, characteristically (as we shall see presently) avoids the public context, setting his episode at an intimate symposium in the temple of Ephesian Artemis: Clitophon's relationship of primary significance is with his family, not his civic community. Nevertheless, his act of narration is envisaged, as in Chariton, in terms of mastery of trauma and maturation. In language that clearly alludes to Chariton, Sostratus encourages Clitophon to surmount his embarassment (*aidōs*) over the 'grievous' events that have befallen him.[110] The act of narration consigns trauma to the past, and translates the suffering of experience into the pleasure of narrative: 'a narration of events past provides more entertainment than grief for one whose sufferings are over'.[111] Even more explicitly than in Chariton, this passage marks narration as a therapeutic act that separates narrated past

---

[106] μετὰ δὲ τὴν ταφὴν εὐθὺς ἔσπευδον ἐπὶ τὴν κόρην, 1.15.1.   [107] Pearcy (1978).
[108] Below, pp. 159–63.
[109] Hägg (1971) 124–36; Reardon (1994); Morgan (2004d) 493–502. The other major work of imperial Greek homodiegetic narrative is the *Ass*, at least in its pseudo-Lucianic and Apuleian forms, and probably also in 'Lucius of Patrae' (the papyrus fragment *P. Oxy.* 4762 is narrated heterodiegetically).
[110] λέγε, τέκνον Κλειτοφῶν, μηδὲν αἰδούμενος. καὶ γὰρ εἴ τί μοι συμβέβηκε λυπηρόν, μάλιστα μὲν οὐ σόν ἐστιν ἀλλὰ τῆς Τύχης, Ach. Tat. 8.4.4 ~ μηδὲν αἰδεσθῇς, ὦ τέκνον, κἂν λέγῃς τι λυπηρότερον ἢ πικρότερον . . . , Char. 8.7.4. The symposium so far, we have been told, has been dominated by *aidōs* (ἦν ὅλον τὸ συμπόσιον αἰδώς, 8.4.1).
[111] τῶν ἔργων παρελθόντων ἡ διήγησις τὸν οὐκέτι πάσχοντα ψυχαγωγεῖ μᾶλλον ἢ λυπεῖ, 8.4.4.

from narrating present.[112] Yet Clitophon is no Chaereas. Whereas the latter takes the opportunity to create a story celebrating his own heroic virility, Achilles' manipulative hero slyly refashions his account into one of sexual sobriety, censoring out his indiscretion:

> When I came to the part about Melite, I elevated my own role, reshaping the story into one of chaste self-control, although I told no outright lies . . . one of my actions in the plot alone I overlooked, namely the 'respect' (*aidōs*) I subsequently paid to Melite.[113]

In other words he glozes over the fact that having refused sex with Melite for the entire time that he believed Leucippe to be dead, he succumbed immediately after discovering she was alive (replaying, more outrageously, Callirhoe's strategic omission of her secret communications with Dionysius: 8.4.11). The euphemistic use of the word *aidōs*, here translated 'respect', confirms the point that Clitophon is prone to refashioning language for his own purposes: when (in the passage discussed in the previous paragraph) Sostratus anticipated Clitophon's *aidōs*, it is unlikely that he was thinking of adultery behind his daughter's back.

Clitophon continues explicitly to refashion his story in accordance with his own agenda. Presently he tells us that 'I elevated [Leucippe's] role too, even more than I had done mine',[114] in an attempt to win her favour. He soon returns to the theme of his own chastity, with a breathtakingly captious formulation: 'and as for me too, if there be such a thing as virginity in a man, I have retained it up to the present day, as far as Leucippe is concerned'.[115] The double qualification means that his claim to virginity is once again not an 'outright lie' – but it is certainly misleading in the mouth of an adulterer and visitor to prostitutes (2.37.5).

Given that it is Clitophon who (via the unnamed primary narrator) tells most of the story, these observations have repercussions for the entire erotic narrative. Clitophon's self-censorship in the passage quoted above

---

[112] In the analogous passage in Chariton, Hermocrates simply says that 'the brilliant end overshadows all of the previous events' (τὸ . . . τέλος λαμπρὸν γενόμενον ἐπισκοτεῖ τοῖς προτέροις ἅπασι, 8.7.4); it is a question of Chaereas' stature in the eyes of others, not of his own psychological therapy. The idea that narrative can have a therapeutic role is traditional (Hes. *Th.* 98–103, with Walsh (1984) 22–4), but usually the effect is on others: I know of no Greek parallel for this idea of a talking cure.
[113] ἐπεὶ δὲ κατὰ τὴν Μελίτην ἐγενόμην, ἐξῇρον τὸ πρᾶγμα ἐμαυτοῦ πρὸς σωφροσύνην μεταποιῶν καὶ οὐδὲν ἐψευδόμην . . . ἓν μόνον παρῆκα τῶν ἐμαυτοῦ δραμάτων, τὴν μετὰ ταῦτα πρὸς Μελίτην αἰδῶ, 8.5.2–3.
[114] ἐξῇρον καὶ τὰ αὐτῆς ἔτι μᾶλλον ἢ τἀμά, 8.5.5.
[115] εἴ τις ἄρα ἐστιν ἀνδρὸς παρθενία, ταύτην κἀγὼ μέχρι τοῦ παρόντος πρὸς Λευκίππην ἔχω, 8.5.7.

(8.5.2–3) is strikingly recursive. For a start, the scene alludes to the arch-narrator himself, Odysseus, who seems to pass over his sexual relationship with Circe when recounting his adventures to Penelope (*Odyssey* 23.321). The language, moreover, seems self-reflexive: the word translated 'plot' is *dramata*, literally 'dramas' (the very word used to denote the romances themselves by Byzantine times);[116] 'reshaping' is *metapoiein*, another knowingly technical term, used of illicit tampering with authoritative texts.[117] How much tampering has gone on in the transmission of the narrative as a whole? Achilles thoroughly subverts the paradigm of the first-century romance, replacing its Hellenocentric naturalism with a tricky, elusive, metaleptic, decentred, self-subverting discourse.

ART AND INTERPRETATION

Achilles' emphasis upon filtering and mediation is paralleled in an approximately contemporary text, Longus' *Daphnis and Chloe* – at one level a very different kind of text, but, despite the generic blending of Alexandrian pastoral motifs and the absence of adventuring themes, still recognisably romantic in its emphasis on the love and maturation of a heterosexual couple.[118] The two works have much in common (it is more than likely that one author read the other, although it is hard to be confident which is the prior):[119] both begin with an unnamed painter visiting a sacred space, and subsequently seeing a painting;[120] in either case, an interpreter arrives to explicate the painting, and the explication becomes the remainder of the narrative. Longus' use of the painting motif is developed from Xenophon of Ephesus, who describes Anthia and Habrocomes as dedicating a *graphē*

---

[116] Agapitos (1998) 128–32.
[117] E.g. in a marginal note at Hebrews 1:3 (ἀμαθέστατε καὶ κακέ, ἄφες τὸν παλαιόν, μὴ μεταποίει), cited at Haines-Eitzen (2000) 110.
[118] The generic hybridity of *Daphnis and Chloe* has been widely discussed: see especially Hunter (1983) 59–83, Zeitlin (1990) 421–30 and Pattoni (2004).
[119] Alvares (2006) explores similarities and differences; see also von Möllendorff (2009) 153–6.
[120] As discussed above (p. 80), Achilles' painting is not actually located in the temple precinct, at least as the text (which may be corrupt) stands. Longus' painting has been widely discussed. Some have taken it as a *Beglaubigungsapparat*, i.e. a device to procure the reader's belief in the plausibility of the tale: Imbert (1980) 210–1 (arguing for a specifically Stoic interpretation of the text's aesthetics); Wouters (1989–90). The opposite view has also been maintained, namely that the author is pointing, Platonically, to the distance of his text from reality: Blanchard (1975) 40–1. A number of readers see an ironic tension between the fictionality of the text and the pseudo-historical *Beglaubigungsapparat*: cf. Perry (1967) 109–11; Hunter (1983) 38–52; MacQueen (1985) 133; (1990) 15–23; Zeitlin (1990) 434–5. See also Mittelstadt (1967), hypothesising parallels with contemporary painting; Philippides (1983). Kestner (1973) focuses the opposition of the spatial and temporal. Ecphraseis in the romances generally are discussed by Billault (1979), (1990); Zimmermann (1999); cf. also Debray-Genette (1980), Dubel (1990) and Whitmarsh (2002b) on Heliodorus.

(a picture, or perhaps a written text) containing all their experiences, in the temple of Artemis (5.15.2). Similarly, Daphnis and Chloe are said at the end to decorate the cave of the Nymphs, set up images (*eikonas*), which we are implicitly invited to identify with those described by the narrator at the outset (4.39.2): Longus' is another 'self-begetting' romance.[121]

That Longus' narrative is the verbal transcription of an artwork creates different kinds of metaleptic effects. As in Chariton and Xenophon, the very process of the romance's own creation, its 'self-begetting', is dramatised. At one level, the artwork is equivalent to the narrative. When the narrator expresses his desire 'to compose in response to the composition' (*antigrapsai tēi graphēi*)[122] the Greek plays on the fact that the same word, *graphē*, can mean both 'painting' and 'written text'. The narrator is offering to 'compose' (*-graphein*) in response to a 'composition' (*graphē*).

But emphasis is also placed on the *difference* between the painting and the narrative: the key lexeme here is the prefix *anti*-appended to the verb *graphein* ('compose'). I have translated it 'in response to', its most neutral rendering: it could also mean 'in exchange for' or even 'in competition with'. In other words, it marks not the *identity* between painting and romance, but an indeterminate play between identity and difference. This phrase calls on us to weigh the likenesses and unlikenesses between the two media.

It is important, then, to catch the nuances underlying the narrator's account of how he came to write. 'When I had seen and wondered at (*thaumasanta*) these and many other things, all erotic', the narrator comments, 'a desire seized me to compose in response to the composition.'[123] The text emphasises the psychological processes, the (erotic and aesthetic) motivation that underlies this particular intermedia presentation. What is described is a two-stage process: initial wonder (*thauma*), followed by a desire to respond to the painting. As Froma Zeitlin notes, a comparable passage in Lucian's *On the hall* distinguishes between the practice of 'commoners' and 'men of culture' in response to spectacles:[124] the former merely gaze in silence, whereas the educated viewer 'will try as much as

---

[121] Kellman (1980); above, p. 62.
[122] ἀντιγράψαι τῆι γραφῆι, 1. *pr.* 3. The phrase also points to the artistic qualities of the narrative: its word-painting, compositional finesse, elegant structure and neat framing. See further Hunter (1983) 38–52; Zeitlin (1990) 430–6.
[123] Πολλὰ ἄλλα καὶ πάντα ἐρωτικὰ ἰδόντα με καὶ θαυμάσαντα πόθος ἔσχεν ἀντιγράψαι τῆι γραφῆι, 1. *pr.* 2–3. I have adopted the conventional punctuation *contra* Reeve, who begins a new sentence after ἐρωτικά.
[124] οὐχ ὁ αὐτὸς περὶ τὰ θεάματα νόμος ἰδιώταις τε καὶ πεπαιδευμένοις ἀνδράσιν, *De dom.* 2. See Zeitlin (1990) 432–3 n. 47; also, with different emphasis, Billault (1979).

he can to linger and respond to the sight with speech'.[125] A facility with language is the primary diagnostic of elite behaviour.[126] Artworks involve the viewer in a power relationship, which has wider implications for one's social standing: the disempowered are subdued into passive silence, mere 'wonder',[127] while the empowered respond actively and emulously. A number of roughly contemporary texts dramatise the intellectual's ability to translate art into language (e.g. Lucian's *Heracles*, the *Imagines* of the two Philostratoi, and the *Descriptions* of Callistratus).

The silence of the awestruck viewer, conversely, replicates the silence of the artwork itself: in their mute inertia, the two mirror each other.[128] Pictures are incommunicative, aporetic; they require linguistic supplementation in order to signify. When Longus' narrator describes the content of the painting, he lists a series of depictions, but without any awareness of them: 'On it [the painting]: women, some giving birth and others swaddling, children being exposed, sheep nurturing, shepherds rescuing, youths courting, a landing of pirates, an enemy attack.'[129] This sentence mimics the incomplete narrative cognition experienced by the viewer of an artwork: it can represent discrete episodes, but not the relationships between them. Painting operates in spatial dimensions alone; it cannot represent time (as Gotthold Lessing's *Laokoön oder die Grenzen der Malerei* famously showed). Longus represents the achronic nature of the picture in terms of syntactical absence: the sentence lacks both the main verb that would organise the episodes into a coherent meaning, and the connecting particles that would articulate the relationships between

---

[125] πειράσεται δὲ ὡς οἷόν τε καὶ ἐνδιατρῖψαι καὶ λόγωι ἀμειψάσθαι τὴν θέαν, *De dom.* 2.
[126] For this theme in imperial Greek literature, see esp. Schmitz (1997) 91–8.
[127] The disempowering effect of *thauma* is a key theme of ps.-Long. *De subl.* 1.4: 'the combination of wonder and astonishment always *has power over* the merely persuasive and pleasant. This is because persuasion is on the whole something we can control, whereas amazement and wonder *exert invincible power and force* and get the better of the reader' (πάντη δέ γε σὺν ἐκπλήξει τοῦ πιθανοῦ καὶ πρὸς χάριν ἀεὶ κρατεῖ τὸ θαυμάσιον, εἴγε τὸ μὲν πιθανὸν ὡς τὰ πολλὰ ἐφ' ἡμῖν, ταῦτα δὲ δυναστείαν καὶ βίαν ἄμαχον προσφέροντα παντὸς ἐπάνω τοῦ ἀκροωμένου καθίσταται). The *nil admirari* theme is strong in Philostratus' *Apollonius*: see Whitmarsh (2004a) 433–5.
[128] Cf. Ach. Tat. 3.15.6, where Clitophon sententiously discourses on the effects of awe (*ekplēxis*, closely related to *thauma*), rationalising the myth of Niobe by explaining that she became motionless in her shock 'as though turned into stone' (ὡσεὶ λίθος γενομένη); Luc. *Imag.* 1, where Lycinus claims to have been almost turned to stone by *thauma* on beholding Panthea (a woman he will later compare to various artworks), and predicts his interlocutor would also have become 'more immobile than statues' (τῶν ἀνδριάντων ἀκινητότερον). In the latter case, there is also an obvious *double entendre*.
[129] γυναῖκες ἐπ' αὐτῆς τίκτουσαι καὶ ἄλλαι σπαργάνοις κοσμοῦσαι, παιδία ἐκκείμενα, ποίμνια τρέφοντα, ποιμένες ἀναιρούμενοι, νέοι συντιθέμενοι, λῃστῶν καταδρομή, πολεμίων ἐμβολή, 1 *pr.*2.

them. Indeed, the only temporally significant words in the sentence are the present-tense participles, which indicate an iterative state rather than its duration. To convert the painting into narrative would be to supply a temporal structure, hence to give it meaning.

The translation of pictorial into narrative representation, then, is as an act of intellectual control that also has consequences for the social positioning of the subject.[130] This is the significance of the two-stage response of Longus' narrator: initial wonder, a response available to anyone, followed by an assertion of intellectual and social mastery, 'composing in response to the composition': the narrator is vying, competitively, with his source.[131] This power play is all the more important in that this is a rural setting, and 'rustic' (*agroikos*) in this period is conventionally used as the antithesis of 'educated':[132] the literary reaction to the painting thus demarcates him from those around him. The elite status of the narrator is consolidated by the only 'fact' we learn about him, which is that he entered the grove 'while hunting in Lesbos':[133] hunting is a typically moneyed pastime. In the course of the romance, we meet a number of other hunters visiting from the city, with little sympathy for or understanding of the countryside. In book 2, some 'rich young Methymnaean men, wishing to pass the vintaging season having exotic fun',[134] put in nearby to hunt hares; their aggressive behaviour leads to war between Mitylene and Methymna, and to Chloe's abduction. In book 4, Astylus ('City-boy'), the son of the estate owner Dionysiophanes (also Daphnis' father, it will emerge), is described in terms that markedly recall the Methymnaean playboys of book 2: 'he set about *hunting hares*, as you would expect from a *rich young man*, devoted to luxury, who had come to the countryside to enjoy *exotic* pleasure'.[135] A social gulf thus opens up between the primary narrator and the subjects of his narrative – in much the same way as the cultural gap that divides Achilles' narrator from his Phoenician subject.

Also comparable is the mediation between the local and the panhellenic. Achilles' narrator, as we have seen, represents himself as interpreting

---

[130] Pandiri (1985) emphasises the political angle; see further Saïd (1999) 97–107; Whitmarsh (2008) 77–9.
[131] This agonistic desire to outdo one's own source is grounded in imperial Greece's culture of literary emulation: compare e.g. ps-Long. *De subl.* 13.4 on Plato as Homer's 'antagonist', with Whitmarsh (2001a) 59–61.
[132] Whitmarsh (2001a) 100–8.   [133] ἐν Λέσβωι θηρῶν, 1 *pr.* 1.
[134] νέοι Μηθυμναῖοι πλούσιοι διαθέσθαι τὸν τρυγητὸν ἐν ξενικῆι τέρψει θελήσαντες, 2.12.1.
[135] περὶ θήραν εἶχε λαγωῶν, οἷα πλούσιος νεανίσκος καὶ τρυφῶν ἀεὶ καὶ ἀφιγμένος εἰς τὸν ἀγρὸν εἰς ἀπόλαυσιν ξένης ἡδονῆς, 4.11.1. οἷα might be taken as an internal reference marker alluding to the earlier νέοι... πλούσιοι.

Phoenician cult for the sake of a Greek readership. Longus' narrator is even more explicit: his work serves, he hopes, 'both as a dedication to Eros, the Nymphs and Pan, and as a pleasurable possession for all men'.[136] The Longan narrator presents himself as shuttling between the local and the general: transforming an object of local cult, physically embodied in a specific locale, into a panhellenic literary work destined for 'all men'. A work, moreover, that now has a general applicability to all humanity: 'it will cure the sick, console the grieving, remind one who has loved, and provide a preliminary education for one who has not; for absolutely no one has escaped Love, nor ever will . . . '[137] The phrasing here casts the text as a work of formal instruction,[138] and thus marks a total generic transformation of the sacred tale.

Set alongside this transformative, panhellenising impulse, however, is a desire to mimic the religious qualities of the original painting. The text is imagined not only as a 'pleasurable possession for all men', but also as a 'dedication' to the deities of the grove. This dedicatory function replicates the cultic role of the painting itself, 'dedicated' by Daphnis and Chloe in the grotto.[139] The narrator is attempting to achieve two different, even conflicting aims: *both* to transform the local cultic painting into a panhellenic work of literature *and* to preserve the religious essence of the artwork.[140] This paradoxical duality lies at the heart of *Daphnis and Chloe*. Scholarship on *Daphnis and Chloe* has tended to be bipolar, seeing it *either* as pious *or* as sophistic,[141] but this is a work that manages to be both detached and sympathetic, ironic and sincere, sophisticated and religiose. Against the well-known passages that play to the reader's sense of superiority

---

[136] ἀνάθημα μὲν Ἔρωτι καὶ Νύμφαις καὶ Πανί, κτῆμα δὲ τερπνὸν πᾶσιν ἀνθρώποις, 1 *pr.* 3. Longus' Thucydidean allusions: Valley (1926) 101–2 has the details; see Cueva (1998) and Trzaskoma (2005) for interpretation.

[137] ὃ καὶ νοσοῦντα ἰάσεται καὶ λυπούμενον παραμυθήσεται, τὸν ἐρασθέντα ἀναμνήσει, τὸν οὐκ ἐρασθέντα προπαιδεύσει· πάντως γὰρ οὐδεὶς Ἔρωτα ἔφυγεν ἢ φεύξεται . . . 1 *pr.*3.

[138] Comparable is e.g. Galen's assertion of the educational value of epitomes and aphoristic collections: 'This kind of instruction is fitting for primary learning itself, and for remembering things that one has learned are necessary, and afterwards for reminding one of things one has forgotten' (εἴς τε γὰρ αὐτὴν τὴν πρώτην μάθησιν καὶ εἰς τὴν ὧν ἔμαθέ τις [ὠφεληθῆναι] μνήμην καὶ εἰς τὴν ὧν ἐπελάθετό τις μετὰ ταῦτα ἀνάμνησιν ὁ τοιοῦτος τρόπος τῆς διδασκαλίας ἐπιτήδειος, *Comm. Ad Hipp.* Aphorismoi = XVII.2 p.355.6–10 K).

[139] ἀνάθημα, 1 *pr.* 3 ~ ἀνέθεσαν, 4.39.2. The painting, it is true, is 'dedicated' in a cave that is not mentioned in the proem, but this is hardly a decisive objection.

[140] Morgan (2004a) 147 notes the contrast, relating it to a wider distinction he perceives between aesthetic and religious approaches to the text; cf. Merkelbach (1988) 138 for the 'two levels' (*zwei Ebene*) on which the text can be read. As will be clear, my position is that we are asked to read on both 'levels' simultaneously.

[141] Pious: Rohde (1937), Chalk (1960), Merkelbach (1988); sophistic: e.g. Rohde (1914) 534–54, Anderson (1982) 41–9, Goldhill (1995) *passim*.

by teasing the young lovers' naivety,[142] we need to set the passages where the natural world is presented as a medium for divine communication. Events are pregnant with meaning: a wolf attacks the sheep (1.11), billy-goats fight (1.12.1), a cicada nestles between Chloe's breasts (1.26). The inability of urbanites to read nature is dramatised at one point, where the Methymnaean raiding party fails to interpret the weird phenomena that ensue after their capture of Chloe:[143]

> These phenomena were intelligible to anyone with any sense, namely that they were visions and sounds sent by Pan by way of signalling something to the sailors; but they could not interpret the reason, for no temple of Pan had been plundered[144]

Longus here explicitly describes a god's intention to communicate with mortals through signs manifested (Pan is 'signalling something') in the natural world. Humans' capacity to read these signs is problematic: *that* Pan is communicating is clear, but *what* he is communicating the sailors fail to 'interpret' (*sumbalein*, cognate with *symbolon*, 'symbol'). The correct interpretation (that the kidnap of Chloe is the root cause) is given to the captain, Bryaxis, by Pan in a dream-epiphany (2.26.5). This is subsequently confirmed by the sight of Chloe wearing a pine wreath, which he takes as a 'symbol' (*symbolon*, 2.28.2). This episode constitutes a programmatic reminder that *Daphnis and Chloe* is a textual exegesis of Lesbian mystery cult, an expression of the power of the rustic gods as displayed in the natural world: interpretation should never be superficial. The Methymnaeans represent the aggressive rapacity of the urban world; their inability to construe divine meaning warns the text's urban readers not to underestimate the forces that inhabit the countryside. We are learning, in the course of our textual pilgrimage, to become good readers, which means to read sympathetically.

---

[142] E.g. their interpretation of Philetas' euphemistic advice (2.9–11) and Daphnis' fear of 'wounding' Chloe (3.19).

[143] The scene borrows elements from Euripides' *Bacchae* (Merkelbach (1962) 209). The dolphins attacking the ship are borrowed from *HhBacch.* 48–50; Dalmeyda (1934) 45 n. 1 additionally notes that Longus is punning on δελφῖνες = lead weights for dropping on enemy ships. The narrative event – abduction of woman leads to divine vengeance – looks to the rape of Chryseis at the beginning of the *Iliad* (Hom. *Il.* 1.11–12; 93–6); there is perhaps also allusion to the weird phenomena that follow the desecration of Protesilaus' cult-site at the conclusion of Herodotus' *Histories* (Hdt. 9.116–22, esp. 116.3: ἐν τῶι ἀδύτωι γυναιξὶ ἐμίσγετο).

[144] συνετὰ μὲν οὖν πᾶσιν ἦν τὰ γινόμενα τοῖς φρονοῦσιν ὀρθῶς, ὅτι ἐκ Πανὸς ἦν τὰ φαντάσματα καὶ ἀκούσματα μηνιόντός τι τοῖς ναύταις, οὐκ εἶχον δὲ τὴν αἰτίαν συμβαλεῖν (οὐδὲν γὰρ ἱερὸν σεσυλήτο Πανός)..., 2.26.5. The phrasing suggests the riddling of archaic poets: cf. esp. Bacch. 3.85, Pind. *Ol.* 2.85, *Pyth.* 5.107.

At the same time, however, such passages need to be set against Longus' relentlessly ironical presentation of the countryside as a place of naivety, fundamentally lacking in the *paideia* (education/civility) that is so constitutive of elite urban living. This duality is Longus' equivalent to Achillean metalepsis: throughout the text, readers find themselves constantly shuttling back and forth between empathetic identification with the rustics, attuned to nature as they are, and condescension towards their impossible naivety. Longan metalepsis forces us to adopt two incommensurable perspectives at once, of the knowing and the naive, 'one who has loved' and 'one who has not'.

In this elevation of the religious function, Longus is very different to Achilles. In *Leucippe and Clitophon*, the association between the cult of Sidonian Ištar and the erotic narrative is indirect at best: the painting provides the initial impetus for the narrative, but the two tell different stories (at the literal level at least).[145] In Longus' case, by contrast, the painting is thematically coextensive with the narrative, and also an object of cult, attracting those who come 'as pilgrims to the Nymphs and spectators of the picture'.[146] Parallels for this kind of literary description of sacred viewing are widely attested in the period (Pausanias provides numerous examples).[147] Another sacred feature not found in Achilles is the mediatory role of the exegete (*exēgētēs*) whom the narrator seeks out to explicate the painting. Again, this kind of exegetical role can be paralleled, particularly in Pausanias' *Description of Greece*, which is richly populated with *exēgētai* and *periēgētai* prepared to share their local knowledge with passers-by.[148] Such figures might in some cases be little more than tourist guides,[149] but in other instances they are counted among the sacred personnel of the

---

[145] For the subtle proleptic qualities of the painting, see Bartsch (1989) 40–5; Morales (2004) 38–48; Reeves (2007).

[146] τῶν μὲν Νυμφῶν ἱκέται, τῆς δὲ εἰκόνος θεαταί, 1 *praef.* 1. For ἱκέτης = 'pilgrim' cf. LSJ s.v., and Naiden (2006) 94 (although Longus does not say that the pilgrims come to heal love-sickness: that is rather the narrator's wish for his own work, and a reworking of Theocr. 11.1–3 (also ~ Long. 2.7.7)).

[147] On the importance of the visual focal point in imperial religious pilgrimage see Petsalis-Diomidis (2006), and specifically on art Elsner (1996). Whether Pausanias can be counted a pilgrim remains a matter of debate (for the positive case see Elsner (1995) 125–55; Rutherford (2001); Hutton (2006) 295–6); I prefer to see the pilgrim (in the extended sense) as one of the many roles Pausanias adopts, rather than as his dominant identity.

[148] Paus. 1.13.8, 1.31.5, 1.34.4, 1.35.8, 1.41.2, 1.42.4, 2.9.8, 2.23.6, 2.31.4, 4.33.6, 5.6.6, 5.10.7, 5.15.11, 5.18.6, 5.20.4, 5.21.8, 5.21.9, 5.23.6, 7.6.5, 9.3.3, 10.10.7, 10.28.7, with Jones (2001) (valuable comments too at Winkler (1985) 234–6). As is often noted, ps.-Cebes' *Tabula* is the primary literary model for an exegete explaining a picture.

[149] Plut. *De Pyth.* 395a-b, 396c, 397d, 400d–f, 401e, with Jacquemain (1991). Strab. 17.1.29 writes of exegetes who explain sacred matters to outsiders (ἐξηγηταὶ τοῖς ξένοις τῶν περὶ τὰ ἱερά).

cult site, perhaps even with formal religious duties.[150] It is impossible to determine precisely the status of the exegete. But the most important point is that Longus places heavy emphasis upon the process of the narrative's transmission, as it travels from lived reality to devotional painting to cultic exegete to panhellenic narrator, and finally to reader.

If the first-century romancers emphasised the characters' own retrospective retooling of their narratives, their successors emphasise second-order *mediation*. Romance is (deliberately) caught in the act of its own artificing, as it is filtered through different layers of creative reception. Achilles draws attention to both his narrators' self-interested, partial narration; Longus to the chains of multimedia transmission that lead from life to its narrative representation. What this focus on mediation insists on most forcibly is the *politics* of reception: at every stage, listeners and readers transform the story, in accordance with their own agendas. And, of course, we too as readers are invited to reflect on our own investment in these stories (particularly in *Daphnis and Chloe*, where the text's class differentials repeatedly invite us to self-disclose as elite voyeurs of rural poverty, like the Methymnaean playboys).

TRANSFORMING NARRATIVE

The second-century romances respond to their first-century predecessors, then, by placing much greater emphasis upon the proliferation of cultural perspectives, and upon the interpenetration of different narrative subjectivities. I want to turn now to consider closural dynamics. As we saw in the previous chapter, Chariton and Xenophon use a centre–periphery spatial model, drawn from myths of passage rites. The effect of this is to present the return as reintegration: the Greek community, compromised at the outset, is finally restored to an equilibrium that is implicitly imagined as its natural, proper state. In second-century narrative, as we have already seen, the roles of both Hellenism and the *polis* are greatly diminished: the experiences of the individual are central, rather than the eternal health of the city. What is more, as we shall see now, the motif of restoration, of a return to the same, is correspondingly de-emphasised; instead, the focus is upon the *transformations* wrought by the events of the narrative.

---

[150] On the official status of exegetes (only attested at Olympia), see Jones (2001) 37 (making the link to Longus' exegete); also Merkelbach (1988) 140–1. Exegetes are also attested in the actual process of cultic initiation, guiding initiands towards the true sacred meaning of their experiences (Dio Chr. 12.33).

The most visible sign of this shift is the relocation of the marriage. In Chariton and Xenophon (and indeed in *Metiochus and Parthenope*, to judge from the Persian version), the lovers marry at the beginning; they are then separated, before a final reunion at the end. In the subsequent romances, with the possible exception of Iamblichus' *Babylonian affairs* (although this is unclear),[151] the marriage is shifted to the end. The conclusion of the romance, therefore, no longer marks the recovery of the initial state before the travels, but the transition to a new state.

In line with this concern for transformation, the second-century romances develop a new language to articulate accession into erotic maturity, that of initiation. We need to be careful here, since the English word 'initiation' conflates what are for the Greeks two very different forms of passage rites: coming of age and entry into the brethren of a mystery cult.[152] The first-century romances are centrally about the former, and not at all about the latter. In the romances of the second century and later, by contrast, *erōs* is repeatedly imaged in terms of the mysteries (*telos/teletē, muēsis*).[153] This connection itself goes back to Plato,[154] but its introduction in the context of the romance marks a significant development. The marriage that (now) ends the romance is hereby marked in terms of the acquisition of a new identity. The mysteries were imagined to mark the death of the old self and the birth of the new. These effects are described by the orator Sopater (fourth century CE): 'I saw that initiatory rite (*teletē*), which all of you initiates (*memuēmenoi*) understand, and emerged from the sanctuary a stranger to myself.'[155] In Burkert's terms, 'mystery festivals

---

[151] Photius begins his story with the claim that they are (to use Stephens and Winkler's translation) 'deeply in love with each other within the bounds of matrimony, and they are in fact being married [or betrothed?]' (νόμωι γάμου ἐρῶντες ἀλλήλων καὶ δὴ καὶ ζευγνύμενοι, *Bibl.* 74a = 190 SW). Does this mean they were actually married? There are four reasons to withhold certainty: (a) as Stephens and Winkler indicated, ζευγνύμενοι can mean 'betrothed' as well as 'married'; (b) νόμωι γάμου need not mean 'in the legitimacy of marriage', a kind of hendiadys; it might well mean 'in the manner of marriage'; (c) if νόμωι γάμου does refer to marriage, then it is hard to make sense of the second phrase. It is both pleonastic and bathetic to write 'they were married, and actually they really were yoked'; (d) the next event in Photius' summary is the attempt of the wicked king Garmos to force Sinonis to marry him, which suggests that she is not married to Rhodanes yet: although wicked kings can happily pursue married women, it would perhaps be odd to have one seeking to *marry* a newly-wed.
[152] Graf (2003) 4, 9, with references.
[153] Zeitlin (2008) 102–3. Such allusions are sagaciously hunted by Merkelbach (1962) and (1988); see further below on Achilles.
[154] Esp. Pl. *Symp.* 210a; cf. 202e-203a, 215c; fuller list and discussion at Riedwieg (1987) 2–29; see also 30–69 on the *Phaedrus*.
[155] ξενιζόμενος ἐπ' ἐμαυτῶι ('surprised at myself', thus Innes and Winterbottom (1988) 95, is too weak), 114.26–115.1 Walz.

should be unforgettable events, casting their shadows over the whole of one's future life, creating experiences that transform existence'.[156]

The Platonic analogy between sex and initiation is recurrently invoked by Achilles. Clitophon is, the unnamed narrator observes upon first meeting him, 'recently initiated into the god's cult (*teletē*)'.[157] When Clitophon reveals his designs on Leucippe's virginity, he asks her to allow Aphrodite to serve as their 'mystagogue' (2.19.1), and in the Melite episode, again, the goddess's 'mysteries' are repeatedly alluded to.[158] Beneath this mysteriosophic language lies an artful wordplay. The Greek word *telos* (cognates are used in all three contexts cited above) means both 'ritual' and 'end'. In the context of erotic narratives, a ritual initiate is also someone who has experienced the end of the story. The conclusion of the narrative is indeed a *telos* in this double sense. Leucippe and Clitophon 'consummated our much-prayed-for marriage rites, and went off to Tyre',[159] before proceeding to Byzantium. The verb *epiteleō* ('consummate') suggests both the enactment of sacred liturgy and the conclusion of the narrative of romantic love.[160] The first meaning is primary elsewhere in Achilles,[161] but the second is also present: the adjective 'much prayed-for'[162] signals that the wedding is also the *telos* of the romance plot, marking the dissolution of the erotic and narrative tension.

Clitophon is counterposed, in his desire for sexual initiation, to his pederastic cousin Clinias: 'two years older than myself; he had been initiated (*tetelesmenos*) into the cult of Eros';[163] he is addressed as 'an initiate for longer than me, and you are already more familiar with the mysteries (*teletē*) of Eros'.[164] Clinias' principal role in the plot is to play the 'restraining friend' role (compare Polycharmus in Chariton, Hippothous

---

[156] Burkert (1987) 89. On mystery religions in general, see esp. Burkert (1987).
[157] οὐκ μακρὰν τῆς τοῦ θεοῦ τελετῆς, 1.2.2.
[158] For mystic imagery used of sex elsewhere in Achilles, see 5.15.6, 5.16.3, 5.25.6, 5.26.3, 5.26.10, 5.27.4; cf. also 8.12.4. Achilles' initiatory motifs are discussed by Merkelbach (1962) 114–60, though his criteria for inclusion in the category are overgenerous and his interpretation overliteral.
[159] τοὺς πολυεύκτους ἐπιτελέσαντες γάμους ἀπεδημήσαμεν εἰς τὸ Βυζάντιον, 8.19.2.
[160] For these two senses of ἐπιτελέω, see LSJ 1.1 and 11, respectively.
[161] 7.12.3: . . . ὅσων οὐκ ἐπετέλεσαν τὴν θυσίαν οἱ θεωροί. Two MSS (W and M) give ἀπετέλεσαν, but all editors print ἐπετέλεσαν, 'a technical term for discharging a religious duty' (Vilborg (1962) 122).
[162] This is how I take πολύευκτος (cf. 4.17.4 (ἡ πολύευκτος ἠὼς ἀναφαίνεται); also e.g. Hdt. 1.85.8 → D.S. 9.33.2, *Anth. Pal.* 14.79, Xen. *Cyr.* 1.6.45, [Luc.] *Cyn.* 8, and esp. Hesych. Π 2849 (τίμιον, πολυπόθητον)). The meaning 'accompanied by many prayers' is theoretically possible but unparalleled.
[163] δύο ἀναβεβηκὼς ἔτη τῆς ἡλικίας τῆς ἐμῆς, ἔρωτι τετελεσμένος, 1.7.1.
[164] ἀρχαιότερος μύστης ἐμοῦ καὶ συνηθέστερος ἤδη τῆι τελετῆι τοῦ θεοῦ, 1.9.7.

Transforming romance

in Xenophon),[165] but the mysteriosophic imagery adds two components. The first is metanarrative. As an initiate, one who has already attained the *telos* of his own romance, Clinias is ideally placed to advise Clitophon on the 'routes' (1.9.7) to sexual success. It is thus to Clinias that Clitophon initially turns for an *erōtodidaskalos*, a 'teacher of desire'. Secondly, and relatedly, initiatory language introduces the play between insider knowledge and ignorance that lies at the heart of all mystery cult.[166] The tension between Clinias' knowingness and Clitophon's ignorance is pronounced: Clitophon blurts out his sufferings, all hackneyed erotic symptoms (sleeplessness, imagining Leucippe constantly: 1.9.1–2), concluding that 'there has never been such a misfortune'.[167] This too has a metaliterary aspect: Clinias' reply that this is 'nonsense' (1.9.2) bespeaks both his sexual and his literary knowingness: these are, of course, entirely standard *topoi* in the erotic repertoire.[168] An even stronger example comes when his boyfriend Charicles announces his impending marriage. Clinias turns straightaway to literature to warn him of the risks:

If you were vulgar and uncultured (*idiōtēs . . . mousikēs*), you would be unaware of the plots (*dramata*) of women. But as it is, you could even instruct others in the myths that women have supplied to the stage: Eriphyle's necklace, Philomela's banquet, Stheneboea's slander, Aerope's theft, Procne's murder . . .[169]

Distancing himself, like many an elitist of the imperial age, from the uneducated masses,[170] Clinias displays his education to make his point: in addition to the Attic tragedies checked off here, he refers elsewhere to the arch-misogynist Hesiod, to Homer and to Herodotus.[171] Clinias' status as initiate means not only that he knows about sex, but also that he knows about knowing about it.

---

[165] Below, pp. 206–10.
[166] The Iolaus fragment (SW 368–71) draws out the pedagogical implication: Iolaus 'learns' (μανθάνει, 3; ἐμεμαθήκει, 36) the cult secrets that are 'taught' (διδάσκειν, 3; διδαχθέντι, 7; διδάσκεται, 35–6) him.
[167] οὐ γέγονεν ἄλλο (cf. O'Sullivan (1978) 317) τοιοῦτον ἀτύχημα, 1.9.2.
[168] For sleeplessness, see e.g. Long. 1.13.6, 1.14.4, 2.9.2, 3.4.2, 4.29.4, 4.40.3; for envisaging, Ap. Rh. *Arg.* 3.453–8; Virg. *Aen.* 4.3–5; Char. 2.4.3, 6.7.1.
[169] ἀλλ' εἰ μὲν ἰδιώτης ἦσθα μουσικῆς, ἠγνοεῖς ἂν τὰ τῶν γυναικῶν δράματα· νῦν δὲ κἂν ἄλλοις λέγοις, ὅσων ἐνέπλησαν μύθων γυναῖκες τὴν σκηνήν· ὅρμος Ἐριφύλης, Φιλομήλας ἡ τράπεζα, Σθενεβοίας ἡ διαβολή, Ἀερόπης ἡ κλοπή, Πρόκνης ἡ σφαγή, 1.8.4.
[170] For the opposition ἰδιώτης – πεπαιδευμένος see esp. Luc. *Dom.* 2, *Lex.* 24; Philostr. *VA* 3.43, and further Schmitz (1997) 89–91.
[171] 1.8.2 = Hes. *Op.* 57–8; also τὸ τῶν γυναικῶν γένος (1.8.1) ~ γένος . . . γυναικῶν (Hes. *Th.* 590). Homer's Chryseis and Briseis are referred to at 1.8.5, and Odysseus and Penolope at 1.8.6; Herodotus' Gyges and Candaules story (important for the romancers: Tatum (1997)) at 1.8.5.

In a later speech, he again connects desire with learning and sophistication: Eros, Clinias opines, is a 'self-taught sophist'.[172] What he means, on the most literal level, is that lovers can improvise on the spur of the moment. But the phrase works on another level too, by reinforcing the analogy between erotic experience and literary competence, in the form of sophistic expertise. This message is underlined by the medium: the phrase is a knowing allusion to Plato and Xenophon.[173] Even the description 'self-taught' is ironically learned: in the first instance it alludes to Phemius, the bard who plays in Odysseus' household,[174] but it may also allude to Dio Chrysostom, who claimed – his eye glinting as brightly as Clinias' – to be 'self-taught in wisdom' (a phrase itself borrowed from Xenophon).[175] The phrase thus triggers a playful reflection upon the ratio of instinct and instruction involved in sexual initiation. Another twist follows shortly. When he describes sleeping with Melite in the make-shift boudoir of his prison cell, Clitophon borrows Clinias' phrasing: 'Eros is a self-made, improvising sophist.'[176] It is a delicious paradox that this celebration of the organically creative power of desire itself rests upon the reuse of a distinctive phrase that this selfsame romance has already rendered a cliché (and a phrase that itself has, as we have seen, a hypotextual history).

Erotic initiation, then, is a game with high stakes: it implicates the reader too in the quest for both literary sophistication and social prestige. Like Achilles' Clinias, Longus' erotic teachers, Philetas and Lycaenion, have mystagogic aspects.[177] Both claim to be divulging god-sent truths. Philetas has witnessed an epiphany of Eros: 'I have come to reveal (*mēnuein*) to you what I have seen', he comments, 'to announce to you what I have heard'.[178] The language of 'revelation' suggests the mysteries, and there is also an echo of the cultic 'things said' (*legomena*), 'things shown' (*deiknumena*) and 'things done' (*drōmena*). His disquisition on the nature and power of Eros (2.7) is the most powerful and authoritative statement of the erotic

---

[172] αὐτοδίδακτος... σοφιστής, 1.10.1.
[173] Pl. *Symp.* 203d; Xen. *Cyr.* 6.1.14. Eros as a teacher (*didaskalos*) occurs in Euripides' first *Hippolytus* (fr. 430 N²).
[174] *Od.* 23.347; cf. also Pind. *Ol.* 2.86–7.
[175] αὐτουργοὶ τῆς σοφίας, Dio Chr. 1.9 ~ Xen. *Mem.* 1.5; on Dio's slipperiness here see Whitmarsh (2001a) 161.
[176] αὐτουργὸς... ὁ Ἔρως καὶ αὐτοσχέδιος σοφιστής, 5.27.4.
[177] See Merkelbach (1988) 164–6, 176–8, though much of his evidence is far-fetched; also MacQueen (1990) 53–4, 73–4. Chalk (1960) sees *Daphnis and Chloe* as a devotional work; Rohde (1937) is more measured, seeing the text as a second-order literary expression of a religious truth. See further n. 141. For the structural pairing of Philetas and Lycaenion, see Stanzel (1991) 161–2 and Morgan (2004a) 209–10 (also noting her links with Dorcon and Gnathon).
[178] ἥκω δὲ ὑμῖν ὅσα εἶδον μηνύσων, ὅσα ἤκουσα ἀπαγγελῶν, 2.3.2.

principle driving the narrative, and it focuses upon cosmic theology (his first words are 'Eros is a god', 2.7.1).[179] Although Philetas' instruction is incomplete (focusing, perhaps, on the things said at the expense of the things shown and done), it is a nevertheless a crucial formative moment in the education of the young lovers.[180]

Parallel to the Philetas episode in book 2 is the Lycaenion episode in book 3:[181] she provides the acts (*erga*) of Eros to complement the words (*onomata*) supplied by Philetas.[182] This episode is heavily marked with the language of teaching,[183] which can be used in mystic contexts, but here seems more neutral, reactivating the association between sex and knowledge that the narrator drew in the preface (1 *pr.* 4: the text 'will provide a preliminary education', *propaideusei*). If Philetas' erotic instruction was coded as religious, this appears to be a more practical lesson. The only soteriology here is fraudulent: she handles her young charge '*as though she were truly about to teach* (*didaskesthai*) *something great and truly heaven-sent*' (the narrator thereby implying, of course, that it is not).[184] Between the two of them, Philetas and Lycaenion represent the ambiguity of Longan narrative, which equivocates metaleptically between the sacred and the profane.

The crucial point, however, relates to the metanarrative significance of this language of education and instruction. Philetas and Lycaenion are instruments of narrative teleology, in a double sense. In terms of the kinetics of plot, they supply knowledge that Daphnis and Chloe need in order to achieve the consummation that they crave. But they also, in their states of superior knowledge, point to the lack that the lovers must make good before the plot can complete. This cognitive lack is remedied in conclusion, as 'Daphnis did one of the things that Lycaenion had taught (*epaideuse*) him, and then for the first time Chloe learned (*emathen*) that what happened in the woods were just shepherds' games'.[185] Like all acts of closure, this final act of instruction has powerful implications for the identities of the central figures. Here, the pedagogical relationship also

---

[179] Morgan (2004a) 177–84, esp. 179–80. [180] παιδεύσας, 2.8.1; παιδευτήριον, 2.9.1.
[181] On the parallelism see Morgan (2004a) 209–10 (also noting her links with Dorcon and Gnathon).
[182] I argue at Whitmarsh (2005f) that the portrait of Philetas mobilises readers' awareness of stories that the Hellenistic poet Philetas/Philitas of Cos was sagacious, sometimes without reward, in his pursuit of words.
[183] διδαξαμένην, 3.17.2; μαθητήν; διδάξω, 3.17.3; διδάξαι τὴν τέχνην, 3.18.1; διδάσκεσθαι, 3.18.2; παιδεύειν, 3.18.3; μαθοῦσα, 3.18.4; ἐπαιδεύσε, 3.18.4; ἐρωτικῆς παιδαγωγίας; πεπαίδευτο, 3.19.1; μαθεῖν; ἐπαίδευσε, 3.19.2; ἀρτιμαθής, 3.20.2.
[184] ὥσπερ τι μέγα καὶ θεόπεμπτον ἀληθῶς μέλλων διδάσκεσθαι, 3.18.1.
[185] ἔδρασέ τι Δάφνις ὧν αὐτὸν ἐπαίδευσε Λυκαίνιον, καὶ τότε Χλόη πρῶτον ἔμαθεν ὅτι τὰ ἐπὶ τῆς ὕλης γενόμενα ἦν ποιμένων παίγνια, 4.40.3.

naturalises social hierarchies (coinciding as it does with the consummation of marriage, imagined as the acculturated form of 'natural' sex). This act of teaching also marks Daphnis' final assumption of a position of dominance over Chloe, as he becomes the teacher (just as Xenophon's Ischomachus constructs his hierarchical relationship to his wife in terms of education).[186]

Daphnis and Chloe and *Leucippe and Clitophon* self-consciously revise the paradigms established by Chariton and Xenophon in a number of ways. There is certainly (as much criticism has emphasised) much greater store laid by 'literary' self-reflexivity, signalled by the use of ecphrastic description, intertextual depth, the use of philosophical and literary-critical terminology, the deployment of Atticising diction, and so forth.[187] What I have sought to show in this chapter is that these features are not simply epiphenomenal responses to shifts in literary aesthetics (the emergence of the so-called 'Second Sophistic'), but part of a larger package of narrative reorientations, all expressing a revised conception of the paradigms of identity subtending the romance form. It is a question not just of 'literariness', but of an awareness of the mediated, self-consciously non-natural status of narration. The focus on the text as an artefact directs our attention towards the constructedness not just of narrative itself, but also of the stories that we choose to tell about who we are. Whereas Chariton and Xenophon see identity as (fundamentally) a stable core of selfhood that can be recovered within traditional civic structures after times of strife, the second-century romancers see it as mutable, likely to be moulded by life.

The second-century romances, then, are *transformative*. We can see this everywhere in the stories incorporated into the central narrative. Achilles' Callisthenes, notably, starts out as a rogue rapist, but ends up changing his personality entirely: 'everyone marvelled at his sudden transformation from a worse character to an entirely excellent one'.[188] A subtler example is Longus' Lampis, who is 'forgiven' for his actions, implying contrition (Long. 4.38.2). At a subtler level still, Achilles and Longus fill their romances with embedded narratives of mythical metamorphosis, which reinforce towards the thematic centrality of the transformation theme.[189] This is

---

[186] On progressive marginalisation of Chloe in books 3 and 4 see Winkler (1990) 114–18.
[187] From among myriad studies of these features see especially Hunter (1983) on *Daphnis and Chloe*; more generally, Billault (1991) and Morgan and Harrison (2008).
[188] ὥστε θαυμάζειν ἅπαντας τὸ αἰφνίδιον οὕτως ἐκ τοῦ χείρονος εἰς τὸ πάνυ χρηστὸν μετελθόν, Ach. Tat. 8.17.5. Laplace (2007) 705–42 discusses the transformation theme in Achilles Tatius, but overstates her position by arguing for thoroughgoing character change in *Leucippe and Clitophon*.
[189] Ach. Tat. 1.1.13 (Zeus), 1.5.5 (Daphne), 5.5.5 (Procne), 8.6.7–9 (Syrinx), 8.12.8 (Rhodopis); Long. 1.27 (Pitys), 2.33.3–34 (Syrinx), 3.23 (Echo). These narratives cannot be taken as straightforwardly

a world in which character is not necessarily set for life: individuals can reshape themselves in the light of their experience, and others can reappraise their evaluations. This interest in the metamorphosis theme reflects not only literary trends (the popularity of *Ass* narratives, the collection of tales by Antoninus Liberalis), but also the newer conceptions of character change embedded in the works of biographers (notably Plutarch, whose account of Themistocles' change of character Achilles may have followed).[190]

This transformative dynamic makes for greater self-consciousness about closure. As we have seen, the marriage is relocated to the end, where it can figure newly acquired identities. We have also considered the heavy exploitation of the ambiguities of the word *telos* ('end'/'initiation'), particularly by Achilles. It is in this context that we should locate *Leucippe and Clitophon*'s celebrated resistance to closure. The text concludes with the lovers marrying and sailing from Tyre to Byzantium together; but in the framing narrative that begins the text, which seems to take place soon afterwards,[191] Clitophon is in Sidon, inexplicably despondent and without Leucippe. This puzzle has been widely discussed: particularly convincing are explanations that allude to Platonic precedent and the anticlosural, experimental aspects of the romance.[192] As we have also seen in this chapter, the second-century romances are specifically concerned with the problematisation and relativisation of narrative: they dramatise the absence of final meaning, and the difficulty of locating a single cultural vantage on the narrative. But anticlosurality is not just a formal, literary choice: it also has implications for the identity politics of the romance. Marriage, it implies, is neither the absolute end of the story nor the natural destiny of the human subject.

---

paradigmatic, since they generally involve (a) females only and (b) sexual violence, in pointed contrast to the romance plot (Winkler (1990) 118–21; Morales (2004) 178–84); even so, the insistent return to the metamorphosis theme is striking.

[190] The notable cases of Plutarchan character change are Philip V of Macedon (in *Aratus*), Sulla and particularly Sertorius: see Swain (1989) 64–6. Themistocles' character change: Ach. Tat. 8.17.1 ~ Plut. *Them.* 2.7.

[191] 'To judge by the look of you, it is not long since your initiation (*teletēs*) into the god's cult' (1.2.2; the god in question being Eros, Aphrodite's son); Repath (2005) 260–1. The Greek text is quoted above, n. 157.

[192] Fusillo (1997); Repath (2005), with full bibliography at 250–1 n. 3.

CHAPTER 3

Hellenism at the edge
Heliodorus

> When day had just begun to smile, and the sun was beaming down onto the peaks, men armed like bandits crept over the summit of the hill that overlooks the so-called Heracleiotic mouth of the Nile, where it pours into the sea...[1]

Practised readers of the romance – even after Achilles Tatius' flamboyant opening – would have been bamboozled by the beginning of Heliodorus' *Charicleia and Theagenes*. These first words unsettle. We begin with a striking, disorientating metaphor, which would become famous in Byzantine times. How do we read the day's enigmatic 'smile'?[2] Is it benign, mocking, or threatening? More generally, what is the narrative context? Other romances open straightforwardly with diegetic material establishing the parameters of place, characters and sometimes period.[3] For sure, Heliodorus gives us some orientating markers here, but they are notably hazy: temporality (just after sunrise – but on what day, why?), geography (the 'so-called' Heracleotic mouth of the Nile) and prosopography ('men armed like bandits' – but are they really bandits?).

Matters do not become any clearer after this. The focalisation shifts to the bandits, as they attempt to decipher the scene before them: a laden ship, and the shore strewn with signs of feasting and carnage.[4] The panorama is aporetic to them: after having surveyed the ship and the shore, 'at a loss (*aporountes*) as to what had happened'.[5] It is as if we had reached book 22 of the *Odyssey* without the earlier narrative to prepare us. They then spy a beautiful young woman and man, 'a sight more aporetic (*aporōteron*) than

---

[1] Ἡμέρας ἄρτι διαγελώσης καὶ ἡλίου τὰς ἀκρωρείας καταυγάζοντος, ἄνδρες ἐν ὅπλοις λῃστρικοῖς ὄρους ὑπερκύψαντες, ὃ δὴ κατ' ἐκβολὰς τοῦ Νείλου καὶ στόμα τὸ καλούμενον Ἡρακλεωτικὸν ὑπερτείνει..., Hld. 1.1.1.
[2] Discussed at Whitmarsh (2005e), where references to Byzantine imitations can be found. The phrase is found once in earlier literature, in the *Praeparatio Sophistica* of Phrynichus the Arab (93–4 de Borries); a similar expression at Philo, *De mutatio nominum* 162.
[3] See Chapter 2 n. 37.   [4] Bühler (1976); Winkler (1982) 95–106; Whitmarsh (2002b) 117–19.
[5] τὸ γεγονὸς ὅ τι ποτέ ἐστιν ἀποροῦντες, 1.1.8.

108

the previous one'.[6] Their aporia is ours too. Who are they, and how did they get there? The girl, whose name we learn is Charicleia, does explain their story presently (1.22.2–5) – but this explanation turns out to be a deception. The full story will not be revealed until half way through the text (5.32), when Calasiris, the Egyptian priest who has arranged the two young lovers' elopement from Delphi and shepherded their journey through Egypt, discloses it. This perplexing beginning, deliberately resisting the reader's 'primordial need for certainty at the beginning' of a narrative,[7] is not just a hermeneutic game for the reader.[8] It is also a calculated defamiliarisation of the genre, an affront to the naturalistic rules of the Greek romance. This text forces us to read the genre, and the Hellenocentric assumptions upon which it is predicated, through fresh eyes – literally, since the eyes of Egyptian bandits are our only guide at the opening of this text.

This defamiliarisation of the genre is linked to the exceptional literary–historical position occupied by this text. *Charicleia and Theagenes* is antiquity's longest, latest and arguably greatest romance. The date is uncertain, but the fourth century remains the likeliest candidate.[9] Like the second-century romancer Iamblichus and Lucian, and like the male protagonist of *Leucippe and Clitophon*, Heliodorus was a Hellenised Syrian: as he reveals at the end of the text, 'a Phoenician man from Emesa, of the race of Helios, the son of Theodosius, Heliodorus'.[10] Emesa (modern Homs, in Syria) lay on the east bank of the Orontes, on the edge of the central Syrian steppe, around 70 km inland from the 'properly' Phoenician coast.[11] Emesa had grown to rapid prominence in the imperial period, and apparently rapidly under the empire to one of the most important towns of the region. Its most famous export was the cult of 'LH'GBL (Elahagabal), a local Ba'al-type god who achieved international prominence thanks to the Emesene empress Julia Domna (whose father had been a priest of the cult) and her son, the emperor Elagabalus (218–22), who introduced his worship to Rome. The first part of the name derives from the Aramaic '*elahā*' meaning 'god' (from the same root as 'Allah'), but the Greeks identified it with the Greek Helios,

---

[6] θέαμα... τῶν προτέρων ἀπορώτερον, 1.2.1.   [7] Said (1975) 49.
[8] Winkler (1982) 96–9; more generally Hunter (1998).   [9] See appendix.
[10] ἀνὴρ Φοῖνιξ Ἐμισηνός, τῶν ἀφ' Ἡλίου γένος, Θεοδοσίου παῖς Ἡλιόδωρος, 10.41.4. On Iamblichus, see above, p. 75.
[11] On ancient Emesa, see esp. Chad (1972); Millar (1993) 300–9. Greek sources are vague and inconsistent on the distinction between the coastal Phoenicians and the inland Arabs ('Phoenician' is, in any case, a catch-all term bestowed by the Greeks). Bowie (1998) notes that Heliodorus strategically dots various kinds of φοῖνιξ – the phoenix bird, the date palm, the blood-red colour – through his text (see also Winkler (1982) 157).

hence the form Heliogabalos.[12] Heliodorus' name and his descent 'from the race of Helios' are thus eloquent testimony to his Emesene origins, and may even point to a hereditary priesthood. In fact, a bilingual inscription from Athens gives us a clue as to what his Semitic name may have been: the Phoenician equivalent given for 'Heliodorus' is 'BDŠMŠ: 'Abdshamash, 'Servant of Sun'.[13]

The romance is set not in Phoenicia but in Africa;[14] even so, it is dominated by Helios, the sun-god from the famous smile of daybreak, through the episodes (narrated in flashback) built around the oracle of Apollo (∼Helios) at Delphi, to the closing scenes in Ethiopia, the ancient land of the sun,[15] and culminating with the author's own reference to 'the race of the sun', discussed above. Helios/Apollo dominates proceedings throughout, along with his counterpart Artemis/Selene/Isis, to the almost total exclusion of the rest of the Greek pantheon.[16] The solar emphasis of the romance reflects not only a debt to Xenophon of Ephesus (whom, as we shall come to see, Heliodorus treats as the romancer *à degré zéro*), but also the author's background in west-Asian religion. It may not, indeed, be fanciful to see a figurative representation of Emesa in Meroe, the utopian Ethiopian kingdom where Heliodorus' narrative culminates: both are centres of sun-cult standing on great rivers.[17]

It is possible too that the centrality of solar cult reflects changes in the religious landscape of late antiquity, but the dating remains problematic: estimates vary from the second to the fourth centuries CE.[18] Most scholars prefer a third- or fourth-century date, which would locate Heliodorus in the

---

[12] *GBL* probably means 'the mountain', suggesting an original identification with the cosmic mountain (Starcky (1975–6) 503–4 insists on 'god consisting in the mountain' rather than 'god from the mountain') rather than, or perhaps in addition to, the sun. There is, however, some controversy over this: see Altheim and Stiel (1966) 127–9, Frey (1989) 45–6, and for the doubt esp. Millar (1993) 304–5 (citing personal communication from Sebastian Brock). A Palmyrene stele records the Semitic form of the god's name (Starcky (1975–6)).

[13] *KAI*[3] 53 (= vol. 1 p. 13). It is also possible, however, that the *Helio*- element translates Aramaic '*elahā*' (as in Heliogabalus). The *–dorus* ending, meanwhile, seems to render the Semitic theophoric form *'BD*, 'servant of' (as in the modern Arabic name 'Abdullah).

[14] Is Heliodorus a Phoenician writing of north Africa, playfully recompensing for the Phoenician romance of the Alexandrian Achilles Tatius?

[15] On the solar traditions underlying Heliodorus' representation of Ethiopia, see Lesky (1959), esp. 38.

[16] Bargheer (1999) is a thorough, if banal, treatment. Despite its ostensible contribution to a section on sun-cult, Kövendi (1966) provides only a pedestrian literary appreciation. The central role of Apollo/Artemis also invokes the precedent of Xenophon of Ephesus.

[17] Altheim (1942) draws useful parallels between Heliodorus' theology and Emesene sun-cult. Heliodorus' Meroe may be romanticised, but the city was real enough, the powerful capital of Kush (in modern Sudan). Heliodorus' representation of the historical city is discussed by Hägg (2000).

[18] See appendix.

aftermath of the Severan promotion of the solar cult of Elagabal.[19] Rohde wanted to squeeze him into the narrow window of the reign of Aurelian (270–5), who revived Elagabal in the form of Sol Invictus.[20] A slender majority of scholars, however, locate the text in the fourth century, some in the even briefer reign of Julian (361–3), who attempted to disestablish Christianity; his philosophical writings (particularly his hymn *To Helios the king*) share with Heliodorus an interest in neoplatonism and solar cult.[21] But to seek a single determinant for Heliodorus' preoccupation with the god who shared part of his own name is too reductive. Helios is inevitably an overdetermined figure; and there is certainly no call to believe that the romancer was closely allied with imperial ideology.

Charicleia and Theagenes represents a new stage in the history of the romance. It is, for a start, extremely ambitious: substantially longer than any other extant romance (although Iamblichus' second-century *Babylonian affairs*, now mostly lost, was almost certainly longer),[22] and much more narratologically complex, in terms of flashback and embedded narration (although again Antonius Diogenes' lost *Wonders beyond Thule* offers a precedent).[23] Stylistically, it is much more elaborate and ornate.[24] This presentational sophistication matches the thematic scale and scope of the work, which approaches the cosmic. Beginning on the Mediterranean coast of Egypt, the narrative takes us (partly under the guidance of Calasiris, an Egyptian priest) up the Nile, through Egypt to Ethiopia, home of solar cult. This journey is presented as a mystic pilgrimage for characters and readers alike.

The erotic narrative shares these religious–mystic associations. Achilles Tatius, as we have seen, borrows the Platonic imagery of sex as initiation, but in the context of a narrative in which (for Clitophon at any rate) sexual urges are to be satisfied as quickly as possible. Heliodorus uses the same Platonic resources to a much more elevated effect: exceptionally for a Greek romance, both lovers remain 'pure' until they are married, in pointed contrast to the base adulterers who populate the text.[25] Perhaps Heliodorus is

---

[19] If the date is later in the third century, then the Ethiopians' trouncing of the Persians at Syene in book 9 might be taken to invoke the successful Roman defence of Emesa against the invasions of the Parthian king Šāpūr I in CE 252, an event commemorated pseudo-prophetically in the thirteenth *Sibylline oracle* (where the Parthians are also named 'Persians').
[20] Rohde (1914) 493–6.   [21] Esp. Bargheer (1999).
[22] With most scholars, I take the *Suda*'s βιβλίοις λθ' (i.e. 39) as an error (*Suda* s.v. Ἰάμβλιχος 1), on the basis that Photius *Bibl.* cod. 94 only describes sixteen.
[23] Discussed esp. by Hefti (1950); Winkler (1982); Morgan (2004e).   [24] Mazal (1958).
[25] On Platonic features, see esp. Sandy (1982). For sexual 'purity' (καθαρότης), see 1.8.3, 1.25.4, 6.9.4, 8.9.12, 10.7.7, 10.8.2, 10.9.1, 10.22.3; cf. 7.8.6 for the inverse (Arsace). For the Cnemon story as a

directly responding to Christian moralism,[26] and certainly he is developing ideas already to be found in third-century neoplatonist theology, taking its place within a culture vigorously debating the relationship between sexual morality and spiritual health. Before she meets Theagenes, indeed, Charicleia is described as 'reverencing virginity and holding it close to the immortals'[27] – a phrase that is unimaginable, in its association of abstinence with godliness, in any of the earlier romancers. The narrative proper concludes with Charicleia and Theagenes assuming priesthoods and entering Meroe 'so that the more mystic parts of the marriage could be consummated more joyously in the city':[28] in closure ('consummated', *telesthēsomenōn*, has metanarrative overtones),[29] religious and erotic fulfilment fully converge, to the extent that the sacerdotal installation and the marriage seem to be fused into the same telestic process. Heliodorus promotes initiation from a subordinate metaphor for sex to an equipollent institution.

MYTHIC PARADIGMS: CENTRE AND PERIPHERY

As the brief discussion above has already shown, *Charicleia and Theagenes* is fusion of the generically distilled themes of the first-century romance (infatuation, separation, travel, oppression, reunion in marriage) and a more ambitious religious, cultural, even (in the non-technical sense) philosophical myth-history. Mythic paradigms are important to all of the romancers,[30] but whereas the others use them primarily as resources for literary play, Heliodorus approaches them as the fundamental paradigm for life itself. Most important in structural terms is Homer's *Odyssey*.[31] The narrative

'prolonged portrait of perverted, immoral, simply bad love', see Morgan (1989a) 107–11, at 107; Morgan proceeds to offer the Arsace narrative as another example of 'loving badly' (112).

[26] As claimed by Ramelli (2001) 124–41; Morgan (2005) sees Heliodorus as part of an anti-Christian backlash. The well-known ancient tradition that the author of *Charicleia and Theagenes* was also the bishop of Tricca in Thessaly begins with Socrates' *Historia ecclesiastica* (5.22 = Hld. T 1 Colonna; cf. Tt. 3, 14 Colonna), but the report is already treated with caution there (cf. λέγεται), and few modern scholars would place absolute faith in it (cf. Dörrie (1938) 275–6).

[27] ἐκθειάζουσα μὲν παρθενίαν καὶ ἐγγὺς ἀθανάτων ἀποφαίνουσα, 2.33.5; see further below, pp. 150–5.

[28] τῶν ἐπὶ τῶι γάμωι μυστικωτέρων κατὰ τὸ ἄστυ φαιδρότερον τελεσθησομένων, 10.41.3.

[29] In the manuscript tradition, Greek works often conclude with the word *TELOS* (much as 'THE END' rolls up at the end of films); Heliodorus wittily exploits this convention, using a cognate form in the sense not of 'conclusion' but of 'ritual practice'.

[30] Cueva (2004), offers some reflections: see now esp. Lefteratou (2010).

[31] See Keyes (1922) on the structural similarities, although his theories concerning the composition of the *Aethiopica* are suspect. More generally, see Feuillâtre (1966) 105–114; Garson (1975); Fusillo (1989) 28–32; Whitmarsh (1998), (1999). The Memphitic episode in book 6 also rests heavily upon the Oedipus tragedies. Charicleia's guiding (χειραγωγούμενος, 6.11.4) of Calasiris looks to Antigone and Oedipus at the beginning of Sophocles' *Oedipus at Colonus* (an allusion missed by Paulsen

Hellenism at the edge

opens with the lovers on the Egyptian shores of the Mediterranean, just as Odysseus is on the shore of Calypso's island Ogygia when the *Odyssey* begins; and, again as in the *Odyssey*, the explanation for this state of affairs is given in retrospective, embedded narration (cf. Hom. *Od.* 12.447–53).[32] Calasiris, the narrator in question, is indeed a notably Odyssean figure: a stoical wanderer, wise and experienced but afflicted by sufferings, an artful narrator who is capable of deception and showmanship.[33] These similarities are not accidental. On Zacynthus, Calasiris dreams to receives a dream-visitation from Odysseus himself. The hero castigates the priest for his failure to pay honours to him while passing near 'the island of the Cephallenians' (5.22.2);[34] he then warns that 'you will suffer the same troubles as me',[35] before passing on Penelope's best wishes to Charicleia, since she exalts 'chastity' (*sōphrosunē*) above all (5.22.3). This is clearly an explicit signal to the reader that the travels and trials that befall Heliodorus' lovers are to be read against the paradigm of the *Odyssey*.

If *Charicleia and Theagenes* is a rewrite of the *Odyssey*, however, it is a rewrite from a distinctively non-Greek, self-consciously marginal perspective. At one point, Calasiris claims that Homer himself was an Egyptian:

'Different peoples may attribute Homer's origins to different places, my friend; and we can allow the wise man every city. But the truth is that Homer was a compatriot of mine, an Egyptian, and his hometown was Thebes, 'Thebes of the hundred gates', to borrow his own phrase [*Ili.* 9.383]. Ostensibly his father was a high priest, but in actual fact it was Hermes, whose high priest his ostensible father was: for once, when his wife was sleeping in the temple performing some

---

(1992)). When they arrive on the battlefield, their intervention is heavily modelled on Euripides' *Phoenissae*: Paulsen (1992) 164–72 discusses the complex web of intertextual and metatheatrical motifs here; see also Fusillo (1989) 41–2. Calasiris' and Charicleia's intervention is modelled on Jocasta's and Antigone's arrival too late at Eur. *Phoen.* 1427–79: Fusillo (1989) 41, Paulsen (1992) 262 n. 90. (Diggle brackets all references to Antigone in the Euripidean passage.) Elmer (2008) 413–16 rightly cautions that Odyssean allusions arise primarily in the Calasiris sequence, and that the importance of Herodotus for the novel's final third has not been fully recognised by scholarship. The *Odyssey* remains, however, the only text explicitly identified as a narrative hypotext for the wanderings and return of Charicleia (see main text).

[32] On the Homeric debt, see Rohde (1914) 474; Keyes (1922) 44.
[33] On the characterisation of Calasiris see esp. Sandy (1982).
[34] Carefully chosen words: in Homer, 'Cephallenians' is the generic name for different islanders under Odysseus' command (*Il.* 2.631); the precise Homeric location of the specific island of Cephallenia, however, was the subject of debate (Str. 10.2.10, 13–14). I take the entire scene of Odysseus' appearance as a Heliodorean–Odyssean refashioning of Philostr. *VA* 4.16, where Achilles appears to Apollonius at Troy, asking him to put right the Thessalians' neglect of his shrine; cf. also *Her.* 53.19–23, with Follet (2004) 227 on the historical event behind Achilles' 'retribution' (i.e. punishment for flouting imperial restrictions on the production of purple).
[35] τῶν ὁμοίων ἐμοὶ παθῶν αἰσθήσηι, 5.22.3.

ancestral ritual, the god coupled with her and fathered Homer, who bore on his person a token of this unequal union; for, from the moment of his birth, one of his thighs was covered with a shaggy growth of hair. Hence, as he wandered his way around the world, particularly through Greece, performing his poetry, he was given the name (*ho mēros* = 'the thigh'). He himself never spoke his true name, nor did he name his city or his descent, but the name was fabricated by those who knew of his deformity.'

'What was his purpose in concealing the land of his birth, Father?'

'It may be that he felt ashamed of being an exile, for he was banished by his father, after the mark he bore on his body had led to the recognition of his illegitimacy at the time when he came of age and was being enrolled as a priest. Or possibly this may be another example of his wisdom, and by concealing his true place of origin, he was claiming the whole world as his own.' (3.14.2–4)

Homer's homeland was the subject of famously intense (and wilful) speculation throughout antiquity; it was well known that a number of different cities laid claim to him.[36] Enlisting the aid of an outrageous etymology,[37] Calasiris now appropriates him for Egypt. Although this is neither the first nor the last appearance of this claim in Greek literature,[38] its importance is double-weighted in the context of a narrative that works as a Nilotic refiguration of the *Odyssey*. Indeed, Homer's biography, as presented here, bears a remarkable similarity to Charicleia's story:[39] a tale of contested paternity, foreign travel necessitated by a physical defect, and wandering.[40] Homer's life also resembles that of Calasiris, who was driven by fear of sexual scandal from his priestly Egyptian home (2.24.5–25.6). The exile theme (which will be further discussed in Chapter 6) also has a wider relevance: all of Heliodorus' major characters suffer some kind of expatriation.[41]

Charicleia and Theagenes, then, can be read as the *Odyssey* that Homer would have written had he lived his days on the fertile banks of the Nile.

---

[36] E.g. Dio Chr. 47.5, 55.7 (discussion at Kindstrand (1973) 113–14); Paus. 10.24.3; Philostr. *Her.* 18.1–3; *Anth. Plan.* 292–302. The Homereion of Ptolemy IV in Alexandria paraded statues representing all the *poleis* that laid claim to Homer's birthplace (Ael. *VH* 13.22). In a gesture similar to that of Calasiris, the Syrian Lucian claims that Homer was Babylonian (*VH* 2.20).
[37] Possibly derived ultimately from Eur. *Bacch.* 294–7: Anderson (1979). [38] Sinko (1906).
[39] As noted by Winkler (1982) 102–3; Anderson (1982) 38; Fusillo (1988) 21–2; Bartsch (1989) 145. Calasiris' account also suggests the birth of Alexander as presented in the *Alexander Romance* (1.4–12).
[40] Characters refer to their lives of wandering (ἄλη / πλάνη): 2.24.5, 5.16.2, 5.2.7, 6.15.4, 7.8.2, 7.13.2, 7.14.7. This theme will be further discussed in chapter 6 below.
[41] Cnemon (1.14.1), Theagenes (2.4.1), Cnemon's father Aristippus (2.9.3), Calasiris (2.25.4, 3.16.5), Charicles (2.29.5), Sisimithres (2.32.2), and Charicleia (4.18.2) are all described as exiles. Comito (1975) treats this theme, albeit without insight. See further below, pp. 220–3.

Homer, Calasiris and (implicitly) Heliodorus himself are linked by a thematic chain of exoticism, priesthood and deracination. This has significance for the geographical structuring of the text as a whole. The *Odyssey* is the paradigm of the centre–periphery structure that we have associated with the ephebic romance. Heliodorus' romance, by way of contrast, is shaped around a linear north–south axis.[42] The protagonists frequently express their feelings of disorientation at their seemingly random travels,[43] but in fact their trajectory is unwavering and consistent: up the Nile we proceed, edging inexorably towards the exotic kingdom of Ethiopian Meroe, at the edge of the world as it was known to the Greeks. Since Homeric times, the Ethiopians had been the 'most distant of (*eskhatoi*) men' (Hom. *Od.* 1.23).[44] Homer's centre–periphery construction of geography is regularly echoed by characters in the romance: the necromantic corpse, for example, prophesies that Charicleia will end up 'at the most distant (*eskhatois*) limits of the earth' (6.15.4).[45] Heliodorus also refers, in the reflexive self-revelation that we considered above, to the end of his narrative as a *peras*, a word that regularly denotes the furthest boundary of the world: 'such was the *peras* of the story of the *Ethiopian affair of Theagenes and Charicleia*...'.[46] In reaching the end of this romance, the reader has also attained the limit of human ken.

In one sense, then, the linear shape of *Charicleia and Theagenes* reverses the spatial paradigm of the Odyssean return narrative, also used by the first-century romancers, which distinguishes the geographical hub (Greek space, narrated at the beginning and end) from the non-Greek periphery ('abroad', narrated in the middle). In another sense, however, *Charicleia and Theagenes* remains a centre–periphery text: from the Ethiopians' vantage, this is precisely a story about expatriation into an unfamiliar foreign space, and subsequent home-coming. Charicleia is the girl, says her father Hydaspes, 'whom [the gods] exiled from her home land to the ultimate limits (*perata... eskhata*) of the earth' (10.16.6).[47] This reorientation is all the more striking when we consider that it is Delphi – for Greeks, the 'navel' (*omphalos*) or 'hearth' of the world – to which Hydaspes is referring.

---

[42] Szepessy (1957) 244–54; Létoublon (1993) 108–9; Fusillo (1989) 29.
[43] Above, n. 40.   [44] See further Romm (1994) 49–54.
[45] γῆς ἐπ' ἐσχάτοις ὅροις, perhaps a tragic quotation (it fits an iambic trimeter: Rohde (1914) 480 n. 3). Even Charicleia submits, wondering how Thisbe might have travelled ἐκ μέσης τῆς Ἑλλάδος ἐπ' ἐσχάτοις γῆς Αἰγύπτου (2.8.3); eschatic language also at 2.28.2, 4.14.2.
[46] τοιόνδε πέρας ἔσχε τὸ σύνταγμα τῶν περὶ Θεαγένην καὶ Χαρίκλειαν Αἰθιοπικῶν..., 10.41.4.
[47] ... ἣν ἐξῴκισαν [*sc.* οἱ θεοί] τῆς ἐνεγκούσης ἐπὶ πέρατα γῆς ἔσχατα, 10.16.6. This technique is perhaps borrowed from Ap. Rh. 3.678–80, where the Colchian Chalciope uses the language of the edge of the earth (ἐπὶ γαίης / πείρασι) in such a way as to imply that Colchis is central.

Charicleia and Theagenes is a linear narrative for its male, Greek protagonist, but a centre–periphery narrative for his female, Ethiopian counterpart. Like the second-century romancers, but even more radically, Heliodorus plays off against each other distinct cultural perspectives, and hence forces his readers to interrogate their own. When we reach the end, we have learned to reassess our expectations, of not only the generically conventional structure of the romance, but also the received (Greek) mapping of the world.

The other major mythic narrative can be dealt with more briefly. The story of Perseus' rescue of Andromeda from an Ethiopian sea-monster is the subject of the painting that causes Charicleia to be born white (4.8.3–5; 10.14.7; see also 10.6.3).[48] Given the loss of Euripides' celebrated play (and the difficulty of interpreting Aristophanes' lurid parody in the *Thesmophoriazusae*), it is hard to be certain how much direct intertextual engagement Heliodorus is undertaking. The broad themes, however, are clear from Apollodorus' summary of the Perseus narrative in *Library* (2.34–49). This version is clearly ephebic:[49] it narrates Perseus' transition from early manhood, at a time of personal threat, to a recognised, propertied, settled, married state. As with Jason, Heracles and Bellerophon, when Perseus comes to manhood (*endrōmenou*, 2.36) he is sent off on a challenging mission by a jealous ruler who wants him dead (Polydectes, the brother of the king of Seriphus, who has designs on his mother Danae). After his Gorgon-slaying adventures and rescue of Andromeda, he returns to Seriphus, kills Polydectes, and ultimately founds a dynasty at Tiryns.

It is also a story about the psychosexual stabilisation of gender relations, about the transition from a period of anxious defence of his (perpetually harassed) mother to the acquisition of a bride – via the destruction of a deadly female figure, who represents the terrors of female sexuality (hence Freud's famous analysis in *Das Medusenhaupt* (1922), which reads Medusa as a figure for castration anxiety). The myth also manifests a clear centre–periphery structure, with the Gorgons and the sea-monster figuring the threats to be found in peripheral space. Heliodorus' Theagenes, like Perseus, achieves manhood (as we shall see in the following section, *Charicleia and*

---

[48] On Heliodorus' treatment of the myth, see Billault (1981). The myth is also found in pictorial form at Ach. Tat. 3.6.3–7.9: see Morales (2004) 174–9, with references. The best-known version in antiquity was Euripides' *Andromeda*, now largely lost, which featured a celebrated *donna abandonata* aria and an Ethiopian escape plot: for the Ethiopian setting of Euripides' play, see Wright (2005) 129, on the basis of Ar. *Thesm.* 1098. For other Ethiopian versions, see Eratosth. *Cat.* 15–17, Apollod. 2.4.3–5, Philostr. *Imag.* 1.29.3. An alternative tradition, apparently later, locates the rescue in Joppa, modern Jaffa: Paus. 4.35.9, Joseph *BJ* 3.420, Str. 16.2.28, Conon *FGrH* 26 F1.40.

[49] Cf. John Tzetzes *ad* Lycophr. 838, 15 (πρὸς ἥβην ἐλαύνοντος).

Theagenes has significant ephebic elements) and rescues his beloved, before taking her home. Once again, however, the geographical model of the canonical myth has been reversed, as Ethiopia becomes the homeland and Greece the foreign space.

REFORMING NARRATIVE

The primary narrative template that *Charicleia and Theagenes* rewrites, however, is that of the romance – or, more specifically, that of Xenophon of Ephesus, which serves throughout as a foil for Heliodorus' extravagant experiments. Like Xenophon's Habrocomes, the young Charicleia holds love and marriage in contempt (2.33.4, 3.17.5).[50] The account of the Thessalian ritual of propitiation at Delphi, where Charicleia and Theagenes fall in love, closely reworks Xenophon's description of the Ephesian procession at the outset of *Anthia and Habrocomes*,[51] also taking the opportunity to lard the scene with additional opulent, ecphrastic detail.[52] This description is presented by Calasiris to the eager narrator Cnemon, whose interruptions, refusing to allow his narrator to skip over detail and controlling the rhythm of the narrative (especially 2.32.3, 3.1.1, 3.2.3, 3.12, 4.3.4, 4.4.2), have been much discussed: Cnemon is playfully set up as kind of (anti-)model reader, revelling indulgently in the sumptuous technicolour description.[53] What has not been noted, however, is that Cnemon's interventions also have an intertextual function: it is the more lavish account that they prompt that allows Heliodorus to mark the distance between his festival scene and its skeletal model. Heliodorus' romance, twice the length of Xenophon's, is also (its author hints) twice the romance.

---

[50] Xen. Eph. 1.1.4–6; cf. also line 60 of the major papyrus fragment of *Metiochus and Parthenope* = SW 86 = HU 25 (with 29 n. 21). The 'marriage rejection' motif is also found at *Joseph and Aseneth* 2.1.

[51] Noted briefly by Gärtner (1967) 2080–1 (*non vidi* Schnepf (1887)). In Xenophon, Anthia appears first and is acclaimed by the dazzled spectators for her beauty (ἐκπλήξεως... καλή, 1.2.7), before being eclipsed by Habrocomes (πάντες ἰδόντες Ἀβροκόμην ἐκείνων ἐπελάθοντο, 1.2.8); in Heliodorus it is Theagenes who dazzles the spectators with his beauty (ἐξεπλήττε... κάλλους... κάλλος, 3.3.8), and is then 'defeated' (cf. ἡττηθῆναι, 3.4.1) by Charicleia. Xenophon's maidens and ephebes process 'in line' (κατὰ στίχον), carrying τὰ ἱερὰ καὶ δᾶιδες καὶ κανᾶ καὶ θυμιάματα (1.2.4); in Heliodorus, the Thessalian girls preceding the ephebic procession hold a dance 'in line' (στιχήρη, 3.2.2), bearing κανᾶ πεμμάτων τε καὶ θυμιαμάτων (3.2.1); the torch (λαμπάδιον, δᾶιδων, 3.4.6) is held by Charicleia. Anthia wears a χιτὼν ἁλουργής (1.2.6), Charicleia a χιτῶνα... ἁλουργὸν (3.4.2); Anthia's girdle (ζωστὸς εἰς γόνυ, 1.2.6) is elaborated into a lengthy ecphrastic description in Heliodorus (3.4.2–4); Anthia has κόμη ξανθή, ἡ πολλὴ καθειμένη, ὀλίγη πεπλεγμένη, 1.2.6, Charicleia κόμη... οὔτε πάντηι διάπλοκος οὔτε ἀσύνδετος, 3.4.8; both have bright eyes, although there are no linguistic parallels (Xen. Eph. 1.2.6 ∼ 3.4.6).

[52] Hardie (1998); Whitmarsh (2002b) 119–21.

[53] Winkler (1982) 140–4; Morgan (1991), 95–100; Hardie (1998); Hunter (1998) 53–6; Morgan (2004e) 535–8. See further below, pp. 172–5.

Again as in the first-century ephebic romances, the effect upon Charicleia and Theagenes is presented as a form of sickness (3.7.1, 3.11.1, 3.18.2, 4.5.2). Again we meet the paradox that the festival, the ritual designed to engineer social cohesion,[54] leads to erotic malady, and ultimately to chaos within the community, namely when the Aenianians kidnap Charicleia. The importance of this event to the entire polity, indeed, is stressed: an assembly is called (4.19), and the general Hegesias passes motions to pursue the Thessalians and kill them, banning any of their descendants from future rites (4.20.2–3). The charge to recapture them involves all the Delphians, including women, children and the aged: 'the entire city (*polis*) was keenly aggrieved at Charicleia's abduction',[55] applying itself 'collectively' (*pandēmon*) to the pursuit (4.21.3). This emphasis upon pandemic cohesion in the face of erotic crisis will be familiar from Chapter 1.

Charicleia and Theagenes is not, however, an ephebic romance, at least in the first-century sense. The wounds inflicted upon the Delphic community are not healed at the end; Charicleia is not reaggregated into the community. In fact, Charicles does reappear at the end to demand the restitution of his 'daughter' (10.34.3–4); but he admits defeat, and ends up reconciled to her new (and indeed old) identity as an Ethiopian princess. This episode serves to bring into focus the whole question of true and false beginnings – and hence the metageneric question, of whether this will be a Xenophontic centre–periphery romance, or a new kind of work that images the act of initiation as a journey to a wholly unfamiliar space (a journey that is, in Charicleia's case at least, also a kind of return). If Charicles represents the expectations of the first-century romance, the claims he stakes are partial and deceptive: 'When Hydaspes bade him state more clearly what he meant, the old man (who was really Charicles) concealed the truth of Charicleia's origin (*genous*) . . . he set out the story, summarising only the harmless parts'.[56] Charicles, who embodies the homing instinct of the conventional romance, is forced into compression and falsification of the true story. The ending of *Charicleia and Theagenes* thus rests upon a settlement between two different generic forces, one established and the other wholly new, each represented by a different claimant to Charicleia's paternity. The tension between the two is expressed by Theagenes, who,

---

[54] Heliodorus' festival is an ἐναγισμός, a ritual expiation of the pollution entailed by the murder of Neoptolemus at Delphi (2.34.7; see Hilton (1998) *ad* 3.1.1).
[55] πᾶσα ἡ πόλις ὑπερήλγησε τὴν Χαρικλείας ἀφαίρεσιν, 4.21.3.
[56] καὶ τοῦ Ὑδάσπου σαφέστερον λέγειν ὃ βούλοιτο κελεύοντος, ὁ πρεσβύτης (ἦν δὲ ἄρα ὁ Χαρικλῆς) τὰ μὲν ἀληθέστερα τοῦ γένους τῆς Χαρικλείας ἀπέκρυπτε . . . ἐξετίθετο δὲ ἐπιτέμνων ἃ μηδὲν ἔβλαπτε καὶ ἔλεγεν . . . , 10.36.1.

Hellenism at the edge 119

when asked by Hydaspes to explain Charicles' accusations that he abducted Charicleia, states:

All the charges are true. I am a bandit, a kidnapper, a rapist and a criminal – that is, as far as he is concerned; but to you I am a benefactor.[57]

Theagenes is caught between two narrative systems: he is the destroyer of one (Xenophontic) family romance, and the creator of another (Heliodorean) one. It is the second that wins out. The two fathers are hierarchically differentiated, in that Hydaspes is (to use Charicleia's words) 'my natural parent', whereas Charicles is 'adoptive'.[58] The celebration that concludes the narrative is arguably the most powerfully closural scene in classical literature, with disputes resolved, crowds cheering joyously, and Ethiopians and Greeks (including Charicles) alike sharing in the procession in celebration of the marriage and investiture of the two lovers as priests of Selene and Helios.[59] The priest Sisimithres declares that 'these things have been brought to pass through the assent of gods'.[60] Even Charicles recognises this ending, acknowledging it as the fulfilment of Pythian Apollo's prophecy, given him early on and repeated here (2.35.5 ∼ 10.41.2).[61] When the oracle was first given, the narrator had commented that 'prophecies and dreams are usually judged by their outcomes (*telesi*)':[62] that 'outcome' is effectuated in the end, the *telos*, of the narrative itself. The ending is thus signalled as a moment of truth and destiny, on many levels. Heliodorus implicitly constructs his as the true romance aretalogy of Helios and Selene, in implicit contrast to the weak, etiolated version of Xenophon.

NILOTIC NARRATIVITY

In this romance of initiation and defamiliarisation, the Nile plays a central role.[63] The river not only supplies the template for a Conrad-esque sense

---

[57] ἀληθῆ ... πάντα τὰ κατηγορηθέντα. λῃστὴς ἐγὼ καὶ ἅρπαξ καὶ βίαιος καὶ ἄδικος περὶ τοῦτον, ἀλλ' ὑμέτερος εὐεργέτης, 10.37.1.
[58] τὸν μὲν φύσει γεννήσαντα / τὸν δὲ θέμενον, 7.14.6 (also referring to Calasiris as a third father: cf. 2.23.2); see also 10.16.2 for Hydaspes' 'natural' parentage. On the theme of contested paternity see Whitmarsh (1998) and Elmer (2008).
[59] 10.41; cited as a paradigm case of total closure by Fowler (1997), with Morgan (1989b) more generally on closural mechanisms in Heliodorus. See further, Chapter 5 below.
[60] θεῶν νεύματι τούτων οὕτω διαπεπραγμένων, 10.40.1.
[61] The oracle is further discussed below, pp. 201–3.
[62] χρησμοὶ ... καὶ ὄνειροι τὰ πολλὰ τοῖς τέλεσι κρίνονται, 2.36.2.
[63] On the metaliterary role of the Nile, see esp. Plazenet (1995) 20–1; Whitmarsh (1999) 25–9; Elmer (2008) 432–47, who reads the quest for the origin of the Nile as a metatextual search for the origins of both Charicleia and the Heliodorean narrative itself.

of journey and destination as the narrative progresses upstream, but also figures the hermeneutic mystery itself. Greeks had been fascinated by this river since at least the time of Herodotus: as the priest Calasiris points out during a discussion of it, 'every Egyptian tale or story is most alluring for Greeks to listen to'.[64] Two questions in particular baffled Greek writers: why does it flood in summer,[65] and where are its sources?[66] These questions came to emblematise the enterprise of philosophical pilgrimage. Indeed, as one commentator has noted, the mystery in effect *constitutes* its significance for Greeks.[67]

An important intertext for the Nilotic narrative is Philostratus' *Apollonius of Tyana*, the importance of which for Heliodorus has often been noted.[68] The Philostratean sage's travels to India, Egypt and Cadiz constitute a *voyage initiatique* establishing his cosmic wisdom,[69] and his search specifically for the source of the Nile is a key moment in his quest for wisdom (6.17, 26). Intriguingly, this is the one quest that remains unfulfilled. Damis, the mysterious figure upon whose eyewitness account Philostratus claims to have based his narrative, finds the noise from the cataracts 'difficult and intolerable to perceive',[70] and so cannot proceed to the sources. Only Apollonius and his Egyptian companions continue, and even they can only behold the sources: the road up is 'impossible (*aporon*) to travel, impossible (*aporon*) to be conceived of'.[71] The protective shroud that Philostratus weaves around the sources of the Nile gives them an air of sacred taboo.

Heliodorus too offers stories about the sources of the Nile. In the second book, the Egyptian priest Calasiris reveals to the Delphians that the Nile originates in the southern mountains of Ethiopia, and offers an explanation for the flooding based around the Etesian winds (2.28.2–3). This is construed as a grand revelation, given that he accessed the information (he claims) in holy books that 'only prophets are allowed to read and

---

[64] Αἰγύπτιον... ἄκουσμα καὶ διήγημα πᾶν Ἑλληνικῆς ἀκοῆς ἐπαγωγότατον, 2.27.3.
[65] Aesch. *TGF* 3 fr. 300; Arist. *De inund. Nil.* = frr. 246–8 Rose; Nearchus *ap.* Strab. 15.1.25; Diod. Sic. 1.36.7; 1.38.1–41.10; Strab. 17.1.5; Luc. *Bell. Civ.* 10.219–331; Philostr. *Apoll.* 2.18; 6.1. See in general Postl (1970).
[66] Hdt. 2.34.1; Σ Ap. Rh. 4.269; Diod. Sic. 1.37; Strab. 17.4.1; Verg. *Georg.* 4.291–3; Sen. *Quaest. Nat.* 4a; Plut. *Mor.* 897f; Arr. *Anab.* 6.1; Ael. Ar. 48 *passim*.
[67] 'the Nile must remain elusive: this is the reason for its fame': Murphy (2004) 144. See also Plazenet (1995) 20–2, at 21: the Nile is 'la mesure du discours vrai'.
[68] On the importance of *VA* for Heliodorus, see Rohde (1914) 466–73; Bowie (1978) 1664–5; Anderson (1986) 230–1; 234; on his use of Philostratus more generally, Bowie (2008) 32–3 (also below, n. 101).
[69] Elsner (1997) 28–32. [70] χαλεποῦ... καὶ οὐκ ἀνεκτοῦ αἰσθέσθαι, 6.26.1.
[71] ἄπορον μὲν ἐλθεῖν, ἄπορον δὲ ἐνθυμηθῆναι, 6.26.2.

understand'.[72] As with all of Calasiris' portentous posturing, these claims are multilayered: readers cannot divine whether this is earnestly meant – there is in fact nothing recondite in this explanation[73] – and if not, whether the joke is on the internal audience or on us too.

Nevertheless, the invocation of the mysterious origins of the Nile plays an important kinetic role in the plot. In response to Calasiris' revelations about the Nile, Charicles now proceeds to tell Calasiris privately of how he travelled to Egypt, met an Ethiopian, and was entrusted by an Ethiopian with the care of the girl Charicleia (2.29–33). As a priest and surrogate father of Charicleia, Charicles serves as a doublet for Calasiris. Indeed, their stories show a kind of chiastic parallelism:[74] both lose their wives and, seeking solace for domestic grief, travel abroad for philosophical purposes, Calasiris to Delphi and Charicles to Egypt, 'to research (*kath' historian*) the cataracts of the Nile':[75] the reference to *historia* in Egypt underlines the Herodotean flavour, and subtly reinforces the link back to Calasiris' Etesian hypothesis.

Investigation into the Nile's mystery is thus woven into the text. It is in the context of these philosophical questing narratives that Charicles explains how he first came into contact with Charicleia. When we might be expecting disclosures about the sources of the Nile, it is upon *her* origins that narrative deliberates. When the Ethiopian ambassador initially hands over the girl, Charicles is not given the full story, but has to leave 'stunned and reeling, and like those who suffer a heavy blow, because I did not know the girl's story (*ta kata tēn korēn*): who she was, where she was from, or who her parents were'.[76] This sentence contains a double allusion, to both the titling convention for a romance (*ta kata*, or *peri*, + girl's name)[77] and the standard Homeric request for identification, 'who are you and where are

---

[72] μόνοις τοῖς προφητικοῖς καὶ γινώσκειν καὶ ἀναγινώσκειν ἔξεστι, 2.28.2.
[73] The Etesian hypothesis is already found in Herodotus (2.20). What is more, Calasiris provokes the Delphian priest Charicles to answer that he heard the same thing from the priests at Catadoupy (2.29.1) – which suggests that the information is hardly restricted even with Heliodorus' narrative universe. For Calasiris' mystic theatricality, see 3.17.1 (τερατεύεσθαι), and more generally Sandy (1982) 143–6; Winkler (1982) 145–6.
[74] At least, on Calasiris' first account of his journey abroad, which he has just given. Notoriously, he later claims to have been mandated by Persinna, the Ethiopian queen, to search for her daughter (4.8): see Hefti (1950) 72; and for attempts to resolve it. Winkler (1982) argues that it dramatises Calasiris' deceptive narration; Baumbach (1997) goes further, arguing that he invents the entire visit to Meroe.
[75] καθ' ἱστορίαν τῶν καταρρακτῶν τοῦ Νείλου, 2.29.5.
[76] ἀνιαρῶς ἄγαν διατεθεὶς καὶ ὥσπερ οἱ βαρεῖάν τινα πληγὴν εἰληφότες ὅτι δὴ μοι γνῶναι μὴ ἐξεγένετο τὰ κατὰ τὴν κόρην τίς ἢ πόθεν ἢ τίνων, 2.32.3.
[77] Whitmarsh (2005b).

you from?'[78] This knowing literariness reminds us that her origins are still a mystery for us too, and to re-emphasise the metanarrative significance of this moment, Heliodorus has Cnemon interrupt: '"No wonder", said Cnemon, "I myself am disappointed not to have heard – but perhaps I will"';[79] to which Calasiris replies that he will indeed hear. Cnemon plays the role of hyperappetitive narratee, in tension with Calasiris' artfully controlled manipulation of narrative flow. His butting in here characterises the response of a certain style of reader, desperate to know where Charicleia comes from, but forced to wait. The mystery of Charicleia's origins, and the central mystery of the text, thus borrows from the association of the Nile with recondite sources.[80]

The Nilotic pilgrimage narrative structures the geographical hierarchy of religions, with Greece at the bottom, Egypt in the middle and Ethiopia on the top (rather as *Callirhoe* ranks Sicily, Ionia and Persia).[81] Each corresponds to one of Charicleia's three 'fathers': Charicles, Calasiris, and her biological parent Hydaspes (as Chariton, again, associates each zone with a different lover of Callirhoe). There is also a sense of serial proportionality: Ethiopia is to Egypt what Egypt is to Greece. In the Greek tradition, philosophers travel to Egypt for their initiation.[82] The Egyptian Calasiris, however, travels to Ethiopia 'out of desire for the wisdom that they have':[83] similar phrases are used of Greek wise men who travel to Egypt.[84] Heliodorus implicitly trumps his predecessors (especially Xenophon) who present Egypt as a land of religious miracles: his own text goes one stage further.[85] It is significant, in this connection, that the first eight books are set in Egypt: this is the standard length for a prose narrative, to judge by Chariton, Achilles and Philostratus' *Apollonius*, consolidating the impression that the final two Ethiopian books constitute an appendage to the Egyptian *logos*.

The representation of Ethiopia is, however, complex and ambiguous. It is certainly idealised as a utopian community, characterised by the perfect

---

[78] τίς πόθεν εἰς ἀνδρῶν, sometimes with πόθι τοι πόλις ἠδὲ τοκῆες (Hom. *Od.* 1.170, 7.238, 10.325, 14.187 etc.); well discussed by Webber (1989) 3–7.
[79] μὴ θαυμάσηις, ... ἀσχάλλω γὰρ καὶ αὐτὸς οὐκ ἀκούσας, ἀλλ' ἴσως ἀκούσομαι, 2.32.3.
[80] Winkler (1982) 151–2 points to the various correspondences between the tale of Charicleia and Heliodorus' account of the ebbs and flows of the Nile.
[81] Esp. Dowden (1996) 280–3.
[82] E.g. Porph. *Vit. Pyth.* 11–2; Iambl. *Vit. Pyth.* 18–9. Pythagoras is sometimes said to have travelled to the sources of the Nile: see e.g. Diog. Laert. 9.36. On Egypt as the land of philosophical initiation, see André and Baslez (1993) 283–5.
[83] ἐπιθυμίαι τῆς παρ' ἐκείνοις σοφίας, 4.12.1.
[84] E.g. ἵνα τῶν ἐνταῦθα νομίμων καὶ παιδείας μετάσχωσιν, of Homer at Diod. Sic. 1.96.2.
[85] An idea already present in Apollonius' Nilotic journey: see esp. Philostr. *VA* 6.22.

justice of the gymnosophists, the Ethiopian royal advisors (see especially 10.10.3–4).[86] We also, however, find markers of cultural primitivism. The wrestling match between Theagenes and the giant Ethiopian dramatises cultural difference in an agonistic context, with the superiority of Greek intellect winning out over the dehumanised 'monstrous and bestially harsh lump'.[87] The culturally paradigmatic status of the match is brought out not only in the use of the phrase 'the Ethiopian' to identify the wrestler (10.31.4, 6), but also in the name of the wrestler's patron, Meroebus, seemingly chosen to identify him as an eponym for 'Meroe'. Theagenes, meanwhile, manages to defeat him 'in that he was a man familiar with gymnasia and oil since his youth, and skilled in the competitive art belonging to Hermes'.[88] The episode looks not only to epic precedent for the use of a wrestling match as a ritualised sublimation of competitive instincts (notably that between Telamonian Ajax and Odysseus at Hom. *Il*. 23.700–39), but also more generally to a series of mythical wrestling matches between Greeks and monstrous others (particularly Heracles vs Antaeus and Polydeuces vs Amycus).[89] Another negative marker is the practice of human sacrifice: although disapproved of and ultimately abolished by the gymnosophists, its long history of association with the most wild and uncivilised spaces (notably in Euripides' *Iphigenia in Tauris*) necessarily reflects badly on Ethiopian culture. (It is possible too that with the abolition of human sacrifice the Emesan Heliodorus means to remind us that Phoenicians too had a reputation for this practice, and might claim to have abandoned it.)[90]

This is not the only ambiguity. Both the idealisation and the barbarisation are strategies of 'othering' Ethiopia (as is the heavy emphasis,

---

[86] For utopian themes, see Szepessy (1957), Alvares (2002) 16–21.
[87] ὄγκον... πελώριον καὶ θηριωδῶς τραχυνόμενον, 10.31.5; cf. ὠγύγιος ἄνθρωπος, 10.25.1. On this episode, see esp. Morgan (1998) 72–7, tracing the complex interactions between this episode and Theagenes' Pythian exploits (4.2.1, 4.4.1–2); also König (2005) 134–5, seeing humour in the mismatch between Theagenes' vigour here and his passivity elsewhere.
[88] οἷα δὴ γυμνασίων ἀνὴρ καὶ ἀλοιφῆς ἐκ νέων ἀσκητὴς τήν τε ἐναγώνιον Ἑρμοῦ τέχνην ἠκριβωκώς, 10.31.5. Morgan (1998) 62 discusses other 'cunning' words used of Theagenes here: κατασοφίσασθαι (10.31.5), ἐσκήπτετο, ἐσχηματίθετο (10.31.6). This theme looks to Odysseus' guile in his wrestling match with Telamonian Ajax (Hom. *Il*. 23.700–39: πολύμητις... κέρδεα εἰδώς, 709; δόλον, 725), even if that contest is ended before a result issues. He also notes, however, (74–5) that the Greek Theagenes is the champion of the Ethiopian crowd, and that this victory marks his entry into Ethiopian society.
[89] For the monstrosity of Amycus, see Ap. Rh. *Arg*. 2.1–100 and Theocr. 22 (esp. 55–72).
[90] There is a human sacrifice scene in Lollianus' *Phoenicica*, although it is unclear whether that episode is actually set in Phoenicia. For the idea that Phoenicians have abandoned the practice, compare Philo of Byblus *FGrH* 790 F3b (where the past tense ἔθυον implies obsolescence, if it is Philo's rather than Porphyry's).

unparalleled in the other Greek romances, on the language barrier).[91] But despite some Herodotean references to differences in custom (*nomos*),[92] there is no attempt to represent an 'authentic' Meroitic culture: what Heliodorus gives us instead is an Ethiopian world filtered through Greek stereotypes of otherness.[93] The Ethiopian names reflect a promiscuous mixture of different non-Greek cultures: Hydaspes is named after a river in India (important for the Alexander tradition);[94] Persinna's name seems to be a bastardised feminine of 'Persian'; Sisimithres alludes to the Iranian cult of Mithras. At the level of religion, the Ethiopian Hydaspes claims to honour the 'local' (*egkhōrios*) gods Helios, Selene and Dionysus, and heroes Perseus, Andromeda and Memnon, as 'founders' of their race (10.6.3).[95] Had he wanted to choose deities to mark cultural alterity, Heliodorus could have done so easily; but he opted instead for recognisable Greek deities and heroes. The solar and lunar traditions surrounding Ethiopia we have already considered. Dionysus is a telling choice, as the deity who embodies alterity in dialogue with Hellenism, ever in transition between the familiar and the other. Perseus and Andromeda, too, signal the marginality of Ethiopia, belonging (as we have seen) to a classically Hellenocentric hub–periphery narrative. Perseus is thoroughly Greek and, while Andromeda is represented in some traditions as black, Heliodorus has chosen to represent her as white (his whole plot turns on this fact, which explains how Charicleia was born white).[96] Memnon, meanwhile, is the archetypal Ethiopian in the Greek literary tradition, since the Epic Cycle. This seems to be an example of what Spivak calls 'an abyssal specular alterity', 'the self othering the other, indefinitely'.[97] A Greek text reads Ethiopians reading themselves as Greeks would: Ethiopia is not so much an absolute other as a space where the patterns of mimicry and inversion traditionally ingrained in Greek representations of the other are played out to lurid effect.

An important model here is (once again) Philostratus' *Apollonius*, in which the sage travels to India and Egypt in search of wisdom: in India in particular, he learns of the insufficiency of Greek wisdom in relation

---

[91] 10.9.6; 10.15.1; 10.35.2; Winkler (1982) 104–5 and Slater (2005).
[92] 9.1.5, on different ways in which gold is imagined (νομίζεται) among Ethiopians and others; 10.6.3.
[93] Hägg (2000) pushes the evidence for authentic Meroitic features to its limits.
[94] The name is used of a 'dark' (*fuscus*) slave – perhaps Indian (Parker (2008) 157) – in Horace (*Sat.* 2.8.14); it may also recall 'Hystaspes', a common Persian name (which appears as 'Hydaspes' in the A recension of the *Alexander Romance* as the name of a Persian satrap (1.39.7–8)).
[95] 10.6.3 names only the heroes, but the three are named as τοῖς πατρίοις ἡμῶν θεοῖς at 10.2.2; cf. also 4.8.3: ἡμῖν πρόγονοι θεῶν μὲν Ἥλιος τε καὶ Διόνυσος ἡρώων δὲ Περσεύς τε καὶ Ἀνδρομέδα καὶ Μέμνων ἐπὶ τούτοις. Cf. also 9.1.4 for θεοῖς τοῖς ἐγχωρίοις.
[96] For the traditions surrounding Andromeda's colour, see Dilke (1980).   [97] Spivak (2004) 118.

to Brahmanic thought.⁹⁸ The voyage to India represents a challenge to received perspectives, requiring us to look at the world from a different vantage. This cultural reversal is itself, however, not straightforward, since the Indians' cultural superiority is constructed in markedly Greek terms. The king Phraotes reads Euripides (2.32), locals speak Greek (3.12), and we come across statues of Greek gods (3.13). Brahmanic philosophy too looks suspiciously Greek: their social theory is Platonic, their cosmology Stoic, and their utopian communism Cynic.⁹⁹ Philostratus' text is strangely duplicitous, at once radically challenging *and* reinforcing the Isocratean idea of Hellenism as a universal set of values.¹⁰⁰

IDENTITY FICTIONS

What this points to is a conception of identity not as an innate essence but as the product of human culture, forged in the perceptions of others. Alongside Heliodorus' narrative of Charicleia's return to her true, 'natural' homeland runs a recurrent interest in the possibilities for fictionalising identity. Calasiris is first seen on the banks of the Nile in Greek garb, and mistaken for a Greek by Cnemon (2.21.4–6; see also 4.16.9).¹⁰¹ As we have seen above, Homer, the author-figure par excellence, is miraculously reinvented as an Egyptian (3.14.2–4). At one point, Theagenes is credited with an ingenious argument for proving that Achilles was in fact a compatriot of his, an Aenianian, that is to say, from his own hometown (2.34.2–8). This, Theagenes claims, demonstrates that his race is 'truly Greek'.¹⁰² By Heliodorus' day, Aenis had grown into a small but significant Thessalian *koinon*; its history, however, was shadowy, and any traces in the mythical record exiguous.¹⁰³ Theagenes' sophistic argumentation recalls the strategies used by cities with marginal claims to Greekness to link themselves to

---

⁹⁸ Philostr. *VA* 3.18, 3.27.1; cf. 2.29.2. On Philostratus' *Weltbild*, see Elsner (1997).
⁹⁹ On these points more generally, see König and Whitmarsh (2007) 19–20.
¹⁰⁰ Parker (2008) 288–94.
¹⁰¹ This passage alludes to another instance of cultural misreading, the opening of Philostratus' *Heroic tale*, where the vintner mistakes the Phoenician for a Sybarite. ὁ Κνήμων ""Ελλην δὲ' εἶπεν 'ὁ ξένος;' 'Οὐχ "Ελλην' εἶπεν 'ἀλλ' ἐντεῦθεν Αἰγύπτιος.' 'Πόθεν οὖν ἑλληνίζεις τὴν στολήν;' 'Δυστυχήματα' ἔφη 'τὸ λαμπρόν με τοῦτο σχῆμα μετημφίασε.' (Hld. 2.21.4) ~ Ἀ. Ἴων εἶ, ξένε, ἢ πόθεν; Φ. Φοῖνιξ, ἀμπελουργέ, τῶν περὶ Σιδῶνα καὶ Τύρον. τὸ δὲ Ἰωνικὸν τῆς στολῆς ἐπιχώριον ἤδη καὶ ἡμῖν τοῖς ἐκ Φοινίκης. Ἀ. Πόθεν οὖν μετεσκεύασθε; (Philostr. *Her.* 1.1). Cf. also μεταμφίασαι at *Her.* 4.9. The theme of cultural travesty in the *Heroicus* is discussed in Whitmarsh (2009a) 216–19.
¹⁰² ἀκριβῶς Ἑλληνικόν, 2.34.2.
¹⁰³ The Ἐνιῆνες make only a single appearance in Homer (*Il.* 2. 749); Strabo's discussion emphasises their obscurity (9.4.11, 9.5.22).

famous 'mothercities' via invented myths and genealogies, a process that was given new impetus by Hadrian's Panhellenion.[104] It is possible, indeed, that Heliodorus is exploiting (even parodying) a Procrustean argument that was current in his own day, designed to furnish Aenis with a mythical prehistory to match its current status.

Most significantly of all, Charicleia, the emblem of the text,[105] looks Greek, and is continually referred to as such[106] – until we discover that she is ethnically Ethiopian. The wanderings of the lovers take us through a succession of false fatherlands and false fathers, until we reach the truth at the end. Like Homer in the passage we have discussed (3.14.2), Charicleia must make do with 'an apparent father'. The first is the Greek Charicles, who educated her and gave her his very name (2.33.3). At the end, when addressing Hydaspes, he refers to himself as 'a father not just in name, but I have become one too',[107] a paradoxical phrase that exposes its own captiousness (how can one 'become' a father?). The second is Calasiris, whom she describes as 'who seems to be, and is, my father' – another phrase that begs questions (how can one reconcile 'seeming' with 'being'?).[108] Calasiris himself, in response to a question as to whether they are 'in reality' (*tōi onti*) his children, describes how the lovers are his 'unmothered children', how the travails of his soul bore them, and how 'their disposition towards [him] was considered (*enomisthē*) nature (*phusis*)'.[109] This paradoxical opposition of culture (*nomos*) and nature (*phusis*), the blazons of sophistic speculation, parades the thematically central opposition between natural and artificial parentage, and hence identity too.[110] When Calasiris dies, Charicleia bewails her fate:

'O Calasiris,' she cried mournfully. 'No more may I call anyone Father, the best of names, for heaven has made it its sport at every turn to deny me the right to address anyone as my father. My natural (*phusei*) father I have never seen; my

---

[104] Curty (1995) presents the inscriptional evidence; see further Jones (1999), with 106–31 on the Roman period. I discuss the Aenianian claim more fully at Whitmarsh (1998) 101–4 (where I exaggerate their insignificance in imperial times).
[105] On Charicleia's metonymic relationship to the text, see W. Stephens (1994) 71–3. Philip the Philosopher (T XIII Colonna) casts his allegory of Heliodorus as a defence of 'Charicleia's' virtue. There is a joke along the same anthropomorphic lines in the margins of the title page of the Marcian MS of Heliodoros known as Z: ἡ Χαρίκλεια χαράν γε πάντως ἀποδίδει οὐ κλέος.
[106] 7.11.4; 7.12.4; 8.3.2; 8.3.5; 8.17.3; 10.7.5.
[107] μὴ μόνον ὀνομαζόμενον ἀλλὰ καὶ γεγενημένον, 10.34.4.
[108] τὸν δοκοῦντα καὶ ὄντα πατέρα, 7.13.1. The phrasing perhaps alludes to Favorinus' famous claim to excel in 'both seeming Greek and being one' (Ἕλληνι δοκεῖν τε καὶ εἶναι, *Cor.* 25): discussion at Whitmarsh (2001a) 119–20.
[109] παῖδες ἐμοὶ ἀμήτορες γεγονότες... φύσις ἡ διάθεσις ἐπ' αὐτοῖς ἐνομίσθη, 2.23.2.
[110] Rohde (1914) 489 n. 1 on the sophistic echo.

adoptive father, Charicles, I have alas betrayed; now I have lost the man who took me into his care, cherished me, and saved my life.'[111]

Despite her indication that there is a genuine ambiguity in her multiple parentage (*which* is she to call her father?), Charicleia acknowledges that there is, beyond the plethora of false fathers, one true, original begetter. This is the man who is by nature (*phusei*) her father. Although she has only ever known exile and constructed homelands, she nevertheless retains a strong sense that there is a true parent and origin; and it is towards the revelation of true, natural parentage that this narrative progresses. At 9.24.8, Charicleia observes that the recognition tokens she carries cannot constitute absolute proof, whereas 'maternal nature (*phusis*) is an undeniable token' of parentage.[112] Persinna does indeed accept her immediately, on production of the band at any rate (10.13.1). But Hydaspes requires much more proof, before finally his own parental nature overtakes him:[113]

Finally, he was defeated by all-conquering nature (*phuseos*): not only was he convinced that he was a father, but he also betrayed a father's feelings.[114]

Heliodorus now sets up the expectation that falsity and artifice will be supplanted, at the conclusion, by the truth and naturalness of genetic parentage. At one level, as we have seen, Hydaspes and Persinna are validated as natural parents by authorial comment. There is a twist, however. This emphasis upon natural parenthood stands in tension with the story of Charicleia's artificial conception. The climax of the recognition scene in the final book comes with the display of the painting of Andromeda, the sight of which at the moment of conception caused Charicleia to be born white. The Ethiopian princess's identity is finally confirmed when Sisimithres places the two side by side and the crowd marvels at 'the accuracy of the likeness', a phrase that invokes the discourse of realistic art criticism.[115] The whole scene is a reversal of the normal expectation, that a painting's truth is guaranteed by its resemblance to the subject: in this case, it is the reverse, the girl's identity is established through her resemblance to the artwork.

---

[111] Ὦ τὸν Καλάσιριν,' ἀνεκάλει κωκύουσα, 'τὸ γὰρ χρηστότατον ὄνομα καλεῖν ἀπεστέρημαι πατέρα, τοῦ δαίμονος πανταχόθεν μοι τὴν τοῦ πατρὸς προσηγορίαν περικόψαι φιλονεικήσαντος. τὸν μὲν φύσει γεννήσαντα οὐκ ἔγνωκα, τὸν δὲ θέμενον Χαρικλέα, οἴμοι, προδέδωκα, τὸν δὲ διαδεξάμενον καὶ τρέφοντα καὶ περισωίζοντα ἀπολώλεκα . . .', 7.14.5–6.

[112] ἀναντίρρητον γνώρισμα . . . ἡ μητρῶια φύσις, 9.24.8.

[113] Hydaspes makes further reference to his parental φύσις at 10.16.7.

[114] . . . τελευτῶν ἡττήθη τῆς τὰ πάντα νικώσης φύσεως καὶ πατὴρ οὐκ εἶναι μόνον ἐπείθετο ἀλλὰ καὶ πάσχειν ὅσα πατὴρ ἠλέγχετο, 10.16.2.

[115] τὸ ἀπηκριβωμένον τῆς ὁμοιότητος, 10.15.1; cf. ps.-Long *De subl.* 36.3. See more fully Whitmarsh (2001a) 85–7, and Reeve (1989) on the ancient traditions surrounding 'maternal impression'.

Countering the emphasis upon nature, then, is a focus upon the procreative power of art. The central conceit underlying Heliodorus' narrative is an extension, to a grand scale, of the parable found in Dionysius of Halicarnassus' *On imitation*: a rustic wife looked at paintings while having sex with her ugly husband, so as to produce beautiful children (fr. 6.1 U-R).[116] This story, for Dionysius, instantiates the triumph of culture over nature, of artful creation over genetics. Analogously, the scene that culminates *Charicleia and Theagenes* seems to show us that Charicleia's true point of origin is not her 'natural' father, but the artificial painting. Heliodorus' Ethiopia is a place of deep truths; but one of those truths is that mimetic artefacts possess an unopposable reproductive force, which can exceed mere nature.

Overall, the text associates cultural, mimetic identities with Greek more than any other. There is an implicit suggestion that the narrative is philosophically realist, peeling away the false layers of Charicleia's identity until we reach her true, natural, Ethiopian self. We can read *Charicleia and Theagenes* as the supplanting of a false, Hellenocentric, centre–periphery romance with a true, linear, Ethiopo-centric text. And yet the very ideality, the constructedness of Heliodorus' Ethiopia (discussed earlier), casts doubt on the ontological status of Ethiopian identity too, suggesting that this may perhaps also be another illusion. We could also point to the language of wonder (*thauma*)[117] and incredulity[118] that surrounds the revelation of Charicleia's identity: does this playfully signal the unreality of this narrative edifice? Perhaps this kind of doubt is simply a postmodern reflex, born of a reluctance to admit any essential truths. Certainly, the neoplatonist philosophy with which the text is suffused is itself fundamentally essentialist.[119] But romance is not philosophy: it may incorporate passages that speak of natural or true selves, but is also tends to expose and deconstruct these claims, pointing to an alternative conception of identity founded on the fictive power of the word.

---

[116] See further Whitmarsh (2001a) 73; (2002b) *passim*, esp. 115–16.

[117] Wondrousness: θαῦμα and cognates at 9.22.2, 9.22.4, 10.9.1, 10.9.4 (θάμβος), 10.12.1, 10.13.2 (θάμβος), 10.13.3, 10.15.1, 10.16.6, 10.30.5, 10.34.2, 10.35.2, 10.39.3; ἔκπληξις at 10.15.1, 10.30.7. On the wonder provoked by this recognition, and literary recognitions generally, see Cave (1988) 17–21, 44–5.

[118] Hydaspes at one point comments precisely that Charicleia's birth occurred 'against all plausibility' (παρὰ τὸ εἰκός, 10.14.5). At 10.13.1, the narrator (focalising through Persinna) calls the revelation 'the unexpected, unbelievable event' (τὸ τῶν παρ' ἐλπίδας ἄπιστον), and Persinna is said to fear Hydaspes' 'suspicion and disbelief' (ὑποψίαν τε καὶ ἀπιστίαν, 10.13.1; at 10.15.1, he is said to 'disbelieve no longer' (οὐκέτι... ἀπιστεῖν).

[119] Dowden (1996) bases his 'serious' reading of Heliodorus on the truth claims inherent in the philosophical undertow.

ALLEGORY AND METALEPSIS

If *Leucippe and Clitophon* and *Daphnis and Chloe* played with the convergence between narrative and ritual *telos* (end/initiation), Heliodorus takes this association to a whole different level. The end of *Charicleia and Theagenes* promises not just a *telos* to the erotic plot, but also a higher revelation of secret wisdom: the mystery of Charicleia's birth is aligned with the mystery of the Nile's sources, both arcane truths. The transformation theme that is so prized in the second-century romances is thus expanded in its scope: not only are the characters metamorphosed by their experiences, but also we as readers are promised our own far-reaching transformative event. The transformative effect of the narrative on the characters is thus shared by readers too.[120] In contrast to earlier romances (with the exception of the mystical Jewish *Joseph and Aseneth*), *Charicleia and Theagenes* offers its availability to be read as an *allegory*, a narrative encoding a final truth below the surface of the text.[121]

Heliodorus marks the transition to Ethiopia carefully. The beginning of book 9, where Syene (modern Aswan) is surrendered to Ethiopian control, marks a significant juncture. Such coincidences between textual segmentation, geographical boundaries and narrative meaning are not new to the genre: Chariton (as we saw in Chapter 1) uses the beginning of book 5 (and the second half of the romance) to mark the transition to Persian territory; the arrival at Alexandria that begins book 5 of *Leucippe and Clitophon*, again, 'has the earmarks of a new beginning'.[122] Heliodorus is subtler in his use of book divisions, but there is nevertheless a broad correlation between geography and clusters of two books (1–2 are primarily localised in Egypt, 3–4 in Greece, 5–6 in Egypt, 7–8 in Persian-dominated Egypt, 9–10 in Ethiopia). The transition to book 9 may have been experienced particularly keenly by ancient readers, since the standard length for a Greek romance seems to have been eight books (thus Chariton, Achilles, Philostratus' *Apollonius*).

The beginning of book 9 is significant at the thematic level as well as the paratextual. Just as readers cross the frontier into this new section

---

[120] As Elsner notes of Philostratus' *Apollonius*, 'the act of writing about pilgrimage is a surrogate form or repetition of the ritual' ((1997) 29).
[121] Ancient allegory is the subject of a number of recent stimulating discussions. Lamberton (1986) offers an excellent account of philosophical and theological allegories in late antiquity (see 149–52 on Heliodorus). Dawson (1992) considers allegory as a means of controlling and mediating cultural authority. On allegory and literary criticism, see Ford (2002) 67–79 for the classical period, and more generally Struck (2004). The diverse essays in Boys-Stones (2003) are also important. Most (2007) reflects on Heliodorus and/as allegory.
[122] Nimis (1998) 110; see further Whitmarsh (2009b) 44–7 and above, pp. 51–2.

130 *Part 1 Returning romance*

of the text, the surrender of Syene re-establishes the northern border of Ethiopia. We have earlier learned that the war is particularly over the 'contested' (*epimakhon*, 8.1.1) city of Philae,[123] 'subject to dispute' (*amphibolon*, 8.1.2) between the Ethiopians and the Egyptians on the grounds of different definitions of national borders: 'the Ethiopians define the borders of their country by the cataracts, the Egyptians considering that they should additionally allocate Philae to themselves because the act of settlement by the [Egyptian] exiles constituted an invasion'.[124] There is an implicit contrast here between natural, geophysical boundaries and those that derive from human creativity. The narrator's language subtly suggests the tendentiousness of the Egyptian claim: the Egyptians 'believe' that they should 'allocate' the land to themselves, whereas the Ethiopians simply align their territory with a natural geophysical feature. Heliodorus seems to be activating the cultural preference, which goes back to Herodotus (and probably beyond),[125] for states that recognise the integrity of physical space. Events at the beginning of book 9, then, serve to re-establish the rightful boundary between Egypt and Ethiopia: with the surrender of Syene comes the acknowledgement, on the part of the Persian satrap Oroondates, of the justice of Ethiopian territorial claims (9.6.5).

The beginning of book 9 is marked in temporal as well as spatial terms. The capture of Syene coincides with the summer solstice, when the Egyptians begin the Neiloa, the festival marking the first signs of the flooding of the great river (9.9). Both facts are, of course, highly significant: given the metaliterary roles that Heliodorus accords Helios and the Nile, the fact that the one is at its peak and the other swelling to bursting-point nicely figures the climactic stage of the narrative.

Tellingly, it is at this point that we meet the text's major indication of allegorical self-reflexivity, the digression on the reasons for the Egyptians' apotheosis of the Nile. The Nilotic allegory is distinctive in that it represents a rare case of intrusion into the narrative by the otherwise reclusive primary narrator;[126] in fact, this is by some distance his most substantial intervention in the whole text. Collectively, these features reinforce the impression that the transition to Ethiopia marks a particularly significant new phase in the text. Although Heliodorean allegoresis has received a fair amount of

---

[123] Notoriously, Heliodorus is unaware that Philae is actually an island.
[124] τῶν μὲν τοῖς καταρράκταις τὴν Αἰθιοπίαν ὁριζομένων, Αἰγυπτίων δὲ καὶ τὰς Φίλας κατὰ τὴν προενοίκησιν τῶν παρ' ἑαυτῶν φυγάδων ὡς ἂν δορυαλώτους ἑαυτοῖς προσνέμειν ἀξιούντων, 8.1.2.
[125] Herodotus' preference for natural boundaries is discussed in Romm (1998). The Persian invasion is already imagined as a transgression of the Hellespont in the *parodos* of Aeschylus' *Persians*.
[126] 'Heliodorus' primary narrator is an elusive figure. For much of the time he shows rather than tells' (Morgan (2004e) 526–33, at 526).

Hellenism at the edge

attention in recent scholarship on Heliodorean allegory, this has focused almost exclusively upon Calasiris' expositions, particularly his exegesis of Homer (3.12–15).[127]

'The Egyptians', we are told, 'manufacture the Nile's divinity (*theoplastousi*), and treat it as the greatest of the deities'.[128] This first explanation for this rests upon the river's status as a 'reflection of heaven', in that it waters the soil without the need for rain. Existence derives from wet and dry elements, and the Nile embodies the wet. As has long been recognised, this explanation borrows substantially but mischievously from the Jewish Platonist Philo.[129] This account, however, is immediately deflated. Not only is it presented as a contrivance ('manufacture... divinity'),[130] but it is also associated with 'the common people'.[131] The hierophantic stakes are thus upped; Heliodorus' Ethiopic narrative promises to take us deeper into the mysteries than the vulgar Egyptian account. As we cross the border, we also penetrate deeper into the truths of nature, realising that what we previously took to be revealed wisdom was in fact a smokescreen. We now proceed to a second stage of exposition:

This much they disclose to the public (*dēmosieuousi*), but to the initiates they reveal that the land is Isis and the Nile Osiris, under alternative names. The goddess longs for her husband when he is away and rejoices at his union with her, mourns his renewed absence and despises Typhon like a mortal enemy. There is I imagine a school of natural philosophers who do not denude to the uninitiated the allegorical subtexts sown within these stories; rather they guard them in the guise of a myth, initiating (*telountōn*) more clearly only those who are at the higher grade and already within the temple with the fiery torch of truth. May the gods look kindly on what I have said; the more mystic parts (*mustikōtera*) should be honoured with secrecy and silence, while events draw to a close in sequence at Syene.[132]

---

[127] The Nile passage is not discussed by e.g. Lamberton (1986) 149–52, Dowden (1996) or Hunter (2005), and only mentioned in passing by Most (2007) 166. See, however, Sandy (1982) 157–60 and Winkler (1982) 151–2.

[128] θεοπλαστοῦσι τὸν Νεῖλον Αἰγύπτιοι καὶ κρειττόνων τὸν μέγιστον ἄγουσιν, 9.9.3.

[129] Ph. *De vit. Mos.* 2.195–6: τῆς γὰρ χώρας οὐχ ὑετῶι καθάπερ αἱ ἄλλαι νιφομένης, ἀλλὰ ταῖς τοῦ ποταμοῦ πλημμύραις εἰωθυίας ἀνὰ πᾶν ἔτος λιμνάζεσθαι, θεοπλαστοῦσι τῶι λόγωι τὸν Νεῖλον Αἰγύπτιοι ὡς ἀντίμιμον οὐρανοῦ γεγονότα καὶ περὶ τῆς χώρας σεμνηγοροῦσιν ~ Hld. 9.9.3: θεοπλαστοῦσι τὸν Νεῖλον Αἰγύπτιοι... ἀντίμιμον οὐρανοῦ τὸν ποταμὸν σεμνηγοροῦντες... I write 'mischievously', since Heliodorus seems to be jibing at Philo's Alexandrian background: in spite of his Judaism, he is being bracketed with other theoplastic 'Egyptians'.

[130] θεοπλαστοῦσι, 9.9.3. The claim that they 'divinise' (ἐκθειάζουσιν, 9.9.4) the Nile also implies scepticism. The Egyptians' fondness for divinisation is a running theme: elsewhere we read of animals (ἐκθειάζεται, 2.27.3) and the Neiloa festival itself (ἐξεθείαζον, 9.22.5).

[131] ὁ πολὺς λεώς, 9.9.3.

[132] καὶ ταυτὶ μὲν δημοσιεύουσι, πρὸς δὲ τοὺς μύστας Ἶσιν τὴν γῆν καὶ Ὄσιριν τὸν Νεῖλον καταγγέλλουσι, τὰ πράγματα τοῖς ὀνόμασι μεταλαμβάνοντες. ποθεῖ γοῦν ἀπόντα ἡ θεὸς καὶ χαίρει συνόντι καὶ μὴ φαινόμενον αὖθις θρηνεῖ καὶ ὡς δή τινα πολέμιον τὸν Τυφῶνα

132 *Part 1 Returning romance*

Allegory, particularly in connection with Egyptian mythology, routinely distinguishes between demotic and initiated comprehension: for example, in his own account of the Isis and Osiris story, Plutarch divides 'the myths that all can freely hear' from 'those that are preserved by being concealed in mystic sacraments, and the secret liturgy of initiations, and unpermitted for the masses to see'.[133] In the Heliodorus passage, however, there are *three* groups of interpreters. The first is 'all and sundry', the *dēmos*, who interpret the divinity of the Nile in purely physical terms; the second are the initiates who know of the connection between the inundation and the myth of Isis and Osiris (including, no doubt, Plutarch, who reports it at *Isis and Osiris* 366a); and the third is the higher initiates, who understand the full meaning of the myth. Our narrator leads his readers to the second stage, but no further, theatrically stopping himself before he divulges too much. This is a productive position to occupy for an allegorical text, which must simultaneously demonstrate the existence of a secret and mask that secret from view. After all, a secret is a paradox, epistemologically speaking: it may be known *of*, but cannot be fully known, if it is to remain a secret. (Similarly, as we saw in the previous chapter, Longus represents his narrator as both explicating and preserving the religiosity of the sacred painting in the nymphaeum.) Readers of Heliodorus are positioned in the provocative, liminal space between, on the one hand, the 'all and sundry' who are wholly unaware of the existence of deeper meanings, and the initiates who fully understand what these are. This interpretative liminality mirrors the geographical liminality of Syene. Heliodorus borrows this allusive approach to sacred exegesis from a long tradition of Greek writers who use ritual silence to mark the ineffable: to mark the presence of extreme religious intensity, the absence of linguistic explication is a more powerful index than language itself.[134]

How do we read this passage in the wider context of the narrative? Does it mean that *Charicleia and Theagenes* is meant 'seriously' as an allegory?[135] Support for this position might be sought in the existence of an ancient

---

ἐχθραίνει, φυσικῶν τινῶν, οἶμαι, ἀνδρῶν καὶ θεολόγων πρὸς μὲν τοὺς βεβήλους τὰς ἐγκατεσπαρμένας τούτοις ὑπονοίας μὴ παραγυμνούντων, ἀλλ' ἐν εἴδει μύθου προκατηχούντων, τοὺς δὲ ἐποπτικωτέρους καὶ ἀνακτόρων ἐντὸς τῆι πυρφόρωι τῶν ὄντων λαμπάδι φανότερον τελούντων. τοῦτό τοι καὶ ἡμῖν εὐμένεια μὲν εἴη τῶν εἰρημένων, τὰ μυστικώτερα δὲ ἀρρήτωι σιγῆι τετιμήσθω, τῶν κατὰ Συήνην ἑξῆς περαινομένων, 9.9.4–9.10.1.

[133] ὧν πᾶσιν ἔξεστιν ἀνέδην μυθολογουμένων ἀκούειν... ὅσα τε μυστικοῖς ἱεροῖς περικαλυπτόμενα καὶ τελεταῖς ἄρρητα διασῶιζεται καὶ ἀθέατα πρὸς τοὺς πολλούς, 360e–f.

[134] E.g. Hdt. 2.171.2; Call. fr. 75.4–5; also Pausanias 1.38.7, 2.17.4, 2.35.8, 4.33.4–5, with Elsner (1992) 20–2.

[135] Merkelbach (1962) 282–3 seems to take our passage as evidence for the allegorical status of the romance as a whole. The most recent 'serious' reading is Dowden (1996).

allegoresis of *Chariclea and Theagenes*, attributed to the mysterious (and undatable) Philip the Philosopher.[136] But Philip's allegoresis itself has its own playful cunning, as Richard Hunter has demonstrated.[137] Should we then concede that the higher truth is simply a metanarrative device?[138] But this polarity seems ultimately reductive and anachronistic, depending on a sacred–secular opposition that has only limited validity for ancient polytheism.[139] Heliodorus is not a liturgical writer, but nor is he secular; neither the powerfully metanarrative role of this allegorical episode nor the comic elements to be found elsewhere reduces the climactic significance of the final books as a celebration of solar cult (emblazoned in Heliodorus' very name, and which his home town of Emesa had done so much to promote).

With the proviso that metanarrativity is not definitively antireligious, let us proceed to explore it in more detail. There are indeed strong hints in the passage cited above that foreshadow a convergence of the wider narrative and the allegorical exposition.[140] The story of Isis and Osiris offers itself as a variety of romance narrative:[141] 'the goddess longs for (*pothei*) her husband when he is away and rejoices at his union with her (*sunionti*)'. The language of desire (*pothos*) and sexual congress (*sunienai*) is marked. Another erotic suggestion is the narrator's claim that the natural philosophers do not 'denude' (the verb is *paragumnein*) the mysteries to the uninitiated. This hints at the nudity of the bedroom, from which prurient onlookers are excluded.[142] The sexualisation of mystery imagery is actualised, at the narrative level, in the final chapters of the romance, where the marriage of Chariclea and Theagenes is preceded by their assumption of the priesthoods of Selene and Helios. Selene is a regular *interpretatio*

---

[136] T 13 Colonna, translated at Lamberton (1986) 306–11. On this text, see Gärtner (1969); Lamberton (1986) 148–56; Sandy (2001); Tarán (1992); Hunter (2005). The text as we have it (the ending is missing) makes no explicit reference to our passage.

[137] Hunter (2005); see also Lamberton (1986) 152 (Philip's exposition 'verges at times on parody').

[138] 'It is not that Heliodoros is any kind of believer but merely that he must employ beliefs to illustrate the comedy of composing a romance. There has to be some Noble Message or other at the end, any one will do.' Winkler (1982) 157; similarly ludic readings in e.g. Anderson (1982), Goldhill (1995), Hunter (1998).

[139] Scullion (2005) pushes hard the evidence for an ancient conception of the secular, but I remain unconvinced that this is secularism in a modern sense.

[140] Most (2007) sees in the romance structure of home-coming a narrative actualisation of the hermeneutic process of allegory, which 'always tells a story of restoration, of restitution, of return to an origin thought lost' (164).

[141] Kerényi (1927) argues (see esp. 64–6, 88, 218, 223–38) that the Isis and Osiris myth is the basis for all romance narratives of love and separation. But this is the wrong way round: it is not that the myth powered the invention of the romance genre, but that Heliodorus has romanticised the myth.

[142] The bedroom of Persinna and Hydaspes contains a picture of Andromeda 'naked' (γυμνήν, 4.8.5); Arsace 'denudes' (ἀπογυμνοῦσα, 7.9.3) herself in her bedroom, albeit in sexually frustrated grief.

Graeca of Isis, and Osiris as Helios also appears, even if less commonly.[143] As the narrative closes, we leave the two lovers in a torchlit procession (compare the 'torch of truth' in the Nile allegory), with the 'more mystic parts of the wedding ritual about to be performed with more magnificence within the city'.[144] Just as in the Nile allegory the narrator revealed the myth of Isis and Osiris but kept secret 'the more mystic parts', so here the 'more mystic parts' of the romance (*muthos*) are kept from our view. This is not just coyness about sex (as, arguably, it is when readers are left at the bedroom door at Xen. Eph. 1.8.3); it replicates exactly the dynamics of the Nile allegory, with the reader taken so far and left to guess at the rest. The beginning of book 9 thus offers a strategically partial revelation of the end, at both the allegorical and the narrative levels: it designates a mystery, in the form of an absence. We must read on, into this new, closing phase of the text. Teleology is inscribed both at the narrative level (with the reference to events at Syene 'drawing to a close', *perainomenōn*) and the allegorical, where the language of 'initiating' (*telountōn*) as ever contains within it the idea of the end (*telos*). At the start of book 9, readers are asked to look forward to the 'close' of the text (*peras*, cognate with *perainein*), at the world's ultimate limit.[145]

The Nilotic allegory is reprised when Hydaspes enters Syene during the Neiloa (9.22), and this episode too conjures interesting metatextual effects. Here, the Egyptian priests show him their Nilometer, a well that also measures the rise and fall of the water table (such devices did exist, and were seen as technological marvels), and their horoscopes (9.22.3–4). The king is unimpressed: 'these things were not exotic (*xena*) to Hydaspes, and he did not especially marvel at them, for the same things happened in Ethiopian Meroe'.[146] The Ethiopian king's lack of wonder here contrasts with the fascination for Egypt shown earlier by Greeks, when Calasiris visited Delphi (2.27.3). Egypt is only wondrous when approached from the north. Hydaspes' *ennui* is compounded when the priests offer etymologies, numerologies and natural-historical disquisitions on the Nile (9.22.5–6): 'these miracles are not Egyptian things (*Aigyptia*) but Ethiopian things

---

[143] For Isis and Osiris as moon and sun, see Diod. Sic. 1.11.1; Plut. *De Is. et Os.* 372d–e (an equation that, Plutarch claims, τοῦ πιθανοῦ μέτεστι); Diog. Laert. 1.10, which may derive from Hecataeus (cf. *FGrH* 264 F3A).

[144] τῶν ἐπὶ τῶι γάμωι μυστικωτέρων κατὰ τὸ ἄστυ φαιδρότερον τελεσθησομένων, 10.41.3.

[145] In the closing *sphragis*: 'such was the close of the story of the *Ethiopian affair of Theagenes and Charicleia...*' (τοιόνδε πέρας ἔσχε τὸ σύνταγμα τῶν περὶ Θεαγένην καὶ Χαρίκλειαν Αἰθιοπικῶν..., 10.41.4). On the play between narrative and geographical *peras* see above, p. 115.

[146] καὶ ταῦτα μὲν ὁ Ὑδάσπης οὐ σφόδρα ὡς ξένα ἐθαύμαζε· συμβαίνειν γὰρ τὰ ἴσα καὶ κατὰ Μερόην τὴν Αἰθιόπων, 9.22.4.

(*Aithiopika*)', he counters, before insisting that it is Ethiopia that is worthy of their reverence.¹⁴⁷ This comment is in part an act of territorialism, insisting, in this contested space, on the supremacy of Ethiopia. But it also compounds the sense that Egypt occupies only an intermediary position in the allegorical schema: those (Greeks) who reverence its marvels should readjust their sights. Finally, in this most self-reflexive of texts, Hydaspes' words can be read as a play on the title of the text we are reading.¹⁴⁸ This is not just an Egyptian story like so many predecessors; it is an *Aethiopica*, the ultimate Greek romance.

Charicleia and Theagenes is, indeed, the 'ultimate' romance in every sense. Not only does it take us to the furthest reaches of human habitation, it also transforms the genre inimitably, offering an irreducibly polymorphous fusion of the comic and the mystic, the traditional and the exotic, the naturalistic and the mimetic. It is no surprise that this was (on the fourth-century dating, and assuming no lost works) the last Greek romance composed for half a millennium.¹⁴⁹ Like Ovid, another writer whose centrality to later literary traditions derives from the self-consciously marginal position he assumed for himself, Heliodorus pushes his chosen genre to the very limit, allowing no room for imitation and development. My central aim in this chapter, however, has been to demonstrate that this emphasis upon limits and marginality is, among other things, an allegory of life as a process of cultural estrangement and refamiliarisation. This text, with its relocation to the end of the world and its radical denaturalisation of the kind of Greek paradigms that we see in the first-century romances, looks more to late antiquity than to the classical past: to a world, that is, dominated by thoughts of otherworldliness, mortification and the rejection of established norms.

---

[147] ἀλλ' οὐκ Αἰγύπτια ταῦτα... ἀλλ' Αἰθιοπικὰ τὰ σεμνολογήματα, 9.22.7.

[148] The full title was probably τὰ περὶ Θεαγένην καὶ Χαρίκλειαν Αἰθιοπικά or similar (as the *sphragis* gives it: see 10.41.4, with Whitmarsh (2005b) 596–8). That it could be abbreviated to Αἰθιοπικά is clear from the earliest reference, in the fifth-century Socrates *Ecclesiasticus* (*Hist. Eccles.* 5.22).

[149] Musaeus' *Hero and Leander*, a hexametrical epyllion, does, however, have strong generic affinities (as the romance-echoing title, τὰ καθ' Ἡρὼ καὶ Λέανδρον, demonstrates).

PART II

Narrative and identity

CHAPTER 4

Pothos

The story told so far has been diachronic, describing (broadly) a shift from first-century romances preoccupied with the corroboration of civic Hellenism to Heliodorus' fourth-century *Charicleia and Theagenes*, which offers a radical challenge to Hellenocentric conceptions of identity. In this second section, I want to consider instead the durability of the romance narrative as a form of cultural expression (without sacrificing alertness to variety). Why was it felt that the romance continued to offer meaningful perspectives upon life over such a long period, despite the huge social and cultural upheavals between the first and the fourth centuries? My argument in this section is that the romance structure is both expressive and supple. It embodies a particular way of expressing the relationship between self and society, one that could be identified over a long period as characteristically Greek, while also accommodating the radical changes that Greek identity underwent over four centuries.

This chapter addresses the role of desire in the narrative economy of the romances. My aim here is not so much to diagnose the romances as concretisations of sexual *mentalité* in wider imperial culture – a task that has occupied much recent scholarship[1] – as to map out the multiple modes of desire that motivate the plot, and to use that as a basis for a cultural–historical account of the romance form (a project that will cover the next three chapters). My premise here is that the romance is, most fundamentally, a tale of desire fulfilled (fulfilled for the protagonists, at any rate). Sexual compatibilisation is, as we have seen, synchronised with (different varieties of) home-coming, an inscrutable serendipity that implies a powerful link between sexuality, the community, and the cultural–ethical values enacted by the protagonists.

Two principles are fundamental. The first is that desire is more than the urge to satisfy a physical craving. Rather, it is constituted, as Lacan

---

[1] Foucault (1990); Konstan (1994); Goldhill (1995); Haynes (2003); Morales (2008).

would put it, in the realm of the symbolic, where language and socialisation displace biological drives into specific cultural forms.[2] Narratives of desire are thus (also) socially normative: sexuality emerges in the interstices between the primal and the socialised selves.[3] For Lacan, the yearning for union with another person (or, as he would put it, 'the other') figures the fantasy of return to a pre-Oedipal state of maternal wholeness. The modes of desire dramatised in the romances also invoke ideas of the restitution of identity, albeit in different ways: the self is defined principally in relation to community rather than constituted solely within the psyche, since the desired wholeness is the integrated society rather than the child's bond with her or his mother. (This distinction between psychoanalytic and romantic is in line with the difference that Christopher Gill traces between post-Cartesian 'subjective–individualist' and older 'objective–participant' models of identity.)[4] The romancers are also more optimistic, presenting their erotic nosography in terms of a trauma that can be healed, whereas Lacan sees the subject's entry into the symbolic as the point of irrevocable alienation.

If, as Althusser claimed,[5] one of the roles of art is to translate ideology (which can be challenged) into abstract truth (which cannot), then the romance seems at first sight designed to naturalise and legitimise the traditional, dynastic structure of the Greco-Roman aristocracy – at a time when that structure was progressively threatened by ideals of radically anti-sexual asceticism (as embodied, for example, in Christian martyrologies like *Paul and Thecla*).[6] The notorious tendency of the romance to move from a world of oppressive hostility towards a 'happy ending' (discussed in more detail in the following chapters) suggests a process of narrative distillation, simplifying and resolving the morally, politically and culturally complex questions raised in the central part of the text. Chariton's narrator promises in his *intervento* at the start of his final book that there will be 'no more piracy, slavery, legal process, fighting, wasting away, warfare, or capture in this [book]; only legal love and lawful marriage'.[7] This prolepsis emphasises the transition from conflict to harmony, from complexity to resolution, from a world of status fluidity (in which enslavement or capture in war is

---

[2] Lacan's most lucid discussion of the nature of desire is in 'La signification du phallus', at Lacan (1971) 103–15. His value and limitations for classicists are discussed by Janan (1994), (2001); Porter and Buchan (2004).
[3] Lacan (1971) 110: 'le désir n'est ni l'appétit de la satisfaction, ni la demande de l'amour, mais la différence qui résulte de la soustraction du premier de la seconde'.
[4] Above, p. 41.   [5] Althusser (1984).   [6] For this interpretation, see esp. Cooper (1996).
[7] οὐκέτι ληιστεία καὶ δουλεία καὶ δίκη καὶ μάχη καὶ ἀποκαρτέρησις καὶ πόλεμος καὶ ἅλωσις, ἀλλὰ ἔρωτες δίκαιοι ἐν τούτωι <καὶ> νόμιμοι γάμοι, 8.1.4. See above, pp. 59–60, 65.

a possibility) to one in which identity is underpinned by law. This sense of closure is encapsulated in the final phrase, which in effect embodies a single concept (by hendiadys): 'legal love and lawful marriage'. The proper satisfaction of erotic urges – in the right place, at the right time, with the right people, in the right way – thus emblematises the whole complex of social, psychological, cultural and narrative closure.

As Althusser also argued in the same essay, however, art and literature also have the capacity to multiply perspectives on the ideology that they inhabit, to '"see" it from the *outside*, makes us "perceive" it by a distantiation inside that ideology'.[8] This leads us to this chapter's second fundamental principle: that desire is complex, paradoxical, sometimes contradictory.[9] While the romances certainly can (and should) be seen as normative in the way we have described, legitimising not only the institution of marriage but also the cluster of values (civic, aristocratic, often Hellenocentric) that here accompany it, there are also powerful cross-currents. The romances dramatise not only the dominance of the marriage plot but also *the processes* whereby that dominance is achieved; they show us the losers in love, the narrative roads not taken, the possible alternatives. They view the centrality of normative ideology both, as Althusser would have it, from the inside and without.

DESIRE, ETHICS, NARRATIVE

In Greek, 'desire' is denoted principally by three interrelated words: *pothos, erōs, himeros*.[10] Their etymologies are debated by modern scholars[11] and had seemingly become obscure already by the imperial period: commenting on a statue group personifying the triad, Pausanias expresses doubt as to whether they could be semantically distinguished from one another (1.43.6).[12] The romancers, however, use them in distinct ways. *Himeros* is a rare and *recherché* word, only appearing twice in the corpus.[13] It is upon *erōs* and particularly *pothos* that we shall focus here: not in terms of

---

[8] Althusser (1984) 177, specifically of Balzac and Tolstoy.
[9] See also Carson (1986) 77–97 (esp. 83–5) on paradox as central to romance accounts of *erōs*, with a different emphasis.
[10] The literary evidence for their collocation and differentiation is weighed by Headlam (1922) 358–60.
[11] Kloss (1994); Weiss (1998).
[12] This group was made by Scopas for Megara; the same sculptor also created a Pothos and Aphrodite for Samothrace (Plin. *NH* 36.25). One or other of Scopas' Pothoi is often assumed to have been the model for a Roman statue type representing a male nude: see Lattimore (1987) (with literature) on the reconstruction of the original.
[13] Char. 8.4.11, of the Egyptian sailors' 'affection' for Chaereas; Hld. 3.4.4, in a poeticising ecphrastic description.

wider cultural resonance (the history of sexuality)[14] or the literary history of sexual poetics,[15] but as a metanarrative force, a cipher for the romantic plot. *Pothos* in particular always creates a space for narrative potentiality: it marks an absence to be remedied, a gap to be filled, a crisis to be resolved, a journey to be undertaken. The primal meaning is not narrowly sexual; perhaps deriving from an Indo-European root denoting the activity of praying, it marks a sensation of separation from that which one craves, a yearning for what is absent.[16] This emphasis is notably central to Plato's pseudetymology in the *Cratylus*: 'it pertains not to that which is present, but to that which is elsewhere (*allothi pou*) and distant (*apontos*)' (*Crat.* 420a).

The relationship between *pothos* and its satisfaction is one of the most fundamental models for Greek narrative. Homer's *Odyssey* revolves around the twin urges of Odysseus' *pothos* for home and his family's *pothos* for him;[17] the *Iliad* operates a more complex web of *pothoi*, encompassing the Achaeans' *pothos* for the withdrawn Achilles and the pain of loss.[18] This association with mourning and bereavement (predicated, like sexual desire, on a keen sensation of absence) is, indeed, a persistent feature of the tradition. In the *Homeric Hymn to Demeter*, Demeter is described as 'wasting away in desire (*pothōi*) for her deep-girdled daughter' (201, 304), abducted to the underworld. In Aristophanes' *Frogs* it is a *pothos* for Euripides that stirs Dionysus to descend to Hades (53, 55, 66, 84 etc.). Death is the most extreme and intraversible (except in myth and fiction) gulf of separation between desirer and desired.

Pothos, indeed, has a more general association with destruction, for its subject as well as its object. It is a destabilising emotion, which can also portend tragedy for the desirer. The epithet *lusimelēs* (limb-loosing), found in early Greek poetry, is shared between *pothos* and *thanatos*.[19] This reflects in part the paradigmatic status of the Trojan War, where the *pothos* of Paris

---

[14] Above, n. 1.   [15] Fusillo (1989) 179–234.   [16] Weiss (1998) 32–4.
[17] Odysseus' *pothos* for home: *Od.* 13.219 (compare ἱέμενος at 1.58–9, and the travelling Telemachus' *pothos* for his home and parents at 4.596); Anticleia's death out of *pothos* for Odysseus: 11.196, 202 (perhaps echoed at Xen. Eph. 5.15.3); Penelope's *pothos* for her husband: 1.343–4, 14.144, 18.204, 19.136.
[18] Achaeans' *pothos* for Achilles: *Il.* 1.240; Achilles' *pothos* for the dead Patroclus: 24.6 (cf. more generally for *pothos* and mourning 5.414, 12.161, 17.439). '*Pothos* is a serious element in the lament for the dead' (Vermeule (1979) 154).
[19] Alcman fr. 3.ii.61–2 Davies; Archilochus fr. 196 West, both building on Hes. *Th.* 910–11 (ἔρος... λυσιμελής). For the association between death and desire in early Greek poetry, see esp. Vermeule (1979) 154–60; and, a general but thought-provoking account, Dollimore (1998) 3–35. More generally, the language of warfare and sex frequently converges (see Rissman (1983), on Sappho).

and Helen is typically blamed for the carnage.[20] Similarly, in Thucydides, a *pothos* for 'distant' (*apousēs*) spectacles and sights motivates the young to support the disastrous Sicilian expedition (6.24.3).[21] In a more ambivalent context, it is a *pothos* for conquest and exploration that is held by Arrian to have spurred on Alexander (*Anab.* 1.3.5; cf. *Ind.* 9), to a campaign that has both glorious and tragic elements. Both Thucydides and Arrian link *pothos* to a desire for movement, expansion, boundary-crossing, transgression; and both accounts have plausibly been read as deriving from 'quietist' critiques of imperialism.[22]

Pothos also, however, points to the devastating psychological effects upon its subject, particularly the male subject, who is normatively expected to be autonomous and self-controlled. Desire weakens, etiolates, reduces. In philosophy, as Nussbaum has influentially demonstrated, desire is treated from as early as Aristotle as a pathological mental state to be corrected by philosophical reflection.[23] It is in Hellenistic and post-Hellenistic philosophy, however, that it becomes a central issue. The schools dominant in the first two centuries CE (when the pre-Heliodorean romances were being composed), the Stoics and the Epicureans, viewed sexual desire as threatening to the philosopher. The early Stoics wrote enthusiastically on *erōs*,[24] which they seem to have seen (following Plato's *Symposium*) as a socially constructive desire for the good; they distinguished it, then, from the passions (*pathē*), i.e. irrational and unnatural movements of the soul or excessive urges,[25] false beliefs that should be 'cured' by philosophy.[26] *Pothos*, by constrast, is seen as an erotic 'appetite' (*epithumia*) for what is absent,[27] and hence both a distraction and categorically distinct from *erōs*. Epicureans, meanwhile, seem to have distinguished between 'natural' sexual desire, and the kind of emotional overload that comes from obsessiveness.[28]

Stoics and Epicureans alike held that the ultimate good for the soul was happiness (*eudaimonia*), a state of serenity to which violent passions were inimical (although they disagreed as to how to attain it). A passage from the second-century Stoic Epictetus articulating the antinomy between *eudaimonia* and *pothos* also helps to contextualise the models of desire we find in the romances:

---

[20] See e.g. Alcaeus fr. 42 L–P. [21] Cf. Nicias' δυσέρωτας τῶν ἀπόντων (6.13.1).
[22] Ehrenberg (1947) 62–7. [23] Nussbaum (1994). [24] Schofield (1991) 28 lists the titles.
[25] Schofield (1991) 28–31. Zeno's definition of a *pathos* (ἔστι δὲ αὐτὸ τὸ πάθος κατὰ Ζήνωνα ἡ ἄλογος καὶ παρὰ φύσιν ψυχῆς κίνησις ἢ ὁρμὴ πλεονάζουσα) comes at D.L. 7.110.
[26] Nussbaum (1994) 366–72. [27] πόθος δὲ ἐπιθυμία κατ' ἔρωτα ἀπόντος, Stob. 2.10c.7–8.
[28] Nussbaum (1994) 149–54.

It is impossible for happiness (*eudaimonia*) and longing for things not present (*pothon tōn ou parontōn*) to coincide. For that which is happy must possess everything it wants, resembling someone whose appetite is fully satisfied; no thirst or hunger can approach it.

Yet [Epictetus here imagines an objection to his claim] *Odysseus longed* (*epepothei*)[29] *for his wife and wept as he sat on a rock.*

Do you accept Homer and his stories (*muthois*) for everything? If Odysseus really wept, he must have been miserable. What genuinely excellent person (*kalos kai agathos*) is miserable?[30]

The interest of this passage for us lies in its sharpening of the contrast between philosophical and romantic views of *eudaimonia* and *pothos*. Epictetus critiques the Homeric Odysseus, the prototypical yearner for wife and home. Both the Stoic and the romance hero agree that happiness depends on the removal of *pothos*; where they differ is on the means of removing it. Odysseus' method is fundamentally narrative: his *pothos* drives him to set out to sea again, questing after his return home. The philosopher, on the other hand, can simply annul the effect of *pothos* through his own self-sufficiency. *Pothos* thus loses its narrative–dynamic function: rather than creating an absence that future plot will fill, it is simply bypassed. Philosophers, Epictetus makes clear, have no time for romantic 'myths'.

For the Greek romancers, desire is deeply ambivalent. On the one hand, it is the very lifeforce of the romance plot. The destructive effects of sexual yearning, destabilising the household and city, are the very precondition for romantic narrativity; and, conversely, the act of consumption or reunion, the satisfaction of desire, marks the exhaustion of plot. Desire is thus the prerequisite of romance narrativity. On the other hand, *pothos* in the romances is (as ever in Greek culture) a painful and potentially psychologically destabilising sensation of absence. It is

---

[29] My emendation: see following note.
[30] οὐδέποτε δ' ἐστὶν οἷόν τ' εἰς τὸ αὐτὸ ἐλθεῖν εὐδαιμονίαν καὶ πόθον τῶν οὐ παρόντων· τὸ γὰρ εὐδαιμονοῦν ἀπέχειν δεῖ πάντα ἃ θέλει, πεπληρωμένῳ τινὶ ἐοικέναι· οὐ δίψος δεῖ προσεῖναι αὐτῷ, οὐ λιμόν. – Ἀλλ' ὁ Ὀδυσσεὺς ἐπεπόνθει πρὸς τὴν γυναῖκα καὶ ἔκλαιεν ἐπὶ πέτραις καθεζόμενος. – Σὺ δ' Ὁμήρῳ πάντα προσέχεις καὶ τοῖς μύθοις αὐτοῦ; ἢ εἰ ταῖς ἀληθείαις ἔκλαεν, τί ἄλλο ἢ ἐδυστύχει; τίς δὲ καλός τε καὶ ἀγαθὸς δυστυχεῖ; Arr. *Diss* 3.24.17–18. The MSS reading ἐπεπόνθει πρὸς τὴν γυναῖκα is odd, both for the pluperfect and for the banal πρός. I propose thus to read ἐπεπόθει [πρὸς] τὴν γυναῖκα instead. ἐπιποθεῖν is a favoured verb in this section of the *Dissertations* (see 3.24.53, 86, 87). The philosophical implications of this passage are discussed at Long (2002) 191.

crucial to romantic ideology, however, that this pain is (unlike in philosophy) temporary and non-scarring: it is a sign not of moral deterioration, but of the absence of the socialised sexuality that is implicitly presented as necessary for civilised living. The 'happy ending' is the romantic transfiguration of philosophical *eudaimonia*,[31] supplied now not by psychic adjustment but by erotic, social and material satisfaction.

DESIRE AND ROMANTIC NORMS: CHARITON AND XENOPHON

The structure of the romance plot is, as we have often said, simple – primal, even. Desire is generated, frustrated, and then consummated. The generic centrality to the Greek romance of this 'schematic', iterable plot is well known. But 'plot' need not be conceived of as static and inert; reader-response theory has pointed the way to a more dynamic model, according to which literary meaning is cognitively recomposed by the reader in response to the indeterminacies, ambiguities and contradictions of the text.[32] On this interpretation, textual narrative is precisely not a structure, but the space where the reader is invited to structure her or his responses. Desire may be said to have a privileged role in this. In Peter Brooks' influential model of readerly cognition, the reader's craving for narrative design is stimulated by the representation of desire in a text, 'a form of desire that carries us forward, onward through the text'.[33] Brooks' thesis is that the various modalities of desire that we find expressed in narratives serve metanarrative functions, cuing the reader's complex and often contradictory desires for narrative consumption. This sense of the complexity, the opacity, the paradoxical nature of narrative desire will be one of the focal points of this chapter.

Desire is not, however, merely psychosexual. As we have said, it is also (in Lacanian terms) symbolic: it implies a craving for a socialised status, a stabilised relationship to others. Romantic *pothos* intimates an itch not simply for sex, but also for identity. Adapting Lacan, we might say that this *pothos* is the physical urge materially embodied in normative cultural

---

[31] The romancers do use the term *eudaimonia* and cognates, but of general material prosperity and good fortune rather than the psychic serenity of the philosophers. The questions of the extent to which and the ways in which the novels are philosophical remain much discussed: see esp. Morgan and Jones eds (2007).
[32] See esp. Iser (1978) 163–78.
[33] Brooks (1984) 37, with 13–21 on earlier theorists. Brooks' model lies behind Quint (1993), esp. 50–96; see also Mitchell-Boyask (1996).

discourse: sexuality as social praxis. Because it is socially inflected, *pothos* is also culturally variable: we would not expect to find the same ideals of identity expressed in texts composed across a span of three hundred years. So we should begin by mapping out the forms of desire articulated by and attributed to the principal characters of the romances, and the social values encoded in them.

In Chariton, the translation of sexual into social desire is conspicuous. The lovers are married at the beginning, so there is no sexual itch to be satisfied; the primary emphasis is upon the geopsychic gap between self and community. Callirhoe laments primarily for Sicily and her family. When she delivers her great lament on the banks of the Euphrates, it is *pothos* for her homeland (*patris*) and kin (*suggeneis*) that overwhelms her (5.1.3), in the context of a general reflection on the contrast between the barbarian continent of Asia and the Greek Mediterranean.[34] She does, for sure, express regret at the absence of Chaereas (at least, before she believes him dead) – but not before first lamenting her loss of parents, home and freedom (1.11.2–3) and of her father and mother (1.14.6–7). Her ambivalence towards Chaereas may be perhaps psychologically realistic, given that he has only recently kicked her to near-death; but it also points to a wider tendency in this romance to fold erotic desire into the desire for social identity. The same pattern recurs later on, after she discovers he is in fact alive: she laments first not being in Sicily and the absence of family, and only then Chaereas (7.5.2–5).[35]

Moreover, any desire she expresses for Chaereas is strikingly unerotic; rather, hers is an Andromache-like yearning for him as a husband and father (cf. 2.9.4–6), that is to say as part of the nexus of social identity and emotional support that she associates with home. Callirhoe's social desire contrasts with the more straightforwardly erotic instincts of the

---

[34] Above, pp. 51–2.
[35] 'L'amour de la cité d'origine est donc inséparable pour Callirhoé de son amour pour Chéréas: ce sont les deux faces, subjective et objective, d'un même ensemble de valeurs, dont elle est porteuse.' (Daude (1990) 85). It is true that there is at first sight a counter-example at 2.11.1: 'I wish to die the wife of Chaereas alone; this is dearer to me than my parents, fatherland and child – not to have experience of another man' (θέλω... ἀποθανεῖν Χαιρέου μόνου γυνή. τοῦτό μοι καὶ γονέων ἥδιον καὶ πατρίδος καὶ τέκνου, πεῖραν ἀνδρὸς ἑτέρου μὴ λαβεῖν). For the reasons given above, however, I disagree with Montiglio (2005) 233, who in an otherwise excellent discussion generalises from this passage to posit a 'weakening of one's fatherland as an existential reference'. What Callirhoe is in fact primarily doing here is reworking an amatory topos. Montiglio (perhaps following Goold's Loeb note) locates the wrong Homeric hypotext: Callirhoe is not inverting Odysseus' desire for home but retooling Andromache's words to Hector ('*you* are my father, mother and brother...', *Il.* 6.429–30) and their later reception (Sophocles' Tecmessa to Ajax: 'what country could I have except you?', *Aj.* 518).

romance's males: Dionysius, Mithridates, Artaxerxes and even Chaereas, whose general yearning to recover Callirhoe (3.5.9, 4.4.1–2) is on occasion presented in hazily sexual terms (3.3.4–7, where he longs for her *thalamos* or bedroom). The return narrative, however, implicitly corroborates, and lends normative weight to, Callirhoe's privileging of community over the satisfaction of individual desires. *Callirhoe* is antiquity's greatest articulation of the aesthetics of endogamy.

In the romances in general, erotic desire always betokens some kind of desire for identity, but each of the romancers models this in different ways. In Xenophon, what the lovers yearn for most is each other. As they set sail together, Habrocomes addresses as 'more desirable (*potheinotera*) than my soul', and extracts from her an oath to stay faithful 'if we are separated (*apallagōmen*)' (1.11.3–4). That oath, with all its implications, defines the narrative arc. When characters 'remember' it (2.1.5;[36] cf. 3.8.1, 3.8.7, 5.8.4), readers too are encouraged to do the same: the oath also constitutes a contractual promise on the text's part that the lovers will remain faithful to the end, as well as a metanarrative markers of the *pothos* that will only be satisfied in the closing scenes, the desire to 'get' each other back (*lambanein*, 5.5.11; *apolambanein*, 2.3.2, 3.3.2). In an Iliadic touch, that *pothos* slopes into quasi-mourning for the absent other: thus Anthia can be found 'lamenting for (*thrēnousa*)' Habrocomes (2.10.1), and Habrocomes imagines Anthia dying out of *pothos* for him (5.8.4). The distance between Chariton and Xenophon can be seen clearly in the episode where Habrocomes returns home without Anthia: he may think of his fatherland and his parents, but what he bewails is that he is returning 'alone', and will be seen by his parents 'without Anthia' (5.10.4). Even so, in Xenophon, the lovers' desire for each other is (after their marriage) not specifically erotic: it is the oath mentioned above, the compact of fidelity, that structures their *pothos* for each other. The emphasis is not on the itch for physical sexual release but, as we have said, it is on restoration of the marriage, on 'getting back' one's spouse. And as in *Callirhoe*, the location of that restoration in the lovers' homeland implicitly privileges the endogamous perpetuation of the local community. The slide between sexual desire and the socialised desire for community is visible in the occasional eroticisation of the relationship to the homeland.[37]

---

[36] If Hemsterhuis' supplement ἀναμνησθῆναι is correct. For the importance of the memory of the marriage vow, see Griffiths (1978) 416.

[37] τῆς πατρίδος ἐπιθυμοῦντες, 1.11.1; cf. 1.10.5, where the desire to 'get back' (*apolambanein*) the fatherland (*patris*) replicates the language used for the lovers themselves, noted above.

SEXUAL *TELOS* AND SOCIAL SERENDIPITY:
ACHILLES AND LONGUS

In the second-century romances, by contrast, consummation is delayed to the end, and becomes the primary object of the lovers' quest. In *Daphnis and Chloe*, the narrative crisis is generated by the lovers' lust for each other, which is retarded by their naive ignorance (and at times their physical separation). There is no expressed wish to return home, not least because they are not aware that they are away from it (after all, they do not know at this point that they are foundlings). The yearnings experienced by the lovers are, then, exclusively erotic: at first they cannot identify them as such ('Chloe had felt nothing unusual other than the appetite (*epethumei*) for seeing Daphnis wash again',[38] 'she had long desired (*pothousa*) to kiss Daphnis'[39]), but presently Philetas teaches them (albeit inadequately) to seek release in physical union (2.7). There are, however, other forces that progressively supervene onto the narrative. As recent scholarship has emphasised, cultural pressures emerge gradually, seeking to harness the lovers' desire to the social institution of marriage.[40] The lovers themselves may initially desire only erotic fulfilment, but others, notably Chloe's foster-parents (esp. 1.19.3; 3.25–31) have more pragmatic thoughts of dowries and social advantage. Accordingly, the lovers' own attentions shift as they recognise the constraints operating upon them, from sex to marriage. The role of the gods is also instrumental: the Nymphs and Pan are said by the narrator to intervene in the plot (communicating principally through dreams) in order to direct it towards their own preferred end (1.7.2, 2.23, 2.26–7, 2.30.4, 3.27.2–5, 4.34.1, 4.35.5). These gods are also desirers: 'we care for Chloe more than you do', the Nymphs tell Daphnis;[41] 'Eros wishes to make a story (*muthos*)' out of Chloe, Pan tells the brigand Bryaxis.[42] The last quotation in particular can be read as a metanarrative exegesis of the traditional role of divine desire in Greek narrative (going back to the controversial 'will' (or 'plan'?) of Zeus at *Il.* 1.5): a story is what the gods want, and what the gods want becomes a story. Amid the diverse desires of all these different interest groups, the happy ending of *Daphnis and Chloe* effects an accommodation: marriage is the meeting-point between the lovers' erotic desire, society's economic and dynastic needs, and the gods' requirements for this story.

---

[38] ἐπεπόνθει Χλόη περιττὸν οὐδὲν ὅτι μὴ Δάφνιν ἐπεθύμει λουόμενον ἰδεῖν πάλιν, 1.13.3.
[39] πάλαι ποθοῦσα φιλῆσαι Δάφνιν, 1.17.1.
[40] See esp. Winkler (1990) 101–26, Teske (1991) and more briefly Morgan (2004a) 11–12.
[41] Χλόης… ἡμῖν μᾶλλον ἢ σοὶ μέλει, 2.23.2.   [42] Ἔρως μῦθον ποιῆσαι θέλει, 2.27.2.

The same pattern can be glimpsed, more obliquely, in *Leucippe and Clitophon*. Clitophon has no interest in the local community (which barely registers in the romance): it is the promise of the performance of 'the act' (*to ergon*) that is the central narrative motor (1.9.5, 1.10.2, 1.10.6). Conversely, the postponement of that consummation – delayed first by Pantheia's interruption of the lovers' tryst, and secondly by the dreams visited upon both Leucippe and Clitophon warning them to wait (4.1.3–8, a rather obtrusive and psychologically underdetermined narrative device) – is a cause of repeated frustration.[43] It is, for sure, not that desire is entirely unrelated to socialisation. As we saw in Chapter 2, foreign lands (particularly Egypt) are presented as barbarian; this implicitly creates the impression of a desire on the part of the narrator (and principal character) for a return home, even if that desire is nowhere explicitly stated, and even if (as again we saw in chapter 2) the Greek–barbarian discourse is unsettled by Clitophon's Phoenician identity. What is more, even if the lovers' civic communities are invisible, their relationships with their parents remain important. Initially, both have seen their parents as impediments to their desire, and have hence willingly escaped from home.[44] The second half of the romance, however, effects a gradual reconciliation with the parents.[45] Desire is anchored here in familial identity, and in the restoration of parent–child relations. But never does either Leucippe or Clitophon take any decision that is said to be motivated by desire for return, community or family. In line with the general neglect of the *polis* in this romance, there is no sense of loss of status or identity, or indeed of its restoration at the end. Finally, as in *Daphnis and Chloe* the gods intervene to protect the marriage narrative: Aphrodite intimates through dreams (4.1.3–8, mentioned above) that she wishes them to delay consummation until the end, and Artemis' dominance at the end of the narrative dimly suggests a religious warning to avoid illicit sex.[46] Overall, however, these hints at the restoration of cultural

[43] Cf. the repeated 'for how long . . . ?' motif: 2.5.1 (μέχρι τίνος, ἄνανδρε, σιγᾷς; where Christenson (2000) ambitiously detects an allusion to Callinus fr. 1.1–3 Campbell), 2.19.1, 5.21.3, 5.21.4, 6.12.3. The phrasing is rhetorical (cf. see most famously Cic. *Cat.* 1.1), but already found in Homer (e.g. *Il.* 24.128–30).

[44] Clitophon: 'I am in the no-man's land between two opposing factions: *erōs* and my father are competing.' (ἐν μεθορίωι κεῖμαι δύο ἐναντίων· ἔρως ἀνταγωνίζεται καὶ πατήρ, 1.11.3). Leucippe: 'I beg you, in the name of the gods of foreigners and locals alike, take me away from my mother's eyes, anywhere.' (δέομαι . . . πρὸς θεῶν ξένων καὶ ἐγχωρίων, ἐξαρπάσατέ με τῶν τῆς μητρὸς ὀφθαλμῶν, ὅποι βούλεσθε, 2.30.1).

[45] First comes the news that Leucippe's father Sostratus had independently proposed the marriage of Clitophon and Leucippe (5.10.3–5.11.2); then Leucippe expresses mild regret for leaving her mother Pantheia (5.18.4); then Sostratus appears on the scene (7.12.3–*fin.*); finally, Clitophon is reunited with his father, Hippias (8.19.3).

[46] For these themes see Bouffartigue (2000).

and religious order are only hints: Clitophon's expressed desire, and indeed (to the extent that we hear of it) Leucippe's too, is primarily for sex.

There is one exception. The erotic narrative culminates with the lovers 'fulfilling our long prayed-for marriage rites',[47] a phrase that, in its deployment of pious language of prayer and rites, contrasts powerfully with the earthier sentiments Clitophon expressed earlier.[48] This is the first time that he has claimed to have desired (even 'prayed for') *marriage*. Has he come to accept the importance of marriage and social institutions? Or is his social conformism here entirely pro tem? Not for the first time in *Leucippe and Clitophon*, we are left guessing. Achilles gestures towards a Longan narrative structure of progressively socialised desire, but his narrator is too flittish to commit to it.

Whereas in the first-century romances *Callirhoe* and *Anthia and Habrocomes* the protagonists' desire for each other is inseparable from, even subordinate to, their desire for socialised living, their counterparts in *Leucippe and Clitophon* and *Daphnis and Chloe* desire primarily sex; marriage and social structure emerge apparently incidentally (for the lovers, at least) as a means to that end, rather than as ends in themselves. Marriage is a pragmatic accommodation between the initially divergent requirements of civilised society and the sexual self: 'I am in the middle zone between two antagonists', comments Clitophon near the start of his narrative, 'Eros and my father are at war!'[49] This shift follows the pattern we identified in Chapter 2, the general shift of emphasis from first-century *polis*-based models of identity towards interpersonal psychology and education (*paideia*) as initiation into civilised living as sanctioned by the gods. Whereas in the first-century romances civilised characters never desire sexual activity outside of the familiar space of the Greek *polis*, the second-century romances present a much more tense and harder-won accommodation between self and society.

CHASTE DESIRE

In Heliodorus, the desocialisation of the lovers' desires is even more extreme. In contrast to other romantic protagonists, Charicleia and Theagenes have only a limited sense of their ultimate destination,[50] and

---

[47] τοὺς πολυεύκτους ἐπιτελέσαντες γάμους, 8.19.2.
[48] Pious language: πολυεύκτους is picked up by εὐξόμενοι τῶι θεῶι, 8.19.3; ἐπιτελέσαντες suggests religious initiation (above, p. 102). Note, however, that γαμεῖν is used as a euphemism for 'have sex with' at 5.20.2!
[49] Ach. Tat. 1.11.2 (see n. 44).
[50] There is one reference to a 'hoped-for land' (ἐλπιζομένης ... γῆς, 5.4.7), which we may assume is Ethiopia.

never express any active desire to go home.⁵¹ In fact, it is not at all clear what 'home' would mean in this text: Charicleia and Theagenes react with delight (*hēdonē*) when they discover that Cnemon is Greek (1.8.6), which implies an emotional attachment to Greece; but of course Charicleia is ethnically Ethiopian, and it is in Ethiopia that the narrative concludes. Moreover, the extent to which Meroe can be said to be a 'society' is limited by its symbolic status as an idealised 'other' space. Scholars have often identified a utopian strain in this romance.⁵² This sense that Heliodorean space is metaphorical rather than 'real', or (better) defines spiritual status rather than cultural identity, is brought out in the Neoplatonic allegoresis of the text by Philip the Philosopher.⁵³ For Philip, Ethiopia signifies the dark, invisible matter from which Charicleia has emerged into the light (~Greece);⁵⁴ and presumably, although the incomplete text that we have does not make this clear, the ultimate return to Ethiopia figures the return of soul to the noumenal realm, whether through death or philosophical ascent. As we saw in Chapter 3, this allegorical aspect is already seeded in Heliodorus' text.

The only positive desire that Heliodorus' lovers express is for each other (e.g. 1.25.4, 5.4.6, 6.8 *passim*); otherwise, their motivation is purely negative, to escape present misfortunes, or (vaguely) to end their life of wandering (6.7.9, and see further Chapter 6 below). They seem to have no geographical destination in mind; they end up where they do thanks to forces beyond their control. Extraordinarily, this is a Greek romance in which neither of the principal characters expresses any interest in home-coming – principally because, as we have noted, it is questionable where 'home' actually is.

If they are uninterested in return, there is also a conspicuous lack of eroticism to their passion for each other. This is an exceptionally chaste text: unlike Chariton's, Achilles' and Longus' protagonists (and unlike Odysseus in Homer's ur-romance), Charicleia and Theagenes remain faithful to each other throughout, displaying an unwavering commitment to the ideals of sexual continence (*sōphrosunē*) and self-mastery. Clitophon, the hero and narrator of Achilles Tatius' romance, chastises himself for his 'untimely' continence,⁵⁵ and describes his transformation into a 'slave to erotic pleasure'.⁵⁶ This kind of behaviour is staunchly repudiated by Heliodorus' lovers. Before meeting Theagenes, Charicleia first refuses marriage completely, preferring instead to 'divinise virginity'.⁵⁷ Even after

---

⁵¹ Charicleia does, however, lament being deprived of οἰκεῖα ('familiar surroundings'?) at 1.8.2.
⁵² Szepessy (1957), esp. 244–51; also e.g. Kuch (2003) 218, and esp. Alvares (2002) 16–21.
⁵³ Ch. 3 n. 136.   ⁵⁴ Colonna (1938) 369.92.   ⁵⁵ ἀκαίρως σωφρονεῖς, 1.5.7.
⁵⁶ δοῦλος… ἐρωτικῆς ἡδόνης, 1.7.2.   ⁵⁷ ἐκθειάζουσα… παρθενίαν, 2.33.5.

submitting to her love for Theagenes, she claims that her love is no 'vulgar or populist lust', but a 'pure and continent (*sōphronōn*) desire (*pothos*)',[58] a polarity that (characteristically for this text) uses the language of social distinction to map ethical differentiation.[59] The primary emphasis is upon Charicleia, but Theagenes too shows self-restraint: when left unchaperoned with Charicleia, he can 'easily contain himself: although worsted by love he was the master of pleasure',[60] a phrase that alludes to (and translates into a positive register) the words of Achilles' Clitophon, cited above.[61]

But for all that it is easy to see how sexual appetitiveness might be stigmatised as vulgar, the idea of a 'pure and continent desire' remains paradoxical and troubling. What does it mean? This is a question repeatedly invoked, but never answered. At 4.10.6, Calasiris is counselling Charicleia as to how she should cope with her desire. The best course, he advises, is to turn to continence (*to sōphron*), as a way of avoiding the 'shameful name of "lust" (*epithumia*)'.[62] Yet in the preceding paragraph, the priest has referred to the omnipotence of Eros, who captures many virgins who are *in other respects* continent (*sōphronōn*). Calasiris seems to suggest *both* that desire necessarily implies loss of self-control *and* that one can react to it in a self-controlled way. In one address to Theagenes, she herself diagnoses the paradox:

There is only one way I know of in which I have not displayed continence (*sōphrosunousa*), namely in my original desire (*pothos*) for you. But even this was legitimate: for I gave myself to you on that first occasion not as one seduced by a lover but as one betrothed to a husband, and I have kept myself up to this point pure and untouched by congress with you. I have repulsed your many attempts, looking instead to the fulfilment of the lawful (*enthesmon*) marriage originally compacted between us and sworn in everything we said.[63]

---

[58] οὐ... δημώδης οὐδὲ νεωτερίζουσά τις ἐπιθυμία / καθαρός τε καὶ σωφρονῶν... πόθος, 6.9.4.
[59] Charicleia's language 'assimilates sexual passion to the radical politics of the lower classes' (Konstan (1994) 95). Cf. 3.3.8, where the δημώδεις γυναῖκες are said to lack self-control in the face of Theagenes.
[60] σωφρονεῖν ῥαιδίως... ἔρωτος μὲν ἐλάττων ἡδονῆς δὲ κρείττων γινόμενος, 5.4.6.
[61] Both passages also echo of Agathon's words at Pl. *Symp.* 196c: εἶναι γὰρ ὁμολογεῖται σωφροσύνη τὸ κρατεῖν ἡδονῶν καὶ ἐπιθυμιῶν, Ἔρωτος δὲ μηδεμίαν ἡδονὴν κρείττω εἶναι.
[62] τὸ... ἐπιθυμίας αἰσχρὸν ὄνομα, 4.10.6.
[63] ἓν μόνον οἶδα μὴ σωφρονοῦσα, τὸν ἐξ ἀρχῆς ἐπὶ σοὶ πόθον· ἀλλὰ καὶ τοῦτον ἔννομον· οὐ γὰρ ὡς ἐραστῆι πειθομένη ἀλλ' ὡς ἀνδρὶ συνθεμένη τότε πρῶτον ἐμαυτὴν ἐπέδωκα καὶ εἰς δεῦρο διετέλεσα καθαρὰν ἐμαυτὴν καὶ ἀπὸ σῆς ὁμιλίας φυλάττουσα, πολλάκις μὲν ἐπιχειροῦντα διωσαμένη, τὸν δὲ ἐξ ἀρχῆς ἡμῖν συγκείμενόν τε καὶ ἐνώμοτον ἐπὶ πᾶσι γάμον ἔνθεσμον εἴ πηι γένοιτο περισκοποῦσα, 1.25.4.

Parallels have, for good reason, been drawn with Christian texts like *Paul and Thecla*, where young female converts are said to renounce the marital relationships expected in their communities for a life of sexual purity with a holy man: the 'lust' that Thecla experiences for Paul (*epithumia*, 9) subtends a narrative not of sexual consummation but of religious conversion (the 'apostolic love triangle', in Kate Cooper's happy phrase).[64] Yet Charicleia's is a case not of sexual renunciation in the service of a god, but of radical sexual ambivalence: her *pothos* for Theagenes is both 'incontinent' (in that she experienced it at all) and 'pure' (in that she has sublimated it into a desire for marriage). In the schizoid moral world depicted by Heliodorus, desire is both a radical threat to moral integrity (as dramatised in the wild lustings of Demainete and Arsace, who exceed the bounds of *sōphrosunē*),[65] and simultaneously the means to spiritual fulfilment through the recognition of the divine kinship of two souls (3.5.4). This paradox of chaste sexuality is nicely captured by the ninth-century commentator Photius, who observes that Heliodorus depicts the 'desire (*pothos*) for *sōphrosunē*' (*Bibl.* 50a17–18).

Charicleia and Theagenes, thus, is differentiated from both the first-century romances, which broadly speaking present sociality as the object of desire, and the second-century romances, which dramatise a pragmatic but serendipitous convergence between sexual urges and social values. What motivates Theagenes, and particularly Charicleia, is a desire not for physical sex but specifically for 'legitimate marriage'.[66] For all that the phrase looks back to the endogamous narratives of the first-century romancers,[67] Heliodorus in fact presents it in a radically new way: not as the bedrock of Greek society, but as the only acceptable psychological compromise between sexual urges and moral purity. The marriage that concludes the narrative is not a legitimation of the Greek social order, but the culmination of a period of willing sexual self-restraint; and, tellingly, the marriage ceremony is indistinguishable from their ordination as priests of Selene and Helios, a conflation that invests the marriage with a sense of piety. At every stage, what Charicleia and Theagenes strive to fulfil is a desire that is *abstracted from* society, not (as in the first-century romances) merely *compatible with* it. Again, Heliodorus demonstrates an affinity with narratives like *Paul and Thecla*, in which the conception of desire initiates not (as in Chariton and Xenophon) a temporary social sickness that can be cured by transition rites, but an irreversible alienation from the traditional structures of Greco-Roman community.

---

[64] Cooper (1996) 51–6; see also esp. Brown (1990a) 155–9 and Burrus (2005).
[65] See esp. 1.9.3, where Demainete's gaze is said to 'stand outside' *to sōphron*.
[66] νομίμωι γάμωι, 6.8.6.   [67] νόμιμοι γάμοι, Char. 8.1.4; γάμον νόμιμον, Xen. Eph. 2.16.7.

The paradox of chaste desire, a desire that denies its own desiring, derives from Heliodorus' fusion of the romance paradigm with contemporary sexual ethics (which are themselves built on the kind of pothophobia we have seen in Stoicism and Epicureanism). The Roman world of the third and fourth centuries witnessed the emergence of radical dogma focusing upon the relationship of an individual to her or his body. In Christian asceticism, as Peter Brown has argued, sexuality becomes the privileged locus of human choice, an 'ideogram of all that [is] most irreducible in the human will', the site of the most important struggle for freedom, in a double sense of both spiritual liberation from the demands of the flesh and social liberation from traditional, 'pagan' Greco-Roman values.[68] This does not necessarily, however, argue that Heliodorus was a Christian (despite claims that go back to the fifth century).[69] Sexual abstinence was not exclusive to Christianity: already in the early third century CE, for example, we find Philostratus representing his holy man Apollonius of Tyana as sexually continent, and indeed demonising the lures of female sexuality.[70] Bodily asceticism was a dominant feature of the Neopythagorean movement that emerged in the third century,[71] and can even be glimpsed (through the literary veil of satirical enmity) in second-century figures like Proteus Peregrinus.[72] It is, I think, undeniable that fourth-century readers would have detected Christian resonances in the exaltation of sexual continence and in particular female virginity (as well as the Charicleia's miraculous rescue from 'martyrdom' at 8.9.9–15),[73] but I see no call to identify Heliodorus as either an active promoter or an opponent of Christianity: I read him as syncretistic rather than particularist, polyphonically universalist rather than partisan, a literary counterpart to culturally hybridising artworks like the Projecta casket and the Via Latina catacombs.[74]

Let us return, however, to Peter Brooks' observation that actorial desire is a motor of narrative. As we have seen, the desire of Charicleia and Theagenes is non-social, even (to the extent that it opens itself to allegory) non-mundane; even the erotic element is bizarrely self-cancelling. It is an extraordinarily *unenergetic* desire. The metanarrative consequence is

---

[68] Brown (1990b), at 481, and more fully Brown (1990a). [69] Ch. 3 n. 26.
[70] Philostr. *VA* 4.25.2–6, the Lamia episode immortalised in Keats' poem of 1819.
[71] Fowden (1982), esp. 36–8.
[72] Francis (1995) is interesting but erratic on this phenomenon. Peregrinus does become a Christian (Lac. *Peregr.* 11–16) but it is only one of many identities temporarily adopted by this problem figure.
[73] Charicleia's rescue from the pyre looks to a martyrological type-scene: cf. *ACM* 1.15, 2.3, 10.21, 12.4–5, and also *Paul and Thecla* 22. But it also has a more traditional heritage, leading back to Croesus on the pyre (Hdt. 1.87.1–2; Bacchyl. 3.23–56) via Xen. Eph. 4.2.
[74] Cf. e.g. Elsner (1998) 750–1.

that Chariclea and Theagenes seem, in comparison to other romantic figures, barely to participate in their own plot. Particularly in the second, more providentialist half of the work,[75] their capacity to act is limited by captivity (they are arraigned by Persian troops at 5.6; Chariclea is subsequently freed, but falls under Persian control in book 7, particularly after Calasiris' death), and they perceive themselves to be subject to forces beyond their control. What is interesting, however, is that they gradually learn to accept this conditioning, moving from angry resentment over their impotence (5.6.2–4, 7.14.7–8, 7.21.3–4) to acceptance of divine benevolence (8.11.5–9, 9.24.3–4, 10.9.3, 10.20.2). The narrative thus vindicates a mode of desire that is primarily passive. Calasiris' words to Nausicles, when the latter proposes to ransom Theagenes, are programmatic in this regard:

Excellent Nausicles, the wise man never stands in need; his will (*boulēsis*) does not exceed his means. He takes from the gods only those things that he knows it is right to ask for. So only tell me where is the man who holds Theagenes: divine intercession will not overlook us, but will give all that we want (*boulēthōmen*) to drive back Persian greed.[76]

Wisdom is here defined not only in terms of self-sufficiency (or *autarkeia*, as post-Hellenistic philosophy often names it), but also to the alignment of human will (*boulēsis*) with divine. The wise desire only that which the gods also desire. If we interpret Calasiris' words as a metanarrative pointer, then we can see that the plot is also driven by a chaste desire: a yearning for narrative closure that is tempered by respect for the gods' (and the author's) inscrutable intentions. In other words, our inescapable desire to know more of the narrative is playfully problematised in a text that associates such desires with uncontrolled excess.

DESIRE AND THE OTHER

We have focused thus far on the passions of the protagonists, but they are of course far from the only romantic figures who articulate desire. The romances are full of love rivals, whose primary narrative role, insofar as they inhibit the lovers in their quest for each other, is to serve as

---

[75] 'The focus of the plot shifts with the conclusion of Kalasiris' retrospective narration at 5.33.3. The impulse of the first half of the plot is primarily hermeneutic... [whereas] from 5.33.4 onwards... the romance becomes end-directed' (Morgan (1989b) 303).
[76] ὦ 'γαθὲ Ναυσίκλεις... οὐκ ἔστιν ὅτε ἐνδεής ἐστιν ὁ σοφὸς ἀλλ' ὕπαρξιν ἔχει τὴν βούλησιν, τοσαῦτα λαμβάνων παρὰ τῶν κρειττόνων ὅσα καὶ αἰτεῖν οἶδε καλόν· ὥστε καὶ φράζε μόνον ὅπου ποτέ ἐστιν ὁ κρατῶν Θεαγένους, ὡς τό γε ἐκ τῶν θεῶν ἡμᾶς οὐ περιόψεται ἀλλ' ἐπαρκέσει πρὸς ὅσον ἂν βουληθῶμεν τὸ Περσικὸν φυγαδεῦσαι φιλοχρήματον, 5.12.1.

blocking figures, i.e. challenges to be overcome (like the obstacles in a folktale) in the course of the narrative *Prüfung*.[77] They are typically figures who are both in positions of superior power over one or both of the lovers, and branded as morally and culturally inferior. In this way they can be clearly identified as expendable opponents of the dominant ideology of the romance; and conversely the fidelity of the protagonists can be demonstrated, in much the same way that the endurance of Jewish and Christian martyrs is dramatised through persecution narratives.[78] Obvious examples include the pirates Corymbus and Euxinus, the barbarian Manto and the bandit Perilaus in Xenophon of Ephesus; the would-be rapist Dorcon, the Methymnaeans and the decadent Gnathon in Longus; the thuggish Thersander in Achilles Tatius; and in Heliodorus the pirates Pelorus and Trachinus, the lustful stepmother Demaenete and the obsessive barbarian Arsace. Such figures of cultural and ethical otherness clearly, at one level, represent the polar opposite to the norms embodied in the protagonists.[79] This simple, normative picture is not inaccurate: as we have stressed throughout, part of what romance is about is the simplification of moral complexities for ideological purposes. Like the mythical paradigm of the story of the Lapiths and the Centaurs (figured on the cloak worn by Heliodorus' Theagenes, 3.3.5), the romances actively promote marriage at the expense of deviant modes of sexuality.

This, however, is not the final word. The process of identity construction through opposition always invites deconstruction, and the romances are no exception. There are several ways in which this simple process of allocation into 'positive' and 'negative' modes of desire is problematised: not displaced or challenged as such, but (to return to Althusser's phrasing) 'distantiated', 'seen from the outside' as well as the inside. The romantic presentation of alternative focalisers of desires opens up the possibility of counter-ideological identification, rather as (for example) the Iliadic depiction of Thersites, for all its descriptive and narrative execration, raises the possibility of an alternative, sub-elite perspective upon the action.[80] Like epic, the romance can mobilise 'further voices',[81] in addition to the dominant cultural and narrative articulation that triumphs at the end. I identify

---

[77] Or *agresores*, in Ruiz Montero's neo-Proppian account of the novels ((1988) 311–17).
[78] For this comparison see esp. Shaw (1996), Chew (2003). As is noted by Braun (1934) 23–118, (1938) 44–104, there are also many points of contact between the romantic representation of sexual aggression and Hellenistic Jewish versions of the Potiphar's wife story.
[79] See e.g. Scobie (1973) 19–34.
[80] Rose (1988). Whether Thersites is actually represented as sub-elite remains contentious (e.g. Marks (2005)).
[81] Lyne (1987), building on Parry (1963).

three kinds of further voice: (i) deviant desire; (ii) the pederastic; (iii) the viable alternative.

(i) Deviant desire

As we have said, there are a number of predatory, sexually aggressive desirers in the romances, who are usually marked as in some way culturally deviant: barbarians (typically Persians); criminals (pirates and bandits); or, in Longus, city folk, notably the Methymnaeans of book 2.[82] But the very representation of such figures also opens up the possibility of fleeting identification, even if that possibility is eventually discarded. As Stanley Fish argues, alternative interpretative choices are not simply cancelled once they have been proved wrong: 'in the end we settle on the more optimistic reading – it feels better – but even so the other has been a part of our experience, it *means*'.[83] It is, then, open to us to explore the possibility that within the stochastic framework of the normative desire of the protagonists, alternative, deviant models are provisionally available to readers.[84]

Rape is at one level, clearly, perceived by all Greeks as the moral and cultural antithesis of marriage: it defines the behaviour of tyrants, barbarians and animals, the aberrant Centaurs as distinguished from the normative Lapiths. When Chariton's Leonas suggests taking advantage of his status as Callirhoe's owner, he responds with outrage: 'Am I to play the tyrant over a free body? Will Dionysius, famed for his self-control (*sōphrosunē*), rape an unwilling woman, whom not even the pirate Theron would rape?'[85] Rape here finds its place in a matrix of sexual ethics that also organises social and psychological identities: on the one side tyranny and piracy, on the other the magnanimous Greek displaying his *sōphrosunē*.

At another level, however, the romantic representation of sexual aggression can be read as catering to rape fantasy, albeit safely neutralised by generic conventions. Helen Morales sets the numerous unfulfilled threats of violence against women (sixteen times in *Anthia and Habrocomes* alone, on her count) alongside the included reported tales of achieved violence

---

[82] Guez (2001) surveys such figures in Chariton, Xenophon and Achilles.
[83] Fish (1976) 470. See also ch. 1 n. 192.
[84] A theme of Morales (2004) on Achilles, e.g. 95: 'Achilles' moral universe is not sharply polarised and no one character or way of reading is stamped with a clear seal of approval. There is no internal "ideal reader" who serves as a metafictive mode of reading, but by dramatising the various ways of reading, the narrative pre-empts, reflects and positions its own readers.'
[85] ἐγὼ τυραννήσω σώματος ἐλευθέρου, καὶ Διονύσιος ὁ ἐπὶ σωφροσύνηι περιβόητος ἄκουσαν ὑβρίσω, ἣν οὐκ ἂν ὕβρισεν οὐδὲ Θήρων ὁ λῃστής; 2.6.3. This passage has a doublet at 6.3.7–8, where Artaxerxes rejects his eunuch's advice to abuse his position of power of Callirhoe.

(Pan/Syrinx in Longus and Achilles, Zeus/Europa, Apollo/Daphne and Tereus/Philomela), viewing them as alibis for repressed desire for sexual domination.[86] We could extend this category to include also threats of male rape, much less frequent though they are.[87] In general, scholars of the ancient world have a tendency to assume too quickly that literature straightforwardly promotes morality, but even the briefest of reflections on contemporary culture will teach us that audience identification can be complex and multiple: we may aspire to being both Luke Skywalker for his values and Darth Vader for his dark power. 'We are in conflict, even confusion, about what it means to affirm ordinary life... We sympathize with both the hero and the anti-hero; and we dream of a world in which one could be in the same act both.'[88]

Now it is, admittedly, impossible to give anything like an accurate assessment of this phenomenon in terms of the psychological reception of the ancient romances, particularly given how little we know about their readerships; but we should not assume without pause that affective identification took place in a more straightforward way than it does now. If, moreover, we read romantic rapists as channels for (meta)narrative desire, then we can offer a more precise account. The structural opposition between rape and marriage, after all, operates at the narrative level too. Whereas the romance marital plot gradually engineers a *telos* involving consensual marriage in a civilised environment, rape threatens a sudden, spontaneous, unilaterally enforced sexual consummation in a politically marginal space. It is a violation, in every sense, of the principles of deferral and intricate plot management upon which the romance rests. The link with pirates and bandits, recurrent across the corpus (whether by association[89] or in terms of real attempts)[90] is particularly significant here. Where marriage and the family represent stability and social structure, the narrative role of bandits and robbers is quite the opposite: embodying vigorously unpredictable, dynamic narrative energy,[91] they create sudden disorder, rapidly relocating

---

[86] Morales (2008) 53.   [87] Xen. Eph. 1.16; Long. 4.12.
[88] Taylor (1989) 23–4.   [89] Ach. Tat. 6.13.1, 6.21.3–22.2, 7.5.3, 8.5.6.
[90] Xen. Eph. 2.1–5; 2.13; Hld. 1.19.3–21.2, 5.28–9. The last three are technically cases of (attempted) coerced marriage rather than simply sexual violence. Guez (2001) notes that whether a romance represents bandits and pirates as sexual aggressors depends upon strategy, principally whether the erotic challenge rivalry comes from credible social equals (Chariton, Achilles) or from monstrous others (Xenophon, Heliodorus). Romance bandits are discussed by Hopwood (1998); see also McGing (1998). Incidentally, I think I hear in Achilles' references to *peiratai* ('pirates') an etymological pun on the root *peiran*, in the sense of 'make an attempt on a woman's honour' (LSJ s.v. A.IV, the meaning used at Ach. Tat. 2.4.3; also *peira* at 1.10.4).
[91] Kasprzyk (2001) argues brilliantly for the metanarrative role of Chariton's Theron; see also Daude (1990) 80–2, and above, pp. 46–7.

the protagonists and/or changing their social status (typically from free to slave).

When the plot is considered from a metanarrative perspective, it becomes immediately clear that a straightforward moral–cultural distinction between 'good' and 'bad' modes of desire is unsatisfactory. Marriage, sedentary life and kinship may be intuitively and empathetically preferable for many, but they do not make for good stories. Romance plot depends (as we shall see in more detail in the following chapter) on the tension between contrary principles: *both* the centripetal pull of stability and marriage, focalised by the protagonists, *and* the centrifugal push of hostile agents pursuing their own aggressive desires, be they sexual, mercantile or imperial. If it is right that the representation of desire within the text guides the plot's narrativity, then we need also to accept that deviant modes of desire also play their part in the complex plotting of the text. The rapist's desire figures what Brooks calls 'premature discharge', 'the possibility of [narrative] short-circuit', which typically consists in the wrong kind of erotic union.[92] Rape is of course never endorsed morally or successfully achieved, but – to reprise Fish's phrasing – 'the other has been a part of our experience, it *means*'.

(ii) The pederastic

Because of the narrative centrality of marriage to the romances, pederastic relationships are generally marginalised.[93] There is no mention at all of male–male love in Heliodorus. In Chariton,[94] there are a few hints surrounding Chaereas: when he is languishing in lovesickness for Callirhoe, 'the gymnasium yearned (*epothei*) for him' (1.1.10); she responds to his reproaches by alluding to his 'boyfriends' (*erastas*, 1.3.6); and the comparison of his friendship with Polycharmus and Achilles' with Patroclus (1.5.2) is at least suggestive. In all the other romances, by contrast, we have major characters who are defined as pederastic: Xenophon (Corymbus, Hippothous and Hyperanthes), Longus (Gnathon) and Achilles (Clinias). In Iamblichus, there may be a rare case of female–female homosexuality.[95] Some of these are typed as negative, and play the role

---

[92] Brooks (1984) 109.
[93] See, in general, Konstan (1994) 26–30 and Goldhill (1995) 46–111; also Effe (1987) (who sees this marginalisation as a sign of continuity with epic tradition). *Non vidi* Brioso Sánchez (1999), (2003).
[94] Sanz Morales and Laguna Mariscal (2003) observe that Chariton elsewhere alludes to Achilles' mourning for Patroclus in erotic contexts.
[95] Phot. *Bibl.* 77a20–2 = SW 196–7; Morales (2006).

of aggressive love rival discussed in the previous section (Xenophon's pirate Corymbus, Longus' appetitive Gnathon); others (Xenophon's Hippothous and Achilles' Clinias) may be more sympathetically portrayed, but their beloveds die tragically, in apparent contrast to the heterosexual happy ending. For this reason, scholars have often concluded that pederastic lovers in the romances serve primarily as polar antitypes to the heterosexual couple.[96]

This kind of sharp polarisation is undoubtedly found in imperial Greek culture, notably in syncritic debates over the merits of pederasty and heterosexuality (one of which, indeed, can be found in Achilles Tatius, at 2.35–8):[97] these rest on agonistic claims for the superiority of one mode of sexual praxis (as distinct from sexual identity)[98] over another. It is misguided, however, to see the romances in Foucauldian terms as symptomatic of a cultural shift away from a classical model of sexual relationships (promoting a phallocentric hierarchy between penetrated and penetrated, irrespective of the gender of the latter) towards a new, more symmetrical, conjugal ethics.[99] This is a simplification, not simply because the 'classical model' is open to challenge,[100] but also because pederastic love continued to be actively celebrated in the imperial period – as is demonstrated by texts as diverse as Petronius' *Satyrica*, Strato's collection of homoerotic epigrams (to which Rufinus' heteroerotic collection seems to be a response),[101] and the pseudo-Lucian *Amores*. There is no general aversion to pederasty in the imperial period; any *a posteriori* denial of the possibility of pederastic interest in the Greek romance is wrong-headed. In fact, the syncritic debates referred to above can be seen rather as evidence for a Newtonianisation of erotics, whereby pederasty and marriage were being seen as equal and opposite forces. This presumes that so far from legitimising a widely held belief that pederasty was an inferior form of sexual practice, the romances were intervening in a debate that was still live.

Do the romances accommodate a pederastic reading, focalising a form of desire that is alternative to the dominant, marital ideology? The best candidates for figures of pederastic identification are Xenophon's Hippothous

---

[96] E.g. Effe (1987) 101 (*Nebenfiguren*). The *pais* in Lollianus may be a pederastic boyfriend (Winkler (1980) 173–4).
[97] Also in Plutarch's *Amatorius* and the Lucianic *Amores*; for these debates see Goldhill (1995) 46–111; Swain (1996) 118–27.
[98] As Halperin (1994) emphasises, the debates are over the merits of different modes of pleasure and 'stylistics', rather than over the kind of moralised essentialism found in their modern equivalents.
[99] Foucault (1990) 228–32, critiqued by Goldhill (1995); Konstan (1994). Effe (1987), by conbrast, explains the privileging of heterosexual relationships primarily in terms of allegiance to the epic tradition (102–8).
[100] Above, p. 9.   [101] Höschele (2006), esp. 63–5.

and Achilles' Clinias. Hippothous, despite tragically losing his boyfriend, befriends the hero Habrocomes (playing the same role of staunch companion that Chariton's Polycharmus plays to Chaereas);[102] he becomes fortuitously rich, and finally ends up with a new boyfriend, apparently destined to live happily ever after. In one sense, then, the 'rule' that gay lovers in the romances must be doomed is broken already in Xenophon. Despite his first incarnation as both a bandit and a tragic figure, Hippothous metamorphoses into a positive figure, arguably into an icon of elite masculinity; and his pederasty does, in fact, seem to end happily.[103]

Even the story of his passionate affair with Hyperanthes (3.2) can be read in a more positive light. This shares many features with that of Habrocomes and Anthia: it tells of two beautiful young lovers, of approximately equal age,[104] who fall in love and meet at a festival; they remain true to each other despite love rivals and maritime misfortunes. The name 'Hyperanthes', what is more, looks like an attempt to outdo 'Anthia'.[105] This story, it is true, is condensed into a single paragraph of the romance, an act of epitomisation that illustrates the heterosexist priorities of the central narrative; but at the same time, the lack of proportionality points to the arbitrariness of the narratorial choice to privilege the marriage plot. With a different narrator, *Hippothous and Hyperanthes* might have been the primary narrative, with *Anthia and Habrocomes* as the subplot.

Gay subplots, then, can denaturalise the dominant, marital ideology by exposing its constructedness, the economy of selections and prioritisations that underlie any narrative of desire. This is brought out even more vividly in *Leucippe and Clitophon*, where the homodiegetic (i.e. character-bound) narrative mode draws attention to the idiosyncratic emphases of the text. Clitophon, the principal narrator, is far from omniscient, and his distinctive characterisation ('weak, cowardly, pompous, self-serving, gullible, wilfully blind about himself and others') colours much of what he says.[106] Now, that Clitophon's narratorial identity is shaped by his status as an *erōtikos*,

---

[102] On such friendships, see below, pp. 206–10.
[103] Watanabe (2003) emphasises Hippothous' status as an elite male. See also Morales (2008) 48 *contra* the argument of Konstan (1994) 56 that because Hippothous adopts Cleisthenes as his son this necessarily terminates the erotic relationship (the text is opaque: suggestive rather than decisive).
[104] The text is, however, uncertain. τὸ τῆς ἡλικίας ἀλλήλοις [<ὅμοιον> O'Sullivan] ἀνύποπτον ἦν (3.2.4). This has traditionally been taken to mean 'we were not suspected [viz. of pederasty] because we were of the same age', but David Konstan has cast doubt on this ((2007) 31–7). His objections, however, build partly upon the questionable premise that pederastic lovers must always and of necessity be asymmetrical in age.
[105] Konstan (1994) 27.
[106] Morgan (2004d), quotation from 501; see also Hägg (1971) 124–36 on Clitophon's limitations *qua* narrator, and further Whitmarsh (2003), Morales (2004) 78–82, Morgan (2007a).

one subject to sexual passion, is well established;[107] what has not been sufficiently emphasised is that his sexual identity is specifically heteroerotic. This is forcibly underlined in the debate on the ship that concludes book 2, in which he argues *contra* Clinias and Menelaus for the superiority of the love of women over boy love (2.35–8).

Clitophon's narratorial/sexual identity, indeed, is constructed dynamically by distinction from his cousin Clinias. As we shall see more fully in the next chapter, Clinias is constructed as the literary and erotic sophisticate that Clitophon is not, with a better intuitive understanding of the kind of plot in which they are immersed. What concerns us now, however, is that Clinias has his own erotic novella, culminating Hippothous-wise in the tragic death of his boyfriend Charicles in a horse accident ('tragic' in a strong sense, evoking as it does the demise of Euripides' Hippolytus). Again as with Xenophon's Hippothous, there are links with the main narrative. When Charicles' death is announced, Clinias' response – immobility (1.12.2), followed by a shriek (1.13.1) and a lament (1.14.1) – foreshadows directly Clitophon's thunderstruck responses to news of Leucippe's false deaths (particularly the first and third: 3.15.5–6;[108] 7.4.3–6). Clinias' novella offers us glimpses of an alternative eroticism, a narrative in which tragedy is real, rather than melodramatic misprision.

It is in the unequal treatment of these parallel stories that Clitophon's narratorial agenda is most laid bare. Despite burdening Clinias with his own erotic anxieties, Clitophon betrays an astonishing lack of compassion. When Charicles' corpse is brought in, it is 'a most pitiable, pathetic sight... no one present could refrain from tears'.[109] The language of pity and shared grief suggests Clitophon's collusive sympathy, but in what follows this is conspicuous by its absence. Nothing suggests the narrator himself is in tears. The twin laments of Clinias and Charicles' father are reported, with the facetious interjection that 'it was a contest of mourning'.[110] The narrative transition from Clinias' lamentation to the next episode, however, is so brutal that a textual lacuna has been suspected:[111] 'After the burial, I immediately set off hurriedly to see the girl.'[112] The burial is mentioned only in passing, as an impediment to the real aim of getting to the girl 'immediately'. Like its narrator, Clitophon's

---

[107] Morales (2004) 78–82; Morgan (2004d) 496. The unnamed primary narrator (and secondary narratee, i.e. Clitophon's 'addressee') explicitly describes himself as *erōtikos* (1.2.1).
[108] The reference here to the petrifaction of Niobe may to allude to Philemon fr. 102 KA or a common source.
[109] θέαμα οἴκτιστον καὶ ἐλεεινόν... ὥστε μηδένα τῶν παρόντων κατασχεῖν τὰ δάκρυα, 1.13.2.
[110] ἦν θρήνων ἅμιλλα, 1.14.1.   [111] Pearcy (1978).
[112] μετὰ δὲ τὴν ταφὴν εὐθὺς ἔσπευδον ἐπὶ τὴν κόρην, 1.15.1.

narrative betrays an indecent haste in the pursuit of its heteroerotic quarry (and in the neglect of homoeroticism).

The stories of Xenophon's Hippothous and Achilles' Clinias both reinforce the centrality of the marital narrative and expose the narratorial processes that create that centrality. The pederastic desires that would inspire a very different set of narrative priorities are repressed, but the work of that repression is visible.

(iii) The viable alternative

Most romantic love rivals are coded as dangerous and barbaric, but not all. In Achilles, notably, Calligone and Melite are presented as marital alternatives to Leucippe. Clitophon is initially betrothed to Calligone, whom he describes to Clinias as 'beautiful – at least until I saw Leucippe'.[113] She represents the road he would have taken had Leucippe not appeared, and indeed the threat of a most premature form of narrative discharge. Clitophon's impending marriage to her is revealed almost as soon as he starts speaking. Calligone represents too immediate a match, and not only in terms of narrative temporality: as Clitophon's half-sister, she represents the risk of incest, the logical outcome of the romance's instinct towards endogamy.[114] The romance plot, with its emphasis on the isomorphic symmetry of the couple, is haunted by the spectre of sibling incest (Heliodorus' Charicleia and Theagenes also claim to be brother and sister). Clitophon attributes to his father the desire to 'join the two of us [i.e. him and Calligone] *closer* through marriage':[115] the implication of the comparative is that marriage here is a simply the formalisation of the pre-existing familial bond.

This incestuous foreclosure, of course, must be and is prevented, by powerful divine abstractions: 'the Fates, who are mightier than humans',[116] and particularly by a dream-figure, who seems to be a Fury.[117] Clitophon,

---

[113] καλὴν μέν, ὦ θεοί, πρὶν Λευκίππην ἰδεῖν, 1.11.2.
[114] Commentators argue that 'le mariage entre frère et soeur d'un même père était autorisè par la coutume greque' (Garnaud (1991) 6 n. 1; cf. Vilborg (1962) 21), but in fact the examples refer primarily to fifth-century Athens, distinguishing their practice from that of other Greeks (Nep. *Cim.* 1.2; Sen. *Apoc.* 8.3; Minuc. Fel. *Oct.* 31.3; Philo *De spec. leg.* 22 adds the claim that Sparta permitted homometric and forbade homopatric sibling marriage). What is more, all are based on outsiders' perceptions, implicitly or explicitly contrasted with their own culture's practice (Seneca and Philo link it with incest). In any case, the report may simply stem from a hostile tradition on the relationship between Cimon and Elpinice (cf. Piccirilli (1984), although Plut. *Them.* 32 offers an apparent parallel).
[115] συνάψαι μᾶλλον ἡμᾶς γάμωι, 1.3.2. [116] αἱ . . . Μοῖραι τῶν ἀνθρώπων κρείττονες, 1.3.2.
[117] I propose this identification on the basis of the snaky hair, bloodshot eyes and torch: cf. Eur. *Or.* 256 (τὰς αἱματωποὺς καὶ δρακοντώδεις κόρας), with Willink (1986) 127 for further parallels.

we are told, has a terrifying dream: he is joined to (*sumphunai*) his half-sister and intended bride Calligone, up to the belly-button (*omphalou*); a bloody-eyed, snaky-haired female appears bearing a torch and a sword, and cuts the maiden away at his groin (*ixuos*, 1.3.4). The account eerily blends the sexual and the familial: *sumphunai* can suggest erotic combination (cf. 3.17.7, where it seems to mean 'hug'), but also alludes to their common (*sun-*) identity (*phusis*). The joining up to the navel is also suggestive: it necessarily fuses their genitals, but also implies their common umbilical relationship to their family, as though each figures for the other the shared mother they lack. It is, finally, significant that it is a figure with tragic associations who cuts them apart, since tragedy is the genre most closely associated with kinship violations: this intervention prevents the romance from an illicit, polluting union with a genre with which it seems at this point to have too much in common.

Melite too is 'truly beautiful',[118] a description that marks her (like Calligone) as a potential alternative to Leucippe. In this case, Clitophon does in fact marry. When he learns that Leucippe is still alive, he denies to Satyrus that this is a real marriage, on the grounds that it is as yet unconsummated (5.20.2–3); but he then proceeds to consummate it anyway. The marital relationship is significant in narrative terms, because it casts Melite as a potential *telos*. This point is explicitly made by Leucippe in her epistolary reproach to Clitophon: have I gone through all this suffering, she asks rhetorically, 'so that you can become what you have become to another woman, and I to another man?'[119] This idea that the beloved might be substituted by another seems to renege on the romance's generic contract, of absolute commitment to one individual.

---

[117] *LIMC* s.v. *Erinys* offers numerous parallels from the visual arts for snaky hair (nos. 11, 12, 20, 21, 27, 38, 39, 41–4, 49, 50, 52, 59, 63–4, 69, 70, 74, 85, 104–5), torches (23, 26, 31–3, 35, 58, 71–3, 75, 87, 92, 94–5, 100, 102, 109, 111), and both (9, 55, 57, 61, 90, 99). See *LIMC* 842 for discussion of these features, and 841–2 for whips, swords and spears (although I have found no parallel for a ἅρπη). Cf. also Vergil's Allecto, snaky-haired, and with (not bloody but) *flammea... lumina* (*Aen.* 7.448–50), who carries a torch, which she thrusts into Turnus' breast (7.455–6). The Furies are sometimes linked with the Fates (e.g. in Aeschylus' *Eumenides, passim*). Alternative identifications of the figure have been offered, but without any real evidence. Merkelbach (1962) 116 claims Isis, but without any credible basis (his reference to 'Xen. Eph. III.2.4' should no doubt read 1.12.4, but there too the figure is unidentified). Bartsch (1989) 86 comments that 'she may well be Fate herself'; Morales (2004) 52 n. 62 refers to a 'tradition of hybrids and monstrosities like the *mixoparthenos*'. The description of the figure seems to be drawn from Xen. Eph. 1.12.4, while Clitophon's reaction (περιδεής... ἀναθορὼν ἐκ τοῦ δείματος, 1.3.5) alludes to Xerxes' dream at Hdt. 7.15.1 (περιδεής... ἀνά τε ἔδραμε ἐκ τῆς κοίτης).

[118] τῶι ὄντι καλή, 5.13.1.

[119] ἵνα σὺ ὃ γέγονας ἄλληι γυναικί, καὶ ἐγὼ τῶι ἑτέρωι ἀνδρὶ γένωμαι, 5.18.4.

As a number of scholars have noted, Melite strikes an unusual figure in the gallery of romantic love rivals: mature but beautiful, powerful but sympathetic, an active erotic agent who is seemingly free from the usual stigmas associated with sexually dominant women.[120] She is hardly a 'realistic' figure, if by that we mean verisimilar; rather, she mirror-inverts the usual stereotyped sex roles, actively controlling the gaze, and assimilating her love objects (as Clitophon usually does) to comestibles and artworks.[121] She does, however, stand outside the idealised generic conventions of romance, which typically pit idealised love object against aggressive love rival: she is neither. Because she is generically anomalous, however, she is destined to be discarded unceremoniously. We never discover what happens to her: Clitophon's relentlessly egocentric narrative eye flits away from her as soon as she ceases to impact upon him. Even so, she offers (like the pederasts discussed in the previous section) a tantalising glimpse of an alternative sexual narrativity, one less constrained by the idealised marital economy of the romance plot: a world in which marriage is not the happy ending of the adventure of adolescence but the beginning of a new phase.

Melite is often compared to Longus' Lycaenion, in that both are mature, married women, seemingly less trammelled by society.[122] In fact, she is modelled most closely on Chariton's Dionysius, who initiates the romance corpus' other great second marriage. The intertextual relationship between the two is clearly signalled by the letter (mentioned above) in which Leucippe recriminates against Clitophon for marrying Melite: the precise allusions to Chaereas' letter to Callirhoe (attacking her for marrying Dionysius) emphasise the structural parallel between the two situations.[123] Indeed, this reinforces the sense of Melite's gender transgression, since she is playing Dionysius to Clitophon's Callirhoe.

Chariton's second marriage episode plays on the theme of doubling and iteration, even more than Achilles' does. For Callirhoe, Dionysius becomes a proxy for Chaereas, a second father for her child (cf. 2.11.2 for his 'two fathers'); for Dionysius, meanwhile, Callirhoe is the revenant of his first

---

[120] Cresci (1978); Robiano (2002).   [121] Morales (2004) 220–6.
[122] Robiano (2002); Morales (2004) 220–1.
[123] διὰ σὲ τὴν μητέρα κατέλιπον καὶ πλάνην εἱλόμην· διὰ σὲ πέπονθα ναυαγίαν καὶ λῃστῶν ἠνεσχόμην· διὰ σὲ ἱερεῖον γέγονα καὶ καθαρμὸς καὶ τέθνηκα ἤδη δεύτερον· διὰ σὲ πέπραμαι καὶ ἐδέθην σιδήρωι καὶ δίκελλαν ἐβάστασα καὶ ἔσκαψα γῆν καὶ ἐμαστιγώθην, ἵνα σὺ ὃ γέγονας ἄλληι γυναικί, καὶ ἐγὼ τωι ἑτέρωι ἀνδρὶ γένωμαι· μὴ γένοιτο. ἀλλ' ἐγὼ μὲν ἐπὶ τοσαύταις ἀνάγκαις διεκαρτέρησα, σὺ δὲ ἄπρατος, ἀμαστίγωτος γαμεῖς, Ach. Tat. 5.18.4–5; ἐγὼ μὲν ἐπράθην διὰ σὲ καὶ ἔσκαψα καὶ σταυρὸν ἐβάστασα καὶ δημίου χερσὶ παρεδόθην, σὺ δὲ ἐτρύφας καὶ γάμους ἔθυες ἐμοῦ δεδεμένου. οὐκ ἤρκεσεν ὅτι γυνὴ γέγονας ἄλλου Χαιρέου ζῶντος, γέγονας δὲ καὶ μήτηρ, Char. 4.3.10.

wife: 'I dreamed I saw [my first wife] clearly, grander and lovelier than ever', he says, the morning after Callirhoe arrives.[124] Again like Melite, Dionysius is a plausible second spouse, sitting uncomfortably in the polar romance economy of idealised youth and execrated love rivals: widely hailed as the dominant Ionian in station, culture and wealth (2.1.5, 2.4.4, 2.5.4, 2.11.2, 3.6.5, 4.4.3, 4.6.4, 8.7.9), he behaves towards Callirhoe with generosity and restraint. He even replicates the love-sickness, passivity and propensity towards suicide of a young romance lover.

Yet marriage cannot simply be reproduced like this, at least not in a romance plot. Callirhoe's decision to marry him is born not of erotic attraction but of pragmatic calculations (*logismoi*, 2.11.4) of the options available to her, given that she finds herself both enslaved and pregnant. Chariton's Ionia is a place where, for Callirhoe, ethical ideals are compromised by material necessities, and clear moral vision is impossible. (This sense of moral complexity is further underlined by the spatial liminality of Ionia, discussed in Chapter 1.) Her soliloquy at 2.11.1–3 illustrates this beautifully: addressing Chaereas, in the form of an image, and her unborn child, she imprecates them 'let us deliberate as to what suits us all collectively'.[125] She then recognises that her own desire to die rather than remarry is countermanded by her baby's putative desire to live: 'you cast a vote contrary to me, my child'.[126] This act of moral deliberation is philosophically defensible, corresponding as it does to the Stoic concept of 'the proper function with circumstance' (*to kathēkon peristatikon*): after proper reflection, a decision is taken on rational grounds to perform an action that would not normally be 'proper'.[127] Such calculations are alien to the romantic ethos, however, which demands an absolute alignment between desire and erotic praxis.

Callirhoe and Dionysius, then, is a novella that cannot end well. Dionysius ends the story heartbroken, seeking 'solace' (*paramuthion*) in his long journey home, the position of political authority entrusted to him by the Great King, and in the representations (*eikonas*) of Callirhoe at Miletus (8.5.15). Although Callirhoe has been compared to artworks from the very start (1.1.1) as a means of troping her beauty, these images have a different flavour: they signify as ersatz substitutes, markers of absence, consolations for the absence of the real Callirhoe (as her own *eikōn* of Chaereas does at

---

[124] εἶδον αὐτὴν <ὄναρ> ἐναργῶς μείζονά τε καὶ κρείττονα γεγενημένην, 2.1.2.
[125] βουλευσώμεθα περὶ τοῦ κοινῇ συμφέροντος, 2.11.1.
[126] ἐναντίαν μοι φέρεις, τέκνον, ψῆφον, 2.11.3.
[127] *SVF* 3.495–6; LS 59E. I thank Thomas Bénatouïl for pointing me to this connection.

2.11.1). Dionysius' second marriage replicates his first – by offering not the plenitude of life, but the *telos* of mourning.

Dionysius is not, then, an adequate marriage partner for Callirhoe; happy second marriages do not feature in the romantic script. Yet, nor is it the case that the restitution of the first marriage simply involves the recovery of a state of original bliss. Callirhoe's tactical gamble on her second marriage is also now part of her story; and the memories of this risk destabilising the happiness of the reconciliation. In the final book, Callirhoe sends a message to Dionysius, her second husband, promising that 'I am with you in spirit through the son we have in common.'[128] This letter, although nobly motivated ('it seemed to Callirhoe right and generous to write to Dionysius'),[129] is a forceful reminder that a woman who has married twice, and convinced her second husband that her first husband's child is his, can never fully escape her past. *Callirhoe* is not a straightforward tale of desire satisfied, for the reason that the desires of its protagonist are conflicted. Not only is she still implicated in the pragmatic deception of Dionysius as to the fatherhood of 'the son we share', not only is she still capable of intimate language with him ('I am with you in spirit'), not only does her phrasing manage to suggest to Dionysius that she left him unwillingly (8.5.14), but also the sending of this secret letter involves her in a fresh intrigue behind Chaereas' back: 'this was the only thing she did apart from Chaereas: she took care to conceal it, knowing of his innate jealousy'.[130] Both the reminders, of the son that she has farmed out to Dionysius and of Chaereas' jealousy (and hence of his brutal attack on her in book 1) serve as 'Aphrodisian footnotes', intratextual signals reminding us that the joyous resolution at the end is nubilated by a morally complex past that cannot be entirely effaced.

Chariton's is a multilayered and subtle narrative, the ending of which has a literary, ideological and emotional complexity belying the apparently simple, comic-style restoration of the idealised Greek marriage that took place at the start. Dionysius figures much of that complexity, by introducing the themes of duplication, iteration and substitution that haunt the final reconciliation. The narrative sophistication lies in the combination of a circular plot, in which the *telos* is a return to the beginning, with a linear plot, in which maturity brings with it experience and memories that cannot be expunged.

---

[128] εἰμὶ ... τῆι ψυχῆι μετὰ σοῦ διὰ τὸν κοινὸν υἱόν, 8.4.5.
[129] ἔδοξε ... Καλλιρόηι δίκαιον εἶναι καὶ εὐχάριστον Διονυσίωι γράψαι, 8.4.4.
[130] τοῦτο μόνον ἐποίησε δίχα Χαιρέου· εἰδυῖα γὰρ αὐτοῦ τὴν ἔμφυτον ζηλοτυπίαν ἐσπούδαζε λαθεῖν, 8.1.4.

READERLY DESIRE

There is, then, on the one hand certainly a strongly normative dimension to the narrative arc of romantic desire. Romances teach us, implicitly, that certain kinds of desire are better than other kinds. In the first-century romance, the distinction is between endogamous and exogamous desire. The second-century romance enacts an ethical compatibilisation between the urges of premarital sexuality with the requirement of marriage. Heliodorus plays off vulgar, appetitive desire against its sublimated, divine counterpart. There is, as we have noted, a conservative, socially consolidatory element to all romance, in that the return on which it is predicated implicitly legitimises a prior status quo. Homer's *Odyssey*, in this respect as in so many, points the way: a narrative of restoration of the patriarchal, aristocratic *oikos*, and of the peace of the Ithacan community. In the *Odyssey* as in the romances, the erotic narrative of desire fulfilled is overlain with moral values.

But, as we have also seen, this will not do as a complete reading, either of the *Odyssey* or of the romances. Within the normative narrative of desire properly fulfilled are a number of other more or less successful erotic subplots. In the *Odyssey*, these are limited primarily to the archipelago narrative: the stories of Calypso, Nausicaa and Circe are bounded both territorially by island coastlines and episodically by their sequential discreteness.[131] In the romances too, we can choose either to follow the teleological thrust of the normative narrative, or choose to explore the microecologies of desire that are narrated en route. Readers of romance are given *both* the ineluctable teleology of marital ideology *and* the toolkit for deconstructing it.

Can we then map out the ways in which the reader is activated as a desiring agent within the text? The famous Byzantine epigram in iambic trimeters on Achilles Tatius by Photius or Leon the philosopher, as Helen Morales has shrewdly observed, points the way to different interpretative strategies of romantic narrative:[132]

> A bitter love, but a continent (*sōphrōn*) life
> The story of Cleitophon reveals.
> But the most continent (*sōphronestatos*) life of Leucippe
> Amazes everyone, how she was beaten,
> Shorn and abused,
> And (greatest of all) endured three deaths.
> If you too wish to be continent (*sōphronein*), friend,
> Do not look at the depiction's marginal sights (*parergon thean*),

[131] Mossman (2010) discusses the poetics of island narratives.   [132] Morales (2004) 227–8.

> But first learn the destination of the narrative;
> For it marries off those who desire (*pothountas*) prudently.[133]

As Morales proceeds to observe, the poet encourages us to read for the end, for the marriage and the normative moral virtue of continence (*sōphrosunē*), but also adverts to (while appearing to disparage) the 'incidental sights' of the text. The poem builds up a series of contrasts, between *sōphrosunē* and its implied opposite, between visual pleasure ('depiction[134] ... sights') and moral 'learning'. In fact, one of the controlling oppositions is borrowed from the romance structure itself, namely the metaphor of the journey: the poet sets a straightforward, linear journey towards 'the destination of the tale' against the 'marginal sights', where *parergon* implies deviation from a course. The opposition is clearly hierarchical, since the language of *sōphrosunē* is so visibly normative, and since the imperatives directly interpellate the reader into that normative evaluative framework. But the conditional clause ('*if* you too wish to be continent...') also offers a degree of choice, predicated upon the reader's own wishes: what if we decide against a continent reading of the poem? Indeed, we might even say that the poem subverts its own *prima facie* insistence on *sōphrosunē*, by insisting that any attempt to read *Leucippe and Clitophon* as though it were a Heliodorean narrative of chaste desire will inevitably involve wilful myopia. Indeed Photius, if he is the author, well understood the 'excessively shameful and impure contents' of Achilles' romance.[135]

This opposition between teleological and deviant readings will occupy us for much of the remainder of this book, where I shall argue that the romances theorise their own reading strategies. For now I want to focus more narrowly upon the role that the epigrammatist gives to the reader's own will: the kind of reading we produce, he perceptively observes, is dependent upon what kind of person we want to be ('If you too wish to be continent...'). Readers too have desires, and these do not necessarily map onto the dominant, marriage-based ideology of the return narrative.

---

[133] Or 'marries off prudently those who desire'. Ἔρωτα πικρόν, ἀλλὰ σώφρονα βίον / ὁ Κλειτοφῶντος ὥσπερ ἐμφαίνει λόγος·/ ὁ Λευκίππης δὲ σωφρονέστατος βίος / ἅπαντας ἐξίστησι, πῶς τετυμμένη / κεκαρμένη τε καὶ κατηχρειωμένη, / τὸ δὴ μέγιστον, τρὶς θανοῦσ᾽ ἐκαρτέρει. / εἴπερ δὲ καὶ σὺ σωφρονεῖν θέληις, φίλος, / μὴ τὴν πάρεργον τῆς γραφῆς σκόπει θέαν, / τὴν τοῦ λόγου δὲ πρῶτα συνδρομὴν μάθε· / νυμφοστολεῖ γὰρ τοὺς ποθοῦντας ἐμφρόνως, *AP* 9.203.

[134] *Graphē*, a word the ambiguity of which (text/painting) is already toyed with in the romances (Xen. Eph. 5.15.2 and esp. Long. 1 *praef.* 1, retaining εἰκόνος γραφήν (V) *contra* Brunck's εἰκόνα γραπτήν). See above, pp. 93–4.

[135] Cf. *Bibl.* 66a: τό ... λίαν ὑπέραισχρον καὶ ἀκάθαρτον τῶν ἐννοιῶν.

Counter-ideological modes of reading can be dramatised in the romances themselves.[136] In *Charicleia and Theagenes*, the brigand Thyamis interprets a dream: he 'drags the interpretation towards his own will (*boulēsis*)',[137] and 'using his appetite (*epithumia*) as an interpreter' (1.19.1).[138] Clearly, this passage represents (as Winkler notes)[139] a negatively coded manifestation of interpretative desire: in contrast to (his father) Calasiris, who in the passage we have seen matches his will (*boulēsis*) to the gods, Thyamis – at this point marked as a barbaric, low-status character – sees his will driven by his appetite. Indeed, Thyamis' aggressive exegesis is presented in language that actually mimics the rape that he is contemplating: 'to drag' (*helkein*) is sometimes found euphemistically in this sense.[140] The romances, as we have seen, frequently portray an unambiguous pothic hierarchy, setting civilised, reciprocal passions that are ultimately successfully consummated above forceful, barbaric, asymmetric passions that typically end in frustration or tragedy. But, even if alternative interpretative desires such as those of Thyamis are repressed, they continue (as we saw in the previous section) to resonate.

How do the romances engage the reader's desire for heretical interpretations? One technique, emphasised by Simon Goldhill, is euphemism, which provokes us to supplement the narrative gaps for ourselves. Goldhill's example is Longus 3.18, where Daphnis is sexually initiated by Lycaenion, in language that is discreet and allusive: she 'guided him to the road that he had sought for so long; thereafter she tried out nothing strange, for nature herself taught what remained to be done'.[141] Longus, Goldhill notes, 'holds up a veil that depends upon the reader's *sōphrosynē* [self-control] for its continuing existence as a veil'.[142] A comparable example occurs in Heliodorus: when Charicleia and Theagenes are left alone unchaperoned, they embrace, but only with 'pure (*katharois*) kisses': and, we read, whenever Charicleia discovered her lover 'stirring' (*parakinounta*) and 'becoming manly' (*andrizomenon*) she reminded him of his oaths (5.4.5). This sentence need not have an obscene meaning: Achilles Tatius, for example, uses *andrizesthai* in a context where Clitophon is merely

---

[136] See esp. Morales (2004) 83–95 on Achilles Tatius' Conops, Callisthenes and Thersander.
[137] ἕλκει πρὸς τὴν ἑαυτοῦ βούλησιν τὴν ἐπίλυσιν, 1.18.5.
[138] He later reinterprets the dream, again incorrectly: 1.30.4.
[139] Winkler (1982) 118–19, aptly comparing 2.36.1, where the Delphians interpret the oracle 'each according to his own will' (ὡς ἕκαστος εἶχε βουλήσεως).
[140] E.g. Lys. 1.12; Lib. *Prog.* 11.5; Nonn. *Dion.* 8.69, 16.330, 33.356 etc.
[141] ἐς τὴν τέως ζητουμένην ὁδὸν ἦγε, τὸ δὲ ἐντεῦθεν οὐδὲν περιειργάζετο ξένον· αὐτὴ γὰρ ἡ φύσις λοιπὸν ἐπαίδευε τὸ πρακτέον, 3.18.4.
[142] Goldhill (1995) 26.

steeling himself for a more courageous approach to Leucippe (2.10.1).[143] The juxtaposition with *parakinein*, however, is provocative: not only is the verb used intransitively[144] of intense passion, but *kinein* both unprefixed and prefixed (albeit not, to my knowledge, with *para-*) is very frequent as a synonym for *binein*, 'fuck'.[145] As Duncan Kennedy reminds us, obscenity is often a function of interpretation rather than inherent meaning, since sexual discourse tends towards the metaphorical – or, better, confuses our sense of what is metaphorical and what is literal.[146] Once we appreciate this, the question becomes not 'is there an obscene sense or not?', but 'what kind of readers would choose what kind of sense?' Heliodorus supplies us with an immediate answer to this answer, commenting that Theagenes 'drew back without difficulty, and easily submitted to self-control (*sōphronein*): although worsted by love he was master of his pleasure'.[147] Can we, like Theagenes, control our desire? Even if we can, our experiment with the alternative code of sexual ethics that is suddenly withdrawn from view cannot be erased from memory: in Fish's words, 'the other has been a part of our experience'.

Readerly desire is closely associated in particular with vision and visualisation (as the Photius epigram, with its animadversion not to 'look' at the 'marginal sights', has already suggested). Ancient rhetorical theory defined this as *enargeia* (or *evidentia* in Latin), an affective response to particularly vivid description (or *ecphrasis*);[148] the psychological effect was often called *phantasia*, a term that seems to have begun life as a technical term of Stoicism, but became more generally associated with the powers of the imagination.[149] Much work has been devoted to exploring the metanarrative role of visualisation in the romances, particularly in Achilles Tatius, where, as Helen Morales has emphasised, Clitophon's 'scopophiliac' narratorial habits simultaneously stigmatise and invite illicit modes of

---

[143] As also in Paul's celebrated encouragement to the Corinthians to 'stand in faith, be manly (*andrizesthe*)' (στήκετε ἐν τῆι πίστει, ἀνδρίζεσθε, 1 Cor. 13:16). The usage at 4.1.2, however, may well have 'a sexual sense' (O'Sullivan (1980) 27).

[144] As I take it here, with Morgan ('becoming too ardent'), rather than implicitly transitive ('deale with her over wantonly', Underdowne; 'sa [viz. Charicleia's] vertu mise en péril', Maillon). For the intransitive sense, LSJ s.v. II.3.

[145] Henderson (1991) 151–2.   [146] Kennedy (1993) 57–63.

[147] οὐ χαλεπῶς ἐπανήγετο καὶ σωφρονεῖν ῥαιδίως ἠνείχετο ἔρωτος μὲν ἐλάττων ἡδονῆς δὲ κρείττων γινόμενος, 5.4.5.

[148] *Ecphrasis* has been widely discussed in recent years, but predominantly in the modern sense of the description of artworks (see esp. two special issues of journals, *Ramus* 31 (2002) and *Classical Philology* 102 (2007)). See, however, now Webb (2009), a comprehensive survey of *ecphrasis* as 'vivid description' (with 178–85 on the Greek romances); also Nünlist (2009) 153–5 and 194–8 on the Homeric scholia.

[149] Webb (2009) 107–30; also Watson (1988) on the Stoic term.

reading-as-viewing.[150] In particular, the figure of Callisthenes, who 'fell in love through hearsay', is both pilloried for his shamelessness (*akolasia*) and, implicitly, presented as a potential model for readerly identification.[151]

The most explicit case of *enargeia* is the well-known passage at the beginning of Heliodorus' third book, where Cnemon's request to the secondary narrator Calasiris for more details is expressed as a desire to become a 'spectator' (*theatēs*, 3.1.1). Calasiris responds here by linking his desire to become a 'viewer (*theōros*) from the wings' to his identity as an Athenian,[152] an association that looks back to the Thucydidean Cleon's accusation that the Athenians are 'spectators of words' (*theatai logōn*, Thuc. 3.38.4).[153] In due course, Cnemon claims actually to see Charicleia and Theagenes before his eyes:

'That's Charicleia and Theagenes!' cried out Cnemon.

'Where on earth are they?' begged Calasiris, thinking that Cnemon had seen them. 'Show me, I beg you by the gods!'

'Father,' replied Cnemon, 'I fancied I could see them even in their absence, so vividly (*enargōs*) and as I know them from my own eyes did your narrative present them to me.'[154]

Critics have of course identified this episode as a recursive dramatisation of ecphrastic modes of reading–viewing, and hence focused on its status as a paradigm for the implied reader (much as ps.-Longinus saw the Euripidean Orestes' delusions (Eur. *Or.* 255–7; *IT* 291) as figurative of the mental illusion conjured up by a dramatic audience, and indeed by the poet).[155] Winkler claimed that Cnemon serves as a parodic inversion of the ideal reader; his role is 'to illustrate the comedy of misreading'.[156] Other scholars

---

[150] Goldhill (2001) 167–72, 178–80; Morales (2004). Froma Zeitlin's book on visual culture is keenly anticipated (see, for now, Zeitlin (2003)).
[151] Ach. Tat. 2.13.1; Morales (2004) 88–95. Cf. also Philostr. *Her.* 54.4, with Grossardt (2006) 739 for parallels and Whitmarsh (2009a) 224–5 for discussion.
[152] ἐκ παρόδου θεωρὸς γενέσθαι βεβούλησαι, σὺ μὲν Ἀττικὸς ὤν..., 3.1.2. On this passage, see Kövendi (1966) 183; Winkler (1982) 142–3; Bartsch (1989) 120–2; Morgan (1991) 95–9; Hardie (1998) 26–33.
[153] Cf. also the distinction at Pl. *Resp.* 476b between philosophers and οἱ ... φιλήκοοι καὶ φιλοθεάμονες.
[154] "οὗτοι ἐκεῖνοι Χαρίκλεια καὶ Θεαγένης" ἀνεβόησεν ὁ Κνήμων. "καὶ ποῦ γῆς οὗτοι δείκνυε πρὸς θεῶν" ἱκετεύων ὁ Καλάσιρις, ὁρᾶσθαι αὐτοὺς τῶι Κνήμωνι προσδοκήσας. ὁ δὲ "ὦ πάτερ, θεωρεῖν αὐτοὺς καὶ ἀπόντας ὠιήθην, οὕτως ἐναργῶς τε καὶ οὓς οἶδα ἰδὼν ἡ παρὰ σοῦ διήγησις ὑπέδειξεν", 3.4.7.
[155] 'The poet himself saw the Erinyes, and all but forced the audience also to spectate what he imagined (*ephantasthē*)' (ἐνταῦθ' ὁ ποιητὴς αὐτὸς εἶδεν Ἐρινύας· ὁ δ' ἐφαντάσθη, μικροῦ δεῖν θεάσασθαι καὶ τοὺς ἀκούοντας ἠνάγκασεν, *de Subl.* 15.1).
[156] Winkler (1982) 143.

take his intervention as a positive model for the reader of romances.¹⁵⁷ Both simplify the position. If we look to other episodes of appetitive visualisation, both in the romances generally and in Heliodorus, we see that it is particularly associated with lustful, barbaric and low-class figures. In Chariton, the Persian king Artaxerxes is said to have 'burned terribly as he painted and moulded images [of Callirhoe] in his mind'.¹⁵⁸ There is here an implicit association between erotic fantasy and louche, Persian opulence. In Heliodorus, Cnemon's stepmother Demainete – a model of uncontrolled lust, which is visible in her very eyes ('her gaze went beyond the chaste (*tou sōphronos*)')¹⁵⁹ – imagines her beloved in his absence: 'now I imagine (*phantazomai*) seeing him, I deceive myself that I can hear him in my presence'.¹⁶⁰ Elsewhere in the high-minded Heliodorus, immoderate viewing is always a sign of psychic disturbance born of moral weakness.¹⁶¹ It is, then, reasonable to take Cnemon's fantasy (with Winkler) as an analogous case of the hyperaffectivity stigmatised elsewhere.

But there is a subtler question to ask here than simply whether Cnemon represents a positive or negative model for reader response. The crucial point is that his response, like all cases of fantastic visualisation in the romances, dramatises reading *as desire*.¹⁶² His apperception of the lovers 'even in their absence' (*kai apontas*) invokes the play between absence and (the yearning for) presence that is, as we have seen, so central to the Greek concept of *pothos*. Ecphrastic moments play simultaneously to readers' (/viewers') desire to experience physical presence and to their awareness of necessary absence.¹⁶³ Eroticism lies in the play between the two, a phenomenon that Roland Barthes compares to the 'flash' of striptease, 'the staging of an appearance-as-disappearance'.¹⁶⁴ David Halperin expands:

---

[157] Bartsch (1989) 120–2; Morgan (1991) 99; Hardie (1998) 26.
[158] ταῦτα ἀναζωγραφῶν καὶ ἀναπλάττων ἐξεκαίετο σφόδρα..., Char. 6.4.7. Note that Chaereas too can be found Καλλιρόην ἀναπλάττων ἑαυτῶι (4.2.8).
[159] τὸ βλέμμα τοῦ σώφρονος ἐξιστάμενον, 1.9.3. For Demaenete as the inverse of the Heliodorean romantic ideal, see Kövendi (1966) 183; Winkler (1982) 106–7; Morgan (1989a).
[160] νῦν δὲ ὁρᾶν φαντάζομαι, παρόντος ἀκούειν ἀπατῶμαι...1.15.4. Analogously Achilles' Clitophon, who styles erotic pursuit as the renunciation of σωφροσύνη (1.5.7), claims πάντα Λευκίππην φαντάζομαι (1.9.1).
[161] Other Heliodorean examples of negatively coded viewing include the pirate Pelorus ('monstrous') at 5.31.1–2; and the 'vulgar women' (δημώδεις γυναῖκες) in the Delphic parade, who are awestruck by everything they see (ἐξέπληττε μὲν δὴ καὶ πάντας τὰ ὁρώμενα) and hence cannot conceal their psychic passion with self-control (τὸ τῆς ψυχῆς πάθος ἐγκρατείαι κρύπτειν ἀδύνατοι, 3.3.8). See further Whitmarsh (2002b) 121–2.
[162] For ecphrasis as a stimulant of desire see Elsner (2004) 158–63 and esp. 175–8.
[163] Webb (2009) 169–72, highlighting this theme particularly in ecphraseis of the dead.
[164] Barthes (1975) 10.

Narrative itself is erotic insofar as the illusion of dramatic immediacy it provides typically serves to collapse the distance between the occurring and the recounting of an event, or between the characters in a tale and its audience, while the very fact of narrative serves to consolidate that distance, to institutionalize and perpetuate it. For narrative itself is a sign of the gap that has opened up between the 'now' of a telling and the 'then' of a happening, a gap that demands to be continually crossed and recrossed, if we are to succeed at reconstituting in imagination, however fleetingly, the lost presence of a past that is forever slipping away from us. By endlessly abolishing the distance it interposes and interposing the distance it abolishes, narrative at once satisfies and (re)generates desire. . . .[165]

The *success* of ecphrasis – its allure, its desirability – thus consists in its *failure* (to cross the gulf between representation and reality, to create presence). Elsner writes of the Philostratean *Imagines* that 'the dynamic of desire in Philostratean ekphrasis can never be separated from the repeated demonstration of its failure'.[166] Ecphrasis equivocates between the creation of the illusion of reality and its *almost-creation*. Aelius Theon's much cited textbook account of ecphrasis begins by defining it as 'a speech that vividly (*enargōs*) brings before the eyes what is being depicted', but presently refines the account, referring to 'the faculty of making things described *almost* (*skhedon*) visible' (my emphasis).[167] The addition of that tell-tale 'almost' acknowledges that there is inevitably a textual residue, a trace of the immateriality of the word.

So although we can read Cnemon's visualisation of Charicleia and Theagenes as a token of his appetitive characterisation, we must also see it as a dramatisation of the play between absence and presence that is fundamental to all experiences of receiving narrative. Indeed, contrary to Winkler's distinction between naive narratee and sophisticated narrator, the yearning for the physical presence of Charicleia and Theagenes is shared also by Calasiris, whose excitable response ('Show me, I beg you by the gods!') bespeaks his own anxious desire. Presently, he chides Cnemon for the 'sweet deception' (*hēdeias apatēs*) he has practised, 'how you fluttered me up when you made me think that you could see my beloveds (*philtatous*) and were going to show (*deiknunai*) them to me!'[168] This is reinforced by a further accusation of deceit (*exapatan*), on the grounds that 'you have no ability to show me them present before me'.[169] Calasiris succumbs as

---

[165] Halperin (1992) 106. [166] Elsner (2004) 176.
[167] λόγος περιηγηματικὸς ἐναργῶς ὑπ' ὄψιν ἄγων τὸ δηλούμενον, *Prog.* 118.7–8; τοῦ σχεδὸν ὁρᾶσθαι τὰ ἀπαγγελλόμενα, *Prog.* 119.28–9 Spengel. Webb (2009) 168 compares Nikolaos *Prog.* 70.5–6; further examples at Becker (1995) 27–8.
[168] ὅπως με ἀνεπτέρωσας ὁρᾶν τοὺς φιλτάτους καὶ δεικνύναι προσδοκηθείς, 3.4.9.
[169] οὐδαμοῦ δεικνύναι παρόντας ἔχεις, 3.4.9.

much as Cnemon to the illusionistic fantasy of presence, which is signalled in the contemporary-sounding, quasi-technical emphasis upon the language of 'deception' (*apatē*, especially 'sweet deception') and 'showing' (*deiknunai*).[170] Calasiris' desire for the real sight (*thean*, 3.4.10) of Charicleia and Theagenes mirrors Cnemon's desire to view them ecphrastically through description; but both converge at the moment of the illusion.

It will be objected, of course, that an eroticised reading of this passage is problematised by the fact that neither narrator (Calasiris) nor narratee (Cnemon) relates to Charicleia and Theagenes, the subjects of the description, in an explicitly erotic way. This is true, although both are by nature *erōtikoi*, capable of being seduced by beauty. But despite Calasiris' parental role, the description he offers of the two is unmistakeably sexualised, from Theagenes' gently wafted locks (3.3.6) to the body-hugging, snaky breast-band worn by Charicleia (3.4.4). References to their beauty[171] and visual impact on the spectators[172] underline their availability to the desirous gaze. Even if Calasiris' desire for his wards is primarily protective, it acknowledges the erotic, and even shades into it (compare the references to 'my darling (*melēma*) Theagenes' (3.3.4), and 'my beloveds' (*philtatous*, 3.4.9)).

This ecphrastic passage thus serves as a complex, multilayered *mise-en-scène* of readerly desire. Although it is partly an ironical comment on Cnemon's appetitive cognition, it also showcases Heliodorus' astonishingly self-reflexive, theoretical approach to narrative description. For Calasiris' luscious description is also, of course, a narrative fireworks display on Heliodorus' part – especially when considered as an intrageneric agon with its romantic model, the Ephesian parade in *Anthia and Habrocomes*.[173] Indeed, so far from merely dismissing ecphrasis as smoke and mirrors, the passage subtly suggests a mystical power underlying it. When Cnemon cries out 'That's Charicleia and Theagenes!', the phrasing evokes the language of divine epiphany.[174] There is much, indeed, that is epiphanic about the description, as Charicleia is assimilated to Artemis, and Theagenes to both Achilles and Apollo; the pervasive imagery of brilliant light suggests

---

[170] Cf. Philostr. Jun. *Imag.* pr. 4 on the 'sweet (*hēdeia*) deception' (ἡδεῖα... ἀπάτη) in confronting 'things that do not exist as though they did' (τοῖς οὐκ οὖσι ὡς οὖσι), language that distantly evokes Gorgias' famous claim that in tragedy 'the deceived is wiser than the undeceived' (ὁ ἀπατηθεὶς σοφώτερος τοῦ μὴ ἀπατηθέντος), since 'to be easily captivated by the pleasure (*hēdonē*; cf. Philostratus' *hēdeia*) of words calls for sensitivity' (εὐάλωτον γὰρ ὑφ' ἡδονῆς λόγων τὸ μὴ ἀναίσθητον, F23 DK = Plut. *Mor.* 348c). For *deiknunai* in the sense of 'represent' cf. Luc. *Imag.* 5 (where the context suggests that δεικνύτω has this meaning).

[171] ὡραιότητος... καλὸν κάλλιστον... κάλλους... κάλλος (Theagenes, 3.3.7–8); κάλλος (Charicleia, 3.4.1).

[172] ἐξέπληττε... πάντας τὰ ὁρώμενα (3.3.8); περιβλέπτους (3.4.8).

[173] Above, p. 117. [174] οὗτοι ἐκεῖνοι Χαρίκλεια καὶ Θεαγένης, 3.4.7.

divinity.[175] Calasiris' descriptive powers are thus implicitly aligned with the power of the invisible gods to materialise. The affinity between representation and epiphany is further underlined in the description of Charicleia's breastband, on which, Calasiris says, 'you would have said the snakes did not *seem* to move but actually did move'.[176] Inspired representation creates the illusion of movement, challenging (what Lessing (1985(1766)) called) 'the limits of art' – an achievement that looks to Hephaestus' magical artworks in the *Iliad*, the automatic tripods and (especially) the shield of Achilles.

Readerly desire is, then, not simply a function of base appetite, but also an acknowledgement of the magical power of narrative to confront the reader with another world. The crucial points to re-emphasise is that while modes of desire are inevitably vehicles of moral and cultural definition – they divide into proper and improper – they can be conflicted and contradictory. While it is undeniably true that the dominant trajectory yokes desire to an inevitable teleology of civilised marriage, romantic plot is best considered as a space in which multiple, divergent desires are orchestrated relatively openly. Identification with alternative desires is part of the experience of romance; and even if such identifications are ultimately repressed, they are not entirely neutralised.

---

[175] See esp. 3.4.6 on the 'beam' (σέλας; looking to Hom. *Il.* 18.214) emitted by Charicleia's eyes. On the play between light and dark in the entire Heliodorean episode, see Hardie (1998) 38–9; Whitmarsh (2002b) 120. For beauty and 'divine radiance' as features of epiphany see Richardson (1974) 252.

[176] εἶπες ἂν τοὺς ὄφεις οὐ δοκεῖν ἕρπειν ἀλλ' ἕρπειν, 3.4.4. At Whitmarsh (2002b) 124 n. 52, I discuss the possibility that Cnemon is the 'you' being addressed here, given his habit of confusing representation with reality.

CHAPTER 5

Telos

If desire is the central figure for romantic plot, then closure, consummation, is its aim. The settled marriage that concludes the romances is the *telos* for which characters and readers alike aim. The ending thus occupies a privileged position in relation to the narrative, as critics of narrative have recognised since antiquity. For Aristotle, the *telos* is (or should be) both rational and ethical, the merited outcome for a subject of a particular moral complexion.[1] In Barbara Herrnstein Smith's classic study of poetic closure, the end is seen to satisfy a psychological need for structure.[2] For Frank Kermode, the need for closure is a reflex of mortality, both an intimation of the inevitable death of the individual and an attempt to give meaningful shape to the vastness of eternity.[3] Postmodern accounts, by contrast, have seen closure not as the culmination but the abnegation of narrative, fundamentally antipathetic to the free play of textual possibility.[4]

The romance, we have seen, rests upon a flexible but consistent narrative structure. A firm boundary is drawn between settled home life and the turbulent fluidity, insecurity and threat faced by travellers abroad. (*Leucippe and Clitophon*, which hints at continued turbulence for its protagonist after the end of the narrative proper, subverts this pattern; but subversion also affirms the generic expectation.) This distinction is expressed through the narrative form of the romances: it is the beginnings and ends that are closely identified with secure identity, and the central, liminal phase in the middle with change and uncertainty. The relationship between the middle and the ending, thus, has an especially privileged place in the romance's literary, cultural and ideological apparatus, as the place where the lovers achieve (or retrieve) their final state, as mature, settled members of their communities. The narrative management of the three phases of

---

[1] Poet. 1452b–53a. [2] Smith (1968). [3] Kermode (1967).
[4] Miller (1981), esp. 98 (cited above, p. 61).

initiation (separation, marginalisation, aggregation), 'the concord books arrange between beginning, middle and end',[5] lies at the heart of the romance's vision of personal and social identity.

The romances are narratives of return and restitution, a primal pattern that can be traced back through the *Odyssey* to our earliest, Mesopotamian literary texts, and can be found in folklore cross-culturally.[6] This kind of narrative, allegorising the resolution of chaos and uncertainty into a civilised order that rewards 'proper values', clearly plays to a universal psychological need. From the early modern English romancers, who use the template of the biblical book of Job to endorse Christian narratives of suffering and redemption ('virtue rewarded'),[7] to the modern Harlequin or Mills and Boon,[8] the generic 'happy ending' has been widely associated with the legitimation of (a conservative conception of) the social order, particularly in terms of gender and class roles.

From this perspective, it is right to emphasise, with most scholars, the strongly closural nature of the romances.[9] Yet, we should pause at this point: what exactly do we mean by 'closure'? The term is associated in modern critical discourse with at least three different phenomena:

- a sense of resolution at the end of a narrative, with all the loose ends tied up nicely;
- a limitation of interpretative possibilities, as opposed to more 'open', pluralist texts;
- the prescriptive enforcement of an ideological worldview.

Although there is a family resemblance between these phenomena, there is no necessary connection between them. Narrative resolution can generate complex interpretative issues, which may in turn be culturally challenging (as, for example, in *Crime and punishment*). Interpretative closurality, moreover, can itself be ideologically challenging.[10] The once-fashionable post-structuralist association of open, polymorphous discourse with subversion is vulnerable to the charges of both cultural elitism (in that pluralist

---

[5] Kermode (1967) 178.   [6] Above, p. 15.
[7] Parrinder (2006) 106–25.   [8] Radway (1987), esp. 65–7.
[9] See esp. Lowe (2000) 222–58, arguing that the genre has 'a strong sense of destination and closure . . . and a teleological shaping of time and space' (223); also Fusillo (1997) and Fowler (1997), who uses *Charicleia and Theagenes* as an example of closure *in extremis*. The invention of the term is usually credited to Smith (1968). Fowler (1989), (1997) offers an excellent survey of the issues, as well as the relevant bibliography. See also more generally Roberts *et al.* (1997), which includes a useful bibliographic discussion (275–7).
[10] Feminist criticism, for example, has moved away from the lionisation of 'an aesthetically self-conscious literature which subverts conventions of representation', and towards celebrating the constructive impact of works (particularly narrative texts) that are more formally conventional: see Felski (1989), at 180.

art is typically the preserve of moneyed, white males)[11] and a paradoxical mirroring of mainstream liberal economics: the 'customer' (reader) is always right.[12] In this respect, soi-disant avant-gardists can come surprisingly close to those nineteenth-century romantics who privilege aesthetic individualism over the supposed automatism of the masses.

The final problem is that there is no agreed standard for measuring degrees of 'closurality'. Scholars' pronouncements tend to reflect their own political and aesthetic judgements upon the texts in question (and their general outlook), rather than any intrinsic properties. Does the end of the *Iliad*, where Achilles pities Priam and returns Hector's body, mark the transcendence of heroic values by mortal self-awareness?[13] Or is this accommodation undercut by the reminders of the carnage to come once the truce is over? Or in the case of Vergil's *Aeneid*, does Aeneas' defeat of Turnus mark a satisfyingly vengeful dominance over military enemies, or the dangerous victory of his passion over his reason?[14] The answers given to these questions have tended to reflect the intellectual predisposition of the readers in question, whether towards seeing literature as a reflection of social norms or as a detached commentary upon them. But it is, clearly, equally unsatisfactory to conclude that there is a free choice between these alternatives, that all is up to the reader.[15]

With the Greek romances, too, we see radically divergent critical judgements on closurality and its significance. At one extreme, Kate Cooper points to the role of marriage (or its restoration at the end), identifying it as 'a mechanism of narrative resolution'.[16] This narrative resolution, Cooper argues, is inseparable from ideological function: 'The peculiar power of romance to create complicity meant than an author could rely on readers to see in a tale of young lovers an allegory of the condition of the social order – and to be influenced by his views of how that order should be perpetuated.'[17] Other critics, however, take the contrary tack, emphasising the romances' apparently gleeful renunciation of form and narrative direction, to argue instead for constitutive openness. Bakhtin's theory of

---

[11] See e.g. Eco (1979) 52–5; 107–24, 144–72, associating 'open' textuality with baroque poetry, the symbolists and Brechtian drama, and 'closed' with popular fiction and cartoons.
[12] As noted by Fowler (1997) 7.
[13] The position taken, for different reasons, by e.g. Rutherford (1982) and Seaford (1994).
[14] For recent contributions to the debate, see Martindale (1993) 35–54, (1997); Fowler (1997); Thomas (2000), (2001); for a historicist counter-response, see esp. Galinsky (1993–1994). Hardie (1997) 142–51 argues that both readings are seeded in the text.
[15] As e.g. Kennedy (1992), esp. 41.
[16] Cooper (1996) 31. See also, with more qualification, Haynes (2003) 156–62.   [17] Cooper (1996) 31.

heteroglossia (sometimes translated as polyphony),[18] which presents romances as fundamentally unresolved tissues of competing narrative voices, has been influential, even though Bakhtin himself sees the Greek romances as only primitively heteroglossic. Thus, for example, Steve Nimis presents 'the unfolding of a text [of an ancient romance] as a *managerial* process that deploys various heterogeneous elements into a fabric with multiple and contradictory effects', seeking to explore 'how an author negotiates this heterogeneity, manages it, articulates it, operates within it, without seeking to reduce it to a spurious unity'.[19] Once again, this aesthetic judgement can be a political one too. Following Bakhtin, Nimis ties the centrifugality (as he sees it) of romance discourse to a relativisation of authority within late Greek society, born of a 'more fragmented social order'.[20] On this reading, the romances emerge as dynamic and progressive rather than conservative artefacts, even antithetical to established codes of behaviour.

The challenge, then, is to come up with an account of the romance plot that can explain how such divergent readings can be generated. To do this, I propose to build on the findings of the previous chapter, where we concluded that texts pit the normative desire for stable matrimony against the subversive desires for illicit pleasure. On this reading, plot is not a fixed structure but a matrix of possibilities,[21] the space in which readerly desires are mobilised in diverse, sometimes contradictory ways. The question, then, is not whether the romances are open or closed, but how they manipulate, structure and play off against each other the contrary narrative drives towards resolution and deferral, how the closural settlement stands in relation to the open potentiality of the narrative. It is, thus, also misguided to ask whether the romances are socially conservative or not; the issue is how the disruptive energy of narrativity relates to the normative drive towards the aristocratic marital *telos*.

OPEN AND CLOSED CASES

Towards the beginning of *Anthia and Habrocomes*, the fathers of the two lovers, at a loss to explain their children's pining, consult the oracle of

---

[18] Bakhtin (1981), esp. 259–422. The value of this essay to scholarship on the ancient romance is discussed by Branham (2002), and the contributors in Branham ed. (2005).
[19] Nimis (1994) 401; cf. (1998), (1999), (2001), (2003). Nimis' position (at least in relation to Achilles) is supported by Morales (2004) 36, 69. Fusillo too borrows Bakhtin's contrast between the 'staticità impersonale dell' epica' and the 'dinamismo aperto del romanzo', which he locates primarily at the level of intertextuality (Fusillo (1989) 26). Whitmarsh (2005d) critiques neo-Bakhtinianism.
[20] Nimis (1994) 407.   [21] As proposed by Miller (1981) and Brooks (1984).

Apollo at Colophon. The response suggests to them that they should marry the children and then send them abroad on a journey. The start of that journey marks the beginning of the liminal phase. The two sets of parents react differently to the departure, and to the oracle that motivated it:

Now Lycomedes and Themisto [Habrocomes' parents], recalling everything – the oracle, their son, the period abroad – threw themselves to the ground in despair (*athumountes*). Megamedes and Euippe [Anthia's parents], on the other hand, while they experienced the same emotions, felt more cheerful (*euthumoteroi*), since they looked to the outcomes (*telē*) of the prophecy.[22]

At the level of the realist fiction, this passage describes two reactions to events: one set of parents wallow in helplessness (*athumia*) in the face of the seemingly insurmountable obstacles ahead, while the others combine these feelings with a more spirited confidence (*euthumia*) in the eventual outcome. At a metanarrative level, meanwhile, the parents represent two different models of reading romance narrative. Megamedes and Euippe look to the end of the narrative, to closure and resolution (*telē*); Lycomedes and Themisto to the interminable, unresolved middle. The two groups of interpreters are further contrasted in terms of their emotional reactions: the Greek words translated as 'despairing' (*athumountes*) and 'more cheerful' (*euthumoteroi*) are both rooted in *thumos*, denoting vigorous energy. In metanarrative terms, *thumos* marks hermeneutic energy: the desire to read on.[23]

Strikingly, there is no ranking of the two modes: although generically practised external readers will of course be aware that the happy ending is bound to come, Xenophon implies that affective absorption in the immediate crises of the narrative is as legitimate and anticipated a response as a more detached awareness that we are reading a work that ultimately promises a positive outcome. This point needs emphasising, since the idea of emotionally absorbed reading picks up an important motif in ancient literary criticism. Gorgias of Leontini famously wrote of the literary experience (perhaps more narrowly of tragedy), that 'the one who is deceived is wiser than the one who is not deceived... for to be to be easily captivated

---

[22] ἐν τούτωι μὲν οὖν ὁ Λυκομήδης καὶ ἡ Θεμιστώ, πάντων ἅμα ἐν ὑπομνήσει γενόμενοι, τοῦ χρησμοῦ, τοῦ παιδός, τῆς ἀποδημίας, ἔκειντο εἰς γῆν ἀθυμοῦντες· ὁ δὲ Μεγαμήδης καὶ ἡ Εὐίππη ἐπεπόνθεσαν μὲν τὰ αὐτά, εὐθυμότεροι δὲ ἦσαν, τὰ τέλη σκοποῦντες τῶν μεμαντευμένων, 1.10.7.

[23] Intriguingly, however, by the end of the narrative both sets of parents have died out of old age and *athumia* (5.15.3): not even the cheerier Euippe and Megamedes could sustain themselves right up to the *telos*.

by the pleasure of words calls for sensitivity'.²⁴ The wise reader of tragedy – and, no doubt, of the romance too – willingly submits to the fiction.

Readers of Xenophon need to be doubly directed, both driven energetically forward towards the generically required happy ending and passively immersed in the turbulence and indeterminacy of the moment. Supposedly the most maladroit of the romancers, Xenophon still pre-empts modern theoretical definitions of romance as 'a form that simultaneously quests for and postpones a particular end',²⁵ as well as Brooks' famous distinction between 'the death instinct, the drive towards the end' and the principle of traumatic repetition that 'retards the pleasure principle's search for the gratification of discharge'.²⁶

The relationship between these two urges, the closural and the centrifugal, can be presented at times in a Brooksian sense, in terms of *reading* for the plot. At other times, however, it seems to be a case of different modalities of *writing*. In a sense, the author is the plot's first 'reader': translating the raw material (what narratologists call *fabula*) into narrative is itself an act of cognitive creativity akin to reading, and involving the same play between onward progress and procrastination. This is clearly visible in a passage that we have seen before, from the beginning of book 8 of Chariton's *Callirhoe*, where the narrator proclaims that this is the last book, and foretells the happy ending of the romance plot (8.1.2–5).²⁷ Many of the closural motifs (reconciliation, reunion, the healing of divine anger) have already been discussed in Chapter 1 and do not need recapping here. The important point to note here is that Chariton identifies his final book as the start of a new phase: the narrative register shifts, from the wearisome divagatory section of the middle to a more joyous, structured, teleological phase. Aphrodite's arrival will, we are told, put an end to the phase in which Chaereas has 'wandered (*planētheis*) through countless sufferings'.²⁸ This language of wandering – here conspicuously invoking the 'much-suffering' (*polutlas*), wandering Odysseus – is, as we shall see in greater detail in the following chapter, closely tied in the romances to the experience of centrifugal endlessness. The narrator also contrasts the 'grim' (*skuthrōpōn*: see below) events of previous books – 'piracy, enslavement, law-suits, fighting, despair, warfare, captivity' – with 'legitimate love and legal marriage' (8.1.4).

---

²⁴ ὁ δ' ἀπατηθεὶς σοφώτερος τοῦ μὴ ἀπατηθέντος... εὐάλωτον γὰρ ὑφ' ἡδονῆς λόγων τὸ μὴ ἀναίσθητον, fr. 23 DK = Plut. *Mor.* 348c; see further above, p. 175, n. 170.
²⁵ Parker (1979) 4, quoted above p. 18.
²⁶ Brooks (1984) 102. See also Miller (1981), esp. x–xiii, 265–8.
²⁷ Above, pp. 59–60, 65–6; see further Fusillo (1997) 215–16.
²⁸ διὰ μυρίων παθῶν πλανηθείς, 8.1.3.

The division between the two phases replicates, in a different form, the tension we identified above in the Xenophon passage: the circular, repetitive, endless world of the romance is associated with misery and suffering, and the ending with optimism. The key difference is that Xenophon dramatises different *responses* to plot by internal characters of the same event, whereas Chariton marks a shift in *compositional form* as we enter the *teleutaion suggramma*: the 'last book', the 'book of closure'. But the difference is, in the final analysis, illusory: it is not (as Steven Nimis argues) that the romance author has been composing with no sense of where his story will end up,[29] but that the sense of greater authorial control at this point – figured in the assertive use of the peritextual book division[30] – is a cue to the reader, a signal that we are now to play Megamedes and Euippe rather than Lycomedes and Themisto. Indeed, Chariton explicitly directs his readers in this way: 'I also think that this last (*teleutaion*) book will be the most pleasurable for my readers'.[31] Pleasure thus supplants misery in the final book.

The romances are never simply plural, open-ended, heteroglossic, untroubled by thoughts of ending: the promise of closure overhangs the wandering narrative. As we shall see repeatedly in this chapter, the 'Xenophon's parents' paradigm repeatedly plays out, across the corpus, conflicting responses to the oppressive demands of romance narrative. Despite this, however, there is a sense in which the romance is constitutionally linked to wandering, and the closural settlement is simply a cancellation of this. Let us return to the Chariton passage, and consider in more detail the narrative context. Tukhē (Fortune), we are told, 'was planning to enact an event that was not just paradoxical, but outright grim (*skuthrōpon*)',[32] namely to make Chaereas sail away before recognising Callirhoe. Tukhē, to whom we shall return in the next chapter, represents the principle of narrative inventiveness, the malevolent supplier of surprises. Both 'grim' and 'paradoxical' events are repeatedly marked in the central part of the narrative.[33] The use of the word 'grim' (*skuthrōpos*) foreshadows the narrator's own subsequent promise to avoid *skuthrōpa* in his final book,

---

[29] Nimis (1994), (1999) (with 224–5 on this passage).   [30] Whitmarsh (2009b).
[31] νομίζω δὲ καὶ τὸ τελευταῖον τοῦτο σύγγραμμα τοῖς ἀναγινώσκουσιν ἥδιστον γενέσθαι, 8.1.4.
[32] ἔμελλε... ἔργον ἡ Τύχη πράττειν οὐ μόνον παράδοξον ἀλλὰ καὶ σκυθρωπόν, 8.1.2.
[33] Action or actors marked as *paradoxos*: 1.1.2, 1.1.4, 2.8.3, 3.2.7, 3.3.2, 3.4.1, 4.1.12, 5.9.8. For *skuthrōpa* see 3.9.8 (σκυθρωπότερα... τὰ πρῶτα), 4.4.2 (ἡ φιλόκαινος Τύχη δρᾶμα σκυθρωπὸν ὑμῖν περιτέθηκε), 8.7.3 (τοῖς πρώτοις καὶ σκυθρωποῖς), 8.8.2; the word itself also appears frequently in non-reflexive contexts in the first seven books (1.4.5, 1.12.6, 2.1.8, 2.5.7, 2.11.4, 3.10.1, 4.2.7, 4.3.11, 4.5.10, 5.6.11, 5.8.10, 7.6.9). *Skuthrōpos* denotes an inappropriate resistance to the expectation of happiness (Halliwell (2008), index s.v., esp. 39 n. 101).

and the intention to 'enact an event' (*ergon... prattein*) may even recall the literary-critical use of the word *praxis* to denote narrative action.[34] Chariton thus identifies two forms of plot construction: the episodic narrative governed by a malignant, paradox-loving deity, which might in principle continue indefinitely; and the benevolent, providential design of Aphrodite, which supervenes on Fortune's plotting. Commentators have long recognised the metanarratorial aspects of Tukhē,[35] but in fact, the authorial intention is schizoid here, enfolding both Tukhē and Aphrodite: this bifurcation of identities is another instance of double-directed narrative plotting.[36]

Because of this double-direction – and because of sheer practicalities, because no one has ten tongues, ten mouths, an unbreakable voice and a heart of bronze (or the literate equivalent) – narrative can never be endless. And yet Chariton here gestures towards the possibility that it might be: what if Aphrodite had not intervened? What if Chaereas had not recognised Callirhoe? Romance turns on such razor's-edge serendipities, which play off the fantasy of endless narrative improvisation against the inevitability of closure. This is the only instance in the whole romance corpus in which the narrator alludes directly to a counterfactual scenario, an alternative chain of events that might have ensued.[37] As Gerald Prince observes, such instances of what he calls 'disnarration' sharpen readers' senses of the value systems that different narrative modes can embody: 'The disnarrated guides meaning by constituting a model that allows texts better to define themselves, to specify and emphasize the meanings that they wish to communicate, and to designate the values they develop and aspire to.'[38] In this case, the disnarrated represents a narrative without the promise of closure.

Let us borrow an analogy from Freud. Romances are, of course, mimetic of life: their physical and cultural world is more or less that of their target readers (notwithstanding historical displacement in some cases). When we read realistically, as though there is a direct correspondence between our

---

[34] It is the central term in Aristotle's *Poetics*, e.g. (LSJ s.v. II).
[35] Bowie (1985) 128: 'the author... intervene[s] in the thinly disguised *persona* of Tyche, manipulating the plot in the required direction'.
[36] Similarly, Apuleius' narratorial controller is *both* 'blind Fortune' (11.15) *and* the providential Isis (see e.g. Winkler (1985) 107–8). See further below, p. 249.
[37] This alternative narrative, indeed, would have a formal elegance to it: Chariton contrasts Callirhoe with Ariadne, a ring composition linking back to 1.6.2, where she is compared to the sleeping Ariadne (cf. also 3.3.5). I am not convinced by Cueva (2004) 16–24 that Plutarch's *Theseus* is the source for the Ariadne motif. For such counter-factuals in epic, see de Jong (1987) 68–81 and Louden (1993).
[38] Prince (1992) 28–38, at 38.

perceptual-consciousness and the world being described, we engage our readerly ego. The ego is, however, also played on by other vectors of desire. Aphrodite represents the narratorial superego, the voice of generic and cultural conscience:[39] it is she who decrees that the romance must end with reunion and a return to Sicily. Tukhē, meanwhile, figures the id: 'a chaos, a cauldron full of seething excitations... filled with energy reaching it from the instincts, but it has no organisation, produces no collective will, but only a striving to bring about the satisfaction of the instinctual needs'.[40] As we shall see throughout this chapter, the romance ego is the site of an ongoing conflict between superego and id.

CURIOSITY AND CLOSURE

One imperial Greek narrative (if not a romance in the same sense) that conspicuously avoids any markers of closurality is Lucian's *True stories*, which concludes with a promise that 'what happened on land I shall narrate in the following books'[41] – a promise that is unredeemed. This false prolepsis signals closure as mere interruption (perhaps a nod towards Thucydides, whose *Histories* breaks off mid-flow), a serious violation of the narrative contract. The narrative of *True stories* is driven by a spirit of free invention (a tale of 'things that do not exist at all, and could not even exist in the first place')[42] and, particularly, of *periergia*, 'curiosity':

the reason and pretext for my journey was intellectual curiosity (*periergia*), a desire for novel things (*pragmatōn kainōn epithumia*) and wanting to know what is the end (*telos*) of the ocean and who are the people who live beyond.[43]

The metanarrative significance of *curiositas*, particularly for Apuleius' *Metamorphoses*, has long been noted; recent scholarship has begun to recognise the parallel importance of the Greek equivalents, *periergia* and *polupragmosunē*.[44] Lucian's figure of the endlessly inquisitive protagonist

---

[39] Freud (1973) 98.   [40] Freud (1973) 106.
[41] τὰ δὲ ἐπὶ τῆς γῆς ἐν ταῖς ἑξῆς βίβλοις διηγήσομαι, 2.47.
[42] μήτε ὅλως ὄντων μήτε τὴν ἀρχὴν γενέσθαι δυναμένων, *VH* 1.4.
[43] αἰτία δέ μοι τῆς ἀποδημίας καὶ ὑπόθεσις ἡ τῆς διανοίας περιεργία καὶ πραγμάτων καινῶν ἐπιθυμία καὶ τὸ βούλεσθαι μαθεῖν τί τὸ τέλος ἐστὶν τοῦ ὠκεανοῦ καὶ τίνες οἱ πέραν κατοικοῦντες ἄνθρωποι, *VH* 1.5.
[44] Morales (2004) 84–7; Whitmarsh (2005b) 605–7; Hunter (2009b). Matthew Leigh is engaged on a long-term project on curiosity in both the Greek and the Roman traditions. Ehrenberg (1947) unpacks classical Athenian meanings of *polupragmosunē* as 'restless energy', tracing them to the discourse of expansive imperialism; the development of the term as a moral category, prying into the affairs of others, begins in the Socratic tradition. On later developments of the latter, see Walsh (1988). For *periergia* as a near-synonym for *polupragmosunē* in later Greek, see Hesych. B 146; Γ 652;

looks back to Homer's Odysseus, who 'saw the cities of many men and learned their mind' (Hom. *Od*. 1.3), whose desire for knowledge and profiteering (against the better advice of his companions) gets him into trouble in the Cyclops' cave (see esp. *Od*. 9.224–9).[45] In such narrative contexts, curiosity is a kind of subjectively embodied *tukhē*: a lust for innovation, for the *kaina* ('novel things') that are so central to the erotic romances too;[46] centrifugal, insatiable, potentially endless. In the passage quoted above from *True Stories*, it is, for sure, linked to a desire for *telos* – but the *telos* in question is the end of the ocean, the most marginal space of all. This is anything but a returning romance.

Polupragmosunē and *periergia* also play central roles in texts that we would more properly call romances, particularly in *Callirhoe* and *Leucippe and Clitophon*.[47] In Chariton, on whom I focus here (bringing in Achilles for comparison), curiosity drives the plot at two crucial moments near the start, by exposing the erotic desire that protagonists seek to conceal. It is through *polupragmosunē* that the young men of the gymnasium find out about Chaereas' dangerous love for Callirhoe, the daughter of his father's rival (1.1.10). When Callirhoe's failed suitor from Acragas seeks to whip up Chaereas' jealousy against her, he plants various seeds that inspire the *polupragmosunē* of the townsfolk (1.3.3) and Chaereas himself (1.4.4). Like rumour, to which it is closely related in narrative function, curiosity seeks

---

cf. A 6009; Phot. *Lex*. Π 416; *Suda* A 527; B 63. Plutarch in his treatise on *polupragmosunē* uses *periergia* apparently as a synonymous variation: see 516a, 517e, 519c, 521a, 522b. In classical texts, by contrast, *periergia* refers more generally to officiousness or misplaced zeal (as in Thphr. *Char*. 13, the *periergos*). On the lexical history of the Latin *curiosus* and *curiositas*, see Labhardt (1960); Joly (1961); Walsh (1988) 75–6; see also Hijmans (1995). Kenny (1998) offers a lexical survey of terms for curiosity from antiquity onwards; see also Kenny (2004) for an excellent cultural–historical account for the early modern period; Evans and Marr (2006) samples a wider chronology.

[45] Odysseus has already been cited by Lucian as a narrative model, for his fictitious blagging (1.3). Odysseus' *polupragmosunē* is strongly implied at Pl. *Rep*. 620c, where he is said to exchange his life of ambition (*philotimia*) for that of an 'ordinary, incurious (*apragmōn*) man'.

[46] References at Whitmarsh (2005a) 87–8, and more fully Tilg (2010) ch. 5.

[47] As well as, of course, the ps.-Lucianic *Ass*: 15, 45, 56, with Perry (1967) 218; see also *Vit. Aesop*. 55–6 (with Hunter (2009b) 52–3), where, however, it is less instrumental in the progression of the narrative. In Xenophon, Longus and Heliodorus, curiosity is largely deproblematised. For περιεργάζομαι and cognates = 'act energetically' etc. see Long. 1.21.2, 1.28.2, 3.13.4; Hld. 1.28.2, 4.12.2; for πολυπραγμονεῖν = 'enquire', see Xen. *Eph*. 3.9.2, 4.1.2; Long. 4.17.3; Hld. 2.17.4, 2.20.1, 5.2.4, 5.20.6, 7.16.1, 8.3.5; also Philostr. *VA* 5.27.2, 8.23, 31.1. Some of the Charitonian role of curiosity can be seen in two Heliodorean passages: (i) 3.6.2, where Calasiris quizzes Charicles about Charicleia, his *periergia* having been stimulated by what he has heard. (ii) 5.20.6, where Trachinos enquires about Charicleia out of *polupragmosunē*, having fallen in love with her. As in Chariton, the protagonist's beauty cannot remain private, as we learn at 5.19.1 (οὐδὲ ἐπὶ τῆς ἐρημίας ἀνενόχλητον εἶχεν ἡ Χαρίκλεια τὸ κάλλος), where ἀνενόχλητος revives the Charitonian language of the public sphere as the site of exposure (see below).

to expose to the public the intrigues that their subjects want to repress.[48] In Plutarch's terms, curiosity is 'a desire to discover things that are hidden and concealed'.[49] It is implicitly cast as transgressive, immoral, problematic – but at the same time a device indispensible to the development of the plot.

Curiosity is also crucial in stimulating the *narration* of plot. This may apply to narrators, ever inquisitive for new material, like Lucian's protagonist in the *True stories*, or the fourth-century historians Theopompus and Ephorus, known for their *polupragmosunē* towards the salacious gossip of court history.[50] It can equally well apply, however, to narratees, eager to hear. The curious, Plutarch tells us, love to hear sensational narrative (*De cur.* 516d, 517e–f), particularly the latest gossip, the 'novelties' (*kaina*, 519a–b). In Achilles' *Leucippe and Clitophon*, Clitophon listens with curiosity to a (false) story told in the Ephesian prison cell, since 'a man who is down on his luck is an inquisitive being (*periergon*) in relation to the problems of another'.[51] This is a clever *mise-en-abyme*, since of course Clitophon's own narratee is listening to the sufferings of another (and is himself described elsewhere as *periergos*) – just as we, the romance's readers, are doing.[52]

In Chariton, the prime example of a such a narratee is Dionysius, who 'out of curiosity' (*polupragmonōn*) begs Callirhoe to 'narrate' (*diēgēsai*) her story – even, he adds, 'if you have done something terrible'.[53] Curiosity is the force that draws narrative out of its jealously protective guardian.[54] Initially, she gives only her name, before bursting into tears (2.5.6–7); but in response to his curious probing she does reveal all, albeit 'reluctantly' (*molis*), and in abridged form (2.5.10). This episode as a whole

---

[48] For rumour, see 1.5.1, 2.3.8, 3.2.7, 3.3.2, 3.4.1, 4.7.5, 5.2.6; *cf.* 8.1.11, and Nimis (2003) 260–1; Schmeling (2005) 40–2. Tilg (2010) ch. 7 on the metapoetics of Chariton's rumour is particularly illuminating; my interpretation differs from his in that I see *phēmē*, like curiosity, as another variety of the narratorial id, rather than as coextensive with the entire narratorial voice.

[49] φιλοπευστία τῶν ἐν ἀποκρύψει καὶ λανθανόντων, *De cur.* 520c.

[50] Polyb. 9.1.4 = *FGrH* 70 T18b (Ephorus); Phot. *Bibl.* cod. 176 120b = *FGrH* 115 T2 (Theopompus). Flower (1994) 24–5 claims that this accusation (if authentic), namely that Ptolemy wished to execute him for his *polupragmosunē*, relates to unwelcome intervention in public affairs; but this claim rests upon too narrowly prescriptive a definition of the *polupragmōn* ('properly denotes a "meddler"', 24), and ignores the parallel of the accusation against Ephorus.

[51] περίεργον... ἄνθρωπος ἀτυχῶν εἰς ἀλλοτρίων ἀκρόασιν κακῶν, 7.2.3.

[52] Morgan (2004d) 506 notes the recessive narrative play here. The primary narrator looks at the picture of Eros with *periergia* at 1.2.1 (ἅτε δὲ ὢν ἐρωτικὸς περιεργότερον ἔβλεπον τὸν ἄγοντα τὸν βοῦν Ἔρωτα, foreshadowing Leucippe's inquisitive gazing at 2.3.3: περιεργότερον... βλέπειν).

[53] εἰ πέπρακταί σοί τι δεινόν, 2.5.8.

[54] Compare 3.9.4, where Plangon is said to have understood that 'desire is naturally inquisitive and personally inquires curiously after events' (φύσει περίεργός ἐστιν ὁ ἔρως κἀκεῖνος δι' ἑαυτὸν πολυπραγμονήσει περὶ τῶν γεγονότων); and Ach. Tat. 2.20.1, where the *polupragmosunē* of the slave Conops makes it difficult for the attempt on Leucippe's room to 'remain hidden from him' (αὐτὸν λαθεῖν). Morales (2004) 84–7 attractively reads Conops as a figure for the curious reader.

artfully replays the prelude to Odysseus' narration of his adventures in book 8 of the *Odyssey*, substituting pathos and feminine modesty for the Odysseus' cunning self-concealment,[55] and replacing the self-aggrandising male's enormous narrative with the romance heroine's 120 words of edited[56] summary. In view of this intertextual relationship, it is a particularly nice touch that Callirhoe's explanation for her reluctance to tell her story is that 'I do not wish to seem a braggart (*alazōn*), or to relate implausible narratives (*diēgēmata apista*) to those who do not know the truth.':[57] these are precisely the charges that ancient authors level against Homer's Odysseus.[58] Callirhoe's bashful resistance to narration transforms the situational dynamics of the Homeric hypotext: her reluctance means that her narratee has to prompt and probe harder, so that the anticipation of the narrative becomes keener through the delay.

At one level, this passage is clearly self-reflexive: Dionysius serves as an internal narratee, figuring the appetitive reader, keen to extract more from this recalcitrant text (even if his concerns are not exactly ours).[59] Readers of romances have to work harder to get into characters' psychology than readers or audiences of epic. What needs stressing, however, is the tension between Dionysius' curiosity and Callirhoe's reluctance, which is of crucial thematic significance. It plays its part, most obviously, in the normative construction of gender roles in this text, which associates females with silence and interiority; in this respect, it contrasts strongly with Chaereas' narration at 8.7.9–8.11, where the male protagonist surmounts his initial shyness (*aidōs*) to deliver a self-aggrandising account of his deeds.[60] Even more importantly for our purposes, it underlines this text's axial opposition between the individual's desire for privacy and the forces that direct her or him into the public sphere. These anxieties focus (again) particularly

---

[55] ταῦτα λέγουσα ἐπειρᾶτο μὲν λανθάνειν, ἐλείβετο δὲ αὐτῆς τὰ δάκρυα κατὰ τῶν παρειῶν, Char. 2.5.7 (cf. 5.2.4) ~ ἐλάνθανε δάκρυα λείβων, Hom. *Od.* 8.93–5 (cf. δάκρυα λείβων, 8.86). Also εἰπέ [Reardon; εἰπόν F *et edd. al.*; Goold's εἶπόν is impossible] μοι, γύναι, πάντα, καὶ πρῶτόν γε τοὔνομα τὸ σόν, Char. 2.5.6 ~ εἴπ' ὄνομα, ὅττι σε κεῖθι κάλεον μήτηρ τε πατήρ τε, Hom. *Od.* 8.550 (where the request specifically for a name is unparalleled: on the usual formula see Webber (1989)). At 2.5.11 Callirhoe explicitly compares Dionysius to Alcinous. On female silence in the Greek romances, see Anderson (2009), with 16–19 on Chariton (omitting discussion, however, of our passage).

[56] 'she told everything, and was silent only about Chaereas' (πάντα εἰποῦσα μόνον Χαιρέαν ἐσιγήσεν, 2.5.11).

[57] οὐ θέλω δοκεῖν ἀλαζὼν οὐδὲ λέγειν διηγήματα ἄπιστα τοῖς ἀγνοοῦσιν, 2.5.9.

[58] *alazoneia*: Pl. *Hipp. min.* 369e; Polyaen. 1 pr. 8. The proverbial phrase 'address (*apologos*) to Alcinous' = 'lie' has numerous associations (Tümpel (1894)), among them 'lie': see Ael. Ar. 36.88, with Tümpel's comments at 530–1. At Luc. *VH* 1.3–4 the *apologoi* are cited as a paradigm case of fictitious 'blathering' (*bōmolokhia*).

[59] Morgan (2004b) 487.   [60] Above pp. 63–6.

on Callirhoe,[61] who ever seeks privacy. She repeatedly veils herself,[62] an act that both links her intertextually with Homer's Penelope (the primary exemplum of a virtuous wife)[63] and marks her respectability in gendered terms. When she expresses emotions, she seeks a solitary place (*erēmia*) to grieve.[64] Despite his own curiosity, Dionysius is equally sensitive to the need to conceal Callirhoe, particularly at Babylon: 'my one hope of safety', he reasons, 'is to keep my wife hidden (*diaklepsai*): she will be safe if she can be concealed (*lathein*)'.[65] To this end, 'he left Callirhoe in the carriage and closed over (*sunekalupse*) the tent'.[66] Such attempts to conceal are, however, doomed to fail, in a romance in which the private is almost always revealed to the public. It is a fact of nature that the public will discover the truth, however artfully repressed: 'human nature is an inquisitive (*periergon*) thing';[67] 'a crowd is a naturally inquisitive (*periergon*) thing'.[68] Human nature will always triumph over contrived concealment.

This making-public of private affairs is, indeed, central to Chariton's narrative self-reflexivity. In Babylon, we learn that Callirhoe's 'talked-aboutness (*to periboēton*) had even long ago caused Dionysius grief';[69] presently, Callirhoe regrets that she has 'become a narrative (*diēgēma*) for both Asia and Europe'.[70] In Gareth Schmeling's phrasing, she has become a celebrity.[71] And, as Schmeling also implies, there is more: the famous narrative in question is clearly, at one level, the story that we are reading now; Chariton is implicitly celebrating the power of his story to publicise its subject across the known world. We, the readers, are placed in the position of a Dionysius, longing to hear Callirhoe's full story, or that of the Babylonian crowds, jostling to get a glimpse of her. As the author of a new story of a famous woman, moreover, Chariton also self-reflexively positions himself as a new Homer. Callirhoe's reluctant celebrity alludes to Helen's fear, as

---

[61] Compare, however, the case of Theron the pirate, who avoids Athens on the grounds of the city's 'inquisitiveness' (*periergia*), and the fact that its inhabitants are 'curious' (*polupragmōn*, 1.11.6).
[62] 1.1.14; 1.11.2; 1.13.11; 7.6.9; 8.1.7; see further Llewellyn-Jones (2003) 101, 287–8, 303.
[63] Hom. *Od.* 1.334; 18.210. [64] 3.10.4; 5.1.4; 5.9.4; 6.6.2. Chaereas does likewise: 5.2.4; 5.10.6.
[65] μία τοίνυν σωτηρίας ἐλπὶς διακλέψαι [διακρύψαι Reardon] τὴν γυναῖκα· φυλαχθήσεται γάρ, ἂν δυνηθῆι λαθεῖν, 5.2.9.
[66] τὴν δὲ Καλλιρόην εἴασεν ἐπὶ τῆς ἁρμαμάξης καὶ συνεκάλυψε τὴν σκηνήν, 5.2.9; a suitably orientalising allusion to the Panthea episode of Xenophon's *Cyropaedia* (οἱ εὐνοῦχοι καὶ αἱ θεράπαιναι λαβοῦσαι ἀπῆγον αὐτὴν εἰς τὴν ἁρμάμαξαν καὶ κατακλίναντες κατεκάλυψαν τῆι σκηνῆι, 6.4.11).
[67] περίεργον... ἀνθρώπου φύσις, 1.12.6. [68] φύσει... ὄχλος ἐστὶ περίεργόν τι χρῆμα, 8.6.5.
[69] Διονύσιον... καὶ πάλαι μὲν ἐλύπει τὸ περιβόητον τῆς γυναικός, 5.2.7. Cf. 8.8.6 [Chaereas to the Sicilians]: 'By bringing her [to Babylon] Dionysius made Callirhoe famous and admired across all of Asia' (Καλλιρόην... Διονύσιος ἄγων περίβλεπτον ἐποίησε <καὶ> κατὰ τὴν Ἀσίαν ὅλην θαυμαζομένην).
[70] διήγημα καὶ τῆς Ἀσίας καὶ τῆς Εὐρώπης γέγονα, 5.5.3. [71] Schmeling (2005).

expressed in the *Iliad*, that she and Paris will be 'objects of song among generations to come'.[72] Chariton knowingly allows his female protagonist to oscillate awkwardly between the epic paradigms of Helen, the arch-bigamist,[73] and Penelope, the constant wife, and another woman for whom Homer predicts future fame (this time approbative).[74] The two sisters form a dyad, defining the axis of praise and blame for famous literary females.[75]

As ever, however, the forces that govern romance narrative are contradictory. The public perception of Callirhoe, prised away from her by the curious, is not the whole picture. In the interview with Dionysius, she conceals the crucial fact of the existence of her husband ('she told everything, and was silent only about Chaereas').[76] This foreshadows her later deception of Chaereas, in the matter of the letter she sends to Dionysius in book 8.[77] The story told is not always the full one. The crowds have even less of a grasp on the truth. Rumours can be misleading or destructive, such as the story of an epiphany of Aphrodite in the countryside that rages in and around Miletus (1.14.1); or the rumour (*phēmē*) about revolution in Egypt, which causes panic across Asia (6.8.3). The romance narrator gives us greater insight than that offered to the curious public: we see the actors behind closed doors, the person behind the veil, even the intimate thoughts in the hearts of the characters. It is no coincidence that the narrative finishes not in the theatre with Chaereas' address to the people of Sicily, but with Callirhoe's private, solitary prayer to Aphrodite (8.8.15–16).

Curiosity and rumour, then, are metanarrative forces with a complex role in this plot. They mark the transgressive, invasive impulse for knowledge, fully necessary for both the stimulation and the revelation of a story of intrigue. For all that they serve to bring events out into the public domain, however, they do not correspond exactly to the process of 'publication' of the romance. As readers, we are placed in an uncertain, liminal position, as *both* the 'reading public' *and* the private audience who hear much more of the story's truth than any internal narratee does. For this reason, it is important to see the instruments of 'publicisation' that operate within the

---

[72] ἀνθρώποισι... ἀοίδιμοι ἐσσομένοισι, 6.358.
[73] To whom Callirhoe is compared both for her beauty (2.6.1, 5.5.9, 8.1.3) and for her habit of attracting admirers other than her husband (5.2.8). Above, p. 55 n. 156.
[74] Hom. *Od.* 19.108; esp. 24.194–202, where Agamemnon contrasts Penelope's κλέος... ἧς ἀρετῆς with Clytaemnestra's στυγερὴ... ἀοιδή.
[75] Helen contrasted with Penelope: Plut. *Praec. conjug.* 140F, Ach. Tat. 1.8.6. Antisthenes Socraticus wrote *On Helen and Penelope* (Diog. Laert. 6.17). For Callirhoe's oscillation between Penelope and Helen, see Hirschberger (2001) 165–8.
[76] πάντα εἰποῦσα μόνον Χαιρέαν ἐσιγήσεν, 2.5.11.   [77] Above, p. 67.

text not simply as figuring Chariton's own aspirations for the romance,[78] but as tensing against the opposing forces that seek to 'privatise', to repress and conceal. The latter, indeed, are dominant at the end, with Callirhoe's intimate prayer to Aphrodite. Not only is this, as we have seen, a markedly private occasion ('while the masses were in the theatre'),[79] it also marks the cancellation of narrative with an implicit suggestion that Callirhoe will no longer be a worthy subject of narrative: 'I beg you, never again uncouple me from Chaereas, but grant us a blessed life and a shared death.'[80] Ultimately, then, we can read the dynamic play between public and private as another example of the romance's manipulation of centrifugal and centripetal forces within the narrative, and of a contradictory readerly psychology inhabited by *both* an insatiable demand for narrative twists *and* a need for closure.

GODLIKE NARRATORS AND PREDICTIVE TEXTING

It is, as we have said, a simple fact that stories must end. It is also a generically encoded certainty, or at least it became so, that Greek romances will conclude with the joyous reunion of the lovers. The more difficult question is how that ending shapes our reception of the text. On the one hand, we can take it as the culmination of the narrative, where its meaning is finally determined: where Miss Marple, as it were, reveals the identity of the murderer. Others, however, downplay the significance of the end, arguing that it is extrinsic to narrative meaning: 'artificial, arbitrary, minor rather than major chords, casual and textual rather than cosmic and definitive'.[81] In the words of D.A. Miller, the 'closural settlement accommodates the narratable only by changing its status, that is, by putting it in a past perfect tense and declaring it "over". Closure can *never* include, then, the narratable in its essential dimension: all suspense and indecision.'[82] On this interpretation, the ending is simply an arbitrary device for cancelling narrativity, which is fundamentally defined by openness and plurality of potentiality.

For scholars of the Greek romance, these two approaches are best represented by two classic articles on Heliodorus from the 1980s: Winkler's 'The mendacity of Kalasiris and the narrative strategy of Heliodorus'

---

[78] See esp. Tilg (2010) ch. 7. [79] ἕως... ἦν τὸ πλῆθος ἐν τῶι θεάτρωι, 8.8.15.
[80] δέομαί σοῦ, μηκέτι με Χαιρέου διαζεύξῃς, ἀλλὰ καὶ βίον μακάριον καὶ θάνατον ποινὸν κατάνευσον ἡμῖν, 8.8.16.
[81] Brooks (1984) 314. [82] Miller (1981) 98; above, p. 61.

Aithiopika';[83] and Morgan's response, 'A sense of the ending: the conclusion of Heliodoros' *Aithiopika*'.[84] Winkler's Heliodorus is ludic and mischievous. The pleasure of reading lies in the sport of the chase, not in the kill: 'There has to be some Noble Message or other at the end, any one will do.'[85] For Morgan, by contrast, the 'meaning of a story flows back from its ending, which constitutes a goal towards which the narrative can be seen to have been directed'.[86] On this reading, the second half of *Charicleia and Theagenes* is substantively different from the first, progressing as it does towards a satisfying resolution.[87] Clearly, much rests on this question of interpretation, for while Morgan's primary emphasis, like Winkler's, is upon the author's playful literary sophistication, his model opens the way for readings of Heliodorus as ideologically programmatic. Morgan himself gestures towards such a reading in his final paragraphs: although (like Winkler) he sees the text's religiosity as a mere literary device, a 'cypher for the control of its author',[88] he takes its emphasis upon marriage as *telos* as earnest, 'the romance's truest value: the consummation, under the auspices of marriage, of true love'.[89] Such a conclusion would be impossible if, like Winkler, he saw the ending as simply an arbitrary foreclosure of hermeneutic play.

In the light of our discussion so far, it is preferable to see these two readings as accentuating different tendencies within the romances, rather than mutually exclusive choices. Winkler elevates what we have called the narratorial id, Freud's 'seething cauldron' of energies and potentialities. Morgan, by contrast, elevates the superego, the matrix of cultural imperatives that determines the inevitability of the prescribed outcome. (Neither author is unaware of the contrary pressure: the difference, rather, lies in the relative weighting of the two.) These contrary tendencies operate at different levels. Winkler focuses on the hermeneutic efforts of characters on the ground within the narrative, which he sees as mirroring and cuing the reader's responses. Morgan, by contrast, gives much more emphasis

---

[83] Winkler (1982). [84] Morgan (1989b). [85] Winkler (1982) 157.
[86] Morgan (1989b) 299, also acknowledging the Brooksian/Millerian point that 'the ending that we are so eager to reach is the extinction as well as the goal of our pleasure'.
[87] Morgan (1989b) 319, arguing that Heliodorus switches from (in Barthes' terms) the hermeneutic to the prohairetic code. This is essentially the point made by the Byzantine scholar Michael Psellus: 'at the beginning the reader thinks that much of the material is superfluous; but as the narrative proceeds, he will marvel at the author's organisation' (ὁ γέ τοι πρώτως ἀναγιγνώσκων ἐκ περιττοῦ τὰ πολλὰ κεῖσθαι οἰόμενος, προϊόντος τοῦ λόγου, τὴν οἰκονομίαν τοῦ συγγεγραφότος θαυμάσεται, Hld. TXII.17–18 Colonna).
[88] Morgan (1989b) 319. For a neo-theist reading, see Dowden (1996). [89] Morgan (1989b) 320.

to authorial control, taking this as the object of the reader's hermeneutic efforts.

This sense that human action can be interpreted on two levels, of both individual choice and scripted predestination, is fundamental to much Greek narrative reflexivity. Usually it maps onto the polarity of mortal and divine knowledge. Homeric critics write of the principle of 'double determination', whereby the same events can be explained in terms of both the desires and tactical choices made by mortals and divine fiat.[90] This principle reappears in tragedy and new comedy, where the use of divine prologues in particular frames the audience's reception of subsequent events. Nick Lowe defines the conditions under which such a 'control level' can operate in narrative: it must be unilateral (i.e. directing human events without being directed by them); it must be screened from mortals; and it is bound by the rules of plot-type or genre.[91] An excellent example of these conditions comes in the delayed prologue of Menander's *Shield*, spoken by Fortune (Tukhē): 'If something terrible had really happened to these people, a goddess like me could not have come onstage next. But for the moment, they are wandering in ignorance.'[92] The goddess implicitly claims her authority to direct events, and explicitly marks both human ignorance of the 'control plane' and the generic restrictions she represents: put briefly, 'if this really were a tragedy as they think it is, you would not find a comic goddess onstage'. The divine characters know how the play will end, the human ones do not; and the audience is left to negotiate the ironic gulf between both perspectives.

In the Greek romances, in contrast to epic and drama, divine intervention is rare.[93] Accounts of direct supernatural influence, such as Homer's critics found so productively troublesome,[94] are avoided: gods forming councils, greeting favoured mortals, taking part in battles. With some exceptions, the romancers portray a world consistent with conventional physical laws, as a work of history would.[95] These exceptions fall into three classes:

(i) Epiphanies. These are almost never reported directly by the primary narrator. We do rarely find accounts of epiphany reported in a folk

---

[90] Lesky (1961) remains fundamental.   [91] Lowe (2000) 56–8 (at 56), an important discussion.
[92] ἀλλ' εἰ μὲν ἦν τούτοις τι γεγονὸς δυσχερές, / θεὸν οὖσαν οὐκ ἦν εἰκὸς ἀκολουθεῖν ἐμέ. / νῦν δὲ ἀγνοοῦσι καὶ πλανῶνται, Men. *Asp.* 97–9. On the exceptional role given to Tukhē in this play, see esp. Konet (1976).
[93] The most systematic overview of the representation of the gods in the romances is Alperowitz (1992); see also Weißenberger (1997) on Chariton and (with reservations) Bargheer (1999) on Heliodorus.
[94] Feeney (1991).   [95] Morgan (1993) 201–5.

tale[96] or mythical allegory,[97] but of course these are distanced by the very medium in which they are presented. In the later, 'sophistic' romances, gods can be seen in dreams,[98] as they are in Homer (see section (iii) below). In only two cases do gods directly impact on human activities.[99] (a) The first comes at the beginning of book 4 of *Anthia and Habrocomes*, where the hero is being crucified: after a prayer to Helios, 'the god pitied him',[100] and the cross collapses into the Nile; he is then crucified a second time, with the addition of a pyre, and again miraculously saved after a prayer. Although this passage has been interpreted as evidence of an encrypted religious message, it is (in my view) better seen as a case of Xenophontic intertextuality (not impossible, as is often assumed), referencing Herodotus' account of salvation of Croesus on the pyre by a sudden downpour after a prayer to Apollo (1.87.1–2; there are verbal allusions).[101] (b) The other epiphany comes at Longus 2.26–7, where the Methymnaeans who abduct Chloe experience weird sights and sounds by day and night; the narrator comments that 'it was intelligible to everyone with any sense that these apparitions and noises were the work of Pan, and that he was somehow wrathful against the sailors'.[102] To confirm this, Pan himself appears to Bryaxis in a dream, telling him to return Chloe (2.27.3). Again, this is an intertextual collage, with echoes of the Homeric Apollo's 'wrath' against the Achaeans after the abduction of Chryseis,[103] the *Homeric Hymns* to Dionysus and Apollo,[104] and – as the legitimating predecessor of an epiphany in a 'realistic'

---

[96] In Chariton's *Callirhoe*, there is a story (*logos*), which the nurse Plangon repeats to Callirhoe that Aphrodite manifests herself at the shrine of Aphrodite at Miletus (1.14.1, 2.2.5–6, 3.2.17). On the epiphany motif in Chariton see, Hägg (2002).

[97] In *Daphnis and Chloe*, Philetas tells the young lovers that he has seen Eros in his garden that morning (2.3–6).

[98] Ach. Tat. 4.1.4, 4.1.6–7, 7.12.4, cf. 1.3.2–4; Long. 1.7.2, 2.23, 2.26.5–27.3, 2.30.4, 3.27.2–5, 4.34.1, 4.35.5; Hld. 1.18.4, 4.14.2, cf. 5.22.1–3 (Odysseus), 8.11.3 (Calasiris, or perhaps a god in his form). Two dreams in Xenophon of Ephesus (1.12.4, 5.8.6) represent figures who may be divine. See also below, nn. 108–109.

[99] There is additionally a probable case of an epiphany of a saviour god in a battle scene from the fragmentary text that we call *Sesonchosis* (*P.Oxy.* 1826 verso = SW 253), but it is hard to extrapolate with so little of the context surviving.

[100] αὐτὸν ὁ θεὸς οἰκτείρει, 4.2.6.   [101] Above, p. 47.

[102] συνετὰ μὲν οὖν πᾶσιν ἦν τὰ γινόμενα τοῖς φρονοῦσιν ὀρθῶς, ὅτι ἐκ Πανὸς ἦν τὰ φαντάσματα καὶ ἀκούσματα μηνίοντός τι τοῖς ναύταις, 2.26.5. This passage is further discussed above, pp. 47–8.

[103] μηνίοντός ~ Hom. *Il.* 1.75 (μῆνιν Ἀπόλλωνος).

[104] In the account of the weird happenings: *HHDion*. 40 (ivy), 53 (dolphins), and more generally the abduction narrative; at *HHApoll*. 400–3 Apollo turns into an aggressive dolphin. Dolphins also have a more general association with wonder stories, via Arion (Hdt. 1.23–4).

text – Pan's appearance to Phidippides in Herodotus (6.105–6).[105] Even so, this is not simply a literary pastiche: it is the strongest case for a direct epiphany in the Greek romances, and a sign of the dreamier, more mythical world created by Longus.

(ii) Allegorical interventions. In a world in which personified abstractions can be counted as gods, and gods themselves associated with particular qualities (Ares with militarism, Athena with prudence, and so forth), the line between an account of divine intervention and a figurative way of marking a feature in the plot (usually either a psychological change in an individual or a change of narrative organisation) is blurred. Thus, most obviously, the attentions of Eros at the start of Chariton and Xenophon represent the onset of love and the beginning of the erotic plot,[106] and so forth. Chariton's case of Aphrodite overruling Tukhē at the start of book 8 is another example of this phenomenon, figuring the change from episodic to teleological mode, and the end of Chaereas' penance for his anger.[107]

(iii) By far the most important manifestations of a divine 'control plane' are the revelation of divine intentions through dreams and oracles, a central and recurrent feature of romance narrative.[108] These almost always turn out to be true.[109]

Dreams and oracles, thus, form by some distance the most significant category for romance manifestations of the control plane. We should note that this category – let us subsume both under the general heading of 'prophecy' – has quite specific features: through prophecies, gods' intentions (a) are communicated indirectly, in line with the general avoidance of explicit supernatural intervention; (b) require mortals (both characters within the text and readers) to engage in hermeneutic interpretation, which indeed (as so often in Greek culture) may not be fully actuated until the

---

[105] Hunter (1983) 59 also sees an allusion to this Philippides episode in the Nymphs' dream forecast at 2.23.4.
[106] Above, pp. 38–9.   [107] Above, pp. 59–60, 65–6.
[108] Divine appearances in dreams listed above, n. 98. See additionally Char. 2.1.2–3, 5.5.5–7; Xen. Eph. 1.6.2, 2.8.2; Ach. Tat. 1.3.3–4, 2.12.2, 2.14.1, 2.23.5, 3.19.3; Hld. 2.16.1, 2.25.5, 2.26.5, 2.35.5, 10.3.1. Proleptic dreams and oracles are discussed from a narratological perspective by Hägg (1971) 221–42 (on Chariton, Xenophon and Achilles), and Bartsch (1989) 80–108 (on Achilles and Heliodorus). Liatsi (2004) considers two dreams in Xenophon. MacAlister (1992) 70–83 considers romance dreams as symptoms of a general cultural passivity, unconvincingly to my eyes.
[109] The exceptions are Xen. Eph. 2.8.2 and 5.8.6, two dreams that seem not to be realised (Hägg (1971) 231–2). It may be tempting to appeal to the generally uneven texture of *Anthia and Habrocomes* for an explanation for these; but Liatsi (2004) more plausibly argues that Xenophon's dreams can be psychological as well as proleptic, reading 2.8.2 as a reflection of Habrocomes' state of mind at the time (162–71). Hld. 2.16.4 is also puzzling, although proleptic solutions have been proposed (see esp. Bartsch (1989) 99–100).

prophecy is fulfilled; (c) are proleptic, which is to say orientated towards the future.

We can see, then, that prophecies mobilise exactly the same tension between infinite narrative potentiality and goal-orientated teleology that we have been discussing. In Greek literature generally, prophecies tend to work by metaphorical substitution, rather than direct revelation: in Artemidorus' terms, they are 'allegorical' rather than 'theorematic' (his name for dreams that are fulfilled exactly as they are dreamed),[110] signifying by displacement (or 'othering': *alloiōsis*)[111] rather than literally. Thus their interpretation is 'nothing other than the juxtaposition of similarity'.[112] In other words, to decode the dream we need to discover the logic of contiguity upon which the prophetic substitution rests: for example, a thunderbolt hitting the ground nearby stands for impending relocation, since one cannot stand near a thunderbolt (2.9 (p. 110.10–12 Pack)). This means, however, that interpretation is a highly tricky business, since the true meaning can be displaced, in principle, along any number of axes. Artemidorus might want us to believe that the juxtaposition of similarity is an exact science; but he also implicitly concedes that for all but the expert the true meaning is never really secure until the outcome is known. To translate the discourse of prophecy back into metaliterary terms, we have a choice between Morgan's position (the meaning is constituted by the outcome, and then 'flows back' into the interpretative process) and Winkler's (the revelation of meaning is always deferred to an uncertain future).

There was a rich culture of debate in the early imperial period surrounding prophecy, encompassing both traditional and sceptical positions.[113] There are, on the one hand, numerous testaments in the Greek literature of the time (not to mention the epigraphy)[114] to the ongoing belief in the efficacy of prophecy. To list but a few examples: Aristides' *Sacred tales*, Pausanias' *Periegesis*, Astrampsychus' *On oracles* (addressed to Ptolemy Philadelphus but almost certainly imperial), Plutarch's three Delphic dialogues (and no doubt his *On divination*, of which only one fragment

---

[110] δι' ἄλλων ἄλλα σημαίνοντες, Artem. *Oneir.* 1.2, (p. 5.9–10 Pack); cf. 1.2 (p. 4.22–3) and esp. 4.1 (pp. 241.1–242.15).
[111] Artem. *Oneir.* 1.50 (pp. 55.5–57.14 Pack).
[112] οὐδὲν ἄλλο... ἢ ὁμοίου παράθεσις, Artem. *Oneir.* 2.25 (p. 145.11–12 Pack). Similarly, at Ach. Tat. 5.4.1, Menelaus advises that 'interpreters of signs tell us to look at the stories encoded in paintings and assimilate the future to that narrative' (λέγουσι... οἱ τῶν συμβόλων ἐξηγηταὶ σκοπεῖν τοὺς μύθους τῶν εἰκόνων... καὶ ἐξομοιοῦν τὸ ἀποβησόμενον τῶι τῆς ἱστορίας λόγωι, 5.4.1).
[113] See esp. the excellent survey, covering literature and epigraphy, of Bendlin (2006), who locates these debates within the wider cultural context of the contestation of intellectual authority.
[114] Many inscriptions are collected and discussed in Bendlin (2006).

survives (147 Sandbach)), Artemidorus' *Dreambook*, Philo's *On dreams*, Aelian's *On providence* (*pronoia*).[115] It is clear that prophecy remained central to Greek culture. There was, however, also a strong tradition of oracular scepticism, rooted in Cynicism and atomism (early examples can be found in Epicurus – who mischievously appropriated the title 'prophecy' for his own philosophy – Philodemus and Cicero's *On divination*).[116] In the second century, Oenomaus of Gadara composed his anti-oracular *Exposure of frauds*,[117] Diogenes of Oenoanda set up his massive Epicurean inscription (which included a critique of prophecy: frr. 52–4),[118] and Lucian wrote his anti-prophetic texts *Alexander or the false prophet, Astrology, Zeus rants* and *Zeus refuted*. The latter two texts confront the king of the gods with questions about destiny (*heimarmenē*, *Jup. conf.* 1) and providence (*pronoia*, *Jup. trag.* 4),[119] offering the claim (which may derive from Oenomaus)[120] that prophecies of the future are opaque and equivocal, and thus deny humans any real possibility of predicting anything (*Jup. conf.* 14; cf. *Jup. trag.* 31, 43). Specifically, they are 'bivalent' (*epamphoterizonta*, *Jup. conf.* 14), 'thoroughly double-edged and two-faced, like some herms, which are double and the same whichever side you look at them from'.[121]

There is also a philosophical dimension to this debate, reflecting the investigation into the relationship between free will and providential determinism that occupied many thinkers in the Hellenistic and particularly the early imperial periods – not just in Stoicism (the school most closely associated with determinist beliefs)[122] and Epicureanism/atomism (which rules out any predestination),[123] but also among peripatetics[124] and Platonists.[125] For the latter two camps, the kind of mechanistic determinism that they ascribe (sometimes misleadingly) to Stoicism rules out the possibility of

---

[115] Frr. 9–20 Domingo-Forasté. The extant fragments suggest this was centrally concerned with prophecy and religious knowledge, but this emphasis could of course reflect the interest of later excerptors.

[116] Not that Cicero himself was necessarily a critic of prophecy (Beard (1986)).

[117] Hammerstaedt (1988) collects the fragments with commentary; see also (1990). Oenomaus is best dated to the second century: Hammerstaedt (1988) 11–19.

[118] Good discussion of Diogenes on oracles and dreams at Gordon (1996) 105–24, who also notes that fr. 23 mentions the 'ambiguity and tricky obliqueness' (τὸ ἀμφίβολον καὶ ποικίλως πλάγιον) of oracles.

[119] The philosophical background for the former is discussed by Großlein (1998): see pp. 61–9 on prophecy. Criticism of specific cases of prophecy is also in evidence in *Alexander* and *Astrology*.

[120] Thus Hammerstaedt (1990) 2860–1.

[121] ἀκριβῶς ἀμφήκης... καὶ διπρόσωπος, οἷοί εἰσι τῶν Ἑρμῶν ἔνιοι, διττοὶ καὶ ἀμφοτέρωθεν ὅμοιοι πρὸς ὁπότερον ἂν αὐτῶν μέρος ἐπιστραφῇς, *Jup. trag.* 43.

[122] Sources collected and discussed at LS 55, 62; see Bobzien (1998), Frede (2003).

[123] Sources collected and discussed at LS 20.

[124] Most notably in Alexander of Aphrodisias, *On destiny* (*heimarmenē*).

[125] Ps.-Plut. *De fat.* (*tukhē*); Alc. *Didask.* 26; Nemes. *De nat. hom.* 36–8; Apul. *De Plat.* 1.11–12.

chance occurrences, and – more urgently, from an ethical perspective – the responsibility that weighs upon individual humans to contribute towards shaping the future.

We can hear echoes of these debates within the romances themselves. The romancers refer frequently to *heimarmenē*, or 'destiny', a concept widely associated with this kind of debate.[126] Near the beginning of his narrative, Achilles' Clitophon comments that

> The divine (*to daimonion*) often likes to reveal the future to mortals at night, not so that we might deliver ourselves from suffering (for destiny [*heimarmenēs*] is insuperable), but so that we might endure such suffering more easily.[127]

Achilles here gives his principal narrator a ponderously phrased, abstraction-heavy *sententia* that looks like a direct lift from a philosophical handbook (and, indeed, Achilles' very phrase was itself later excerpted).[128] This is not, of course, the key to a coherent philosophical belief-system underpinning the romance, but an example of the kind of daft, pompous sententiousness to which Clitophon is prone. Even so, it testifies to an awareness of the debates over fate and free will current at the time.

It is, however, predominantly through the discourse of prophecy that the romancers figure the relationship between plot and ending. Prophecy, indeed, is a handy figure for plot itself. Reading both is *stochastic*: it involves conjecture and progressive refinement in a field full of random variables. The idea of plot as subtended by prophecy is pre-empted in epic and drama, in the sense that each genre can contain oracles that are instrumental in the development of the narrative (Homer's *Odyssey*, Sophocles' *Oedipus Tyrannus*, *Philoctetes* and *Oedipus at Colonus*), and can begin with divinely authorised prognostications of the outcome, even if these lack the formal properties of prophecies (Homer's *Iliad*; many of the plays of Euripides and New Comedy with divine prologues). It is in the romance, however, that the idea that a prophecy can be coextensive with the plot achieves full form. Near the beginning of Xenophon's *Anthia and Habrocomes*, the two

---

[126] Xen. Eph. 1.10.2 (τὸ εἱμαρμένον); Ach. Tat. 1.3.2, 4.13.5; Hld. 2.24.6, 4.5.1, 4.11.3, 5.6.2, 7.6.5, 8.17.1. Cf. also Char. 2.4.8 (an absurdly lyrical usage by Dionysius).

[127] φιλεῖ δὲ τὸ δαιμόνιον πολλάκις ἀνθρώποις τὸ μέλλον νύκτωρ λαλεῖν, οὐχ ἵνα φυλάξωνται μὴ παθεῖν – οὐ γὰρ εἱμαρμένης δύνανται κρατεῖν – ἀλλ' ἵνα κουφότερον πάσχοντες φέρωσι, 1.3.2.

[128] For parallels, see Theocr. 24.69–70, with Gow (1952) 2.426 on the 'commonplace'. Kerferd (1981) 51 speculates that the belief may go back to Antiphon of Rhamnus in his τέχνη ἀλυπίας. Achilles' phrase is excerpted Ps.-Maximus, *Loci communes* (= *PG* 91, 1000 B) and Michael Apostolius, *Cent.* xvii, 81e. Heliodorus' Calasiris makes a recognisably similar claim (2.24.6–7); see also Iamblichus (the romancer) fr. 34 = SW 210.

lovers' parents, in despair at their children's 'sickness', seek an oracle from Colophonian Apollo. The god replies:

Why do you desire to learn the end of the illness, and the beginning?	1
One illness holds both, and therein lies the cure [or 'solution'].	2
I see terrible suffering for them, and endless tasks.	3
Both will be exiled over the sea, pursued by Lyssa,	4
They will endure captivity at the hands of sea-borne men;	5
For both, the tomb will be their bridal chamber, and the fire will destroy them.	6
But still, after their toil they have a better fate	7
And by the currents of the river Nile afterwards they offer	8
Holy gifts to reverend Isis, their saviour.[129]	9
	1.6.2

This oracle is intimately bound up with the extent of Xenophon's plot, for a number of reasons. I begin with two obvious ones. First, it is not simply proleptic, but kinetic: it is to 'appease'[130] this oracle (and for no other reason) that the parents send their children abroad. It is, literally, a self-fulfilling prophecy. For all that this pretext may seem a weakly motivated narrative expedient (the oracle did not demand their travel, simply predicted it), it is a significant token of the centrality of this oracle to Xenophon's narrative that it both stands outside it (as a metanarrative commentary) and plays an instrumental role within it. The second point is that in general terms this oracle defines (from line 3 onwards) the scope and shape of the narrative to come: sufferings followed by release. The reference to the 'beginning' (*arkhē*) and 'end' (*telos*) of the illness emphasises the analogy with the plot. The fulfilment of the oracle will be the end of the tale, and also the 'cure' for the illness. The list thus serves as a synoptic map of the entire narrative; and, indeed, in what follows Anthia and Habrocomes do periodically cross-refer back to the oracle, measuring their progress against it.[131]

Another reason to think of the oracle as plot-like is the intratextual representation of hermeneutic activity. Although the phrasing is in general relatively descriptive, 'theorematic' (in Artemidorus' terms), it is too compressed to be intelligible to those who do not yet know how the plot will unfurl. The gaps in the narrative demand to be filled, as in real narrative: in

---

[129] I do not print the full Greek text for the oracle, which is seriously disputed: see Zimmermann (1949/50) 256–60, and further below. This translation renders O'Sullivan's text, although I have reservations over ἔνθεν ἔνεστι in line 2.
[130] παραμυθήσασθαι, 1.7.2; also 1.10.3.
[131] 1.7.4, 1.10.3, 1.11.1, 1.12.3, 2.1.2, 3.3.1, 5.1.13; Hägg (1971) 230–1, with 231 nn. 1–2.

Iser's words, 'this is what stimulates the reader into filling the blanks with projections'.¹³² Xenophon re-emphasises this point by portraying internal narratees struggling to make sense:

> The fathers were immediately thrown into perplexity, completely at a loss as to what the problem was. They could not work out the god's utterances, neither what this illness was nor the exile, nor the captivity, nor the tomb, nor the river, nor the divine salvation.¹³³

It is not surprising that the fathers cannot make sense of what they hear: most of the events come in the future.¹³⁴ Their confusion thus marks neither a failure of intellect (as, for example, in the case of Longus' Methymnaeans, who 'could not understand the reason'¹³⁵ for the terrifying portents) nor perversity (like Heliodorus' Thyamis, who 'forced the interpretation' of a dream 'to conform with his own desires'),¹³⁶ but a problem with narrative vantage, which only time can solve. Their failure of interpretation, thus, mirrors and stimulates the external reader's own curiosity at the outset of the primary narrative.¹³⁷

From one perspective, then, the meaning of the oracle is resolved at the end of the narrative: the meaning 'flows back from its ending'. But *are* the oracle's enigmas fully deciphered? Even if we leave aside the problems of textual detail,¹³⁸ lines 6–7 remain unsettling. What does 'for both the tomb will be their bridal chamber' mean? Anthia is buried alive, and Perilaus comments that 'we shall lead you to your tomb as through it were your bridal chamber' (3.7.2); but this does not happen to 'both' of them. Conversely, Habrocomes experiences 'fire' (4.2.8–9), but not Anthia. What is more, after this reference to their death, the following lines suggest salvation. This little hint of soteriological death-and-rebirth serves both to generate a narrative misdirection (neither in fact dies) and to thicken the air of mystery.¹³⁹ Rather than ignoring these lines (or, worse still, excising them as a later interpolation),¹⁴⁰ I propose, that we

---

¹³² Iser (1978) 168.
¹³³ εὐθὺς μὲν οἱ πατέρες αὐτῶν ἦσαν ἐν ἀμηχανίαι καὶ τὸ δεινὸν ὅ τι ἦν πάνυ ἠπόρουν· συμβάλλειν δὲ τὰ τοῦ θεοῦ λόγια οὐκ ἐδύναντο· οὔτε γὰρ τίς ἡ νόσος οὔτε τίς ἡ φυγή, οὔτε τίνα τὰ δεσμὰ οὔτε ὁ τάφος τίς οὔτε ὁ ποταμὸς τίς οὔτε τίς ἡ ἐκ τῆς θεοῦ βοήθεια, 1.7.1.
¹³⁴ The exception is the 'illness': why they cannot understand what this refers to is inexplicable. This is no doubt one of those Xenophontic loose ends that will never be tied up.
¹³⁵ οὐκ εἶχον... τὴν αἰτίαν συμβαλεῖν, 2.26.5. See also above, at n. 102.
¹³⁶ ἕλκει πρὸς τὴν ἑαυτοῦ βούλησιν τὴν ἐπίλυσιν, 1.18.5; see further above, p. 170.
¹³⁷ Hägg (1971) 230–1.   ¹³⁸ Above, n. 129.
¹³⁹ Death and rebirth themes are discussed by Kerényi (1927) 24–43, with 41–3 on Xenophon (this passage is not mentioned).
¹⁴⁰ Zimmermann (1949/50) 257. This drastic solution also involves removing the relevant parts of the fathers' non-comprehending response.

should see them as what Paul de Man calls a 'residue of indetermination', which always results when we attempt to decode figural into natural language.[141]

Xenophon's prophecy thus encodes both narrative's inherent teleology, its end-orientation, and its pleasure in indeterminacy. We can take this point further. The oracle, as we have observed, emphasises the inevitability of the end: it predicts sufferings and exile, but also divine assistance, an 'end' (*telos*) to the illness, a 'cure' (*lusis*), and 'a better fate after their sufferings'. Yet it also foretells *endless* (*anēnuta*) tasks ahead. There is a strange mismatch between the prediction of both end and endlessness: the oracle seems to predict two incompatible futurities.[142] The oracle is not, then, simply a recipe for the impending story, but also a description of the complex, contradictory narrative vectors that drive romance plot, towards both ending and endlessness.

Xenophon's is the most spectacular example of prophetic metanarrative, but there are other cases too. In *Leucippe and Clitophon*, Clitophon begins[143] his story with a proleptic dream, in which he is fused to his half-sister Calligone, and a terrifying female figure cuts them apart (1.3.4). The dream primarily predicts that Clitophon will not marry Calligone, but also subtly portends the entire narrative of erotic separation.[144] In this text, however, the divine control plane is only intermittently referenced, as one would expect in a narrative presented entirely homodiegetically (i.e. by characters within it), and largely from the perspective of Clitophon the agent rather than Clitophon the retrospective narrator.[145] Clitophon, that is to say, is far from godlike as a narrator.

At the other extreme, Heliodorus' *Charicleia and Theagenes* is the most theist of the romances, a narrative in which the control plane becomes progressively more visible, through prolepses revealing divine will.[146] As in Xenophon, one authoritative oracle subtends the narrative. When Calasiris arrives in Delphi, Pythian Apollo announces:

---

[141] De Man (1986) 15.
[142] This incompatibility is underlined if we read λύσις ἔνθεν ἀνυστή (i.e. the positive form of ἀνήνυτα) in line 2 (Abresch, followed by Papanikolaou), instead of the MS ἀνέστη (followed by Dalmeyda) or ἔνεστι (O'Sullivan).
[143] The account of it immediately follows the sentence 'Fortune initiated the drama' (ἤρχετο τοῦ δράματος ἡ Τύχη, 1.3.3).
[144] 'the dream, in its initial position, symbolizes *the concept of "separation"*, in all its appearance in the romance' (Hägg (1971) 238).
[145] Hägg (1971) 237.
[146] Divine βούλησις (and cognates): 2.20.2, 4.15.2, 4.16.3, 7.21.4, 7.23.4, 10.20.2, 10.38.1 (an Iliadic motif, of course). On prediction, prolepsis and prophecy, see esp. Morgan (1989b); Bartsch (1989) 93–108; Futre Pinheiro (1998); Lowe (2000) 249–58.

> Consider her who has elegance (*kharin*) at first but fame (*kleos*)
>   at the end, Delphi, and the goddess' (*theas*) offspring (*genetēn*).
> They shall leave my temple, carve the wave
>   and come to the dark[147] land of the sun (*ēeliou*).
> There they shall garner the great prize (*aethlion*) for the virtue of their lives,
>   a white garland on blackening temples. (2.35.5)

As in Xenophon, this oracle can be seen as a transcription of the literary text. It contains a veiled allusion to the title of the text ('the Ethiopian affairs of Charicleia and Theagenes', 10.41.4), in the cryptic references to the protagonists and the 'dark land of the sun'; and perhaps even to Heliodorus' own name (a poetic form of *helios*, 'sun', is used; and we might take the 'prize' for their virtue as a divine 'gift', *dōron*). It also works as a linear rewriting of the plot. Whereas the narrative that we read is chronologically complex and heavily subplotted, the prophecy offers a straightforward, spatialised model (Charicleia and Theagenes travel from Delphi to Ethiopia), embodying a clear moral of divinely sanctioned 'virtue rewarded'. Romance, as we have frequently noted, is always aware of its potential to be reduced to simple formulae. The simplification here involves reducing the plot to its beginning and its end (the middle represented merely by 'carve the wave'), a process that is obliquely hinted at in the opening lines of the oracle. Charicleia has elegance 'at first' (*en prōtois*) and fame 'finally' (*hustat*): this refers primarily to the order of the elements (*kharis, kleos*) in her name, but can also be taken in a narrative-chronological sense: her elegance is innate but her fame is acquired through the course of (and, at a self-reflexive level, through the medium of) the narrative.

This emphasis on beginnings and ends, shared with Xenophon's oracle, can take us further. Heliodorus' oracle also, again like Xenophon's, initiates the plot, albeit more subtly. Heliodorus' is a narrative with multiple beginning points (also including the opening scenes on the Egyptian coast and the Ethiopian backstory), but one of them is clearly Delphi, where the lovers meet and fall in love at a festival. As we saw in Chapter 3, indeed, Heliodorus mobilises the generically conditioned expectation that a romance will start in this way, by including multiple allusions to the beginning of *Anthia and Habrocomes* in his Delphic episode.[148] We can take Heliodorus' Apollonian oracle, then, as self-consciously reprising the

---

[147] κυανέην, which would conventionally mean 'dark blue', but Homer seems, and more importantly seemed to ancient commentators, to use it on occasion to mean 'black' (*Il.* 24.94, and esp. Σ Hom. *Il.* 1.528, 4.282, 5.345, 11.26 etc.; conversely μέλας can be taken as 'deep blue', Σ 2.825).

[148] Above, p. 117.

dynamic role of the Xenophon's (even if it has only the hermeneutic, not the kinetic role of the latter).[149]

But it is of course the ending towards which this oracle, like all oracles, is primarily orientated. The *telos* of the oracle will also be that of the narrative, and indeed we are explicitly reminded of the prophecy at the end, where Charicles recognises the fulfilment of Apollo's words (10.41.2). Oracle and plot converge in closure. We can go further still. The response to Xenophon's oracle is aporia on the part of the parents, a passage that (as we saw) can be read self-reflexively. Heliodorus's version (directly borrowing Xenophon's language at points) is, characteristically, more knowing in its self-reflexivity:

When the god had spoken thus, the greatest perplexity (*amēkhania*) filled the bystanders, who were at a loss (*aporountes*) as to what the oracle intended to signify. Each pulled the utterance in a different direction, and interpreted it in accordance with his wishes. As yet, no one had fastened on its true meaning, since oracles and dreams are usually judged by their outcomes (*telesi*).[150]

Three features of the bystanders' response are highlighted: (i) it is diverse and multiform; (ii) it is driven by desire (like Thyamis' earlier response to his dream);[151] (iii) it is retroceptive, i.e. the meaning of the oracle is only determined once the *telos* has been reached. We can see here the characteristic signs of the interpretative id in action: the 'seething cauldron' of desire, bubbling out an infinite number of possible futurities.

Calasiris, of course, implicitly opposes this approach to his own, which is to decipher the meaning patiently, and in accordance with the god's will rather than his own.[152] The hermeneutic superego thus stipulates the 'proper', normative approach to reading. But, as ever, we do need to acknowledge the existence of both forces in the romance, even if the one is repressed. The importance of this point becomes clear if we return to the

---

[149] Heliodorus' oracle might be taken to have a kinetic function if we see it as encouraging Calasiris to plan to escape with Charicleia and Theagenes, but this is not explicit.

[150] ταῦτα μὲν ὡς ἀνεῖπεν ὁ θεός, ἀμηχανία πλείστη τοὺς περιεστῶτας εἰσεδύετο τὸν χρησμὸν ὅ τι βούλοιτο φράζειν ἀπορούντες· ἄλλος γὰρ πρὸς ἄλλο τι τὸ λόγιον ἔσπα καὶ ὡς ἕκαστος εἶχε βουλήσεως, οὕτω καὶ ὑπελάμβανεν. οὔπω δὲ οὐδεὶς τῶν ἀληθῶν ἐφήπτετο, χρησμοὶ γὰρ καὶ ὄνειροι τὰ πολλὰ τοῖς τέλεσι κρίνονται, 2.36.2 ~ εὐθὺς μὲν οἱ πατέρες αὐτῶν ἦσαν ἐν ἀμηχανίαι καὶ τὸ δεινὸν ὅ τι ἦν πάνυ ἠπόρουν· συμβάλλειν δὲ τὰ τοῦ θεοῦ λόγια οὐκ ἐδύναντο..., Xen. Eph. 1.7.1.

[151] ἕλκει πρὸς τὴν ἑαυτοῦ βούλησιν τὴν ἐπίλυσιν, 1.18.5; above, p. 170.

[152] See 3.5.7, where he states that the oracle gives him an intimation (*hyponoia*) of the future, but 'I could not yet comprehend any of the subsequent parts of the oracle' (οὐδὲ ἀκριβῶς οὐδὲν ἔτι τῶν ἑξῆς χρησθέντων συνέβαλλον).

oracle, and consider the final line's 'white garland on blackening temples'.[153] What does this mean? *Does* it have an outcome within the narrative? Certainly, Charicleia and Theagenes are 'crowned with white turbans'[154] as they assume their priesthoods and proceed to marriage, but their temples are not 'blackening'. Bartsch proposes that the temples in question belong to Hydaspes and Persinna, from whom Charicleia and Theagenes receive the crowns.[155] This is unsatisfactory because the culmination of the plot (and the reward for the lovers' virtue) is surely the ordination and marriage, when the crowns are *transferred*. For Morgan, Charicleia and Theagenes are becoming Ethiopian by cultural assimilation: 'the white crown makes their white skin metaphorically black'.[156] This is a more attractive interpretation, but cannot be said to be exhaustive (Morgan himself claims only that it is the 'richest' solution).[157] It is better to take this as another residue of indetermination, a sign that literary meaning is not fully determined even in closure.[158]

PARADIGM AND SYNTAGM

I have claimed that despite the ultimate dominance of the superego over the id in closure, both are integral to the experience of the romance plot. It is time to explore this claim in more detail. What is at stake for readers in the choice between these two modes? What kind of readers do we become if we privilege the one or the other? What the superego offers is *meaning*; what the id offers is *vitality*. Let us borrow from Roman Jakobson's famous distinction between metaphor and metonym, or paradigmatic and syntagmatic modes of operation, as reinterpreted for plot by Peter Brooks:[159] 'Narrative operates as metaphor in its affirmation of resemblance, in that it brings into relation different actions, combines them through perceived similarities... Plot is the structure of action in closed and legible wholes; it thus *must* use metaphor as the trope of its achieved interrelations, and it must *be* metaphoric insofar as it is totalizing.'[160] The closural force is paradigmatic in operation: it seeks to tie together all loose strands into a single, tightly ravelled skein, and hence permits the significance of the

---

[153] λευκὸν ἐπὶ κροτάφων στέμμα μελαινομένων, 2.35.5. The similarities are noted and discussed by Winkler (1982) 118–19.
[154] στεφθέντες... λευκαῖς ταῖς μίτραις, 10.41.3.   [155] Bartsch (1989) 102 n. 9.
[156] Morgan (1989b) 318.   [157] Morgan (1989b) 318.
[158] Another example of an indeterminate dream comes in book 2, where Charicleia dreams that a man of savage aspect gouges out her eye (2.16.1–4). See above, n. 109.
[159] Brooks (1984) 90–2.
[160] Brooks (1984) 91. I have corrected an obvious typographical error in the quotation.

narrative as a whole to be grasped, as a totalised expression of cultural values. Thus the *Odyssey* can be said to be 'about' the restoration of the patriarchal household, and the Greek romances to be about the introduction of women and men into legitimate sexual roles within elite, urban, adult society, under the watchful care of benevolent deities.

At the syntagmatic level, events are perceived not in terms of their larger significance in the plot, but as juxtaposed or aggregated in a seemingly arbitrary order. This is life experienced as what Bakhtin calls 'adventure time', with its procession of 'suddenly's and 'just at that moment's.[161] This projects a sense of life as unpredictable, chaotic, threatening, and paradoxical; but also more emotionally engaging, and even (in Achilles Tatius and Longus) free from the overbearing restrictions of the patriarchal household. The romance does not invent the tension between these two modes – which can already be glimpsed in Callimachus and Apollonius, and in Hellenistic scholarship on the *Odyssey*[162] – but it does give it a new, aesthetically definitive centrality.

Modern scholars, who develop their ideas about texts over many readings, whose profession values cohesive, systematic interpretations, and who may look down on affective responses as unintellectual, tend to favour paradigmatic modes of interpretation. We like our urns well-wrought; every detail is expected to contribute to the system. (We saw in the previous section some examples of Procrustean attempts to make perfect sense of Xenophon's and Heliodorus' oracles.) Ancient readers, however, could be (notwithstanding Aristotle's strictures) more tolerant of diversity, of the seductive power of the episodic.[163] Plutarch writes in his *How a young man should listen to poetry* that

Changes in narrative direction furnish stories with an empathetic, surprising (*paralogon*) and unexpected quality. This is what generates the maximum shock and pleasure.[164]

These vicarious emotions – shock (*ekplēxis*), pleasure – are explicitly linked to the kind of sudden changes in narrative direction that we find in the romances, the paradoxical, 'paralogic' features of syntagmatic narration. Surprisingly,[165] Plutarch sees these effects as wholly intrinsic to literary

---

[161] Bakhtin (1981) 89–97, with 92 on 'suddenly' and 'just at that moment'.
[162] Hutchinson (2008) 66–89 writes of 'paratactic' and 'hypotactic' modes of narrative.
[163] A major theme of Heath (1989).
[164] τὸ γὰρ ἐμπαθὲς καὶ παράλογον καὶ ἀπροσδόκητον, ὧι πλείστη μὲν ἔκπληξις ἕπεται πλείστη δὲ χάρις, αἱ μεταβολαὶ παρέχουσι τοῖς μύθοις, 25d.
[165] Van der Stockt (1992) 125–6 observes how unusual this statement is. Hunter (2009a) 190–1 offers the apt parallel of Cic. *Fam.* 5.12.4–5.

creation, and as wholly beneficial. Narrative twists and turns make better philosophers of us, so that 'when we ourselves have met with changes in fortune (*tukhais*) we are not humiliated or disturbed'.[166] In the context of this essay – a reappraisal of the Platonic rejection of poetry, arguing that it can be useful in the education of the young – everything must be seen to serve an ethical function. In one respect, Plutarch's approach is heavily paradigmatic, in that he offers his readers a moral framework that will predetermine the outcome of reading. At the same time, however, Plutarch does acknowledge the sheer pleasure (*kharis*) to be had for the syntagmatic reader, affectively saturated in the narrative moment, absorbed in the thrills of each twist in the plot.

Syntagmatic and paradigmatic modes of reading are repeatedly dramatised in the romances, particularly in the form of dialogues between the despairing (male) protagonist, thoroughly absorbed in the moment, and a counselling friend, who takes a more detached view.[167] In *Callirhoe*, Polycharmus repeatedly 'consoles' Chaereas,[168] holds him back from a rash decision (3.6.5), and forestalls his suicide (repeatedly!).[169] Polycharmus is 'sound of mind' (*sōphronōn*, 3.6.5), 'manly' (*andrikos*, 4.2.3) and – crucially – 'not enslaved to Eros, that harsh tyrant'.[170] It is this absence of emotional engagement that allows him to avoid his friend's thorough affective absorption in the immediate crisis. In particular, it gives him a command of strategy, an ability to manipulate his friend's feelings, to delay tactically, and to plot for the future. In an early case of suicide prevention, he warns Chaereas not to betray Callirhoe (whom he thinks he has killed), that now is the 'proper time' (*kairos*) to bury her (1.6.1). The command of the *kairos* – broadly, the art of knowing the right action for the right occasion – is central to elite Greek ethics in the imperial period.[171] It betokens that certain *je ne sais quoi* that distinguishes the self-controlled from the impetuous, the cultivated from the vulgar. Chaereas is saturated with erotic affect, to the point of near-incapacity to act independently; Polycharmus, on the other hand, can detach himself from the here and now, and plan effectively for the future.

---

[166] αὐτοὺς χρησαμένους τύχαις μὴ ταπεινοῦσθαι μηδὲ ταράττεσθαι, 35d.
[167] The role of friends in the romance is discussed by Létoublon (1993) 93–103 (esp. 95–6 on suicide prevention); Hock (1997), focusing on Chariton; Watanabe (2003) 25–33, on Xenophon. See also Ruiz Montero (1988) 311–17, assimilating the romantic friend to the folkloric 'helper'.
[168] 3.6.8, 4.4.1, 5.2.6 (παραμυθ-); 5.10.10 (παρηγορεῖν).
[169] 1.5.2, 1.6.1, 5.10.10, 6.2.8, 6.2.11, 7.1.7–8. Attempted suicide will be discussed in greater detail below.
[170] μὴ δουλεύων Ἔρωτι, χαλέπωι τυράννωι, 4.2.3.
[171] Whitmarsh (2005a) 28, 37, 55; for wider discussions see Sipiora and Baumlin (2002).

Absorption and detachment are the characteristic styles of the syntagmatic and paradigmatic modes. In Xenophon, this tension is played out in terms of the politics of sexual identity. The role of Habrocomes' buddy is given to Hippothous, who is racked with pederastic love for a young man, now dead, by the name of Hyperanthes: it is he who consoles the protagonist and restrains him from suicide by bidding him 'take heart' (*tharrein*, 3.10.3). So, far from being free from the passion that afflicts the hero, like Chariton's Polycharmus, Hippothous is embroiled in a parallel narrative, which in some respects mirrors Habrocomes' own.[172] The affective detachment from the other's story is thus explained primarily by self-absorption in each's own, and consolidated by the fact of their different sexual orientations.

This differentiation through object-choice is developed with characteristic brio by Achilles Tatius. Clitophon's detached companion is his cousin Clinias, 'after Leucippe, the master of my life'.[173] In fact, there is another major difference between Clitophon and Clinias, in addition to their orientation: Clinias is sexually experienced, where Clitophon is not. He is, Clitophon explains, 'initiated (*tetelesmenos*) into the cult of Eros';[174] later, Clitophon addresses him as one who has been 'an initiate (*mustēs*) for longer than me, and you are already more familiar with the mysteries (*teletēi*) of Eros'.[175] In a narrative that plays so heavily upon the parallels between the different senses of *telos* – ritual initiation, sexual initiation, narrative consummation – this language is highly significant. Sex becomes a metaphor for narrative: readers can be either virgins or initiates. Clinias has already attained the *telos* of his own romance, and it is for this reason that Clitophon entrusts him to guide his erotic instruction (1.9–11).[176] In this narrative, Clinias plays the role of 'second-reader' (to use Winkler's term), one with a keen instinct for how the story is likely to end up.[177] Meaning flows back from the *telos* he has reached.

Clitophon, on the other hand, presents himself as a 'first-reader', naively fumbling his way. 'What should I say?' he asks Clinias, 'what should I do? How should I get my girl? I don't know the routes (*hodous*)'.[178] The hodological metaphor is telling. Roads lead to destinations: this is another reminder that Clitophon has not reached his *telos*. The road in question is at once the romance narrative (which describes a journey), the figurative

---

[172] Above, p. 161.　[173] τὸν μετὰ Λευκίππην ἐμὸν δεσπότην, 3.23.3. See also above, pp. 162–3.
[174] ἔρωτι τετελεσμένος, 1.7.1.
[175] ἀρχαιότερος μύστης ἐμοῦ καὶ συνηθέστερος ἤδη τῆι τελετῆι τοῦ θεοῦ, 1.9.7.
[176] Above, p. 102.　[177] Winkler (1985) 9–11.
[178] τί λέγω; τί ποιῶ; πῶς ἂν τύχοιμι τῆς ἐρωμένης; οὐκ οἶδα γὰρ ἐγὼ τὰς ὁδούς, 1.9.7.

route to the girl's heart, and the anatomical passage that he craves (compare the 'long sought-for route' to which Longus' Lycaenion guides Daphnis during his sexual initiation).[179] Metaphors of roads often of course connote expansive opportunities in novels,[180] but in the Greek romances they tend rather to be intimately physiological, particularly in this text (as in the case of the 'narrow route' (*stenōpos hodos*) that leads to Leucippe's bedroom, Clitophon's description of which is overlain with his fantasies about her: 2.19.3).[181]

Hermeneutically, his sexual-narrative naivety manifests itself particularly in his uncritical affective absorption, his tendency to believe first impressions. This is particularly remarkable when it comes to the series of false deaths undergone by Leucippe. When she is disembowelled by Egyptian bandits, Clitophon sits there gawping out of 'surprise' (*paralogou*, 3.15.5: the word used by Plutarch, in the passage discussed above, to mark thrilling changes of narrative direction), suffering 'shock' (*ekplēxis*), thunderstruck (3.15.6). Readers of course, know full well that the heroine cannot be eviscerated in the third book. Clitophon's initial gullibility may be perhaps forgiveable, but he falls for it twice more. When Leucippe is abducted by pirates in the pay of a love rival, they pretend to sacrifice her and throw her into the sea, in order to hold up the pursuers (5.7). 'This time, Leucippe,' wails Clitophon, 'you have really died.'[182] Even on the third occasion, he shows no understanding of the generic law that the heroine never dies:

Alas, Leucippe, how many times death has torn you from me! Have I ever ceased lamenting you? Am I always to mourn you, as death follows death? All those other deaths were just Fortune's playing games at my expense – only this time, Fortune isn't joking.[183]

Clitophon's inclination is ever to see the situation in hyperdramatic terms. His language of grieving is drawn from tragedy ('Alas', 'lament', 'mourn'). This tragic worldview has five distinctive features. First, it is obviously a misreading. Clitophon fails to see what readers have by now been thoroughly conditioned to see, namely that this is a text in which reports

---

[179] τὴν τέως ζητουμένην ὁδόν, Long. 3.18.4. [180] See esp. Gumbrecht (2006).
[181] Cf. also the dirty priest's insinuation that Thersander 'rented a passageway' (μισθωσάμενος στενωπεῖον, Ach. Tat. 8.9.3). See also Whitmarsh (2010b, 335).
[182] νῦν μοι, Λευκίππη, τέθνηκας ἀληθῶς, 5.7.8.
[183] οἴμοι, Λευκίππη, ποσάκις μοι τέθνηκας· μὴ γὰρ θρηνῶν ἀνεπαυσάμην; ἀεί σε πενθῶ, τῶν θανάτων διωκόντων ἀλλήλους; ἀλλ' ἐκείνους μὲν πάντας ἡ Τύχη ἔπαιξε κατ' ἐμοῦ, οὗτος δὲ οὐκ ἔστι τῆς Τύχης ἔτι παιδιά, 7.5.2.

of Leucippe's death always turn out to have been greatly exaggerated.[184] Second, tragic lamentation is associated with absurd rhetorical orotundity, here and elsewhere in the period.[185] Points one and two thus guarantee that Clitophon's perspective will be read ironically. Third, events are experienced syntagmatically, as a serial chain: 'how many times', 'death follows death'. Fourth, Clitophon (echoing Plato's Athenian in the *Laws*)[186] sees the world as governed by a malevolently ludic Fortune. Unlike Einstein's (but like Hawking's), Clitophon's god does play dice.[187] Fifth, there is a sense of irresolution and endlessness ('have I ever ceased... Am I always to...') – even in the context of death, the ultimate form of closure. The syntagmatic mode, as ever, is associated with the absence of closure.

Clinias, by contrast, assumes the detached position, like Chariton's Polycharmus and Xenophon's Hippothous, and sees the larger picture:

Who knows whether she has come back to life? Has she not died many times before? Has she not been resurrected many times before? Why this haste to die? You will have plenty of leisure to do so once you discover for sure that she is dead.[188]

We can see immediately that Clinias' perspective implies a different approach to time, stressing the *longue durée* rather than the instance. Do not react 'hastily' (*propetōs*), he advises: look to both patterns of the past ('has she not been resurrected many times before?'), and to the possibilities for the future. In particular, he suggests, Clitophon should wait until the outcome ('once you discover for sure') before choosing what to do. This ability to wait, to observe, to think tactically and stochastically, is characteristic of the paradigmatic mode, the drive towards meaning. It is this Polycharmus-like command of the right action for the right time (the

---

[184] In any case, Clitophon the narrator has already told us that this prisoner is an imposter (7.1.3).
[185] LSJ τραγωδεῖν II; see further chapter 6 below.
[186] The individual human as a 'plaything' (*paignion*) of the gods: *Leg.* 644d, 803c; also quoted at Philostr. *VA* 4.36.2.
[187] Cf. 4.9.7 (παιζέτω πάλιν ἡ Τύχη); 5.11.1 (τῆι τῆς Τύχης... παιδιᾶι). For the connection of Fortune with dicing see Plut. *Caes.* 32.8 (Caesar's 'let the die be cast' as a commonplace for those entering εἰς τύχας); note too Pausanias' claim that Palamedes, after inventing dice, dedicated them in the temple of Tukhē at Argos (2.20.3). Tragedy associates unpredictable divine action with dicing: Aesch. *Sept.* 414, Eur. *Suppl.* 330–1, *Rhes.* 183, 446. 'God is quite a gambler': Hawking (2001) 79, quoted at Herrmann (2007) 387. The game-playing aspects of fiction are also emphasised by modern criticism: see Newsom (1988) on gambling, and for Greek narrative Lowe (2000), esp. 31–2.
[188] τίς γὰρ οἶδεν εἰ ζῆι πάλιν; μὴ γὰρ οὐ πολλάκις τέθνηκε; μὴ γὰρ οὐ πολλάκις ἀνεβίω; τί δὲ προπετῶς ἀποθνήισκεις; ὃ καὶ κατὰ σχολὴν ἔξεστιν, ὅταν μάθηις σαφῶς τὸν θάνατον αὐτῆς, 7.6.2.

kairos: 5.11.3) that sets the canny Clinias apart from absorbed Clitophon, and gives him in particular the resources necessary to survive the periodic adversity of romance narrative.

This polarity also dramatises different modes of reading, as detached or absorbed: romances allow us the space in which to find which style we prefer. This choice is not, however, exclusive: to read a romance we need both. The idea of the 'first-reader' is an impossible ideal, not just for knowing scholars who have read a work many times (a 'critical fiction'),[189] but for almost anyone, since no one reads a text without the background of a generic framework (whether inspired by literature or by culture). We always have a sense of how this kind of text works. Indeed, Achilles himself deconstructs the fiction: Clitophon is not just the naive agent within the text, but also the narrator who knows full well how it all turned out.[190] Clitophon the first-reader is an artificial construct of Clitophon the reliving-reader. In fact, even Clitophon the agent is not quite as naive as he seems. In the rhetorical debate over the respective merits of women and boys, he claims that he is a 'first-timer' (*prōtopeiros*) as regards women, but follows it up with the notorious qualification that he has only slept with prostitutes so far (2.37.5). His subsequent account of the pleasures of sex with women, however, is so fulsome that it leads to Menelaus' accusation that Clitophon is 'no first-timer (*prōtopeiros*) but an old man when it comes to Aphrodite'.[191]

But if the idea of the totally naive reader is exposed as an impossible construct, the romance also implicitly discounts an entirely detached, non-engaged approach. Romance readers should not be thinking only about their inevitable happy ending; we need to be absorbed in the characters' emoting, even if at the same time we are ironically distanced from it by our knowledge of what will come. This, I take it, is what is meant by Longus' celebrated claim in his preface that his work 'will remind the one who has loved and educate (*propaideusei*) the one who has not loved'.[192] Like Achilles, Longus uses sex as a metaphor for narrative, so this passage is again in part an allusion to second-readers and first-readers. Second-readers are advised to set aside their knowledge of the *telos*, and read syntagmatically: to re-experience the trials of sexual naivety through Daphnis and Chloe. First-readers, by contrast, are encouraged to read paradigmatically, to search

---

[189] Winkler (1985) 10.　[190] Whitmarsh (2003); Morgan (2007a).
[191] μὴ πρωτόπειρος ἀλλὰ γέρων εἰς Ἀφροδίτην, 2.38.1.
[192] τὸν ἐρασθέντα ἀναμήσει, τὸν οὐκ ἐρασθέντα προπαιδεύσει, 1. *pr.* 3. προπαιδεύσει is the reading of the Vatican MS, and should be preferred as the *lectio difficilior* (the Laurentine has παιδεύσει).

out the meaning, and to look forward to the end (this sense of forward-orientation is brought out by the *pro-* prefix in *propaideusei*, implying a preliminary education that looks forward to a next stage).

The question, then, is not whether the romances are closural or not, but how they play off against each other the conflicting drives towards closure and narrativity. As we have seen throughout, these drives, which are marked in the texts with an extraordinarily self-reflexive prominence, operate simultaneously at the level of plot architectonics and the cuing of readerly responses. In fact, the distinction between narratorial aesthetics and reader response is a false one. In the example of Aphrodite's overruling of Tukhē at the beginning of Chariton's eighth book, this is clearly *both* a token that the narrator is shifting narrative registers, inaugurating the closural phase, *and* a signal to the reader. I write here of the 'narrator', let me be clear, not the 'author'; of an *effet du texte*, the hypostatised figure who embodies the control plane. I do not think that we are in a position to claim (with Nimis) that the real, flesh-and-blood author did not always know where he was going while composing.[193] In part this is because we do not have the evidence – it is hard to extrapolate from text to reality, particularly when there are intra-textual explanations that are more efficient – but it is more because (on my reading) the syntagmatic, 'open' mode, the narrative id, always co-exists with the paradigmatic. For every Clitophon inveighing against the unpredictability of plot, there is always an (explicit or implied) Clinias reasserting the role of design. Their co-dependence is rather as in Aristotle's account of matter and form: the latter gives structure and intelligibility to the former, while the former gives tangibility and substance to the latter.

This co-dependence does not, however, mean that both modes are always equally forceful. The opening of Chariton 8 is an obvious case where the balance of power shifts. It follows that different texts can balance them in different ways.[194] This is particularly visible at the endings, where some romances close down the possibilities for narrativity much more than others. Xenophon, Longus and Heliodorus are cases in point. Each ends with nothing left to happen; in Xenophon, indeed, the main characters are explicitly said to have lived happily ever after (5.15.3–4); Longus too anticipates his lovers' life, apparently unproblematic, for as long as they live (4.39.1). Chariton is more complex: the narrative finishes with Callirhoe praying for a happy life and shared death with Chaereas (8.8.16); but there

[193] Above, n. 29. [194] See also the survey of Fusillo (1997).

is no news on Aphrodite's response, and of course there is the notorious problem that her son is being reared by Dionysius. Most troublesome of all is, as ever, Achilles, whose happy ending is flamboyantly subverted by the initial frame, which shows a despondent Clitophon. The failure to resume the frame at the end is another indication that the whole story has not been told at the end.

But even texts that do end with the total or near-total dominance of the narrative superego cannot cancel the exuberance of the id. Even if the protagonists' stories are over, there are other sympathetic characters in the romance, whose unresolved narratives transect the primary ones: Chariton's Dionysius, Xenophon's Aegialeus, Heliodorus' Thyamis and Charicles. What happens to them? The more we engage with the adventure world, the more we revel in its expansive possibilities, the more we may come to see marriage-as-closure as arbitrary sport-spoiling. *Why* does Aphrodite have to triumph over Tuhkē, so that Chaereas recognises Callirhoe? *Why* are Charicleia and Theagenes captured by the troops of their father – and why are they not sacrificed before they are recognised? (Why do villains not shoot James Bond on the spot, but divulge their plans and leave him to die slowly?) Such generically demanded 'coincidences', forcibly redirecting the plot in the direction in which it 'should' go, can seem to be contrived interventions *ex machina* on the part of an author, the 'equivalent to a fat envelope landing with a thud on the characters' doormat, stamped "author's instructions: follow at once"'.[195] There is room in romances for resistive reading – for *curiosity*.

And what, finally, of ideology? Are the romances 'closural' in the sense of being prescriptive? I have borrowed Freud's id and superego for a reason, since the superego is the voice of culturally enshrined moral normativity. In the romance, closure legitimises heterosexual marriage and the traditional aristocratic household as the right and proper *telos* of existence. Romances are (apart from *Charicleia and Theagenes*) circular: they emphasise a return to the same, the reinforcement of established structures. To this extent, they are ideologically conservative. But the freedom given to the id in the central section loosens up this ideological prescriptiveness, creating the space for more transformative conceptions of romance, and not just for resistive readers. Sameness-but-difference is the mode of operation, within both individual narratives (as we saw in Chapter 1, Xenophon and Chariton explore the question of whether the end marks the restoration of the initial state) and within the genre as a whole: thus over time

[195] Lowe (2000) 58.

we find ideological shifts unthinkable in the first century, towards the more cathectic desire of *Daphnis and Chloe* and *Leucippe and Clitophon*, and the extraordinary Hellenofugality of *Charicleia and Theagenes*. The potential for creating change and transformation will be the subject of Chapter 6.

CHAPTER 6

Limen

In the previous chapter, we considered the status of the end. In this final chapter, I want to consider the middle, the liminal phase: the space of possibility, rapid movement, fluidity of status, anxiety – of *narrativity*, the set of events, thoughts, emotions and possibilities that both enable narration and define the material proper to the genre. Paradoxically, despite the teleology that we traced in the previous chapter – the characters almost always long to leave the adventure world and reach the end – it is the middle that effectively defines the romance form. No one would claim that these texts are 'about' settled domesticity. Their energy and interest derives from pirates, trials and love rivals; that is to say, from liminality.

Liminality brings us to anthropology, and to van Gennep's famous three-stage model of the rites of passage (pre-liminal, liminal, post-liminal). As we have seen (and many others have observed), the novels do indeed rest upon mythic and ritual patterns of separation, marginalisation and reincorporation.[1] It will also be helpful to pause on Victor Turner's idea of liminality as 'anti-structure'. For Turner, the liminal field is imagined in opposition to society's fixed 'states' of identity (such as marriage, adulthood, social roles), and reciprocally defines them. But it is more than an antithesis; it is an experimental space, 'a realm of pure possibility whence novel configurations of ideas and relations may arise', a 'stage of reflection'.[2] Liminality accomplishes two contradictory things at once: it both naturalises the social status quo (by counterposing it to the temporary period of fluidity) and exposes its arbitrariness by positing alternative structures and identities.

The novels' liminal phases are laboratories for experimentation with identity. Chariton's Callirhoe becomes the wife of an Ionian magnate, Chaereas is enslaved and assumes the role of leader of a rebellion against the Persian Great King. Xenophon's Habrocomes becomes a bandit, while

[1] Above, pp. 43–4. [2] Turner (1967) 93–111, at 97, 106.

Anthia, less happily, is coerced into prostitution. Achilles' Clitophon remarries to a wealthy Ephesian, while Leucippe becomes a slave. Heliodorus' Thyamis lives as a bandit before resuming his priesthood. Such status changes are never permanent: remarriages can be shrugged off, nefarious activities pardoned, vulnerabilities unexploited. As in Homer's *Odyssey*, the template for this kind of narrative, the return narrative effaces all trace of the identity reshuffle in the middle. The annihilation of identity that liminality threatens never occurs; in fact romance dramatises what Frye calls the 'conviction... that there is something at the core of one's infinitely fragile being which is not only immortal but has discovered the secret of invulnerability'.[3]

And yet (again as in the *Odyssey*)[4] the liminal narrative reveals both how fragile social identities are – we are never more than one kidnapping away from enslavement – and how brutally societies treat those below. When we meet Achilles' Leucippe enslaved, besmirched and disfigured by shaving and beatings (5.17), we may be consoled that her suffering is only temporary, but we are also confronted with the shocking brutality to which slaves are subjected. The most spectacular example is the status reversal undergone by Lucius in the Greek *Ass* and Apuleius' *Metamorphoses*: he is transformed into a pack animal, situated at the very bottom of the hierarchy of beings, condemned to sufferings that exceed those of slaves.[5]

When Chariton's Dionysius probes Callirhoe (who has been brought to him as a slave) as to her past, she replies:

I beg you, my lord, allow me to remain silent about my fate (*tukhēn*). My former existence was a dream and a myth. I am now what I have become, a foreign slave.[6]

Such laments over the loss of former status are not uncommon in the Greek traditions, particularly in tragedy,[7] but there are two distinctive features here. The first is Callirhoe's absolute contrast, on ontological

---

[3] Frye (1976) 86. See also Bakhtin (1981) 105: 'No matter how impoverished, how denuded a human identity may become in Greek romance, there is always preserved in it some precious kernel of folk humanity; one always senses a faith in the indestructible power of man.'

[4] Rose (1992) 106–12.

[5] For the ways in which Lucius' experiences mirror those of slaves, see Hall (1995) 52–4 (*Ass*); Fitzgerald (2000) 93–111 (Apuleius). Another prose fiction of the imperial period focusing on the experience of slavery (if not quite a novel) is the *Life of Aesop*: on its value for the study of Roman slavery see Hopkins (1993).

[6] δέομαί σου... ὦ δέσποτα, συγχώρησόν μοι τὴν ἐμαυτῆς τύχην σιωπᾶν. ὄνειρος ἦν τὰ πρῶτα καὶ μῦθος, εἰμὶ δὲ νῦν ὃ γέγονα, δούλη καὶ ξένη, 2.5.6–7. εἰμὶ δὲ νῦν ὃ γέγονα invokes the tragic figure that has been named the *pankoinon*, e.g. ἐσμὲν οἷόν ἐσμεν (*Med.* 889; Johnstone (1990), (2000)).

[7] The closest parallel is Andromache's after the fall of Troy (Eur. *Tro.* 639–56).

grounds, between present and past: the present is reality, the past is a 'dream and a myth'. The second is the emphasis upon transformation, in the striking phrase 'I am what I have become.' She brands her achieved identity as true, and her natal one as false. Even if this acceptance of fate may be subverted by her subsequent behaviour – she *does* go on to tell her story, ending with a heroic reassertion of her aristocratic credentials ('if I cannot live as a noble, I choose a free death')[8] – it raises a new prospect, that experience can transform us irrevocably. Perhaps the point of no return really has been reached. The liminal phase dramatises the capacity that identities have to reshuffle themselves. This capacity is already partly realised in Chariton (Chaereas and Callirhoe are not exactly the same people when they return), but much more fully in Longus (Daphnis and Chloe choose to live a pastoral life even after they have been reunited with their urban parents, 4.39.1) and Heliodorus.

Statuses can also be reallocated through strategic fiction and role play. Achilles' Leucippe 'puts on the mask of' (*perithōmai*) a Thessalian called Lacaena (6.16.6). Heliodorus, that great artificer of identity, is particularly drawn to this theme. In book 1, Charicleia tells Thyamis her story: she and her brother Theagenes are noble Ephesians, priestess of Artemis and priest of Apollo respectively, who were shipwrecked en route to a festival on Delos (1.21–2). This is, in fact, the only information that the reader has had about their background, so the first-reader may well also be taken in; it is also a fiction that is deployed repeatedly (5.26.2–4, 7.13, 9.25). The model is the series of Cretan lies told in, again, the *Odyssey*. There seems, indeed, to be a generic self-reflexivity to these 'Ephesian lies', given the centrality of Ephesus to novelistic fiction.[9] Another form of identity manipulation is disguise: Charicleia and Theagenes disguise themselves as beggars (2.19.1), as do Charicleia and Calasiris later (6.10, 6.11.3–4). This of course is another Odyssean touch, although the direct verbal allusions are to tragedy.[10] In a text in which identity is always exposed to questions of artifice, the liminal phase dramatises not so much the possibilities of status reversal as the opportunities for status *refashioning*; and, of course, the intertextual dialogue with the *Odyssey* adds another layer of artful sophistication.

---

[3] εἰ δὲ μὴ δύναμαι ζῆν ὡς εὐγενής, αἱροῦμαι θάνατον ἐλεύθερον, 2.5.12. For the heroic sentiment, cf. Soph. *Aj.* 479–80.

[9] Hunter (2008a) 265. Ephesus is an important backdrop not just to *Anthia and Habrocomes*, which plays such an important hypotextual role in Heliodorus' Delphic episode (above, p. 117), but also to the closing books of Achilles Tatius, and to Petronius' famous 'widow of Ephesus' novella (perhaps a Milesian tale).

[10] Ch.3 n. 31. Their clothing is however Odyssean (esp. the 'rags', ῥάκεσιν, 6.11.3 ~ Hom. *Od.* 19.507, 22.1 etc): Paulsen (1992) 162–4. See further below, p. 221.

The anti-structural agency of the liminal period is embodied elementally in the sea (always a space of unpredictability, 'fluidity');[11] and, as far as human agents go, in the *déclassé* bandits and pirates, human traffickers (always men) who occupy marginal spaces like woods, caves and shores, or semi-civilised villages.[12] Their narrative role is partly to counteract the tendency of the principal characters towards sedentariness, by introducing sudden, rapid change; or, like storms (both in the novel and the epic, its predecessor in this respect),[13] to throw travellers off course, and so to introduce new narrative possibilities. They represent the narrative equivalent of shuffling the pack. It is such figures, chiefly, who engineer status reversal, by capturing and enslaving free agents, particularly (as we shall see) women.

But they are not simply storm-like agents of chaos: they may be selfish, rapacious and invasive, but they are also calculating, especially when it comes to profiteering (another reminiscence of Odysseus – who is, in fact, at one point in the *Odyssey* actually mistaken for a trader).[14] When Chariton's Theron comes across Callirhoe in her tomb, his first instinct is to kill her; but then his thoughts switch to 'gain' (*kerdos*), as he realises that she too has a value ('there is much silver and gold here, but this woman's beauty is worth more (*timiōteron*) than the whole lot').[15] His mental reckoning of price (*timē*) prefaces a torrent of mercantile language from him and his fellow pirates, both in direct speech and focalising through the narrator's words: reciprocal obligation (*kharis*), debt (*opheilein*), selling (*apodidonai, pōlein, pernēmi*), buying (*oninēmi*), goods (*phortion*), profit (*to lusiteles*), gain (*kerdos*), wealth (*ploutos*).[16] Callirhoe has been converted into a chattel, a token of exchange between men. Xenophon's Anthia and Achilles' Leucippe are also bought and sold (Anthia, indeed, is forced into prostitution, the ultimate form of commodification).[17] Heliodorus' Nausicles, a rich Naucratite trader, comes up with a plan to rescue Charicleia,

---

[11] Good discussion at Lalanne (2006) 106–8; Cohen (2006) is a stimulating discussion of the role of the marine chronotope generally in fiction.
[12] Above, pp. 46–7.
[13] Lalanne (2006) 110–14 offers a shrewd discussion of the role of storms and seafaring in the novel.
[14] Odyssean *kerdos*: 13.255, 14.31 etc, with Segal (1994) 181–2. The semantics of *kerd-* words (profit or guile?) in Homer are vigorously debated (e.g. Roisman (1990)), but there is no doubt that the acquisitive Odysseus, at any rate, is associated with profiteering. Odysseus taken for a trader: *Od.* 8.161–4 (NB *kerdeōn* at 164).
[15] πολὺς μὲν ἄργυρος ἐνταῦθα, πολὺς δὲ χρυσός, τούτων δὲ πάντων τὸ τῆς γυναικὸς τιμιώτερον κάλλος, 1.9.6. Theron's guile and metanarrative significance are expertly analysed by Kasprzyk (2001).
[16] Cognates of *apodidonai*, 1.10.5, 1.10.8; *kerdos*, 1.10.8, 1.12.1; *lusitelēs*, 1.10.6, 1.12.9; *oninēmi*, 1.12.9; *opheilein*, 1.10.3; *pernēmi*, 1.10.8; *ploutos*, 1.11.5, 1.11.7; *pōlein*, 1.10.6, 1.10.8; *priasthai*: 1.12.8; *timē*: 1.10.6; *phortion*, 1.10.5, 1.10.7, 1.11.4, 1.11.6; *kharis*: 1.10.3, 1.10.5, 1.12.9.
[17] An analogous passage in the Latin *Life of Apollonius King of Tyre*, 33–6.

'with a trader's pragmatism',[18] by pretending she is the Athenian slave Thisbe (another example of Heliodorus fictionalising identities). Calasiris presently offers Nausicles a 'ransom' (*lutra*, 5.13.2) in return, an amethyst ring. Like Chariton's Theron, Nausicles uses mental arithmetic to reach his decision, showing himself 'delighted at its high value (*polutimon*), judging the gem of equal worth (*isostasion*) to all his equity (*ousias*)'.[19] This exchange will later be subtly recalled when Charicleia bares her arm in front of the Ethiopian people, to reveal an ebony 'circle' (*peridromos*, 10.15.2) on her skin: the ring, it seems, has left its narrative mark on the person, like a permanent price tag.[20]

Unlike in other modes of fiction (such as the *Life of Aesop* and the *Ass* traditions), in romance the commodification of identity is concentrated largely on women. This equivalence between women and money plays a specific role in the novels. The trading of women has an ingloriously long tradition in Greek literature, beginning with the *Iliad* itself (where women are not only captured and bartered like Briseis and Chryseis, but also offered as gifts and prizes).[21] In the novels, however, the free circulation of women is a defining feature exclusively of the liminal phase. For a start, traders represent the antithesis to the aristocratic, dynastic ethics that the novels promote in conclusion. 'What more benighted race could you mention than merchants and ship-renters?' asks Philostratus' Apollonius, citing the fact that they 'sail around' (*perinostousi*), 'mix with' (*anamikhthentes*) lowlife (agents, street-traders) and pursue profit at all costs.[22] Such traders embody the threat to the established order of constant, destabilising movement, the admixture of social classes, the redistribution of wealth.

Commerce, moreover, is a suitable figure for the erasure of familial and social identities in the liminal phase.[23] Money is abstract, impersonal, universal, infinite,[24] 'defined only by its exchange value, capable of unlimited metonymic circulation'.[25] When people become defined by their exchange value rather than by their social and familial identities, they enter into a system where they may be traded freely and repeatedly over the entire

---

[18] ἐμπορικόν τι καὶ δραστήριον ἐννοήσας, 5.8.3.
[19] ἡσθεὶς πρὸς τὸ πολύτιμον, οὐσίας ὅλης τὴν λίθον ἰσοστάσιον κρίνων, 5.15.1. On the gem ecphrasis, see Whitmarsh (2002b).
[20] W. Stephens (1994) 72.   [21] *Il.* 9.128, 23.262, 23.704.
[22] ἀλλ' ἐμπόρων τε καὶ ναυκλήρων κακοδαιμονέστερόν τι ἐρεῖς ἔθνος; Philostr. *VA* 4.32.2.
[23] Turner (1967) 98–9 notes the removal of markers of identity in the liminal phase of Ndembu passage rites: 'characteristic of transitional beings is that they have *nothing*. They have no status, property, insignia, secular clothing, rank, kinship position, nothing to demarcate them structurally from their fellows'.
[24] I adapt these 'features of money' from Seaford (2004) 147–72.   [25] Brooks (1984) 136.

civilised world, and for as long as they retain their worth. The narrative is potentially infinite for as long as the protagonists remain unredeemed tokens of exchange by others. The return home, conversely, marks the heroine's decommodification, and the resumption of identity. It may be a paradox to modern readers that this demonetarisation coincides with marriage (or its restoration), itself a form of commodified exchange between men. But, except in Longus' hand-to-mouth pastoral world,[26] the economics of marriage are never mentioned. Marriage is constructed as the institution where identity is fulfilled as social and psychological destiny, rather than transactionalised.

Trade is thus a cipher for romance narrativity, for the ever-present possibility that individuals might be rapidly relocated and have their roles redefined, against their will. There is, indeed, a second connection between narratives and money. As Winkler notes, both Xenophon and Heliodorus can represent narration as a form of transaction: tales can be '*exchanged in a bargain struck*'.[27] Heliodorus' Cnemon claims a story as 'payment' (*misthos*, 2.23.3–4) for reuniting Calasiris with Charicleia and Theagenes. In Philostratus' *Heroicus*, the Phoenician trader, captivated by his interlocutor's stories, compares them directly to his commercial stock: 'Forget about the ship and its contents! The cargo of the soul is to me sweeter and more profitable (*kerdaleōtera*). Let us consider narrative digressions not as nonsense but as the surplus profit derived from this commerce.'[28] Yet again, there is precedent in Homer's *Odyssey* for this commercialisation of narrative,[29] but the inflection is different here. In Xenophon, Heliodorus and Philostratus, the crucial point for our purposes is that narratives are bartered between *foreigners*. The commercial metaphor enters when narrative is conceived of as crossing boundaries, going beyond its native community. It is hard to ignore the analogy, surely intended, with novelistic literature itself (I include the *Heroicus* in the broader category of the 'novelistic'). This also circulated beyond boundaries, travelling over the Greek-speaking world (papyri of Chariton show a readership in Egypt within 100 years or so of composition).[30] Cost, too, was a factor: at least

---

[26] Long. 3.30–2, with Winkler (1990) 108–10.
[27] Winkler (1982) 109–10 at 109, citing Xen. Eph. 3.1.4, 3.2.15; Hld 2.21.5–7. Cf. also Winkler (1985) 119–22 on Apuleius.
[28] ἐρρώσθω λοιπὸν ἡ ναῦς καὶ τὰ ἐν αὐτῆι· τὰ γὰρ τῆς ψυχῆς ἀγώγιμα ἡδίω τέ μοι καὶ κερδαλεώτερα, τὰς δὲ ἐκβολὰς τῶν λόγων μὴ λῆρον ἀλλ' ἐπικέρδειαν ἡγώμεθα τῆς ἐμπορίας ταύτης, 53.3. See further Whitmarsh (2009a) 224, with references.
[29] 'Old man, the tale you have told is blameless, nor have you spoken a story (*epos*) that is against order and without profit (*nēkerdes*)'. ὦ γέρον, αἶνος μέν τοι ἀμύμων, ὃν κατέλεξας, / οὐδέ τί πω παρὰ μοῖραν ἔπος νηκερδὲς ἔειπες, *Od*. 14.508–9.
[30] Above, p. 11.

by the second century, novels were available in luxurious editions, which would have required serious outlay.[31]

From this more abstract perspective, the high-price buying and selling of women across the Mediterranean and western Asia in the novel's liminal phase can be seen as figurative of the economic condition of the romances (which are named for their female protagonists).[32] But whereas the characters finally achieve stable identities through decommodification, the texts are consigned to endless liminality. Plato's Socrates memorably describes how written texts are like orphans separated from their fathers, 'buffeted all over the place'.[33] This state of wandering and orphanhood, as Derrida observes in his famous commentary on the Platonic passage, is the necessary condition of writing, which enforces an irrevocable break between author and word, destroying the 'self-presence' of language.[34] The text, once written, has passed the point of no return.

THE EXILED SUBJECT

In the passage, which we have already considered on a number of occasions, that opens the final book of *Callirhoe*, Aphrodite intervenes in the plot out of pity for Chaereas – Chaereas who has 'wandered (*planētheis*) from West to East, amid countless toils'.[35] Wandering (*planē*) and roaming (*alē*) are the physical manifestations of the divagatory force that impels the liminal phase of novelistic narrative; they characterise the free-form existence, without structure, direction or point, in contrast to the re-establishment of secure identity at the conclusion of the novel.[36]

As Silvia Montiglio demonstrates (2005), wandering is an ambiguous state.[37] In a culture that associated identity with a settled existence in the *polis*, wandering peoples, nomads (Scythians, Amazons, Arabs), were routinely associated with primitivism. For Greeks, roaming was the condition of the execrated: the low-grade traders we have seen, exiles, the ostracised, mendicants, the touched. Exile, in particular, was a reason to lament ('the

---

[31] Stephens (1994) 413; Cavallo (1996) sees a decisive shift in the second century. The expense needed for luxury bibliophilia is a theme of Lucian's satirical *Against the uneducated book-buyer*.
[32] For *ta kata* + girl's name (or girl's + boy's name) as a generically defining feature of the romance, see Whitmarsh (2005b).
[33] κυλινδεῖται... πανταχοῦ, Pl. *Phaedr*. 275d. [34] Derrida (1981) 82–3.
[35] ἀπὸ δύσεως εἰς ἀνατολὰς διὰ μυρίων πλανηθείς, Char. 8.1.3. See below, p. 226.
[36] πλάνη: Char. 3.9.3, Xen. Eph. 2.14.2, 2.14.4, 3.2.15, 3.3.4, 5.1.3, 5.1.13, 5.8.2, 5.14.1, Ach. Tat. 5.18.4; *Ninus* fr. A.1.16 = SW 32, *Sesonchosis* col. III.1–3 = SW 262. For Heliodorean references, see below, nn. 49–50, 52. See also Montiglio (2005) 221–61 and Lalanne (2006) 109–17.
[37] Montiglio (2005).

most grievous thing (*aniērotaton*) of all', for the seventh-century poet Tyrtaeus, fr. 10.4 West), because it turned a settled status into an itinerant one, in effect removing identity along with the *polis*.[38] In the Hellenistic and Roman periods, philosophers wrote consolations for exiles.[39] On the other hand, roaming is also the condition of superhuman figures, particularly itinerant sages like Anacharsis and Solon, holy-man philosophers like Pythagoreans and Apollonius of Tyana and ascetic Christian monks. As Aristotle puts it, to be one who is by nature without a *polis* (*apolis*) 'is either base, or greater than a human'.[40]

Romance wandering is assimilated to the experience of two key groups of social outcasts, mendicants and exiles. We can be quick with mendicancy, since it only appears in Heliodorus, and only as a disguise for Charicleia and Theagenes (2.19.1), and Charicleia and Calasiris (6.11.3–4). These deliberate pretences are, as we have seen, cases of elective liminality and identity abnegation. The second sequence, as we have also seen, in particular is extremely self-conscious, especially in its use of intertextual reference: they are disguised not only as beggars but also as Odysseus-disguised-as-a-beggar.[41] The sophistication and self-reflexivity is brought to the fore in book 7, when the sons fail (Telemachus-like) to recognise their disguised father when he rushes onto the battlefield (now playing the role of Oedipus in Euripides' *Phoenician women*): they take him, comments the narrator, as *alēthōs alētin*, 'truly a wanderer' (7.7.6). The phrase activates the pun, which goes back to the *Odyssey*, between *alētheia* ('truth') and *alēteia* ('wandering').[42] Greek, like English and the Romance languages, metaphorically associates wandering with falsehood, with 'error': there is thus a playfully paradoxical element in the idea of a true wanderer. The paradoxes multiply when we consider the narrative context: Calasiris may be *disguised* as a wanderer; but he also, as we have seen, really *is* a wanderer. Or is he?

Begging, then, is a theme too overlain with literary precedent to inspire anything other than artful self-reflexivity. Exile, by contrast, is treated

---

[38] On exile and lamentation in the Greco-Roman tradition, see esp. Doblhofer (1987), esp. 21–40 on the Greek context.
[39] The earliest source is Teles fr. 3 Hense = Stob. 3.40.8. On the Greek material, see Whitmarsh (2001a) 133–246, focusing on Musonius, Dio Chrysostom and Favorinus, and with earlier literature; Nesselrath (2007) offers a useful survey of the sources. Claassen (1999) and Gaertner (2007) range across both Greece and Rome.
[40] ἤτοι φαῦλός ἐστιν, ἢ κρείττων ἢ ἄνθρωπος, Arist. *Pol.* 1253a 1–4.
[41] Above, Chapter 3 n. 31; see also pp. xxx on the Oedipal allusions.
[42] The pun is first found at Hom. *Od.* 14.122–7 (esp. 124–5: ἀλῆται ψεύδονται, οὐδ' ἐθέλουσιν ἀληθέα μυθήσασθαι). In a clever twist, Plato's *Cratylus* nicely etymologises *alētheia* as 'holy (*theia*) wandering (*alē*)' (421b).

with more existential seriousness.[43] It is very commonly invoked figuratively to expess the pain of separation from their communities or (more extravagantly) from each other. This slippage between judicial exile and painful separation is facilitated by the vagueness of the Greek terminology: *phugē* denotes evasive action generally, as well as being the specific term for exile. In many cases, it is simply ambiguous whether characters are metaphorically assimilating themselves to those exiled under law or literally referring to themselves as deracinated.[44] At stake, fundamentally, is the question of agency: who has enforced this separation? Nowhere in the novels is one of the protagonists judicially exiled (although it is the fate of some subsidiary characters: Achilles' Menelaus, Heliodorus' Cnemon and Thyamis).[45] Chariton's Callirhoe laments her 'exile' (*phugēn*), but blames non-juridical forces (the sea and the pirate Theron), and accuses Fortune (Tukhē) of 'banishing' her (*phugadeueis*, 5.1.5). In *Charicleia and Theagenes*, where the lovers have voluntarily eloped, Charicleia refers to herself and Theagenes as 'willing exiles (*phugadas*)',[46] a self-consciously paradoxical phrase that neatly condenses the interpretative problem: can one describe as *phugē* a self-willed state?[47] More generally, the shifting, across the novels, of the agents and instruments that dislocate the protagonists points to the complex network of forces that act during the liminal phase, the combination of the active questing and the passive puppeting of the protagonists.

The primary association of exile is with the pain of separation from home and beloved, a pain that provokes in readers both a sympathetic engagement and a prospective anticipation of ultimate reunion. Heliodorus' *Charicleia and Theagenes*, however, also plays with the more positive paradigm of the superhuman wanderer. Concurrent with the central plot detailing Charicleia's return to Ethiopia runs the story of the return of the Egyptian priest Calasiris from exile to his native Memphis. The reason for his exile is not (as we might suppose, for a philosopher-cum-divine)[48] principled

---

[43] Comito (1975) is an eccentric discussion of the topic.
[44] For such ambiguous cases, see Char. 4.1, 6.1.4; Xen. Eph. 1.7.1, 1.7.4, 3.3.1; Ach. Tat. 2.30.1–2, 5.11.1, 5.11.3, 7.14.2, 8.5.6; Hld. 2.4.1, 5.1.1, 5.6.3, 5.18.3.
[45] Menelaus: Ach. Tat. 2.34.6; Cnemon: Hld. 1.14.1 (cf. 2.9.3; 6.2.3); Thyamis: Hld. 1.19.4, 7.2.1, 7.2.5, 7.3.5, 7.4.1. Heliodorus' Thyamis and Calasiris take themselves into exile: see below. See also Ach. Tat. 8.15.2, of Thersander.
[46] φυγάδας αὐθαιρέτους, 4.18.2.   [47] No, according to Philostr. *VS* 488.
[48] Whitmarsh (2001a) 134–7. On the presentation of Calasiris, see in general Sandy (1982); also Anderson (1994) 206–7 for the points of contact with the holy-man tradition. Calasiris' Egyptian provenance is significant: the role of Egyptian priests as authenticators of narrative is familiar from Hdt. 2.99–119, and its imitation at Dio Chr. 11.37. Egyptians who, like Calasiris, commingled native theology with Platonism and Pythagoreanism, could be found as late as the fifth century (Fowden (1982) 46–8). Egypt was also, in the nascent Christian tradition, 'the cradle of monasticism. It was

Limen 223

resistance to the state, but self-critical shame at succumbing to desire for the prostitute Rhodopis (2.25.4) – a characteristically Heliodorean blend of the erotic and the philosophical. As a result of this exile, Calasiris now leads 'a life of roaming' (*bios alētēs*, 2.24.5; cf. *planē*, 2.26.1;[49] which he spreads contagiously to his wards Charicleia and Theagenes).[50] This exile, however, is also a voyage of philosophical self-discovery.[51] It comes, he claims, with a divine mandate: it was this event that allowed him to turn his life over to the gods, whose design it was to save him from the spectacle of his sons' fratricide, and to send him in search of Charicleia (3.16.5).[52] For Calasiris, exile has been the making of his hieratic authority: in this respect, he follows the deeply rooted tradition of those who, like Diogenes and Dio Chrysostom, became true philosophers in exile.[53] That wandering can, for Heliodorus, be a source of redemption is a sign of how far the fourth-century novel has travelled from its first-century beginnings: no longer simply the absence of home, liminality is (or at least can be) a positive, transformative experience. This is a narrative, after all, that does not return 'home' at the end, at least as Greeks would define the idea of home.

DESPONDENCY, TRAGEDY, SUICIDE

Liminal wandering also causes severe unhappiness. In post-classical Greek, the word *aluein* is used of both ambling and distress,[54] perhaps an outgrowth of the deep connection between wandering and despondency in

---

in Egypt that the theory and practice of monasticism reached its highest pitch of articulateness and sophistication' (Brown (1971) 82).
[49] Calasiris' ἄλη also at 4.13.1, 7.7.6, 7.8.2; also πλάνη: 2.22.3, 5.6.2.
[50] 5.2.7, 5.4.7, 5.6.2, 6.7.2, 6.7.9 (Charicleia and Calasiris), 6.8.4, 7.12.2, 7.12.5, 7.13.2, 7.14.7, 8.3.7, 8.9.8. Cf. also πλάνη at 1.25.6, in Charicleia's false narrative. Nausicles (5.2.4) and Cnemon (6.7.5) are also wanderers (they are said by Calasiris to share with him a βίος... πλάνος: 2.22.3); as is Charicles, both before he finds Charicleia (2.29.5) and after he loses her (10.34.3).
[51] Montiglio (2005) 238–9.
[52] Calasiris' exile also, and more obviously, looks to the mythical paradigm of Oedipus: the exile results from sexual transgression, and Calasiris foresees that his sons will battle each other (NB also Thyamis is living in *Egyptian* Thebes: 2.25.6): see further Paulsen (1992) 156–7, and above, pp. 112–13, n. 31. Calasiris' exile also looks forward to that of Homer, now presented as an Egyptian exile (again, linked to Egyptian Thebes) wandering (ἀλητεύων) through Greece (3.14.2–4). By a complex route, this also links back to Dio, who implicitly compares himself (despite the ironic denial) to Homer the fugitive beggar (*Or.* 47.5–7: Kindstrand (1973) 113–15).
[53] Doblhofer (1987) 21–49, André and Baslez (1993) 283–97, Whitmarsh (2001a) 133–80, Montiglio (2005) 180–203.
[54] *LSJ* s.v. ἀλύω. Cf. also Toohey (2004) index s.v. *alus* (although I am uncomfortable with his recourse to modern psychoanalytical analogies).

ancient west Asia.[55] In the novelists, both meanings are active: we find the same verb used of characters wandering mentally (through grief, desire or drunkenness)[56] and physically.[57] Sometimes physical wandering is an outward expression of an internal state. Chariton's Theron can be found 'ambling (*aluōn*)... in a state of thorough mental confusion';[58] and Xenophon's Habrocomes 'traversed the city ambling (*aluōn*), at a loss for news of Anthia, at a loss for resources'.[59] In the latter case, in fact, it is ambiguous as to whether the 'ambling' is mental or physical.

More generally speaking, novelistic liminality is often responded to with an extreme, even suicidal despondency. The novels' protagonists – particularly (but not exclusively)[60] their male protagonists – are prone to expressions of helplessness, to rhetorical lamentation, and to suicide attempts (always curtailed). We do, however, need to be very careful here. A number of recent scholars have seen these as cases of pathological depression, and indeed as symptoms of a wider cultural *anomie* that supposedly afflicted the alienated post-classical Greek world,[61] and sometimes too as a crisis in masculinity (boys, after all, don't cry).[62] Now, while it is certainly true that melancholia emerges as a serious subject for literary reflection in the Hellenistic period (partly as a tool to interpret epic and tragic psychology),[63] there is nothing in the novels to suggest that despondency is a chronic psychopathology rather than a rational (if intellectually misguided) response to immediate circumstances. As we saw in the introduction,[64] this scholarly fiction springs partly from a familiar prejudice against post-classical Greek culture, from an attempt to see analogies for twentieth-century angst, and (perhaps for some) from the lingering effects of a desire teleologically to create a gap in Greek culture that Christianity could later fill.

It is far preferable to read novelistic despondency as a reaction to liminality, to a particular kind of narrativity; it is a form of hermeneutic and

---

[55] Barré (2001), with Kselman (2002). An alternative suggestion for the development of the secondary sense of wandering (mental disturbance is the earlier meaning) may be assimilation to ἀλάομαι (compare the semantic drift of θεραπεύω towards θωπεύω in later Greek).
[56] Char. 2.1.1, 4.2.8 (both grief); Xen. Eph. 1.13.4 (drunkenness); Hld. 3.7.1, 4.7.7 (both desire).
[57] Char. 1.4.3, 1.12.5; Xen. Eph. 5.10.5; Hld. 1.14.3, 2.21.1, 2.30.1, 5.2.2.
[58] ἀλύων [ἀλγῶν MS]... ταραχώδης παντάπασι τὴν ψυχήν, 1.12.5.
[59] περιῄει τὴν πόλιν ἀλύων, ἀθυμίαι [ἀπορίαι MS] μὲν τῶν κατὰ τὴν Ἀνθίαν, ἀπορίαι δὲ τῶν ἐπιτηδείων, 5.10.5.
[60] See e.g. Char. 5.1.4–7; Hld. 6.8.3–6.
[61] MacAlister (1996) 43–52; Toohey (2004) 59–103. Versions of the 'novelistic alienation' thesis in Reardon (1969), Konstan (1994), Morgan (1995), MacAlister (1996), Toohey (2004).
[62] Negative assessments of the male protagonists are surveyed by Haynes (2003) 81–3.
[63] I have learned here from unpublished work by Georgios Kazantzidis.   [64] Above, p. 8.

actorial incapacitation, an inability to see how the plot might be progressed. Let us think back to Xenophon's passage discussed in the previous chapter (1.10.7), in which an optimistic desire for the *telos* is conceived as a manifestation of *thumos*, vigorous hermeneutic/actorial energy. *Athumia*, the absence of *thumos*, is a tell-tale sign of liminal despondency (particularly, as it happens, in Xenophon);[65] it marks an absence of narrative energy, particularly in situations that seem helpless.[66]

This is manifested particularly in the frequent tragic laments.[67] As Morgan notes of Heliodorus, 'their implicit theology sets up a countermodel to the divine providence, manifested by dreams and oracles, that seems on other occasions to be operating to direct the story to its proper ending; they hypothesise a world governed by a malign deity whose sport it is to delude human beings and cause them to suffer'.[68] We can develop this insight. Laments proclaim: (i) *absence of identity*, which comes only with sedentary, *polis*-based life; (ii) *limited self-determination*, a characteristic of the liminal period; (iii) *boundless narrativity*, an existence in which the future could take any number of unpredictable twists and turns; (iv) *endlessness*, the lack of any tendency towards closure. To exemplify this, I want to concentrate upon one particularly rich example, which comes in book 5 of *Charicleia and Theagenes*. The lovers are confronted by a gang of soldiers. Theagenes has had enough:

For how long shall we flee this destiny that pursues us everywhere? Let us yield to fortune, and give in to the current that carries us along! Let us give up this endless errancy, this life of wandering and the god's incessant insults towards us.[69]

Despite the familiarity of the tragic motifs,[70] this is a brilliantly metanarrative passage. What Theagenes protests against is the incessant travel

---

[65] Char. 5.5.5; Xen. Eph. 1.5.2, 1.15.1, 1.16.1, 2.7.1, 3.2.14, 3.9.3, 3.9.7, 5.6.1, 5.6.3, 5.12.3, 5.15.3; Ach. Tat. 4.1.7: Hld. 7.11.10.
[66] On this passage, see above, pp. 180–1. This despondency looks back to Jason's well-known helplessness in the *Argonautica* (cf. Ap. Rh. 1.450–9, 1.1286–9, 3.422–3; but to the *Odyssey* too, cf. Hunter (1993) 10, 19–22). Cusset (2001) emphasises the importance of Apollonius' Jason for the novelists' construction of their male protagonists.
[67] Fusillo (1989) 36–40 offers a good typological analysis of novelistic laments, focusing upon intertextual relations with tragedy; see also Birchall (1996) on rhetorical features. Doulamis (2002) 130–70 offers stylistic analysis of Callirhoe's laments in Chariton; Paulsen (1992) 56–66 focuses specifically upon Heliodorus' laments as tragic motifs.
[68] Morgan (1989b) 303; similar point at Fusillo (1989) 40, and esp. Hefti (1950) 108–10.
[69] ἄχρι τίνος... φευξόμεθα τὴν πανταχοῦ διώκουσαν εἱμαρμένην; εἴξωμεν τῆι τύχηι καὶ χωρήσωμεν ὁμόσε τῶι φέροντι· κερδήσωμεν ἄλην ἀνήνυτον καὶ πλάνητα βίον καὶ τὴν ἀπάλληλον τοῦ δαίμονος καθ' ἡμῶν πομπείαν, Hld. 5.6.2.
[70] Paulsen (1992) 30–1, emphasising also the self-conscious use of theatrical terminology surrounding the passage.

with no hope of homecoming: 'errancy' (*alē*) and 'wandering' (*planē*). The adjective qualifying 'errancy' is *anēnutos* ('endless'), formed by attaching the alpha-privative prefix onto the root of the verb *anuō*, 'I achieve' or 'complete'. (It is also the word used in Xenophon's oracle of the 'endless tasks' facing Anthia and Habrocomes during their travels, 1.6.2.) Theagenes' opening words are 'for how long ...?', a phrase that, for all its familiarity from rhetoric,[71] represents a distinctively novelistic–liminal perception of time as oppressively open and repetitive, fundamentally lacking any anticipation of closure.[72]

The wandering narrative is the antithesis of closurality, travel without any hope of ending. Conversely, closure puts an end to wandering. We have considered many times Chariton's narratorial intervention at the beginning of book 8, where the closural Aphrodite takes over from the liminal Fortune (Tukhē): here, Chaereas is said to have paid his dues 'by wandering (*planētheis*) from West to East, with myriad sufferings'.[73] Xenophon's Anthia, to take another example, greets Habrocomes at their reunion with the words 'Husband and master, I have recovered you, having wandered (*planētheisa*) over much land and sea.'[74] Heliodorus' Charicleia, taking leave of Cnemon, looks forward to 'the end (*telos*) of our wandering (*planēs*)' (6.7.9). The motif of wandering mediates between the characters' affective experience of suffering and the metanarrative signposting of divagatory plot-without-end.

The liminal character's desire for ending, however, will always be frustrated, because of the absence of self-determination. Theagenes, in the passage we have discussed, cannot control his destiny, the only option that he perceives is to 'give in' (*khōrein*) to destiny. He proceeds to imagine himself trapped in an environment without progress, direction or teleology, lambasting the malevolent deity (*daimōn*), inscrutable to the point of anonymity, who plots their progress:

Do you not see how, how he strives to fit together in quick sequence exile and pirates' dens, horrors at sea and worse horrors by land, bandits and war! A short time ago, he held us captive, then arranged for us to be alone and forsaken; he offered us deliverance and an escape to freedom, but now has produced men to

---

[71] Cf. above, Chapter 4 n 43.
[72] Cf. Achilles' use of the comparable μέχρι τίνος (2.5.1, 2.19.1, 5.21.3–4), here signifying sexual frustration.
[73] ἀπὸ δύσεως εἰς ἀνατολὰς διὰ μυρίων παθῶν πλανηθείς, 8.1.3.
[74] ἄνερ ... καὶ δέσποτα, ἀπείληφά σε πολλὴν γῆν πλανηθεῖσα καὶ θάλασσαν, 5.14.1. On the significance of ἀπολαμβάνειν in Xenophon see above, p. 147.

slay us. Such is the wargame he plays upon us, scripting our lives like a theatrical drama.[75]

The theatrical metaphor[76] serves primarily to reinforce the liminal sensation of the absence of self-determination, picking up on the philosophical topos that life is a play in which we do not choose the roles.[77] But it also has an obvious metanarrative application, describing the experience of liminal plot, at least from Theagenes' perspective. This is a narrative that lacks structure, the very inverse of an Aristotelian *muthos*: the sequence of events is determined not by logic or the retributive laws of moral justice, but by an anonymous principle of intensifying accumulation. These are strong markers of what we have called 'syntagmatic' plotting, whereby events gain their significance from their seriality rather than their contribution to any overall pattern. The authoring deity 'fits together' the narrative events in accordance with his own erratic aspiration (*philotimia*), and desire for 'game-playing' (*paizein*).[78]

Faced with malignantly ludic but all-controlling plotting, Theagenes attempts to reassert control:

Why don't we cut short this tragic poem of his and hand ourselves over to those who wish to kill us? Otherwise the deity may strive after some extravagant ending (*telos*) for the drama, and force us to kill ourselves.[79]

The metanarrativity could not be more explicit: Theagenes believes himself to be embroiled in a 'tragic poem'. There are two points to highlight about this passage. First, the concern with self-determination is brought to the fore. Theagenes fatalistically identifies death as the only possible outcome; in such a context, the only way of avoiding the deity's coercive (note 'force', *ekbiazesthai*) power is to accelerate the ending. Second, Theagenes' words are all about closure, about the kind of *telos* that they

---

[75] οὐχ ὁρᾷς ὡς φυγάσι ἐπισυνάπτειν πειρατήρια καὶ τοῖς ἐκ θαλάττης ἀτόποις τὰ ἐκ γῆς φιλοτιμεῖται χαλεπώτερα, πολέμους ἄρτι λῃσταῖς μετ' ὀλίγον, αἰχμαλώτους μικρῷ πρόσθεν εἶχεν, ἐρήμους αὖθις ἀπέδειξεν· ἀπαλλαγὴν καὶ φυγὴν ἐλευθέραν ὑπέθετο καὶ τοὺς ἀναιρήσοντας ἐπέστησε, τοιοῦτον παίζει καθ' ἡμῶν πόλεμον ὥσπερ σκηνὴν τὰ ἡμέτερα καὶ δρᾶμα πεποιημένος, 5.6.3.
[76] Heliodorus' proclivity towards theatrical metaphors is well-known: see Walden (1894), at 4 on this passage; Marino (1990), Paulsen (1992).
[77] Examples at Helm (1906) 44–53, who sees it as a Cynic motif.
[78] For this metaphor, see above, p. 209.
[79] τί οὖν οὐχ ὑποτέμνομεν αὐτοῦ τὴν τραγικὴν ταύτην ποίησιν καὶ τοῖς βουλομένοις ἀναιρεῖν ἐγχειρίζομεν; μή πη καὶ ὑπέρογκον τὸ τέλος τοῦ δράματος φιλοτιμούμενος καὶ αὐτόχειρας ἡμᾶς ἑαυτῶν ἐκβιάσηται γενέσθαι, 5.6.4.

can expect. The deity, he guesses, plans an end that is *huperogkos*: 'extravagant', 'over-weighted', 'tumorous'. It promises an excess, literally, of *ogkos* or 'weight', the quality with which tragedy is often (as indeed elsewhere in Heliodorus) linked.[80] Theagenes' desire to 'cut short' the Gordian knot of liminal narrativity figures in extreme form a (desperate) desire to impose control by determining closure.[81]

The phenomenon of attempted or intended suicide in the novels has received a certain amount of attention in recent years, often seen as another symptom of the supposed spiritual malaise or crisis in masculinity, as though the graves of imperial Greece were full of Chattertons and Werthers.[82] There is very little to support the view of suicide as morbid in ancient accounts, which tend instead to present it as a rational, considered, and even heroic response to extreme circumstances.[83] The same is true in the novels. Theagenes' perspective may be *wrong*, in metanarrative terms, but he is nowhere described as afflicted by a chronic psychopathology. His problem is simply that (like the characters of Menander's *Shield*)[84] he misidentifies the plot as a tragedy and reacts accordingly.

The male characters of the novels are often described as 'passive', but wrongly so. Theagenes' response to the (perceived) syntagmatic nature of the romance plot is an attempt to assert control over the plot, to coerce it into a paradigmatic shape. This involves supplying closure. Suicide constructs death (*teleutē*) as *telos*. This is the real reason why romance heroes never carry through their threats to kill themselves: because suicide is always a form of premature closure, activating what Brooks calls the reader's 'residual fear that... the plot might short-circuit at any moment'.[85] Heliodorus' narrative is both exceptionally long and complex, on the one hand, and strikingly self-aware about the opportunities for narrative compression on the other.[86] Theagenes' attempt to foreclose the plot is a form of

---

[80] Cf. 7.12.1: τὸ τραγικὸν... καὶ ὑπέρογκον. Cf Paulsen (1992) 237 n. 87 on this latter passage (although I do not see that τὸ τραγικόν connotes pomposity here). For tragedy and *ogkos*, see further e.g. Ar. *Ran.* 703; Dion. Hal. *Din.* 7; Jos. *BJ* 7.443; Plut. *Luc.* 21.3; *Nic.* 5.3; *Demetr.* 18.5; *De Pyth.* 407B; Ph. *Mos.* 1.153; *Decal.* 43; [Long.] *De subl.* 3.1.

[81] Cf. esp. Hld. 8.9.8, where Charicleia and Theagenes elect 'to accept any death willingly' (πάντα θάνατον... αὐθαιρέτους δέχεσθαι) so as to relieve them of 'an incurable life, endless wandering, and implacable fortune' (ζωῆς ἀνιάτου καὶ ἄλης ἀνηνύτου καὶ τύχης ἀσπόνδου). That their existence is fundamentally characterised in terms of deficiency is signalled by the series of alpha-privatives.

[82] MacAlister (1996) 53–7c; Toohey (2004) 165–71.   [83] Hill (2004) 1–2.

[84] Above, p. 193.   [85] Brooks (1984) 304.

[86] Hefti (1950) 97–8 on Heliodorus' use of the language of epitomisation and abbreviation in relation to narrative, esp. *epitemnein*: 2.24.5, 2.31.5, 3.14.1, 5.16.5 (ἐπιτεμνόμενος καὶ ὡσπερεὶ κεφαλαιούμενος), 6.2.3, 10.36.1. Note also *kephalaion* at 9.24.3.

Limen

narrative *impatience*, manifesting a desire to end this outstaying liminality, an impetuousness for ending.

As we have said, the syntagmatic force in romance is always counterbalanced by the paradigmatic. Here it is Charicleia who represents the more knowing, resistive interpretation: 'we can take hope from our experience of the past, where we have already frequently survived even more implausible situations (*apistoterōn*)'.[87] Where Theagenes was absorbed in the present, Charicleia looks at the wider temporal picture: she offers a 'hope' (*elpis*) for the future predicated on 'experience of the past' (*tēn peiran tōn parelthontōn*). She plays the role of an adept interpreter of plot, extrapolating from the narrative so far to predict what will happen, using the kind of assumption (that the plotting will be consistent, that the contract established so far will be adhered to) that all romance readers bring to bear. Her reference to 'implausible situations' is also striking, partly because of the generic self-reflexivity (*apistos* is a marker of cunning fictionality),[88] but mostly because it reminds us that there is a narrative pattern even in apparent patternlessness: in romance, the unexpected is, precisely, expected.

Charicleia plays in Heliodorus the role that other novelists give to male buddies (Polycharmus, Hippothous, Clinias).[89] Although she does lament on occasion,[90] she elsewhere shows herself a more optimistic, paradigmatic, detached reader. When Theagenes, imprisoned with Charicleia by the Persian satrap's wife, dreams that Calasiris predicts that they will be set free and end up in Ethiopia, he interprets it to mean that they will die. She, however, offers a more favourable (and literal) perspective, observing that:

familiarity with misfortunes has habituated you to see everything in the worst light, for people are prone to shape their views in accordance with their present circumstances.[91]

Theagenes, in Charicleia's assessment, is displaying the signs of what we have called narrative absorption: he is allowing his 'present circumstances' (*sumpiptonta*) to direct his assessment of the likely outcome. She, on the other hand, adopts a detached perspective, evident in the medium of

---

[87] ἐπιτυχίας ἐλπίδα τὴν πεῖραν τῶν παρελθόντων ὑποθέμενοι, πολλάκις ἤδη καὶ ἐξ ἀπιστοτέρων περιγενόμενοι, 5.7.1.

[88] As in Antonius Diogenes' *Wonders (*apista*) beyond Thule*, and Lucian's *True stories* (1.4, and esp. 1.25). I write 'cunning', because *apista* can be either true accounts that are disbelieved because of their unlikeliness or accounts that should under no circumstances be believed.

[89] Above, pp. 206–10.

[90] See esp. 6.8–9, where she is consoled by Calasiris; also 7.14.4–7.15.1, where she and Theagenes lament together (she takes the lead).

[91] ἡ συνήθειά σε τῶν δυστυχημάτων πάντα πρὸς τὰ φαυλότατον νοεῖν τε καὶ εἰκάζειν παρεσκεύασε, φιλεῖ γὰρ ἄνθρωπος πρὸς τὰ συμπίπτοντα τρέπειν τὴν γνώμην, 8.11.5.

her words as much as the message: the sententious pronouncement upon human nature both arrogates to her the intellectual authority to make such a statement and positions her outside the *hic et nunc* of immediate experience.

Charicleia's prospective vision of the ending of the narrative thus counterbalances Theagenes': whereas he can only see death and tragedy, she has a tendency to predict miraculous escapes and happiness. When captured by the Ethiopians, they willingly submit: he fatalistically, but she because 'she foresaw that they were guided by destiny, and was hopeful of a better outcome'.[92] She also shows an awareness of the narrative amplitude that is generically necessary. When they are brought before the Ethiopian king Hydaspes, she famously resists Theagenes' call to reveal herself immediately: 'a story for which the deity has established complex beginnings must also reach its ends (*telē*) at greater length' (9.24.4).[93]

The novels' representation of despondent lamentation thus characterises a certain way of narrative liminality: it thematises a desire, born of frustration at the relentlessly self-renewing series of disasters (the syntagmatic plot) to impose narrative meaning through premature closure (the paradigmatic plot). At the same time, however, this perspective is always opposed, implicitly or explicitly, to an alternative mode of reading, more patient and hopeful of a happy ending. This binary distribution maps onto a number of other culturally constructed polarities (weak vs strong, youthful vs mature, self-indulgent vs controlled). In generic terms, the distinction is between tragedy and comedy. Although comic genre markers are not so visible, in the way that tragic markers are at the lexical or intertextual levels – the word *kōmōdia* is rare, as are quotations from and direct allusions to the comic poets[94] – it is clear that the 'happy ending' is implicitly coded as comic, particularly in the Menandrian recognition scenes of Longus and Heliodorus.[95] Now, in terms of real literary praxis, happy endings are not

---

[92] [ἡ Χαρίκλεια] συνίει μὲν λοιπὸν ὑπὸ τῶν εἱμαρμένων χειραγωγουμένη καὶ εὔελπις ἦν τῶν βελτιόνων, 8.17.1. I have corrected the obvious error in Rattenbury and Lumb's text at this point.

[93] ὧν γὰρ πολυπλόκους τὰς ἀρχὰς ὁ δαίμων καταβέβληται, τούτων ἀνάγκη καὶ τὰ τέλη διὰ μακροτέρων συμπεραίνεσθαι, 9.24.4. The self-reflexive significance of this passage has long been noted: see esp. Morgan (1989b) 308–9. These words seem to rework *Od.* 23.96–122, where Penelope and Odysseus rebuke Telemachus for attempting to rush their reunion; for the gnomic phrasing, cf. Ar. *Ran.* 1058–9 (ἀνάγκη/μεγάλων γνωμῶν καὶ διανοιῶν ἴσα καὶ τὰ ῥήματα τίκτειν).

[94] Ach. Tat. 8.9–10 (the courtroom speech of the 'Aristophanic' priest) is the exception; apart from a solitary passing reference in Heliodorus (2.23.5; cf. also *kōmikon* at 7.8.1, discussed below), there is no other explicit reference to comedy. Brethes (2007b), however, explores comic motifs in the novels.

[95] Fusillo (1989) 43–55, esp. 53–5 on the comic closure of Heliodorus.

exclusive to comedy,[96] nor do all comedies end with joy unbounded.[97] It is, however, likely that ancient critics opposed them in these terms. An anonymous Byzantine work *On comedy*, which may rest on much older scholiastic traditions, observes that 'the end (*telos*) of tragedy is the dissolution of life, of comedy its consolidation'.[98] Although this firm contrast is indebted primarily to John Tzetzes, it ultimately originates with Aristotle's *Poetics*: in comedy, the greatest enemies 'walk off as friends at the end (*teleutēs*), and no one is killed by anyone'.[99] We can glimpse a trace of this view at Heliodorus 7.8.1, where Calasiris interrupts the potentially fratricidal conflict between Petosiris and Thyamis: 'a contest that had been expected to end in bloodshed turned from a tragic to a comic ending'.[100] This does not mean that the subsequent episode was amusing (in line with modern usage of the word 'comic'), but that the violent outcome foreshadowed in the Oedipal saga (particularly Euripides' *Phoenician women*) has been supplanted with an uplifting re-establishment of social cohesion.

In one respect, then, characters who see themselves as imprisoned within a tragedy are deluded; their fears as to the end in store for them are never justified. Their view of their circumstances is myopic, overabsorbed. Their hyperbole is manifested in part by the contrast provided by the consoling friend, but partly also by the very absurdity of the lamentation. Tragedy is generally associated, in the imperial period, with pompous absurdity; and indeed Achilles Tatius and Heliodorus themselves use the word in this sense.[101] Yet the tragic perspective is not simply a form of false consciousness that will be proven wrong; it also figures one half of the novel-reading experience, namely a 'realistic', affective immersion in the *hic et nunc* of the narrative.

Two more issues. First, what are we to make of the point that tragic despondents are usually male?[102] Elite Greek males, conditioned to expect maximal power and self-determination, were more likely to be aggrieved by their absence. Stoic philosophers addressed such frustrations, advising their addressees to concern themselves only with events that are 'up to us'

---

[96] See Wright (2005) on Euripides' escape tragedies; but the example of Aeschylus' *Oresteia* shows us that tragedies can end joyously even as early as the 450s. Our assumptions about tragic endings might require serious revision if we had more examples of this kind of interconnected trilogy.
[97] Silk (2002) 58–9, in the course of a wide-ranging deconstruction of the comedy–tragedy polarity.
[98] τέλος δὲ τραγωιδίας μὲν λύειν τὸν βίον, κωμωιδίας δὲ συνιστᾶν αὐτόν, *De comoedia* ('Anonymus Crameri' II) = Koster (1975) XIc, 45.56. Koster's notes clarify the debt to Tzetzes to which I refer.
[99] φίλοι γενόμενοι ἐπὶ τελευτῆς ἐξέρχονται, καὶ ἀποθνήσκει οὐδεὶς ὑπ' οὐδενός, *Poet.* 1452a 37–9.
[100] ἀγὼν ὁ δι' αἵματος κριθήσεσθαι προσδοκώμενος εἰς κωμικὸν ἐκ τραγικοῦ τὸ τέλος κατέστρεφε. Further discussion of this passage at Hefti (1950) 112–13.
[101] Ach. Tat. 6.4.4, 8.1.5; Hld. 1.3.2, 2.4.1; further Fusillo (1989) 35.
[102] For Charicleia's two laments, see above, n. 90.

(*eph' hēmin*). The novel can thus be seen as an education in the ontological power-balance between autonomy and determinism. The wellborn male who assumes a powerful, privileged social role at the conclusion has learned the valuable ethical lesson that, in the words of the second-century Stoic Epictetus, 'the gods have made only the mightiest and most powerful thing of all "up to us", namely the proper use of our sense impressions (*phantasiais*); other things are not up to us'.[103] We cannot control the events that happen to us, only how we receive them. Thus Heliodorus' Theagenes proclaims (in a more confident mood) that 'if I must endure suffering, my fortunes and my temperament have often already prepared me to bear all that befalls me'.[104]

Second, one novel arguably does end with tragedy.[105] Achilles' *Leucippe and Clitophon*, as we have seen, has a prologue that seems to subvert its happy ending: here, Clitophon is to be found bemoaning the 'insults I have suffered at Eros' hands'.[106] What these 'insults' might be is left strategically indeterminate. The crucial point for now, however, is the subversion of the standard marriage-as-*telos* motif implies that, exceptionally, the tragic perspective is vindicated in this novel: life really is, apparently, an endless succession of sufferings.[107] Clinias repeatedly consoles his cousin and friend, as a novelistic buddy should; but perhaps he should rather have sought his narrative models in the tragic death of his own boyfriend Charicles (1.12), and of Menelaus' beloved (2.34.1–5). The (apparent) triumph of the tragic mode in Achilles figures the absence of narrative closure in this, the most playful and subversive of the romances.

THE WANDERING NARRATIVE

The novels stage not only the 'reading' of syntagmatic, liminal plotting, but also its active production. The prime example is Heliodorus' presentation of Calasiris' account in books 3–5, by some distance the longest and most developed example of a secondary narrative in the fully extant novels. The point that I wish to emphasise here is the convergence between his

---

[103] τὸ κράτιστον ἁπάντων καὶ κυριεῦον οἱ θεοὶ μόνον ἐφ' ἡμῖν ἐποίησαν, τὴν χρῆσιν τὴν ὀρθὴν ταῖς φαντασίαις, τὰ δ' ἄλλα οὐκ ἐφ' ἡμῖν, Arr. *Diss.* 1.1.7.
[104] εἰ δὲ πάσχειν τι δέοι, φέρειν τὰ προσπίπτοντα ἤδη με πολλάκις ἥ τε τύχη καὶ ἡ γνώμη παρεσκεύασε, 7.21.5.
[105] A second does too, if HU 249–50 are correct in their suggestions about *Metiochus and Parthenope*.
[106] τοσαύτας ὕβρεις ἐξ ἔρωτος παθών, 1.2.1.
[107] Clitophon's words need not mean that he is suffering in the present, only that the story of his past experiences contains suffering (Nakatani (2003) 75–6). Even so, the avoidance of any mention of closure of the tragic phase is eloquent.

representation as a wandering figure and his dilatory narrative style. The narrative is bookended with allusions to wandering. When he and Cnemon enter Nausicles' house, Calasiris immediately invokes a bond between the three men, on the grounds that they share a 'wandering life' (*bios... planos*, 2.22.3): this is the reason, he supposes, why the merchant has agreed to entertain a 'errant vagabond' (*aluonta kai planōmenon*) like himself. In reply, Cnemon asks him what is the nature of this wandering (*planē*, 2.22.4). This question (which will be later echoed by Nausicles)[108] provokes the lengthy embedded narrative of Calasiris' encounter with Charicleia and Theagenes. Calarisis' story, then, is constitutively a *planē*, a tale that (as we shall see presently) wanders in terms of both theme and narration. To this it may be objected that Calasiris only gives a limited answer for now, deferring a full response till after a meal has been had (2.22.5). This deferral, however, is itself part of the narrative strategy, an artful means of increasing anticipation and displaying the speaker's own mastery of the situation. Calasiris may even have borrowed the technique of narrative postponement from Dio Chrysostom, antiquity's most celebrated rhetorical wanderer.[109]

Behind both Calasiris and Dio, however, lies the controlling paradigm of Odysseus,[110] who analogously attempts to postpone part of his narrative during an interruption at *Odyssey* 11.328–84, where he proposes sleep.[111] Calasiris signposts the Odysseanism explicitly, by justifying the break for dinner by noting that 'Homer marvellously named [the belly] "destructive"',[112] alluding to *Odyssey* 17.286–7, where the disguised Odysseus explains his need to beg. Food and sleep, for the Homeric Odysseus, take precedence over all else (he is also the character who, in the *Iliad*, defers Achilles' return to battle until the troops have had time to eat: 19.155–83). The rhythms of the body, the necessary cycles of replenishment, expenditure and rest, arrest and intercut both action and narration. Similarly, Calasiris will later protest that Cnemon is 'not only an insatiable listener... but also impervious to sleep'.[113] For such Odyssean narrators, digressiveness and postponement are the necessary consequences of embodied, human existence.

---

[108] ἡ σὴ πλάνη κάλλιστα ἄν, εἰ βουληθείης, τὴν εὐωχίαν παραπέμποι (5.16.2).
[109] Cf. Dio Chr. *Or.* 1.48, 3.12, 36.27–8; Moles (1978) 96–100, Whitmarsh (2001a) 198, Montiglio (2005) 193–203. On Dio's fame in antiquity, see Brancacci (1986).
[110] Observed by Montiglio (2005) 257.
[111] Hardie (1998) 22 observes the importance of this passage for a later scene, 3.4.1–5.2, where Calasiris breaks off his account of the Delphic procession.
[112] θαυμασίως οὐλομένην ὠνόμασεν, 2.22.5.
[113] οὐ μόνον ἀκουσμάτων ἀκόρεστος... ἀλλὰ καὶ ὕπνωι δυσάλωτος, 4.4.2.

Calasiris is also vulnerable (like Dio) to the charge of wandering in speech.[114] Immediately before Calasiris launches into his three-book long narrative, Cnemon protests about the ad hoc order in which the narrative material has been released so far, protesting about the unnecessary (as he sees it) background detail:

> Enough of herdsmen, satraps, and Great Kings! You nearly tricked me by bringing me straight to the ending (*peras*) of the story with your talk, wheeling on (*epeiskuklēsas*) this episode (*epeisodion*) that, as they say, has nothing to do with Dionysus. Take your narrative back to what you promised. I have found you just like Proteus of Pharos, not that you take on false and fluid forms as he did, but in that you are forever trying to misdirect (*parapherein*) me! (2.24.4)

As so often in Heliodorus, the language of the theatre is employed self-reflexively (if here catachrestically) to discuss the nature of narrative.[115] Cnemon's primary concern in this passage is with organic unity: what he disparages is both Calasiris' use of disconnected, episodic narrative (episodes that have 'nothing to do with Dionysus'), and his lack of respect for chronological sequence, in jumping directly to the 'end' of the narrative.[116] The metaphors are colourful and mixed (note also the reference to Proteus, the metamorphosing god traditionally associated with sophistry),[117] but let us emphasise one in particular, which connects back to the theme of wandering: Cnemon conceives of narrative as a linear procession, from which Calasiris is trying to 'misdirect' him.[118]

What does it mean to accuse a narrative of wandering? In Cnemon's criticism, clearly the focus is upon straying into irrelevance. Yet the criteria for relevance are not always self-evident, especially when a story has just begun. Calasiris asserts in response that he will not 'play the sophist'

---

[114] Dio Chr. *Or.* 1.57, 12.16, 12.38; also 7.1 (πολυλογία), and 5.1, 5.18, 47.8 (ἀδολεσχία); Whitmarsh (2001a) 160 n. 108. ἀδολεσχία is, however, stigmatised in others at 20.3, 27.3, 66.23 (and in the *De garrulitate* of his acquaintance (cf. *Lamprias catalogue* 204, 227), Plutarch).

[115] Above, pp. 229–32, and esp. Paulsen (1992) 148–9, who discusses this passage in terms of narrative retardation. ἐπεισκυκλήσας is the focus of the catachresis: not only is it an unusual choice of verb governing ἐπεισόδιον, but also in standard terminology, εἰσκυκλεῖν strictly refers to the motion of the *ekkuklēma* into the stage building (see Poll. 4.128 on the εἰσκύκλημα). Walden (1894) 39, however, aptly cites the parallel of Luc. *Philops.* 29 (θεὸν ἀπὸ μηχανῆς ἐπεισκυκληθῆναι).

[116] On the distinctively Heliodorean term πέρας, see above, pp. 115, 134.

[117] For Proteus and sophistry, see Pl. *Euthyd.* 288b, *Euthryphr.* 15d, *Ion* 541e (and for his *poikilia*, see Ath. *Deipn.* 258a, Philostr. *VA* 1.4, Nonn. *Dion.* 1.14). The sophist (at least as Lucian presents him) Peregrinus was nicknamed Proteus: see *VS* 563–4; Luc. *Peregr.* 1; *Demon.* 21; *Adv. indoct.* 14. According to the *Suda*, Philostratus ἔγραψε... Πρωτέα κύνα ἢ σοφιστήν (s.v. Φιλόστρατος ὁ πρῶτος, Λήμνιος). It is possible (but I think unlikely) that two works are alluded to here (i.e. Πρωτεύς and κύων ἢ σοφιστής).

[118] Cf. Hunter (1998) 51. This metaphor of deviation also activates the image underlying the etymology of *epeisodion*: see below, pp. 235–40.

(sophisteuōn), but 'provide an account of what follows that is well-ordered *(eutakton)* and relevant *(prosekhē)*'.[119] If we are right that Calasiris is partly inspired by the figure of Dio Chrysostom, then the model for this claim will be the end of the narrative in the *Euboean oration*: 'I have narrated all of this story not pointlessly nor (as some will think) out of a desire for garrulity, but as an example of the life that I set out at the beginning and the life-style of the poor'.[120] In both instances, the claim for relevance is pressed, against the accusations of (imagined or real) interlocutors. A narrative that had seemed to wander turns out to be suitably directed. Part of the lesson, then, is simply that readers need to be patient, and the relevance will emerge. In Heliodorus, however, there is an additional twist. At the beginning of book 3, in a famous passage we have already considered, Cnemon objects once again, this time that Calasiris' narrative is too compressed and undescriptive. Calasiris' defence is that he was confining himself to 'the more important *(kairiōtera)* aspects of the narrative', at the expense of 'extraneous details'.[121] In other words, he is turning the tables on Cnemon, who once castigated irrelevance, but now seems to be insisting that Calasiris fill out his narrative with marginalia.

EPISODE AND DIGRESSION

There is an implicit, normative assumption that a truthful utterance will proceed in a straight line. According to regular Greek idiom, speech should be 'straight' *(orthos)* – not 'crooked' *(skolios)*, like the pronouncements of the powerful according to Hesiod.[122] Narrative particularly attracts the metaphor of paths and journeys, from the Homeric 'paths of song' onwards. These metaphors are heavily pregnant with significance. A story that deviates from its linear path is likely to be viewed as, precisely, deviant. For this reason, the *parekbasis* or 'digression' is a particularly problematic concept. Etymologically speaking, this is a section that 'travels' (-*basis* < *bainō*) 'away from' *(parek-)* the path. Similarly troubling is an 'episode' or *epeisodion*, a 'sidetrack' joining the main route from an unexpected angle (it is *epeisodia*

---

[119] τὴν ἀφήγησιν... εὔτακτον... καὶ προσεχῆ τῶν ἑξῆς παρασκευάζων τὴν ἀκρόασιν, 2.24.5.
[120] ἅπαντα δὴ τοῦτον τὸν λόγον διῆλθον οὐκ ἄλλως οὐδ' ὡς τάχ' ἄν δόξαιμί τισιν, ἀδολεσχεῖν βουλόμενος, ἀλλ' οὕπερ ἐς ἀρχῆς ἐπεθέμην βίου καὶ τῆς τῶν πενήτων διαγωγῆς παράδειγμα ἐκτιθείς, 7.81. Russell (1992) 132 aptly cites the precedent of Pl. *Phaed.* 70c, where Socrates defends himself against the claim that ἀδολέσχω καὶ οὐ περὶ προσηκόντων τοὺς λόγους ποιοῦμαι.
[121] τὰ καιριώτερα τῆς ἀφηγήσεως / τοῖς ἔξωθεν, 3.1.2. Cf. Hardie (1998) 23, with n. 5 for other uses of καιρός in relation to narrative; also Morgan (2004e) 536–7.
[122] *Op.* 194, 219, 221, 250, 258, 262.

that Cnemon accuses Calasiris of introducing in the passage cited above).[123] Digressions and episodes are the technical terms for narrative divagation. In an anonymous tract of rhetorical theory from the imperial period, for example, the use of digression (*parekbasis*) and episodic narration (*epeisodia*) is directly associated with 'wandering away from the subject'.[124]

Episodes, to begin with them, are deeply ambivalent. Greek narrative theory shows a strong normative preference for organic unity. In Plato's *Phaedrus*, Socrates famously decries the fact that the Lysianic speech they are discussing is organised 'randomly' (*khudēn*) (264b), and proposes to the contrary that 'every discourse (*logos*) should fit together as a living organism does with its own body, so that it lacks neither head nor feet, but has both middle parts and extremities, all of which are composed in a manner appropriate both to each other and to the whole'.[125] This normative desire for unity is given canonical shape in Aristotle's *Poetics*.[126] Episodic plots in tragedy, he says, are 'the worst type of 'simple' plot: 'I define an episodic plot as one in which the episodes follow one another in a way that neither plausibility (*eikos*) nor necessity (*anagkē*) admits' (*Poet.* 1451b). In the *Rhetoric*, he accuses Isocrates of trying to conceal bad cases by episodic construction.[127] *Epeisodion* in these passages implies a superfluous scene without structural connection to the main plot. But Aristotle's approach to episodes is in fact 'significantly ambiguous',[128] since he also sees them as essential if one wants full narrative rather than jejune summary.[129] Even so, episodes are necessarily fraught with risk.[130] 'Make sure that the episodes are integral (*oikeia*)', he insists (*Poet.* 1455b13) – an injunction that would not be necessary if they were unproblematically natural to his conception of plot. Episodes stand in the grey area between the intrinsic and the superfluous.

---

[123] On the metaphor, see more fully Race (1978) 183–4; also Friedrich (1983) 41.
[124] ἀπὸ τοῦ πράγματος πλανῶιο (*Anon. Seg.* 67, *RG* 1.436.26–7 = Dilts and Kennedy (1997) 22).
[125] δεῖν πάντα λόγον ὥσπερ ζῶιον συνεστάναι σῶμά τι ἔχοντα αὐτὸν αὑτοῦ, ὥστε μήτε ἀκέφαλον εἶναι μήτε ἄπουν, ἀλλὰ μέσα τε ἔχειν καὶ ἄκρα, πρέποντα ἀλλήλοις καὶ τῶι ὅλωι γεγραμμένα, 264c. The same principle is presently advanced in relation to tragedy (268c–d).
[126] Possibly pre-empted by Protagoras: see *P.Oxy.* 221, with Heath (1989) 157–8.
[127] *Rhet.* 1418a33–8; Heath (1989) 35.   [128] Halliwell (1986) 111.
[129] Thus the *Odyssey* can be summarised briefly, but is very little without its *epeisodia* (*Poet.* 1455b16–23). For the integral role of the *epeisodion*, see *Poet.* 1455a34–b2 (the poet must set out the general shape of the plot, then ἐπεισοδιοῦν καὶ παρατείνειν); and further Nickau (1966), nuanced by Friedrich (1983), esp. 37–43 (the fullest and best discussion); also Tsagarakis (1973) and Heath (1989) 49–54, relating the phenomenon to his larger analysis of unity in diversity in Greek poetics.
[130] Friedrich (1983) 40–1. Aristotle's unitarian approach is best encapsulated in his injunction that plot should be 'a representation of unitary and complete action, and the parts of the action should be so constructed that the displacement or removal of any parts will disturb and disjoint the work's wholeness' (*Poet.* 1451a30–5).

Greek criticism is equally ambivalent about digression.[131] The fourth-century historians Theopompus, Timaeus and Ephorus were decried for their excessive use of the *parekbasis*.[132] Dionysius of Halicarnassus criticises even Thucydides for compromising his *saphēneia* ('clarity'), protesting that his organisation of material by chronological sequence militates against the unified development of narrative (*Thuc.* 9).[133] This concern goes beyond aesthetics, into ethics and ideology (*parekbainein* can be used of ethical deviancy too).[134] Let us take a single example of such a moralising approach to digressions, this time from the preface to a technical work, the text on siege engines of Athenaeus 'the mechanic' (probably from the time of Augustus).[135] Athenaeus is keen to criticise the *polygraphia* ('much-writing') of those authors who expend words and time with no regard for utility: 'when they write copiously (*polygraphountes*) they waste time on useless language, to exhibit their own polymathy; for they leave us their works having filled them with digressions (*parekbaseōn*)'.[136] Digression is not simply self-indulgent, it also offends the utilitarian economics of busy men like Athenaeus and his Roman addressee, Marcellus (possibly Marcus Claudius Marcellus, Augustus' nephew and son-in-law): the controlling opposition is between 'wasting' (*analiskein*: 4, 5) words and time, and 'being thrifty' (*pheidesthai* (bis), *apheidōs*, 3). Time, for Athenaeus, is money. Divagatory writing, for Athenaeus, is an affront to the tight cost–benefit ratio that underlies the discourse of real power.

For all these associations with excess and decadence, however, digressions might also have a more positive status. Oratorical theorists sometimes advise them on tactical grounds. If, for example, one wishes to convey that

---

[131] Well discussed by Billault (1991) 268–74.
[132] Theopomp. 115 *FGrH* T.29.3, T.30.1, T.31.1, with Flower (1994) 167–8; Dion. Hal. *Pomp.* 6.11 (discussed by Fornaro (1997) 264–5); Theon *Prog.* 4 (2.80.27–81.4 *RG*); Ephorus 70 *FGrH* T.23; Timaeus 566 *FGrH* T.19.30. Practising historians often avoid the digressive (e.g. D.S. 1.37.1) or apologise for them (e.g. Plut. *Alex.* 35.16).
[133] Dionysius distinguishes Thucydides from the majority of his predecessors, who 'felt the need to adorn their descriptions of places with mythical episodes' (μυθώδεσιν ἐπεισοδίοις, *Thuc.* 7); Thucydides, on the other hand, 'chose a single theme' (ὑπόθεσιν, 7). Yet Dionysius also criticises his subject for arranging his material by summers and winters, which means that 'the whole book is broken up in this way, and the continuity (τὸ διηνεκές) of the narrative destroyed: predictably, we end up wandering...' (πλανώμεθα cf. also *Ep. Pomp.* 3.13). Thucydides – a Callimachean before his time, on this reading – improves on his predecessors by banishing the episodic, but still fails to avoid the discontinuous and the divagatory. For the *parekbasis* as a threat to *saphēneia*, see also Theon, *Progymnasmata* (= 2.80–1 *RG*).
[134] A usage found prominently in Aristotle: for 'deviant' political systems, see e.g. *EN* 1160a31–2, *Pol.* 1273a21–32, 1279a20 etc.
[135] Whitehead and Blyth (2004), with 15–28 on the date.
[136] πολυγραφοῦντες εἰς οὐκ ἀναγκαίους λόγους καταναλίσκουσι τὸν χρόνον, ὅπως ἐμφήνωσι τὴν ἑαυτῶν πολυμάθειαν· παρεκβάσεων γὰρ πληρώσαντες ἀπολείπουσι τὰ βιβλία, 4.

one is overcome by emotion, one might allow oneself to get 'carried away' from the main theme.[137] A deviation might also provide a kind of figured commentary upon the principal subject: in the rhetorical treatise known as the *Anonymous Seguerianus*, the *parekbasis* is distinguished from the *paradiegesis*, a genuine excursus from relevance: the former, by constrast, operates 'by way of comparison or imitation of the facts'.[138] In other words, digressions have an oblique connection to the main narrative, offering an implicit or explicit commentary, analogy or contrast. Thus, for example, Dio Chrysostom in the passage cited above (7.81) explains that he told the story of his shipwreck on Euboea not out of a desire for garrulity (*adoleskhein*) but to provide an example (*paradeigma*) to support his real point about the preferability of the simple life. Both of these critical tactics, interestingly, involve reasserting the connection with the main narrative, albeit at a deeper level. Digression can be recouped (aesthetically, morally) so long as it can be shown to be relevant – in effect, so long as its very digressiveness can be abnegated. As we shall see, this desire to linearise the novel's digressive tendencies persists in modern criticism on the novel.

Let us turn now to the Greek novels, and in particular to the two most digressive authors, Achilles Tatius and Heliodorus. (Xenophon is perhaps episodic rather than digressive: this distinction will be discussed below.) Achilles' narrator, Clitophon, discourses lyrically on desire in the natural world (1.17–18), the bulls of Egypt (2.15.3–4), the phoenix (3.25), the hippo (4.2), the crocodile (4.19) and Alexandria (5.1); he also reports others' views on aquatic marvels (2.14.6–10), and the hippo and elephant (4.3–5). Heliodorus' primary narrator lards his narrative with accounts and descriptions, principally of cock-crowing (1.18.3), an amethyst (5.13), the skin of elephants (9.18.8), the giraffe (10.27), while his secondary narrator Calasiris also offers disquisitions on the sources of the Nile (2.28) and the evil eye and the ocular genesis of desire (3.7.2–3.8).[139] Not only do these retard the flow of the narrative, but also (as criticism has emphasised since Gotthold Lessing's *Laokoon*) artworks operate in a fundamentally different register to narrative, the spatial rather than the temporal.[140] Descriptions

---

[137] Cf. esp. Hermagoras cited at Cic. *Inv.* 1.97; Quint. *Inst. or.* 4.2.104 (cf. 4.3.5); Aristid. *Panath.* 35; also Sall. *BJ* 4.9. See further Race (1978) 177–9.
[138] καθ' ὁμοίωσιν ἢ μίμησιν τῶν γεγονότων, *Anon. Seg.* 61 (= I.436.7–8 *RG*); Dilts and Kennedy (1997) 20.
[139] We also find in Achilles and Heliodorus numerous brief sententious comments: see esp. Morales (2000) = (2004) 106–30. There are also a few digressions in Longus, but none is longer than a sentence: see 1.30.6 (swimming cows), 2.1.4 (the vines of Lesbos), 4.10.3 (Lesbian wine).
[140] See esp. Lessing (1984 [1766]) 98–103. For discussion of ecphrasis in the novels, see the works cited above, Chapter 2 n. 120.

Limen 239

of artworks within narrative are disturbing because they drive achronic wedges into the midst of a chronological process.

For a long time, scholars considered these features in Athenaean terms, as narrative superfluities designed solely to delectate the intellectually narcissistic reader.[141] More recent readers, however, have emphasised the sophisticated ways in which paradoxographical, zoological or ecphrastic material frames our responses to the larger plot – assuming the kind of compositional sophistication advised by the *Anonymous Seguerianus*.[142] There are three dominant approaches to the integration of digression. One explores the role of descriptive passages as proleptic of the later narrative – a notable example is Bartsch's *Decoding the ancient novel* (1989).[143] Another is to take set-piece descriptions of artworks as structural waymarkers, segmenting the narrative at significant points.[144] Finally, Helen Morales has recently interpreted Achilles' digressive sections as repositories for fantasies of the male sexual dominance that is repressed by the primary narrative: 'a description, whether or not it prefigures an episode which follows it, leaves a deposit, a residue which alters our perception of that episode'.[145] For Morales, the role of many digressions is to fulfil the desire for erotic domination in a context that is safely displaced from the relatively benign world of the primary narrative.

The desire to produce integrated readings, to assume that every detail is at some level 'to the point', may be cognitively intuitive. In the field of pragmatic linguistics, some theorists have seen the presumption of relevance as the most essential and immutable law of communicative situations.[146] But syntagmatic plotting can seem to defy this law. Other critics have seen the novels as designedly digressive and non-linear. Billault has argued that we should see the novelists' digressions as a form of creative exuberance that resists scholarship's attempts to construct unities out of narrative: 'il faut tenter de faire coexister la démarche systématique et totalisante qui est le propre de toute critique et celle, moins rigoreuse et rectiligne, de

---

[141] Cf. e.g. Rohde (1914) 263; Rommel (1923) 82; even Bartsch (1989) finds herself resorting to explaining some passages as unintegrated, included simply because they were 'interesting and of genuine educational worth' (155). Hägg (1971) 108–9 surveys negative approaches to Achillean digression.
[142] Sedelmeier (1959) 113–31 attempts a unified account of Achilles' structure, 'aus dem bunten Gewirr von Ereignissen, Exkursen und thematischen Beziehungen herauslösen' (113). More recent examples of this sentiment are cited at Morales (2004) 96–7.
[143] Bartsch (1989). See also Winkler (1982) on Heliodorus.
[144] Nakatani (2003) 66–74 on Achilles Tatius, also seeing Longus' *aitiai* in a similar light. MacQueen (1990) 15–97 is an ambitious attempt to map out a structure for Longus.
[145] Morales (2004) 183; see more generally 96–151.   [146] See esp. Sperber and Wilson (1995).

240 *Part II Narrative and identity*

la création, dont la digression est une manifestation'.[147] Massimo Fusillo identifies the same tendency, but interprets it slightly differently: in the course of his neo-Bakhtinian argument that the novel is constitutively a 'forma aperta', he points to the novels' inclusion of digressions as evidence for the 'tentazione enciclopedica', born of the desire to fashion the novel into an all-encompassing receptacle for pre-existent genres and nuggets of knowledge.[148]

We can fill out some of the cultural context for this encyclopedism. There was no ancient genre of the 'encyclopedia' as such (no equivalent to Pauly-Wissowa or *Encylopedia Britannica*); what we do have are miscellanies (again not an ancient term) associated with, among other things, radically non-linear modes of literary organisation.[149] Examples include Pamphila's *Historical notes*, Seneca's *Natural questions*, Pliny's *Natural history*, Plutarch's *Sympotic questions*, Favorinus' *Varied history*, Aulus Gellius' *Attic nights*, Achilles Tatius' (lost) *Varied history*, Clement's *Patchwork* (*Stromateis*), Aelian's *Varied history* and *On the nature of animals*, Athenaeus' *Sophists at supper*, Julius Africanus' *Embroiderings* (*Kestoi*).[150] In these, disorganisation is often presented as a positive aesthetic choice. Gellius claims 'I have used the random order (*ordine . . . fortuito*) for my matter that I happened to employ in excerpting it' (*Pref.* 2). Clement presents his material 'as it happened (*etukhen*) to come to my memory, without pruning it either by order or by style, but deliberately scattered all over the place' (6.1.2.1). According to Photius, Pamphila – the only known female miscellanist – explicitly claimed to present her material 'at random' (*eikēi*).[151]

This pleasure in artful disorder reflects the culture of the symposium, where individuals might interpose responses without regard for formal structure. The earliest example of a miscellany of this type seems to have been Aristoxenus' *Varied sympotica* (frr. 122–7 Wehrli). Book II of Callimachus' *Aetia* – a poem programmatically distanced from the 'single continuous song' (fr. 1.3 Pf.) in its prologue – was set around a symposium.[152] The link between miscellanism and sympotic practice is also

---

[147] Billault (1991) 268; his wide-ranging and important discussion at 265–301 has been strangely neglected.
[148] Fusillo (1989) 68–77, at 68. Nimis (1998) sees description in a similar but subtly different light: as provisional experiments with plot on the part of the author. His position thus lies somewhere between the two camps I identify here.
[149] König and Whitmarsh (2007) 31–4.
[150] On which, see Holford-Strevens (2003) 27–36; König and Whitmarsh (2007) 31.
[151] *Bibl.* 119b 27–32. See further Holford-Strevens (2003) 34.
[152] The sympotic culture of Hellenistic poetry is well (if controversially) characterised by Cameron (1995) 71–103.

Limen 241

found in Plutarch's *Sympotic questions* and Athenaeus' *Sophists at supper*.[153] The latter is a particularly intriguing case. If Athenaeus the mechanic decries *polugraphia* as indulgent excess, his later namesake is undoubtedly antiquity's most polygraphic author: in this gross record of conversations structured around meals, luxurious consumption becomes the controlling metaphor for the restrained chaos of table talk.[154] The 'destructive belly' pushes this digressive text to new limits.

The novels are not miscellanies in any generic sense, but there are certainly some markers of this kind of textual organisation. In one fragment, notably, we find both an explicit dramatisation of sympotic table talk and (perhaps) an expression of the principle of arbitrary organisation. In the largest surviving fragment of the novel we call *Metiochus and Parthenope*, Polycrates hosts a symposium where the nature of Eros is discussed. The text is controversial, but the latest editors' view is that Polycrates, or the philosopher Anaximenes (who is also present), proposes a philosophical roundtable with views aired 'according chance' (*kata tukhēn*), i.e. avoiding any particular order of discussion.[155] If this reconstruction is correct,[156] then the implication is that a sympotic miscellany ensued.

In the following, reasonably legible 40 lines, the tension between order and disorder develops. Metiochus begins, after the familiar[157] profession of ignorance (ii 37–9). His praise of Eros is a form of *anaskeuē*, or refutation of traditionally held beliefs: specifically, he challenges the idea that Eros is a young boy. Before he has finished, Anaximenes interrupts and tells Parthenope to speak (ii 62–6). Parthenope attacks Metiochus' account, piqued (the narrator tells us) by the latter's claim to no experience of love, or indeed of any wish for it (ii 66–8; cf. ii 59–60). This disruptive, non-sequential approach to speechifying looks obviously to the hypotext of Plato's *Symposium*, where the guests take turns to praise Eros, improvising a new order when an attack of the hiccups 'chances upon' (*tukhein*, 185d) Aristophanes. Sympotic discourse is capacious and flexible. Indeed, when Socrates himself speaks up, he forewarns that he will speak 'with whatever

---

[153] See esp. Jeanneret (1991) 160–71: table talk 'guarantees that literature can have an exploded structure, proliferating according to no other principle than that of improvisation' (164).
[154] For Athenaeus' slippage between food and words, see esp. Lukinovich (1990).
[155] Col. ii 34 (= SW 84, HU 24): προτι[θεὶς τ]ὴν φ [ιλ]οσόφου ζήτησιν κατὰ τύχην τ[....]. SW 85 translate 'proposing the philosopher's inquiry as chance would have it'. Hägg (HU 28) is more cautious, translating 'pro[posing as a topic] a philosopher's inquiry... by chance...', explaining: 'If "by chance" belongs to the previous sentence, something like "(proceeding) by chance (round the table)" may be implied.'
[156] Maehler (1976) takes κατὰ τύχην with the following sentence ('durch diesen Zufall').
[157] Cf. Ach. Tat. 2.37.5, 'an "Unaccustomed as I am" *topos*' (Goldhill (1995) 85).

words and arrangement of material that happens to (*tukhēi*) occur to me along the way'.[158] Just as Socrates' claim is obviously ironical, however, so the appearance of miscellaneity in *Metiochus and Parthenope* is unconvincing. The two lovers are exploiting the opportunity to flirt, to test out their relationship (as in the analogous episodes in Achilles Tatius: 1.5, 2.9). Anaximenes may even be assuming, under the guise of philosophical disinterest, the role of matchmaker. (In this case, he may well be part of the inspiration for Heliodorus' Calasiris.) The symposium may seem to other participants to be an opportunity to relax the usual expectations of causality and sequence, to indulge a pure digressivism, but at a deeper level (to which the reader has a privileged access), the love plot continues to develop. This play between order and disorder at the thematic level of relevance reflects the ambiguities of the liminal phase, where the paradigmatic, totalising forces that lead towards closure can appear to be muscled aside by the digressive powers of syntagmatic plotting.

LEUCIPPE AND CLITOPHON: DEVIANT DIGRESSION

Achilles Tatius is, without question, the novelist most fond of digressions. Even the generally sympathetic Tomas Hägg writes that 'their subject matter often has only the faintest connection with the plot', and 'the author has not been very careful in his integration of them'.[159] The reasons for their inclusion extend, I think, beyond a mere desire for erudition. Achilles was familiar with the genre of the miscellany, to judge by the report in the *Suda* that he composed, among other things, a *Varied history* (*historia summiktos*), 'recording many great and wonderful men' (A 4695). The title and brief description suggest an anecdotal miscellany, along the same heterogeneous lines as Favorinus' (*pantodapē historia*) and Aelian's (*poikilē historia*). This work seems to have been aesthetically similar to the novel ('his *logos* [in his other writings] is everywhere like the erotic writings'), even if the *Suda*'s phrasing makes it unclear where the points of resemblance lie.[160] The crucial point, however, is that it seems *a posteriori* unlikely that

---

[158] ὀνομάσει δὲ καὶ θέσει ῥημάτων τοιαύτηι ὁποία ἂν τις τύχηι ἐπελθοῦσα, 199b. The text is problematic; I have followed Dover (1980) 46, accepting the reasons given at 132–3.
[159] Hägg (1971) 108–9, at 109. Fusillo (1989) 76 contrasts Heliodorus' digressions, which are all relevant to the plot, with Achilles' 'centrifugal' usage. Bartsch (1989) 172–3 also adverts to this feature, interpreting it in terms of the greater weighting given to narrative indeterminacy in Achilles.
[160] ὁ δὲ λόγος αὐτοῦ κατὰ πάντα ὅμοιος τοῖς ἐρωτικοῖς, *Suda* A 4695. What *logos* actually means here is unclear: are they similar in style, in scurrility, in organisation of material? A second problem is that the *Suda*'s claim that all (πάντα) of Achilles' works resemble *Leucippe and Clitophon* includes *On the sphere*. If this latter text is to be identified with the work *On the universe* (περὶ τοῦ παντός),

the author of a miscellany would have included miscellanea in his novel without thinking through the generic implications.

Digressivism in Achilles is not just an authorial tic, but a narratorial mode that is carefully theorised within the text. An excellent example comes in the first book, where Clitophon pronounces pseudo-scientifically upon the effects of *eros* upon various natural beings and phenomena (1.16–18). The framing of this episode is significant. Firstly, it occurs in the garden. The garden is a particularly marked space in *Leucippe and Clitophon*, where fortuitous natural events can introduce an element of surprise. In this instance, Leucippe 'happened' (*etukhen*, 1.16.1) to be wandering in the garden and to have halted in front of the peacock, and the peacock 'happened by happenstance' (*etukhe…tukhēi tini*, 1.16.2) to fan its tail. Chance happenings provoke chance conversations: an ideal setting for miscellaneous discourse. And yet, as in *Metiochus and Parthenope*, the appearance of chance accidence is an illusion. Clitophon's expositions are not arbitrarily structured: 'wanting to render the girl amenable to *eros*, I began speaking to Satyrus, taking off from the opportunity provided by the bird'.[161] The arbitrary event is but the pretext for a calculated speech. What is more, Clitophon's first words on the subject of the peacock's fan comment self-reflexively upon the tension between randomness and planning. The bird, he opines, has acted 'not without design (*tekhnē*)'; it is, rather, attempting to seduce its mate (1.16.2). Clitophon's sophistical plumage,[162] likewise, is less an excrescence of arbitrary erudition, and more a calculated come-on.

Instructive too are the responses of Clitophon's narratees to his various disquisitions. After the first, he comments that Satyrus 'understood the pretext (*hupothesis*) of my speech',[163] and thereupon asked him for further discussion of erotic natural phenomena (1.17.1). The word *hupothesis*

---

partially transmitted under Achilles' name among the scholia to Aratus (see Maass (1958)), then it is hard to see where the resemblance may lie (Vilborg (1962) 9).

[161] βουλόμενος οὖν ἐγὼ εὐάγωγον τὴν κόρην εἰς ἔρωτα παρασκευάσαι, λόγων πρὸς τὸν Σάτυρον ἠρχόμην, ἀπὸ τοῦ ὄρνιθος λαβὼν τὴν εὐκαιρίαν, 1.16.1. The links between the chance behaviour of Leucippe and of the peacock are emphasised through the word εὐάγωγον (Morales (2004) 185, noting the link to Clitophon's claim that the peacock wants to ἐπαγαγέσθαι its mate (1.16.2); NB also the lexically closer link back to Clinias' advice to work on a girl to make her εὐάγωγον, 1.10.5). On the sexual politics of this section, see more generally Morales (2004) 184–92; also Goldhill (1995) 68–9. The natural–historical sources are discussed by Rommel (1923) 64–73; Vilborg (1962) 33–7. I discuss the garden as a place of opportunities and chance happenings at Whitmarsh (2010b).

[162] For the parallel between the preening sophist and the peacock, Morales (2004) 185 aptly cites Dio 12.2–4; the bird's immoral ostentation is also noted by Tertull. *De pall.* 3.1, Greg. Naz. *De theologia* 24. This bird is, additionally, a subject of sophistic or parasophistic description: see Ael. *NA* 5.21 (cf. ἐπίδειξιν), Liban. *Prog.* 1.3.1–2.

[163] συνεὶς τοῦ λόγου μου τὴν ὑπόθεσιν, 1.17.1.

suggests a meaning 'underlying' (*hupo-* = 'below', *thesis* = 'placement') the literal sense. Satyrus' response to Clitophon's discussion of peacocks distinguishes the superficial concern (zoology) from the *hupothesis*, its core (erotic) meaning. This is an artful lesson in pragmatic, subtextual reading. The choice of the lexeme *hupothesis*, indeed, has a further significance. The word is sometimes used in literary criticism to denote the central plot of a work, in opposition to digressions that wander away from it.[164] So, far from being an arbitrary deviation from the theme, Clitophon's words are fundamentally relevant. And Satyrus is not the only reader capably of pragmatic inference: Leucippe 'subtly signalled (*huposēmainen*) that she was listening not without a certain pleasure'.[165] This is, indeed, an exercise in hyposemantics on both sides, in detecting the true purpose that underlies the apparent casualness of the conversation.

If this is a positive example of the relevance of digressions, however, counter-examples can also be found. Near the beginning of book 4 we encounter another case where the interpretation of digressive description is carefully described. The Egyptian general Charmides, we are told, has fallen for Leucippe, and takes advantage of a fortunate opportunity: 'his men happened (*etukhon*) to have caught a river beast, quite a spectacle'.[166] Like the fanning peacock, the hippo represents an unpredictable arrival from the natural world, which is then turned to the strategic advantage of a randy miscellanist. Again as with the peacock episode, the motivation for Charmides' description of the hippo is explicitly identified with a desire: 'wanting us to stay around for as long as possible, so that he could gratify his eyes, he sought to spin out his discourse (*periplokas... logōn*)'.[167] He describes the beast at length (4.3.2–5), and the techniques used to hunt it. After exhausting this topic, the prevaricant Charmides now turns (encouraged by Menelaus) to elephants, and thereupon to the mysterious qualities of their breath (4.4).[168] The connection between the two beasts is at best tangential.

For all the formal similarities, however, Charmides' attempt to use miscellaneous digression in the service of seduction contrasts unfavourably

[164] Anon. Seg. 62 = *RG* 1.436.12 = Dilts and Kennedy (1997) 20; Σ Dem. 22.124, 23.104; cf. Artem. *Oneir*. 4.22 for the phrase τῆς ὑποθέσεως ἀποπλανᾶσθαι.
[165] ὑπεσήμαινεν οὐκ ἀηδῶς ἀκούειν, 1.19.1.
[166] ἔτυχον ποτάμιον θηρίον ἄνδρες τεθηρακότες θέας ἄξιον, 4.2.1.
[167] βουλόμενος οὖν ἡμᾶς παραμένειν ἐπὶ πλεῖστον, ἵν' ἔχηι τοῖς ὀφθαλμοῖς αὐτοῦ χαρίζεσθαι, περιπλοκὰς ἐζήτει λόγων..., 4.3.2. Cf. the similar phrasing in the peacock scene: βουλόμενος οὖν..., 1.16.1 (n. 161 above).
[168] The sources for these descriptions are discussed at Rommel (1923) 77–80; Vilborg (1962) 80–3.

Limen

with Clitophon's. (It is, appropriately enough, Clitophon *qua* narrator who scoffs at Charmides' dilatory attempts to fill time with irrelevant discourse.)[169] Clitophon's lecture on randy flora and fauna links the eroticism of the natural world to that of the human, and so maintains an inferential link between digression and theme. Charmides', on the other hand, is irrelevant at the level of detail: its only purpose is to keep Leucippe in view for as long as possible. This excursus on pachyderm lore cannot be recouped straightforwardly as an oblique commentary upon the main plot. Even if erotic hints can be glimpsed in the account of the 'capture' of the hippo, it is not clear to whom they would refer;[170] and the elephant is (as Clitophon surmises) gloriously irrelevant. Now, we might in principle wish to distinguish between the motives imputed to Charmides (crude procrastination) and a subtler relevance intended by the author; but, as we have seen, the passage is presented as a lesson in the art of reading irrelevance, and should probably be taken as such.

The most extreme example of irrelevant digression in *Leucippe and Clitophon* is Chaerephon's account of aquatic phenomena (2.14.6–10). Chaerephon is another general (are the military particularly prone to prolixity?), the senior partner in Byzantium of Leucippe's father Sostratus. Sostratus has interpreted an oracle to mean that they should send a sacrifice to Heracles at Tyre. His interpretation is partly based upon a line in the oracle that reads 'where Hephaestus rejoices to have Athena', which he interprets as a reference to a precinct where fire shoots up around an olive tree. Chaerephon expresses his admiration for Sostratus, adding: 'Do not, however, marvel (*thaumaze*) at the nature of fire alone, but also at that of water.'[171] This leads him to describe a spring in Sicily where (apparently) fire can be seen under the water; a Spanish river that makes musical sounds in the breeze; and a lake in Libya where gold is fished out by maidens (2.14.6–10). His words are wholly irrelevant to the matter of the sacrifice, or indeed to anything in the main plot; the only point of contiguity with what has proceeded is the theme of elemental miracles (note *thaumaze*).

---

[169] Clitophon should not, strictly speaking, know this *qua* narrator much about Charmides' motivation, but Achilles does occasionally permit him to know more about his characters than he should. See Hägg (1971) 124–36, esp. 132; also Morgan (2004d) 497.

[170] Morales (2004) 198 argues for a 'paradigmatic relationship' between Leucippe and the hippo on the grounds that (i) the company is said to look at the hippo while Charmides looks at Leucippe (4.3.1); (ii) the hippo is a ἵππον... τοῦ Νείλου (4.2.1), etymologically linking to Leuc*ippe*. But the clumsy, appetitive, thick-skinned beast might be held to be an analogue for Charmides himself; the latter, indeed, is captured (ἑαλώκει, 4.3.1) by Leucippe, as the hippo is trapped.

[171] μὴ μέντοι θαύμαζε τὴν τοῦ πυρὸς μόνον, ἀλλὰ καὶ τὴν τοῦ ὕδατος φύσιν, 2.14.6.

Nor is there any consequence in the narrative: no one responds or reacts in any way. This digression is exquisitely, eruditely,[172] fulsomely, pointless.

Neither Bartsch nor Morales discusses this digression. It has no clear proleptic or metacommentary relationship to the main erotic plot. The point is not that there are absolutely no possible points of correspondence (fire imagery is connected to desire throughout *Leucipe and Clitophon*, music is linked to the stimulation of lust, and fishing with poles could be construed in sexual terms),[173] rather that the ratio of relevance to irrelevance is extremely unfavourable. But the issue is best phrased in terms not of intrinsic textual content but of reception. Digression challenges us to read integratively, 'hypothetically', to construe relevance to the main plot; and there it always contains both elements that are amenable to this process and elements that resist it. In other words, digression is the manifestation of liminality at the narrative–thematic level: to read for relevance is to seek the paradigmatic, totalising meaning that transcends syntagmatic plotting.

OUTRAGEOUS FORTUNE

Digresssion and episodicity are intimately related to Fortune, particularly in Chariton, Achilles and Heliodorus.[174] We have already seen that miscellanism is governed by *tukhē*. Achilles Tatius' zoological and botanological disquisitions in the garden are also occasioned by chance happenings (*etukhen... etukhe... tukhēi tini*, 1.16.1–2). *Tukhē* is the principle that allows for the unpredictability of events during the liminal period, but also threatens to dissolve the plot into a series of episodes with no causal connection. *Tukhē* is a key agent of liminality already in our earliest novel, *Callirhoe*;[175] it is she who is overruled by Aphrodite as we enter the closural phase (8.1.2). *Tukhē* is the narrative id, the force of anticlosural creativity,

---

[172] The final story is adapted from Hdt. 4.195, and contains an allusion to Ctes. *Ind.* 4 (Vilborg (1962) 52).
[173] For fire imagery in Achilles, see O'Sullivan (1978) 378 s.v. πῦρ 2(b). Clitophon is turned on by songs accompanied by the cithara (cf. τὸ ῥεῦμα... ὡς κιθάρα λαλεῖ, 2.14.8) at 1.5.4–7 and 2.1.
[174] Personified *Tukhē* only receives one inconsequential mention in Xenophon (1.16.3) and two in Longus: (3.34.1, 4.24.2). Cf. also *Ninus* A.III.12, 18, SW 33; and possibly Antonius Diogenes SW 150.4. Generally, on fortune in the novels, see Alperowitz (1992) 75–87; Robiano (1984) discusses Chariton and Heliodorus; Bargheer (1999) 148–51, with reservations. Though I emphasise Tukhē's dramatic heritage, Zimmermann (1961) 333–5 rightly insists on the historiographical associations too.
[175] Char. 1.10.2, 1.13.4, 1.14.7, 1.14.9, 2.8.3–6, 3.3.8, 3.8.1, 4.1.12, 4.4.2, 4.5.3, 4.7.3, 5.1.4, 5.5.2, 5.6.8, 6.8.1, 8.1.2, 8.3.5. As is noted by Robiano (1984) 543–4, Chariton also uses the word (as do the other novelists) in the different sense of *sort personel*.

the fiendish devisor of surprising new episodes. At one point in *Callirhoe*, it appears that a settlement may be on the horizon: the Great King of Persia has fallen for Callirhoe, and has the resources to coerce a marriage. *Tukhē*, however, intervenes to prevent the story from ending: she 'quickly transformed all thoughts and talk of *erōs*, by inventing a narrative of most novel (*kainoterōn*) events'.[176] This resourceful creativity is stressed elsewhere, where she is granted the epithet *philokainos*, 'keen on invention' (Char. 4.4.2; cf. 8.3.6).

Tukhē is, then, a figure for the constructive role of liminality: for authorial brinkmanship, narrative exuberance, the ability to generate surprise. But novelistic characters rarely perceive her in such a positive light; with the grimness of a tomb inscription,[177] they see her as aggressive, all-consuming and deathly. In Chariton, she is addressed as 'malign' (*baskanos*, 1.14.7, 4.1.12, 5.1.4). Among the many rhetorical invocations of her in Achilles Tatius, strikingly few are positive.[178] She is 'grudgeful' (*phthonera*) towards humans,[179] and distinctively fond of 'play' (*paizein*).[180] Her creative capacities are construed as aggressive: she 'composed a new (*kainon*) drama to my detriment';[181] and the claim at the start that she 'began the drama'[182] is hedged with ominously fatalistic markers. In Heliodorus too, almost all of the references to Tukhē come from characters who see her as unstable, unpredictable and malevolent.[183] Aside a very few marginal cases,[184] there

---

[176] πᾶσαν δὲ σκέψιν καὶ πᾶσαν ἐρωτικὴν ὁμιλίαν ταχέως μετέβαλεν ... καινοτέρων εὑροῦσα πραγμάτων ὑπόθεσιν, 6.8.1. *Tukhē* thus has an obvious metanarrative kinship with Eros, another lover of paradox (Char. 1.1.4) and novelty (4.7.6).

[177] See T. Morgan (2007) 304–5 on *tukhē* on epitaphs.

[178] 1.3.3, 1.12.5, 1.13.4, 1.13.6, 2.27.3, 3.22.3, 4.1.3, 4.9.5, 4.9.7, 4.15.5, 5.2.3, 5.7.9, 5.9.3, 5.10.4, 5.11.1, 5.11.2, 5.17.3, 6.3.1, 6.13.1, 7.2.1, 7.2.3, 7.3.7, 7.5.2. The following are neutral or positive: 1.9.2, 4.7.3, 5.16.5, 5.26.9, 6.3.6 (in a lying speech), 6.13.2 (in a flattering speech), 7.13.1, 8.7.1. Nakatani (2003) 63–6 notes a decrease in incidence of personified Tukhē (although identifications can be subjective: I include more than he does) towards the end, which he plausibly attributes to a lessening need for plot extension.

[179] 1.13.6, reading φθονερά with Vilborg and O'Sullivan (*contra* πονηρά, with Garnaud); *cf.* ἐφθόνησεν ἡ Τύχη, 5.7.9.

[180] παιζέτω πάλιν ἡ Τύχη, 4.9.7; τῆι τῆς Τύχης παιδιᾶι, 5.11.1; ἡ Τύχη ἔπαιξε κατ' ἐμοῦ ... τῆς Τύχης ... παιδιά, 7.5.2. On narrative and game-playing, see further above, pp. 208–9.

[181] συντίθεται κατ' ἐμοῦ δρᾶμα καινόν, 6.3.1.   [182] ἤρχετο τοῦ δράματος ἡ Τύχη, 1.3.3.

[183] 1.13.2, 1.15.2, 1.19.5, 1.20.1, 1.22.4, 2.21.4, 4.18.2, 5.2.9, 5.4.7, 5.6.1, 5.6.2, 5.7.1, 5.27.1, 6.7.3, 6.8.5, 7.21.5, 7.26.2, 7.26.10, 7.27.2, 8.3.7, 8.6.4 (not spoken by Theagenes, but focalised by him), 8.9.12, 8.16.7, 8.17.3, 9.2.1, 9.6.3, 10.2.1, 10.13.5, 10.16.6, 10.34.6. The following cases are neutral: 2.23.2, 2.31.1, 4.8.6, 4.8.8, 5.8.5, 5.18.9, 5.29.2.

[184] I.e. (i) a reference to personal fate (cf. n. 175 on *sort personel*): 'the Tukhē that marshalled their story ... ' (ἡ κατ' αὐτοὺς ἀθλοθετοῦσα τύχη, 7.12.2; for the athletic metaphor cf. Ach. Tat. 5.2.3, τῆς Τύχης γυμνάσιον); cf. 8.17.5, 9.26.1. (ii) a simile: 'as though Tukhē were improvising the supplication scene ... ' (καθάπερ σχεδιαζούσης ἐν αὐτοῖς τὴν ἱκεσίαν τῆς τύχης, 9.11.6, of the Syenians attempting to elicit Hydaspes' pity).

is only one instance where the primary narrator refers to the goddess's interventions:

> then some figure, whether, I suppose, it was a deity or a Tukhē who adjudicates human affairs, added a new tragic episode (*epeisodion*) to the plot, as if competing with the drama by beginning a new one[185]

In line with the general Heliodorean principle that only characters make strong claims about Tukhē, this passage is carefully circumscribed with markers of non-committal distance ('*some* figure, *whether*, *I suppose*', it was a deity or a Tukhē') and figuration ('*as if* competing'). These markers supply the implicit ironical framing that always accompanies novelistic references to fortune. But the passage is also interesting for its strategic use of the characteristically liminal language of improvisation, creative rivalry and, especially, tragic episodicity.

Let us pause to consider the novelistic association of liminal fortune with tragedy. We have seen throughout this chapter that liminality is associated with feelings of helplessness in the face of the unpredictable caprices of anonymous deities, which are ascribed to tragedy. We have also seen, however, that this perception is always ironically counterbalanced by a suggestion, whether or not it is explicitly articulated by a character, that a happy ending is the likely outcome. The crucial point is that the association of tragic uncertainty with the goddess Tukhē is, predominantly, *not a tragic but a comic motif*.[186] This, indeed, is how the novelists seem to understand Tukhē. For example, the Heliodorean passage that we have just discussed refers to Fortune 'adjudicating' (*brabeuousa*) human affairs, a direct allusion to the goddess's claim in the delayed prologue of Menander's *Shield* ('empowered over all of these matters, to adjudicate (*brabeusai*) and

---

[185] τότε δή πως εἴτε τι δαιμόνιον εἴτε τύχη τις τὰ ἀνθρώπεια βραβεύουσα καινὸν ἐπεισόδιον ἐπετραγώιδει τοῖς δρωμένοις, ὥσπερ εἰς ἀνταγώνισμα δράματος ἀρχὴν ἄλλου παρεισφέρουσα, 7.6.4. The spectacular ecphrastic effects of this passage are discussed by Montes Cala (1992).

[186] The personified Tukhē does not appear in literature before Menander (and indeed her cult is not attested before the fourth century: *IG* II² 333c, with Tracy (1994) 242–3 on the date). On the statuary, see Peine (1998). The cult is invoked repeatedly in Menander: *Asp.* 381, *Dys.* 422, 816, *Epitr.* 223, *Cith.* 40, *Sam.* 116, 297, 445. On fortune in Menander, see generally Vogt-Spira (1992), who links it to developments in the philosophy of cause. The agency of (non-personified) fortune is, for sure, prefigured in tragedy, but tellingly appears there primarily in the late Euripidean 'escape tragedies', which were so influential on Menander and the new comic poets: see the important discussion of Wright (2005) 372–80, with 373–4 on the heavy statistical weighting of *tukhē* words in the escape tragedies. His conclusion that Euripidean *tukhē* is not 'a force at work in the universe but ... a strategy of interpretation which arises out of extreme uncertainty or perplexity' (379) is surely right, and applies equally well to Menander and the romances. Pre-Menandrian philosophers also discuss *tukhē* as a principle of unpredictability: Democritus frr. 68–9 DK, Demetrius of Phalerum frr. 79, 81 Wehrli = 82A–B, 83 in Fortenbaugh and Schütrumpf (2000).

manage them').[187] This allusion further undermines the already ironised suggestion that a tragic episode will be added, by reminding us of the Menandrian context: Fortune has claimed precisely that the apparently gloomy situation is an illusion, and all will turn out well.

Let us remind ourselves briefly of the new-comic background. As in the novels, Tukhē's effects in Menander are often received as hostile[188] and purely aleatory.[189] 'What a variable and wandering (*planon*) thing is Fortune', comments a character in the *Lyre-player*.[190] Elsewhere, she is associated apophthegmatically with unpredictable 'changes' (*metabolai*) in circumstances: again, as in the novel, she represents the power of narrative to redirect itself.[191] Her associations with blindness,[192] opacity,[193] unpredictability,[194] senselessness[195] and ignorance[196] figure both the characters' experience of plot as indeterminate and the ironisation of that experience for the audience who have a generically attuned sense of how that plot will unfurl. In the *Women dosed with hemlock*, a character comments (if the restoration is correct) that 'it would not be right for me to chastise Fortune: for though I have, I admit, called her "blind" in the past, it seems that now she has used her eyes and saved me'.[197] Here a retrospective reading of plot, apparently (the context is uncertain) from the vantage of the *telos*, allows a speaker to code Fortune as a paradigmatic rather than a syntagmatic plotter. These are precisely the techniques developed by the novelists. The last passage, indeed, is echoed by Apuleius, whose narrator Lucius is told during his conversion that he has escaped 'Fortune's blindness' (*Fortunae caecitas*) and is now under the protection of 'Fortune who can see' (*Fortunae... videntis*, i.e. Isis: *Met.* 11.15).[198] The temporal dimension is decisive. Like oracles, Fortune can be seen as opaque when one is embroiled in its effects, and lucid in retrospect. This is why *tukhē* is such an attractive metanarrative figure: it captures both the indeterminacy

---

[187] πάντων κυρία / τούτων βραβεῦσαι καὶ διοικῆσαι, 147–8, also alluded to at Char. 4.5.3. On the prologue of the *Shield*, see p. 193 above.
[188] Bad fortune is lamented alongside personal suffering: *Mis.* 246–8; *Pk.* 810; *Sam.* 398;
[189] And hence closely related to 'randomness' (τὸ αὐτόματον): *Dys.* 545, *Epitr.* 1108, *Mis.* 449, *Pk.* 151, *Sam.* 55, 163 etc. Cf. Philemon fr. 125 KA: οὐκ ἔστιν ἡμῖν οὐδεμία τύχη θεός, / οὐκ ἔστιν, ἀλλὰ ταὐτόματον, ὃ γίνεται / ὡς ἔτυχ' ἑκάστωι, προσαγορεύεται τύχη. See also fr. 178.11–12 KA.
[190] ὡς ποικίλον πρᾶγμ' ἐστὶ καὶ πλάνον τύχη, fr. 8 Sandbach; cf. *Asp.* 18, *Pk.* 802, and frr. 261, 681, 683, 686–7, 860 KA.
[191] Frr. 311, 853 KA. [192] Frr. 682, 711 KA; cf. *Con.* frr. 13–15, quoted below.
[193] *Asp.* 248. [194] Men. fr. 372 KA. [195] Frr. 711, 855 KA.
[196] *Agnoia* delivers the prologue of the *Girl being shorn*.
[197] λελοιδόρημ' ἄρ' οὐ δικαίως τῆι Τύχηι· / ὡς γὰρ τυφλὴν αὐτὴν κακῶς εἴρηκά που, / νῦν δ' ἐξέσωσέ μ' ὡς ἔοιχ' ὁρῶσά τι, lines 13–15 Sandbach.
[198] On the equation of Isis and Tukhē, see Griffiths (1975) 241–4.

and the teleology of plot. This duality is inescapable. Fortune always seems to be duplicitous, an inevitable consequence of Greek views of the human condition and temporality: knowledge, for mortals, always comes too late.

In the Hellenistic and (particularly) Roman periods, Tukhē seems to be haunted by doubleness. A hymn from the Roman period, exploiting the hymnic 'how shall I name you?' motif, encapsulates the problem:

> Multi-coloured, shape-shifting, wing-footed goddess,
> You who share mortals' hearths, all-powerful Tukhē,
> How should we reveal your power and your nature?
> . . .
> Should we call you black Clotho,
> Or Necessity, bearer of swift destiny,
> Or Iris, the swift messenger of the immortals?[199]

The influence of philosophical debates over determinism[200] is evident: the choice is between, on the one side, preordained destiny (symbolised by Clotho, one of the fates, and Necessity), and randomness on the other (Iris, goddess of the rainbow, proverbially associated with inconsistency and change). What is particularly striking is the initial description of the goddess as 'multi-coloured, shape-shifting, wing-footed'. In terms of the sentence, these epithets serve primarily to foreground the difficulty of naming the goddess. But this very elusiveness also points to the inescapably indeterminate nature of the goddess, even in a poem that advances the possibility that we might associate her with a rigidly deterministic view of fate.

Philosophical debates, as we have said, offer one context for explaining this focus on the duality of fortune. A subtler but perhaps more pervasive influence (in that it is plausibly the force that itself shaped the philosophical debates) is the rise of imperialism and theorising about empire. The earliest known treatise on *tukhē*, by the fourth-century Demetrius of Phalerum, seems (to judge from the meagre fragments) to have taken as its theme the rise and fall of great dominions: the unpredicted defeat of Persia, Demetrius tells us, anticipates the future demise of Macedon.[201] History warns us not to expect *imperium sine fine*. The Herodotean theme of the historical mutability of imperial fortunes is here decisively linked to the philosophy of fortune. So it would remain in the Hellenistic and imperial periods. As

---

[199] πολύχροε ποικιλόμορφε πτανόπους θεά / θνατοῖς συνομέστιε, παγκρατὲς Τύχα, / πῶς χρὴ τεὰν ἰσχύν τε δεῖξαι καὶ φύσιν; / . . . πότερόν σε κλῄζωμεν Κλωθὼ κελαινάν, / ἢ τὰν ταχύποτμον Ἀνάγχαν, / ἢ τὰν ταχὺν ἄγγελον Ἶριν ἀθανάτων; *CA* Lyr. adesp. 34.1–3, 8–10.
[200] Above, p. 197.   [201] 81 Wehrli = 82A–B in Fortenbaugh and Schütrumpf (2000).

we discussed at the very beginning of this book, Greek historians repeatedly engage with the question of whether Rome's dominance was due to Tukhē, and if so in what sense. As we saw there, the extant historians all reject the hypothesis that Rome benefited from lucky breaks, and argue instead for Tukhē in the sense of divine favour. What we can see now is that the excluded hypothesis is not simply a viewpoint adopted by real individuals (although it may have been that too), but also the shadow that inevitably follows providentialist accounts of fortune. Any determinist narrative – this is how it is because it had to be thus – is inevitably haunted by the unknowable future, about which the only safe prediction is that it will make a mockery of the claims you press upon eternity. Cnuts who imperially proclaim the end of history invite only posterity's mockery.

What does this imperial context tell us about identity? These theories of empire are, at one level, extrapolations to the political level of an understanding of individual fortune, which goes back to Herodotus and the tragedians: human happiness is subject to flux, happiness should not be announced before the *telos* of life is reached. (For ancient political theory, the health of the empire is closely bound up with the life of the ruler.) Romance offers a more optimistic assessment: stable happiness *can* be achieved through patriarchal marriage, in stable communities (for the first-century novelists, specifically Greek ones). Personal happiness is underwritten by a civilised sociality, and a pantheon that reveals itself, finally, to be provident. This sociality is seen as broadly compatible with hegemony and mastery. Chariton's Persians end up rather benign; Longus' urban landowners turn out to be on the lovers' side. *Charicleia and Theagenes*, indeed, culminates in an imperialist utopia, with the Ethiopian Hydaspes aping the language of idealised Roman rule.[202] The good empire of Meroe is offset against the wicked empire of the Persians. Returning romance represents the re-establishment of the accepted ideological order, the social superego, not just the *nom du père* but also the names of the *patria* (fatherland), the patriarchy, and the *pater patriae* (the emperor in his paternalist guise).

---

[202] Cf. 9.6.2: Hydaspes 'knows how to expugnate his enemies, but naturally pities his suppliants' (πολεμίους τε ἐκπορθεῖν οἶδε καὶ ἱκέτας οἰκτείρειν πέφυκε), which recalls the cliché of Roman imperialism (beat down the foes and spare the defeated: Cic. *De off.* 1.35; Liv. 30.42.17, 37.45.8; Hor. *Carm. Saec.* 49–52; Verg. *Aen.* 6.851–3; Aug. *RG* 26.2). Other signs of benevolent imperialism: 'he does not play the tyrant in victory' (οὐ... τυραννεῖ τὴν νίκην, 9.6.3); 'I do not extend my empire unlimitedly' (οὐδὲ εἰς ἄπειρον ἐκτείνω τὴν ἀρχήν, 9.26.2). Ethiopian kingship is contrasted with Persian hierarchy, which demands prostration (7.19.1–3), and divinises royalty (5.9.2) – whereas Hydaspes refuses the title 'saviour and god' (σωτῆρα... καὶ θεόν, 9.22.7–23.1).

This ideological norming of the romance is not just its *telos*, but also what the characters yearn for. Liminality makes them feel despondent and tragic; it cedes space to threateningly non-urban environments, agency to subelite men and sublunary divinities. It offers opportunities for all kinds of deviance: not just unwarranted deviations from the homeward path, but also counter-ideological modes of desire. Liminal plotting, moreover, makes for bad narrative: it is associated with tragedy, with unaristotelian episodicity, with irrelevancy and digressive extrusions. Like all forms of transition, it exists primarily to define the space between starting-point and destination; it signifies only as interruption, delay, detour. This misery of this liminality creates a *need* for guidance, direction, even governance.

That, at least, is how to read romance paradigmatically. But let us try re-turning it, emphasising the twists and turns, the tropes, the figurality. Liminality is where the genre's exuberance is generated, where it is licensed to confabulate, to redistribute identities, to create anew. We have seen throughout this chapter and the previous one that syntagmatic plotting is associated with gaming, with competition, with theatricality. In short, it can be seen as a variety of *play*, in Huizinga's sense of an activity that initially seems to be a mere interlude or interruption to 'ordinary life', but through habituation ends up constituting the very vitality of existence.[203] Certainly, it is not voluntarily entered into by the protagonists (except in Achilles) – voluntarism is a key definition of Huizinga's idea of play – but (as we saw in Chapter 4) numerous characters with lesser scruples do indulge their own will here. As I see it, these desires generate their own energy, which may (ultimately) not succeed, but are none the less urgent for that. It is for this reason that I have elected to borrow from psychoanalysis to describe the narrative dynamics of the novel. Romance describes different, conflicting kinds of desire. To understand the whole, the romantic psyche (as it were), we need to account for not just the dominant desires but also their structural relationship to the contrary desires that the narrative finally represses.

[203] Huizinga (1949), esp. 27.

Conclusion

> Thereafter introduce the point that marriage is essential for us, humans as we are: for it is the salvation of the family; everything that is good springs from marriage. Then proceed to describe the facial appearance of those who are coming together in marriage. In this part, you will speak of their family and upbringing, their physical beauty and their youth; what fortune has supplied them with, and what their own efforts have. Mention that they themselves were enthusiastic to unite in marriage, and also what their relatives think of the marriage, as well as people outside the marriage, and even the entire citizen body. Say that the marriage is captivating everyone, and that the marriage seems like a holiday, a new moon party, or a public festival for the city.[1]

This passage, which comes from an anonymous *Art of rhetoric* from the imperial period, formulates advice for the student who wishes to give an *epithalamium*, a speech celebrating a marriage that has taken place. It is striking how much it also resembles a recipe for the romance. Marriage is to be presented as indispensable (*anagkaios*) to human life, the foundation of familial and social existence. The egregious beauty of the couple should be stressed, as well as their ancestry and their virtue. Most strikingly of all, it should be claimed that the couple's desire for marriage is matched by that of 'the entire citizen body' (*polis autē dēmosiai*). This collective zeal for a wedding is matched in Xenophon and Chariton ('What a marriage it would be between Habrocomes and Anthia!' Xenophon's Ephesians shout;[2] in Chariton, 'the Syracusans celebrated [the day of the wedding] with more

---

[1] εἶτα ἐπὶ τούτοις ἐπάγειν, ὅτι ἀναγκαῖος ὁ γάμος ἀνθρώποις γε οὖσι· σωτηρία γὰρ τοῦ γένους· καὶ ὅσα ἀγαθὰ ἐκ τοῦ γάμου. εἶτα μεταβήσηι ἐπὶ τὰ πρόσωπα τῶν συνιόντων εἰς τὸν γάμον, ὁποῖοί τινες οὗτοι· ἐν ὧι περὶ γένους ἐρεῖς αὐτῶν καὶ τροφῆς, καὶ περὶ κάλλους σωμάτων καὶ ἡλικίας· ὅσα ἐκ τύχης αὐτοῖς πρόσεστι, καὶ περὶ ἐπιτηδευμάτων· ὅτι σπουδὴν ἔσχον περὶ τὸν γάμον καὶ τὴν σύζευξιν αὐτοί· ὅπως διάκεινται ἐπὶ τῶι γάμωι οἱ οἰκεῖοι, οἱ ἀλλότριοι, ἡ πόλις αὐτὴ δημοσίαι· ὅτι πᾶσι διὰ σπουδῆς ὁ γάμος ἐστίν, καὶ ὁ γάμος ἔοικεν πανηγύρει τινὶ καὶ νεομηνίαι καὶ δημοτελεῖ ἑορτῆι τῆς πόλεως, [Dion. Hal.] *Ars rhet.* 4.2 U-R.
[2] οἷος ἂν γάμος γένοιτο Ἁβροκόμου καὶ Ἀνθίας, 1.2.9.

joy than the day of their victory over the Athenians').[3] Finally, the reference to a 'public festival' (*dēmotelei heortēi*), even if it is only here a comparison, recalls the events at which the lovers meet in Xenophon and Chariton (where exactly the same phrase is used).[4]

Like epithalamia, romances present marriage as the *telos* of civilised living and the hope for the renewal of the community. The collective enthusiasm that they dramatise encourages the readership's complicity. We are to imagine ourselves there cheering Chaereas and Callirhoe or Anthia and Habrocomes when their ship pulls into the harbour, or Charicleia and Theagenes when they head off to their wedding; or, again, singing the epithalamium itself for Daphnis and Chloe. Only the relentlessly non-civic Achilles Tatius avoids such a collectivist celebration of marriage or its re-establishment, no doubt because his relationship to the romance tradition is so oblique. Elsewhere, romance, like the epithalamium, constructs marriage and civic life in the traditional *polis* as the optimal form of existence. Mobilising the paradigm of the return, culturally and psychologically one of the deepest-rooted narratives, the Greek romancers promote a myth of renewal, at multiple levels: the organic (through legitimate sexual reproduction), the civic (through the dynastic renewal of the city), and the narrative (through the circular movement of the story). Romance promotes the compatibility of personal happiness, civic life and cosmic order.

This book has sought to show, however, how that characterisation is only one aspect. What prevents romance from folding into rhetorical epithalamium, and thence into mere normativity, is – precisely – the narrative form in which these tales are embedded. Narrative raises the question of difference, in terms of both spatiality (travel is a metaphor for estrangement) and temporality (how does time transform us?). Narrativity – the condition of narrative possibility – demands detour, deviation, difference; it puts a serious kink in the model of linear transgenerational continuity. Romance, as a form, accommodates *both* the identity-as-sameness that the teleological return implies *and* the transformation necessitated by the polytropic, re-turning narrative of the liminal phase. This ambiguity impacts partly upon the *reception* of the romances: it explains why different critics can read the same texts as conservative or experimental. Romance is an elastic form, accommodating different perspectives, which different readers will emphasise. But it also creates space *within* the romance form for readjustment. Heliodorus is, on any count, a much more 'transformational'

---

[3] ἥδιον ταύτην τὴν ἡμέραν ἤγαγον οἱ Συρακόσιοι τῆς τῶν ἐπινικίων, 1.1.13. See also above, p. 33.
[4] Char. 1.1.4; cf. Xen. Eph. 1.2.2 (ἐπιχώριος ἑορτή).

author than Xenophon. The later texts accentuate the possibilities, already latent in Chariton and Xenophon, for allegorising romance as a narrative of identity metamorphoses: by shifting the marriage to the end, by ramping up the imagery of mystery-cult initiation, by using analogies with pilgrimage; and, most notably of all, by emphasising the artefactual, constructed nature of all story-telling. By the second century CE, romance has lost any pretence of being naive and pellucid (even, or rather especially, in *Daphnis and Chloe*, the most *faux* of all of Greek antiquity's *faux-naif* texts).

I have emphasised (particularly in Part 1) the capacity of romance to respond to historical circumstances. Let me emphasise that the narrative I have told does not correspond to a linear narrative of Greek socio-cultural history in the Roman imperial era. It would be an eccentric and highly limited reading of Greek culture between the first and fourth centuries CE that described a progressive shift from a relatively Hellenocentric outlook towards a centrifugal one. This is the course that the romance took, and the romance forms part of Greek socio-cultural history – but only one part. If we were taking rhetoric, epigraphy, statuary or epigram as our point of departure, we would see very different pictures. As we saw in the introduction, the idea that literary forms are epiphenomena of straightforward paradigm shifts is deeply unhelpful. The crucial point is that cultural forms like literature do not straightforwardly reflect a pre-existing reality (although of course they may contain specific features that do, such as linguistic morphology). Rather, they offer a framework for perceiving it. Indeed the romance, I have argued, supplies more than just a framework; it presents a range of ways of seeing complex questions of culture, ethics and identity, accommodated within a flexible matrix.

I have emphasised that romance explores profound questions about the nature of identity. To what extent does experience change the individual? How do individual events relate to the larger pattern of life experiences? These questions can properly be called philosophical: we could compare discussions like those of Alasdair Macintyre and Charles Taylor (as well as their critics), around the issues of the coherence of life narratives.[5] When we survey the broad range of the Greek romances, two other features worth highlighting emerge. The first is the profound significance not just of narrative but also of *narration*. Telling stories about identity emerges not just as a descriptive but also as a performative act: this is how romance characters express themselves to others and to themselves. This book opened with an example drawn from Xenophon of Ephesus of how one figure

---

[5] Macintyre (1984); Taylor (1989).

tells his story. This is already a complex case, at the thematic level at any rate, but more challenging still are the examples of Chaereas' speech to the assembly at the end of *Callirhoe* and Clitophon's at the end of *Leucippe and Clitophon*.[6] Here, the act of narration of identity is marked as a social act (young men reach rapprochements with their fathers-in-law, and in Chariton's case the entire community too). Telling one's story becomes the vehicle for social reintegration: it offers a version of events that all parties can agree to accept. The process of narration has a therapeutic component: it allows one to transcend the disabling shame (*aidōs*) that afflicts the self-conscious youth, and speak like a man. Yet in both cases (more explicitly in Clitophon's) such retooling of life-stories is overshadowed by deliberate manipulations, deceptions even. Transformations occur not just within narrative but also through narration.

This self-awareness about the creative, fictive power of identity narration in one sense goes back to Homer's *Odyssey*,[7] but finds a new centrality in the romance, particularly from the second century onwards. The doubly embedded homodiegetic narrative of *Leucippe and Clitophon*, the ecphrastic exegesis of *Daphnis and Chloe*, the lengthy narrative of Calasiris and the emphasis on allegoresis in *Charicleia and Theagenes*, all underline the fundamentally mediated nature of romance narration. The effects of this are profound. On the one hand, a relativisation of perspectives. The later romances challenge the casual Hellenocentrism that underlies Chariton and Xenophon (albeit not entirely uncontested), forcing readers to confront their own interestedness in the narrative in question. No reader of *Daphnis and Chloe* can avoid positioning him- or herself between town and country. The same goes for cultural identity in Achilles' and Heliodorus' great romances. This, in turn, provokes a greater sensitivity to the constructedness of identity. The themes of disguise that lurk in the wings of Chariton and Xenophon of Ephesus (for example, in the story of Aegialeus' and Thelxinoe's escape) become central in *Leucippe and Clitophon* and *Charicleia and Theagenes*. It is also in these latter texts, and in *Daphnis and Chloe* too, that the discourse of art and allusion clusters around the principal characters. When Chariton describes Callirhoe as 'the cult-statue (*agalma*) of all Sicily', the metaphor indicates in the first instance supernatural beauty and universal adoration.[8] By contrast, when Heliodorus' Calasiris describes Charicleia and Theagenes in the Delphic

---

[6] Above, pp. 63–6, 91–3. [7] See esp. Goldhill (1991) 36–56.
[8] ἄγαλμα τῆς ὅλης Σικελίας, 1.1.1. This interpretation of the metaphor is encouraged by the subsequent claim that her beauty was divine (τὸ κάλλος οὐκ ἀνθρώπινον ἀλλὰ θεῖον, 1.1.2). On Callirhoe's quasi-divinity, see Hägg (2002) and Schmeling (2005).

parade, together with the illusionistic brooch and cloak that they wear, this contributes to a larger nexus of themes and images connecting narration with deception and desire.[9]

The second point is that romance models different ways of relating self to community. This is crucial. It is emerging with increasing clarity just how small a blip in the history of human thought is the ideal of the self as autonomous, self-sufficient agent. Ancient thought, as Christopher Gill in particular has emphasised, has little sense of such 'subjective-individualist' concepts.[10] Some influential modern philosophers too are revisiting pre-Cartesian views of the self as integrally related to a wider social nexus.[11] What we have seen throughout this book is that romance repeatedly emplots the individual's relationship to a social framework. The precise form of this framework changes. In Chariton and Xenophon it is the *polis* and (as a constitutive part of it) the family. The later romances reconfigure this relationship. In Achilles we find a patriarchal family romance, in which the psychology of obligation and prohibition is explored. In Longus, the dynamic is between the consumer city and the countryside that supplies it. In Heliodorus' more cosmic vision, Ethiopia signifies both as a realisable utopia in this world and as an allegorical figure for philosophical perfection. In each of these cases, romance provides a means of defining individuals, with their doubts, fears, tough decisions and traumas, in relation to a society imagined as stable and eternal, together with the apparatus (familial and theological) that surrounds it. Romance is not the expression of a post-civic individualism;[12] rather, it creates space for individual reflexivity within malleable structures of sociality.

I have placed much weight on the conflicts at the heart of romance models of identity. This conflictedness springs partly from the narrative form itself, which presents the problem of closure in its most extreme form: the returning romance is magnetically drawn towards the inevitable home-coming, but at the same time must strive all it can to postpone that home-coming. Eventually, like a fish swimming against the current of a whirlpool, it submits, exhausted. I have given different names to these counterdirectional forces throughout this book (centripetal and centrifugal, teleological and errant, paradigmatic and syntagmatic); but let us return here to the Freudian metaphors of Part II, of the superego and the id. It is important to re-emphasise that this is an analogy not a claim to the universal value of these categories. But like all productive analogies, it facilitates new ways of seeing phenomena. The Freudian model was

[9] Whitmarsh (2002b). [10] Gill (1996). [11] E.g. Taylor (1989). [12] Introduction, n. 21.

revolutionary because it allowed us to theorise the self in conflict with itself in a non-normative way. Ancient philosophers too imagined bipartite or tripartite models of the soul, but always with an implicit hierarchy: reason (*logismos*) 'should' govern the appetites and the passions, otherwise Plato's chariot will be upturned by its unruly horse. Romance retains this strong sense of the normative, for sure. As we have said throughout, part of the reason for the persistence of the form lies in its moral simplicity: the (almost) unwavering desire expressed by the protagonists for a return to traditional communities and traditional values cues the reader to share that sense of what should and must be done. But as we have also said, romance is sustained by the pleasure of the pause and the detour, which are associated with illicit desires. These desires too form part of the romantic conception of the self. In moral terms, they are stigmatised, and repressed in closure, perhaps even dissipated (although here we must recall the uneasy settlement at the end of *Callirhoe*, and Achilles' apparent subversion in *Leucippe and Clitophon*). But they also embody the principle of transformation and creativity upon which the whole plot rests, and in that sense are presented as integral. The romance model of identity, that is to say, encompasses not only the express desires of the protagonists, but also the contrary wishes of their antagonists, and of the romance itself.

Critics of classical and archaic Greek culture, particularly in the aftermath of structuralism, are attuned to thinking of identity as defined through polarity: Greeks are not-barbarians, men are not-women, the free are not-slaves, and so forth.[13] It is easy to spot such value-laden polarities in the romances, whose narrators and characters alike are as fond as their predecessors of denigrating others,[14] and the generically embedded homing instinct encourages this allocation of identities into self and other. But it would be misleading to think in terms of continuity alone. The romance was born into a world of infinitely greater socio-cultural mobility. In the Roman empire, fortunes could be made; honours could be won; ladders could be climbed; citizenships could be acquired; education opened doors; cults encouraged conversion; sophists could become philosophers. This mobility was, for sure, difficult in practice: it was restricted to a demographically small group, and there were always conservative forces

---

[13] For discussion and bibliography, see Cartledge (1993).
[14] Brief survey of the Greek–barbarian antithesis in the romances at Kuch (2003) 216–18; representations of class are discussed by Kuch (2003) and Whitmarsh (2008).

to belittle a Trimalchio or a Lucian. But it was there. Romance was the medium that best expressed this sense of a Greek culture that was at once deeply rooted and revolutionised by the opportunities provided by a stable world-empire.

One final aspect of what is new about the romance's literary narrative of personal and social identity: we should remind ourselves forcibly that romance is narrative as *text*. One aspect of the romance's continuity with classical culture lies in the frequent recurrence to festival imagery. All of the extant romances bar one (the ever-exceptional *Leucippe and Clitophon*) end with pan-civic parties, celebrating the restoration of the community. It is a crucial image: Xenophon of Ephesus, lest it is too subtly expressed, tells us emphatically that his lovers treated the rest of their lives happily ever after, 'having a festival' (*heortēn agontes*, 5.15.3; cf. 1.10.3). Like so many Aristophanic comedies, the romances conclude with fun and laughter. The difference, however, is that in Aristophanes the festive ritual represented *within* the text is mirrored by that of the Great Dionysia, the institutional framework for the dramatic performance: in the course of a play such as the *Thesmophoriazusae*, 'the space of the ritual performance of the Thesmophoria is transformed into the theater of Demeter'.[15] In the romance, by contrast (whatever Merkelbach may want to claim), festivity is entirely represented; the ritual community is entirely imagined. Readers of these texts, whether we model them as isolated perusers or as members of a mediaeval-style 'reading community',[16] were necessarily removed from the *hic et nunc* of the fictive festival, primarily by the irreducible materiality of the written book (but also by time and space: almost all readers of almost all romances would have felt the difference of the described world). Romance is the product of a world that still construes identity using the festal language of the face-to-face civic community, but in the context of an intercontinental Greek-speaking expanse, impossible to conceptualise in its totality. A similar effect is achieved when Aelius Aristides compares the Roman empire favourably to a chorus, with the emperor as its instructor: the image of the ritual dance, expressing the visibility of the local community to itself, is stretched into an impossible analogy, now covering a body of people that could never literally dance together.[17]

Romance is thus old and new, Greek and Roman, local and global, ritual and textual. It is not determined by history, a mere epiphenomenon of social

---

[15] Tzanetou (2002) 353.   [16] E.g. Manguel (1997) 109–23.
[17] Ael. Ar. 26.29 (cf. 32) Keil; see Bowie (2006) 73–4.

processes; rather, we should think of this literature, much of it gorgeously intricate, in terms of a series of creative and idiosyncratic responses to social processes. But it is very much *of* its time. A complex, supple, sophisticated blend of continuity and innovation, it brilliantly articulates the values of a multicultural Greek community, highly educated and conscious of its past, living in an era of rapid social, political and religious change.

APPENDIX

The extant romances and the larger fragments

This appendix[1] offers a brief guide to the surviving and fragmentary Greek romances (and related texts), together with the main editions used and the date ranges that I have assumed in this book. In every case, dating is uncertain, in some radically so; my assumptions follow current orthodoxy.[2] I have given the titles for the romances proper in the form 'girl's name (+ boy's name)', which I have elsewhere argued to be the norm.[3] Biographical testimony on the individual authors is largely unreliable. For critical discussions of these issues see especially the various essays on individual works in Schmeling ed. (2003). I list here only the editions primarily followed in this book.

Achilles Tatius, *Leucippe and Clitophon*. Probably mid-second century CE, on the assumption that the papyri of the late second century may have been written soon after its composition.[4] The *Suda* (entry under 'Achilles Statius' (*sic*)) records that the author also composed an astronomical work, which is probably the work that survives today among the commentaries on Aratus.[5] The *Suda* also claims that Achilles became a Christian bishop in later life, testimony that is widely (although not universally) suspected. More credence has been given to the *Suda*'s claim (corroborated by the manuscript traditions) that Achilles was Alexandrian, partly on the grounds of his seemingly accurate description of Egyptian fauna; but it is possible that this assumption is merely extrapolated from

---

[1] Which is modelled on and revised from Whitmarsh ed. (2008) 378–84.
[2] The fullest discussion of dates for the earliest romances is Bowie (2002); Tilg (2010) also offers an excellent, detailed account (not limited to Chariton), albeit one angled towards his argument that Chariton is the earliest.
[3] Whitmarsh (2005b), arguing for τὰ περί / κατά + girl's name or girl's name + boy's name.
[4] *Pap. Mil. Vogl.* 124, *P. Oxy.* 3836.
[5] Scholia on Aratus: Maass (1958). All biographical testimonia (in Greek) at Vilborg (1962) 163–8.

the encomiastic description of the city at the beginning of book 5. TEXT: Garnaud (1991)

Antonius Diogenes, *Wonders beyond Thule*, preserved in summary form at Phot. *Bibl.* codex 166. The dating is uncertain, although the author's Roman *nomen* suggests an imperial date (and the combination of names may suggest an Aphrodisian origin).[6] The latest possible date for the work is the middle of the third century CE, when the philosopher Porphyry cites it; it may have been written as early as the late first century.[7] TEXT: SW 101–72, *P.Oxy.* 4760–2.

Chariton, *Callirhoe*. Widely assumed to be the earliest of the extant Greek novels, primarily on the grounds that it largely avoids the Attic dialect (current from the second century CE); current orthodoxy puts it in the mid-first century CE.[8] A reference in the *Satires* of the Neronian poet Persius to a literary work called *Calliroe* (1.134) is widely assumed to refer to our text, but discussion remains open (I myself am unconvinced).[9] Four papyri dated to the end of the second century CE give a *terminus ante quem*.[10] TEXT: Reardon (2004)

Heliodorus, *Charicleia and Theagenes*, more fully *The Ethiopian affairs concerning Charicleia and Theagenes*. Usually dated to the fourth century CE on the basis of perceived borrowings from the emperor Julian; but sometimes put in the third century, and occasionally even the second.[11] According to certain ancient sources,[12] Heliodorus became a Christian bishop, but (as with Achilles Tatius) this is widely doubted. TEXT: Rattenbury and Lumb (1960)

Iamblichus, *Babylonian affairs*. Survives only in fragments and the summary in Phot. *Bibl.* codex 94. Photius implies that the complete work had sixteen books, the *Suda* (entry under the first 'Iamblichus') less plausibly that it had 39. According to Photius, the author claimed involvement in the wars between Lucius Verus and the Parthian Vologaeses III, which occurred between 164 and 166 CE; if not fictional framing, this locates the

---

[6] Bowersock (1994) 38, and now Tilg (2010) 126–7. [7] Bowie (2007) 127–8.
[8] Full discussion and further references at Tilg (2010) 36–79, who tentatively favours the mid-first century CE.
[9] Whitmarsh (2005b) 590 n. 14. [10] *P.Fay.* 1, *P.Oxy.* 1019, *P.Michael.* 1, *P.Oxy.* 2948.
[11] Fourth century: Morgan (2003) 417–21, with further references. Earlier: e.g. Swain (1996) 423–4.
[12] Testimonia I, III in Colonna (1938).

Babylonian affairs in the second half of the second century. Photius tells us that he was a Babylonian, perhaps wrongly: an ancient marginal note[13] (plausibly extrapolated from Iamblichus' own account in the text) reports that he was a Syrian, who learned Babylonian and later Greek. TEXT: Habrich (1960), SW 179–245

Lollianus, *Phoenician affairs*. A Greek novel surviving in papyrus fragments (where, exceptionally, the title and author are identified). To judge from the 'Attic' style, it would seem to have been composed in the second or third century CE; it is possible that the author was one of the three sophists by this name who flourished in the period.[14] TEXT: Henrichs (1972), SW 314–57

Longus, *Daphnis and Chloe*. Nothing is known of the author; even 'Longus' may be a corruption of *logos* ('story'), although it is a *bona fide* name, attested on Lesbos (among other places). Usually dated to the second or third century CE, on the grounds of Atticism and stylistic affinity to works like Lucian and (the equally undatable) Alciphron. There are no certain allusions to the text in antiquity.[15] TEXT: Reeve (1994)

Metiochus and Parthenope. Survives now only in fragments. Wide dissemination in antiquity is indicated by five papyrus fragments, two depictions on mosaic floors in Syrian households, influence upon other literary forms (notably the Christian martyrdom of St Parthenope), and the ultimate transformation of the story, in the eleventh century CE, into the Persian *Vāmiq u 'Adhrā* (perhaps via Arabic).[16] The date is uncertain, but analysis of the style (i.e. the general avoidance of Atticism) suggests the first century CE. It is even possible that the author is Chariton.[17] TEXT: HU, SW 72–100

Ninus. Survives only in three substantial papyrus fragments; the text was probably composed in the first century CE, perhaps even in the first century BCE. TEXT: SW 23–71

Xenophon of Ephesus, *Anthia and Habrocomes*, more fully *The Ephesian affairs concerning Anthia and Habrocomes*. One of the earliest texts: probably

---

[13] Text: Habrich (1960) 2; translated at SW 181. See also ch. 2 n. 30.
[14] For whom see Puech (2002) 327–37.
[15] Bowie (1995), however, argues for allusion in Heliodorus.
[16] These themes are fully discussed by HU.   [17] Tilg (2010) 92–105.

late first or early second century CE (I am, however, still unconvinced that Xenophon is necessarily later than Chariton, as the current orthodoxy holds).[18] Like almost all modern scholars, I reject the theory that the text was epitomised, although it clearly is a different kind of work to the other romances.[19] The *Suda* (under 'Xenophon of Ephesus') reports that, in addition to *Anthia and Habrocomes*, Xenophon also composed a work 'On the city of Ephesus' (unless that is a descriptive gloss on the title of the novel), and other works. TEXT: O'Sullivan (2005)

[18] See e.g. Bowie (2002) 56–7, Tilg (2010) 85–92; and for the contrary view, that Chariton follows Xenophon, see esp. O'Sullivan (1995).
[19] For summary discussion of the epitome theory, together with further literature, see Kytzler (2003) 348–50.

References

Agapitos, P. (1998) 'Narrative, rhetoric, and "drama" rediscovered: scholars and poets in Byzantium interpret Heliodorus', in Hunter ed. (1998): 125–56
Aitken, E.B. and Maclean, J.K.B. eds (2004) *Philostratus's Heroikos: religion and cultural identity in the third century CE*, Atlanta
Alcock, S.E., Cherry, J. and Elsner, J. eds (2001) *Pausanias: travel and memory in Roman Greece*, New York and Oxford
Alexopoulou, M. (2006) '*Nostos* and the impossibility of a "return to the same": from Homer to Seferis', *New Voices in Classical Reception Studies*: internet journal
   (2009) *The theme of returning home in ancient Greek literature: the nostos of the epic tradition*, Lewiston NY
Alperowitz, M. (1992) *Das Wirken und Walten der Götter im griechischen Roman*, Heidelberg
Altheim, F. (1942) *Helios und Heliodor von Emesa*, Amsterdam and Leipzig
Altheim, F. and Stiel, R. eds (1966) *Die Araber in den alten Welt*, Bd. 3, Berlin
Althusser, L. (1984) 'A letter on art in reply to André Daspre', in *Essays on ideology*, London: 173–9
Alvares, J. (1997) 'Chariton's erotic history', *AJP* 118: 613–29
   (2001) 'Egyptian unrest of the Roman era and the reception of Chariton's Chaireas and Callirhoe', *Maia* 53: 11–19
   (2001–2002) 'Some political and ideological dimensions of Chariton's *Chaireas and Callirhoe*', *CJ* 97: 113–44
   (2002) 'Utopian themes in three Greek romances', *AN* 2: 1–29
   (2006) 'Reading Longus and Achilles Tatius in counterpoint', in Byrne *et al.* eds (2006): 1–33
   (2007) 'The coming of age and political accommodation in the Greco-Roman novels', in Paschalis *et al.* eds (2007): 3–22
Amato, E. (2005) *Favorinos d'Arles: Oeuvres*, Paris
Ameling, W. (1986) 'Tyrannen und schwangere Frauen', *Historia* 35: 507–8
Anderson, G. (1979) 'Two notes on Heliodorus', *JHS* 99: 149
   (1982) *Eros sophistes: ancient novelists at play*, Chico
   (1984) *Ancient fiction: the novel in the Graeco–Roman world*, London
   (1986) *Philostratus: biography and belles lettres in the third century AD*, London

(1993) *The second sophistic: a cultural phenomenon in the Roman empire*, London
(1994) *Sage, saint and sophist: holy men and their associates in the early Roman empire*, London
(2000) 'Some uses of storytelling in Dio', in Swain ed. (2000): 143–60
Anderson, M. (2009) 'The silence of Semiramis: shame and desire in the Ninus romance and other Greek novels', *AN* 7: 1–27
André, J.-M. and Baslez, M.-F. (1993) *Voyager dans l'antiquité*, Paris
Asheri, D., Lloyd, A. and Corcella, A. (2007) *A commentary on Herodotus books I–IV*, Oxford
Bakhtin, M. (1981) *The dialogic imagination*, trans. C. Emerson and M. Holquist, M. Holquist ed., Austin
(1986) *Speech genres and other late essays*, trans. V.W. McGee, C. Emerson and M. Holquist eds, Austin
Balot, R.K. (1998) 'Foucault, Chariton, and the masculine self', *Helios* 25: 139–62
Bammer, A. (1984) *Das Heiligtum der Artemis von Ephesos*, Graz
(1988) *Ephesos: Stadt am Fluß und Meer*, Graz
Bargheer, R. (1999) *Die Gottesvorstellung Heliodors in den* Aithiopika, Frankfurt am Main, Berlin, Bern, New York, Paris, Vienna
Barns, J.W.B. (1956) 'Egypt and the Greek Romance', in H. Gerstinger ed. *Akten des VIII. Internationalen Kongress für Papyrologie*, Vienna: 29–36
Barré, M.L. (2001) '"Wandering about" as a topos of depression in ancient near-eastern literature and in the Bible', *Journal of Near Eastern Studies* 60: 177–87
Barthes, R. (1975) *The pleasure of the text*, trans. R. Miller, New York
Bartsch, S. (1989) *Decoding the ancient novel: the reader and the role of description in Heliodorus and Achilles Tatius*, Princeton
Bartsch, W. (1934) *Der Charitonroman und die Historiographie*, Diss. Leipzig
Barwick, K. (1928) 'Die Gliederung der Narratio in der rhetorischen Theorie und ihre Bedeutung für die Geschichte des antiken Romans', *Hermes* 63: 261–87; repr. in Gärtner ed. (1984): 41–67
Baslez, M.-F. (1992) 'De l'histoire au roman: la Perse de Chariton', in Baslez *et al.* eds (1992): 199–212
Baslez, M.-F., Hoffmann, P. and Trédé, M. eds (1992) *Le monde du roman grec: actes du colloque international tenu à l'Ecole normale supérieure (Paris 17–19 décembre 1987)*, Paris
Baumbach, M. (1997) 'Die Meroe-Episode in Heliodors Aithiopika', *RhM* 140: 333–41
Beard, M. (1986) 'Cicero and divination: the formation of a Latin discourse', *JRS* 76: 33–46
Beck, R. (2003) 'Mystery religions, aretalogy and the ancient novel', in Schmeling ed. (2003): 131–50
Becker, A.S. (1995) *The shield of Achilles and the poetics of ekphrasis*, Lanham
Bendlin, A. (2006) 'Vom Nutzen und Nachteil der Mantik: Orakel in Medium von Handlung und Literatur im Zeit der Zweiten Sophistik', in D. Elm von der Osten, J. Rüpke and K. Waldner eds, *Texte als Medium und Reflexion von Religion im römischen Reich*, Stuttgart: 159–207

Benjamin, W. (1970) *Illuminations*, trans. H. Zohn, London
Bhabha, H. (1994) *The location of culture*, London
Bianchi, U. ed. (1986) *Transition rites: cosmic, social and individual order*, Rome
Bierl, A. (2006) 'Räume im Anderen und der griechische Liebesroman des Xenophon von Ephesos', in A. Loprieno ed., *Mensch und Raum von der Antike bis zur Gegenwart*, Munich: 71–103
Billault, A. (1979) 'Approche du problème de l' ἔκφρασις dans les romans grecs', *BAGB* 2: 199–204
  (1981) 'Le mythe de Persée et les *Ethiopiques* d'Héliodore: légendes, représentations et fiction littéraire', *REG* 94: 63–75
  (1989) 'De l'histoire au roman: Hermocrate de Syracuse', *REG* 102: 540–8
  (1990) 'L'inspiration des ΕΚΦΡΑΣΕΙΣ d'œuvres d'art chez les romanciers grecs', *Rhetorica* 8: 153–60
  (1991) *La création romanesque dans la littérature grecque à l'époque impériale*, Paris
Birchall, J. (1996) 'The lament as a rhetorical feature in the Greek novel', *GCN* 7: 1–17
Blanchard, J.M. (1975) 'Daphnis et Chloe: histoire de la mimesis', *QUCC* 20: 39–62
Boatwright, M. (2000) *Hadrian and the cities of the Roman empire*, Princeton
Bobzien, S. (1998) *Determinism and freedom in Stoic philosophy*, Oxford
Bouffartigue, J. (2000) 'Un triangle symbolique: Eros, Aphrodite et Artémis dans la Roman de Leucippé et Clitophon', in A. Billault ed., *ΟΠΩΡΑ: La belle saison de l'hellénisme. Études de littérature antiques offertes au Recteur Jacques Bompaire*, Paris: 125–38
Bowersock, G.W. (1973) 'Greek intellectuals and the imperial cult', in *Le culte des souverains dans l'empire romain. Fondation Hardt: Entretiens* 19: 179–206
  (1994) *Fiction as history: Nero to Julian*, Berkeley
Bowie, E.L. (1970) 'Greeks and their past in the second sophistic', *P&P* 46: 3–41; repr. in M.I. Finley ed. (1974) *Studies in ancient society*, London: 166–209
  (1978) 'Apollonius of Tyana: tradition and reality', *ANRW* 2.16.2: 1652–1699
Bowie, E.L. (1985) 'The Greek novel', in P.E. Easterling and B.M.W. Knox eds *The Cambridge history of classical literature, The Hellenistic period and the empire*, vol. 1.4 Cambridge: 123–39; repr. in Swain ed. (1999): 39–59
  (1991) 'Hellenes and Hellenism in writers of the early second sophistic', in Saïd ed. (1991): 183–204
  (1994) 'The readership of Greek novels in the ancient world', in Tatum ed. (1994): 435–59
  (1995) 'Names and a gem: aspects of allusion in Heliodorus' *Aethiopica*', in D. Innes *et al.* eds, *Ethics and rhetoric: classical essays for Donald Russell on his seventy-fifth birthday*, Oxford: 269–80
  (1998) 'Phoenician games in Heliodorus' *Aithiopika*', in Hunter ed. (1998): 1–18
  (2002) 'The chronology of the Greek novel since B.E. Perry: revisions and precisions', *Ancient Narrative* 2 (2002): 47–63
  (2006) 'Choral performances', in Konstan and Saïd eds (2006): 61–92

(2007) 'Links between Antonius Diogenes and Petronius', in Paschalis *et al.* eds (2007): 121–32

(2008) 'Literary milieux', in Whitmarsh ed. (2008): 17–38

Boys-Stones, G.R. ed. (2003) *Metaphor, allegory, and the classical tradition: ancient thought and modern revisions*, Oxford

Brady, L.R. (2007) *The Aphrodite of Aphrodisias*, Mainz

Brancacci, A. (1986) *Rhetorike philosophousa: Dione Crisostomo nella cultura antica e bizantina*, Naples

Branham, R.B. (2002) 'A truer story of the novel?', in Branham ed. (2002): 161–86

Branham, R.B. ed. (2002) *Bakhtin and the classics*, Evanston IL

(2005) *The Bakhtin circle and ancient narrative*, Ancient Narrative Supplementum 3, Groningen

Braun, M. (1934) *Griechischer Roman und hellenistische Geschichtschreibung*, Frankfurt-am-Main

(1938) *History and romance in Graeco-oriental literature*, Oxford

Brelich, A. (1969) *Paides e parthenoi*, vol. 1, Rome

Brethes, R. (2007a) 'Who knows what? The access to knowledge in ancient novels: the strange cases of Chariton and Apuleius', in Paschalis *et al.* eds (2007): 171–92

(2007b) *De l'idéalisme au réalisme: une étude du comique dans le roman grec*, Salerno

Brioso Sánchez, M. (1992) 'Egipto en la novela griega antiqua', *Habis* 3: 197–215

(1999) 'La pederastia en la novela griega antigua', *ExcPhilol* 9: 7–50

(2003) 'La pederastia en Quéreas y Calírroe de Caritón', in J.M. Nieto Ibáñez ed., *Lógos hellenikós: homenaje al profesor Gaspar Morocho Gayo*, León: I.221–31

Briquel-Chatonnet, F. (1992) 'L'image des phéniciens dans les romans grecs', in Baslez *et al.* eds (1992): 189–98

Brooks, P. (1984) *Reading for the plot: design and intention in narrative*, Cambridge MA and London

Brown, P. (1971) 'The rise and function of the holy man in late antiquity', *JRS* 61: 80–101

(1990a) *The body and society: men, women and sexual renunciation in early Christianity*, London

(1990b) 'Bodies and minds: sexuality and renunciation in early Christianity', in Halperin *et al.* eds (1990): 479–93

Bruner, J. (1987) 'Life as narrative', *Social Research* 54: 11–32

Bühler, W. (1976) 'Das Element des Visuellen in der Eingangsszene von Heliodors Aithiopika', *WS* 10: 177–85

Bürger, K. (1892) 'Zu Xenophon von Ephesus', *Hermes* 27: 36–67

Burkert, W. (1987) *Ancient mystery cults*, Cambridge MA

Burrus, V. (2005) 'Mimicking virgins: colonial ambivalence and the ancient romance', *Arethusa* 38: 49–88

Burton, J. (2008) *'Byzantine readers'*, in Whitmarsh ed. (2008): 272–81

Byrne, S.N., Cueva, E.P. and Alvares, J. eds (2006) *Authority and interpreters in the ancient novel: essays in honour of Gareth L. Schmeling = Ancient Narrative Supplementum 5*, Groningen

Calame, C. (1997) *Choruses of young women in ancient Greece: their morphology, religious role, and social function*, trans. D. Collins and J. Orion, Lanham

Cameron, A. (1995) *Callimachus and his critics*, Princeton

Campbell, M. (1991) *Moschus, Europa: edited with introduction and commentary*, Hildesheim

Capra, A. (2009) 'The (un)happy romance of Curleo and Liliet: Xenophon of Ephesus, the *Cyropaedia* and the birth of the "anti-tragic" novel', *AN* 7: 29–50

Carson, A. (1986) *Eros the bittersweet: an essay*, Princeton

Cartledge, P. (1993) *The Greeks: a portrait of self and other*, Oxford

Cavallo, G. (1996) 'Veicoli materiali della letteratura di consume: maniere di scrivere e maniere di leggere', in O. Pecere and A. Stramaglia eds., *La letteratura di consumo nel mondo Greco-Latino*, Cassino: 13–46

Cave, T. (1988) *Recognitions: a study in poetics*, Oxford

Chad, C. (1972) *Les dynastes d'Émèse*, Beirut

Chalk, H.H.O. (1960) 'Eros and the Lesbian pastorals of Longos', *JHS* 80: 32–55; repr. in Gärtner ed. (1984): 388–407

Chaniotis, A. (2004) 'Under the watchful eyes of the gods: divine justice in Hellenistic and Roman Asia Minor', in S. Colvin ed. *The Greco-Roman East*, Cambridge: 1–43

Chatman, S. (1978) *Story and discourse*, Ithaca

Chew, K.S. (2003) 'The representation of violence in the Greek novels and martyr accounts', in Panayotakis *et al.* eds (2003): 129–41

Christenson, D. (2000) 'Callinus and *militia armoris* in Achilles Tatius' *Leucippe and Cleitophon*, *CQ* 50: 631–2

Claassen, J.-M. (1999) *Displaced persons: the literature of exile from Cicero to Boethius*, London

Cohen, M. (2006) 'The chronotopes of the sea', in Moretti ed. (2006b): 647–66

Colonna, A. (1938) *Heliodori Aethiopica*, Rome

Comito, T. (1975) 'Exile and return in the Greek romances', *Arion* 2: 58–80

Connors, C. (2002) 'Chariton's Syracuse and its histories of empire', in Paschalis and Frangoulidis eds (2002): 12–26

  (2008) 'Politics and spectacle', in Whitmarsh ed. (2008): 162–81

Cooper, K. (1996) *The virgin and the bride: idealised womanhood in late antiquity*, Cambridge MA

Cresci, L., Lalanne, S., Couraud-Lalanne, S. (1978) 'La figura di Melite in Achille Tazio', *A&R* 23: 74–82

Cueva, E. (1998) 'Longus and Thucydides: a new interpretation', *GRBS* 39: 429–40

  (2004) *The myths of fiction: studies in the canonical Greek novels*, Ann Arbor

Culler, J. (1975) *Structuralist poetics: structuralism, linguistics and the study of literature*, London

Curty, O. (1995) *Les parentés légendaires entre cités grecques: catalogue raisonné des inscriptions contenant le terme syngeneia et analyse critique*, Geneva

Cusset, C. (2001) 'Le Jason d'Apollonios de Rhodes: est-il un personnage romanesque?', in Pouderon *et al.* eds (2001): 207–18

Dalmeyda, G. (1934) *Longus, Pastorales (Daphnis et Chloé)*, Paris

Daude, C. (1990) 'Éléments de la modélisation spatiale dans le roman de Chariton', *Recherches en linguistique étrangère, sémiotique, lexicologie, didactique* xv, *Annales littéraires de l'Université de Besançon 421*, Paris: 67–94

Davidson, J. (2007) *The Greeks and Greek love*, London

Dawson, D. (1992) *Allegorical readers and cultural revision in ancient Alexandria*, Berkeley, Los Angeles and Oxford

de Jong, I.J.F. (1987) *Narrators and focalizers: the presentation of story in the Iliad*, Amsterdam

  (2009) 'Metalepsis in ancient Greek literature', in J. Grethlein and A. Rengakos eds, *Narratology and interpretation: the content of narrative form in ancient literature*, Berlin and New York: 87–115

de Jong, I.J.F. and Nünlist, R. eds (2007) *Time in ancient Greek literature*, Leiden

de Jong, I.J.F, Nünlist, R. and Bowie, A. eds (2004) *Narrators, narratees, and narratives in ancient Greek literature: Studies in ancient Greek narrative*, vol. 1, Leiden

De Man, P. (1986) *The resistance to theory*, Manchester

De Temmerman, K. (2009a) 'Chaereas revisited: rhetorical control in Chariton's "ideal" novel *Callirhoe*', *CQ* 59: 247–62

  (2009b) 'A flowery meadow and a hidden metalepsis in Achilles Tatius', *CQ* 59: 667–70

Debray-Genette, R. (1980) 'La pierre descriptive', *Poétique* 43: 293–304

Derrida, J. (1974) *Of grammatology*, trans. G. Spivak, Baltimore

  (1980) 'The law of genre', trans. A. Ronell, *Critical Inquiry* 7.1: 55–81; repr. in J. Derrida, *Acts of Literature*, D. Attridge ed., New York and London: 211–52

  (1981) *Dissemination*, trans. B. Johnson, London

Diggle, J. (1972) 'A note on Achilles Tatius', *CR* 22: 7

Dilke, O.A.W. (1980) 'Heliodorus and the colour problem', *PP* 35: 264–71

Dilts, M.R. and Kennedy, G.A. (1997) *Two Greek rhetorical treatises from the Roman empire: introduction, text, and translation of the Arts of Rhetoric, attributed to Anonymous Seguerianus and to Apsines of Gadara*, Leiden

Doblhofer, E. (1987) *Exil und Emigration: zum Erlebnis der Heimatferne in der römischen Literatur*, Darmstadt

Dodd, D.B. and Faraone, C.A. eds (2003) *Initiation in ancient Greek rituals and narratives*, London

Dollimore, J. (1998) *Death, desire and loss in Western culture*, London

Dörrie, H. (1938) 'Die griechischen Romane und das Christentum', *Philologus* 93: 273–6

Doulamis, K. (2002) *The rhetoric of eros in Xenophon of Ephesus and Chariton: a stylistic and interpretative study*, Diss., University of Exeter

Dover, K. (1980) *Plato, Symposium*, Cambridge

Dowden, K. (1996) 'Heliodorus: serious intentions', *CQ* 46: 267–85
  (1999) 'The passage rite in myth, ritual and the Greek novel', in M. Padilla ed. *Rites of passage in ancient Greece: literature, religion, society*, London and Toronto: 221–43
  (2005) 'Greek novel and the ritual of life: an exercise in taxonomy', in Harrison *et al.* eds (2005): 23–35
Droge, A. (1989) *Homer or Moses? Early Christian interpretations of the history of culture*, Tübingen
Droogers, A.F. (1980) *The dangerous journey: symbolic aspects of boys' initiation among the Wagenia of Kisangari, Zaire*, The Hague
du Gay, P., Evans, J. and Redman, P. eds (2000) *Identity: a reader*, London
Dubel, S. (1990) 'La description des objets d'art dans les Éthiopiques', *Pallas* 36: 101–15
Duff, T. (1999) *Plutarch's Lives: exploring virtue and vice*, Oxford
Eco, U. (1979) *The role of the reader: explorations in the semiotics of texts*, Bloomington
Edwards, D.R. (1991) 'Surviving the web of Roman power: religion and politics in the Acts of the Apostles, Josephus, and Chariton's Chaereas and Callirhoe', in L. Alexander ed., *Images of Empire*, Sheffield: 179–201
  (1994) 'Defining the web of power in Asia Minor: the novelist Chariton and his city Aphrodisias', *Journal of the American Academy of Religion* 62: 699–718
  (1996) *Religion and power: pagans, Jews and Christians in the Greek East*, New York
Effe, B. (1987) 'Der griechische Liebesroman und die Homoerotik: Ursprung und Entwicklung einer epischen Gattungskonvention', *Philologus* 131: 95–108
Egger, B. (1988) 'Zu den Frauenrollen im griechischen Roman: Die Frau als Heldin and Leserin' *GCN* 1: 33–66
  (1994a) 'Looking at Chariton's *Callirhoe*', in Morgan and Stoneman eds (1994): 31–48
  (1994b) 'Women and marriage in the Greek novel: the boundaries of romance,' in Tatum ed. (1994): 260–80
Ehrenberg, V. (1947) '*Polypragmosyne*: a study in Greek politics', *JHS* 67: 46–67
Elam, D. (1992) *Romancing the postmodern*, London
Elmer, D. (2008) 'Heliodorus' "sources": paternity, intertextuality and the Nile river in the *Aithiopika*', *TAPA* 138: 411–50
Elsner, J. (1992) 'Pausanias: a Greek pilgrim in the Roman world', *P&P* 135: 3–29
  (1995) *Art and the Roman viewer: the transformation of art from the pagan world to Christianity*, Cambridge
  (1996) 'Image and ritual: reflections on the religious appreciation of classical art', *CQ* 46: 515–31
  (1997) 'Hagiographic geography: travel and allegory in the *Life of Apollonius of Tyana*', *JHS* 117: 22–37
  (1998) 'Art and archictecture', in I. Eiddon *et al.* eds, *The Cambridge ancient history, the late empire*, AD 337–425, vol. 13, Cambridge: 737–61

(2004) 'Seeing and saying: a psychoanalytic account of ekphrasis', *Helios* 31: 157–85
Elsner, J. and Rutherford, I. eds (2005) *Pilgrimage in Graeco-Roman and early Christian antiquity*, Oxford
Evans, R.J.W. and Marr, A. eds (2006) *Curiosity and wonder from the Renaissance to the Enlightenment*, Aldershot
Fantham, E. (1986) 'ΖΗΛΟΤΥΠΙΑ: A brief excursion into sex, violence, and literary history', *Phoenix* 40: 45–57
Farrell, J. (2003) 'Classical genre in theory and practice', *New Literary History* 34: 283–408
Feeney, D.C. (1991) *The gods in epic: poets and critics of the classical tradition*, Oxford
    (1993) '*Towards an account of the ancient world's concepts of fictive belief*', in Gill and Wiseman eds (1993): 230–44
Fein, S. (1994) *Die Beziehungen der Kaiser Trajan und Hadrian zu den Litterati*, Stuttgart
Felski, R. (1989) *Beyond feminist aesthetics: feminist literature and social change*, London
Feuillâtre, E. (1966) *Études sur les Éthiopiques d'Héliodore*, Paris
Fish, S. (1976) 'Interpreting the Variorum', *Critical Inquiry* 2: 465–85; repr. in Fish, *Is there a text in this class? The authority of interpretive communities*, Cambridge MA: 147–80; and J.P. Tompkins ed. (1980) *Reader-response criticism: from formalism to post-structuralism*, Baltimore and London: 164–84
Fisher, E.A. (1982) 'Greek translations of Latin literature in the fourth century AD', *YCS* 27: 173–215
Fitzgerald, W. (2000) *Slavery and the Roman literary imagination*, Cambridge
Flower, M.A. (1994) *Theopompus of Chios: history and rhetoric in the fourth century BC*, Oxford
Fludernik, M. (2003) 'Scene shift, metalepsis, and the metaleptic mode', *Style* 37: 382–402
    (2007) '*Identity/alterity*', in Herman ed. (2007): 260–73
Follet, S. (2004) '*Philostratus' Heroikos and the regions of the northern Aegean*', in Aitken and Maclean eds (2004): 221–35
Ford, A.L. (2002) *The origins of criticism: literary culture and poetic theory in classical Greece*, Princeton
Fornaro, S. (1997) *Dionisio di Alicarnasso, Epistola a Pompeio Gemino*, Stuttgart and Leipzig
Fortenbaugh, W. and Schütrumpf, E. eds (2000) *Demetrius of Phalerum: text, translation and discussion*, New Brunswick
Foucault, M. (1970) *The order of things: an archaeology of the human sciences*, London
    (1990) *The history of sexuality*, vol. 3: *The care of the self*, trans. R. Hurley, London
Fowden, G. (1982) 'The pagan holy man in late antique society', *JHS* 102: 33–59
Fowler, A. (1982) *Kinds of literature: an introduction to the theory of genres and modes*, Oxford

Fowler, D.P. (1989) 'First thoughts on closure: problems and prospects', *MD* 22: 75–12
  (1997) '*Second thoughts on closure*', in Roberts *et al.* eds (1997): 3–22
Frame, D. (1978) *The myth of return in early Greek epic*, New Haven
Francis, J. (1995) *Subversive virtue: asceticism and authority in the second-century pagan world*, Pennsylvania
Frede, D. (2003) 'Stoic determinism', in B. Inwood ed., *The Cambridge companion to the Stoics*, Cambridge: 179–205
Freud, S. (1973) *New introductory lectures on psychoanalysis*, trans. J. Strachey, London
Frey, M. (1989) *Untersuchungen zur Religion und zur Religionspolitik des Kaisers Elagabal*, Stuttgart
Friedrich, R. (1983) '*Epeisodion* in drama and epic', *Hermes* 111: 34–52
Friesen, S.J. (1993) *Twice neokoros: Ephesus, Asia, and the cult of the Flavian imperial family*, Leiden
Frye, N. (1976) *The secular scripture: a study of the structure of the romance*, Cambridge MA
Fusillo, M. (1989) *Il romanzo greco: polifonia ed eros*, Marsilio
  (1997) '*How novels end: some patterns of closure in ancient narrative*', in Roberts *et al.* eds (1997): 209–27
Futre Pinheiro, M. (1998) 'Time and narrative technique in Heliodorus' *Aethiopica*', *ANRW* II 34.4: 3148–73
Gaertner J.F. ed. (2007) *Writing exile: the discourse of displacement in Greco-Roman antiquity and beyond*, Leiden
Gaisser, J.H. (2008) *The fortunes of Apuleius and the Golden ass: a study in transmission and reception*, Princeton
Galinsky, K. (1993–1994) 'Reading Roman poetry in the 1990s', *CJ* 89: 297–309
Gangloff, A. (2006) *Dion Chrysostome et les mythes: Hellénisme, communication et philosophie politique*, Grenoble
Garnaud, J.-P. ed. (1991) *Achille Tatius d'Alexandrie, Le Roman de Leucippé et Clitophon*, Paris
  (1978) 'Works of art in Achilles Tatius' *Leucippe and Clitophon*', *AClass* 21: 83–6
Gärtner, H. (1967) 'Xenophon von Ephesos', *RE* 9 A.2: 2055–89
  (1969) 'Charikleia in Byzanz', *AandA* 15: 47–69
Gärtner, H. ed. (1984) *Beiträge zum griechischen Liebesroman*, Hildesheim
Geertz, C. (1979–80) 'Blurred senses: the refiguration of social thought', *American Scholar* 49: 165–79
Genette, G. (1977) 'Genres, "types", modes', *Poétique* 32: 389–421
  (1980) *Narrative discourse*, trans. J.E. Lewin, Ithaca
  (1992) *The architext: an introduction*, trans. J.E. Lewin, Berkeley
  (2004) *Métalepse: de la figure à la fiction*, Paris
Geyer A. (1977) 'Roman und Mysterienritual: zum Problem eines Bezugs zum dionysischen Mysterienritual im Roman des Longos', *WJA* 3: 179–96
Giangrande, G. (1962) 'On the origins of the Greek romance: the birth of a literary form', *Eranos* 60: 132–59; repr. in Gärtner ed. (1984): 125–52

Γιατρομανωλάκης, Γ. (1990) Ἀχιλλέως Ἀλεξανδρέως Τατίου ΛΕΥΚΙΠΠΗ ΚΑΙ ΚΛΕΙΤΟΦΩΝ: εἰσαγωγή – μετάφραση – σχόλια, Athens
Gigante, M. (1993) *Nomos Basileus, 2 con un'appendice*, Napoli
Gill, C. (1983) 'The question of character-development: Tacitus and Plutarch', *CQ* 33: 469–87
  (1996) *Personality in Greek epic, tragedy, and philosophy: the self in dialogue*, Oxford
  (2006) *The structured self in Hellenistic and Roman thought*, Oxford
Gill, C. and Wiseman, T.P. eds (1993) *Lies and fiction in the ancient world*, Exeter
Gleason, M.W. (1995) *Making men: sophists and self-presentation in ancient Rome*, Princeton
Gluckman, M. ed. (1962) *The ritual of social relations*, Manchester
Goldhill, S. (1991) *The poet's voice: essays on poetics and Greek literature*, Cambridge
  (1995) *Foucault's virginity: ancient erotic fiction and the history of sexuality*, Cambridge
  (2001) 'The erotic eye: visual stimulation and cultural conflict', in *id.* ed., *Being Greek under Rome: Cultural identity, the second sophistic and the development of empire*, Cambridge: 154–94
  (2008) 'Genre', in Whitmarsh ed. (2008): 185–200
Gordon, P. (1996) *Epicurus in Lycia: the second-century world of Diogenes of Oenoanda*, Ann Arbor
Gow, A.S.F. (1952) *Theocritus*, 2 vols. Cambridge
Graf, F. (2003) 'Initiation: a concept with a troubled history', in Dodd and Faraone eds (2003): 3–24
Green, P. (1982) 'Longus, Antiphon and the topography of Lesbos', *JHS* 102: 210–14
Griffin, J. (1998) 'The social function of Attic tragedy', *CQ* 48: 39–61
Griffiths, J.G. (1975) *Apuleius of Madauros: the Isis book (Metamorphoses, book XI)*, Leiden
  (1978) 'Xenophon of Ephesus on Isis and Alexandria', in M.B. de Boer and T.A. Edridge eds, *Hommages à Maarten J. Vermaseren: recueil d'études offert par les auteurs de la série Études préliminaires aux religions orientales dans l'Empire romain à Maarten J. Vermaseren à l'occasion de son soixantième anniversaire le 7 avril 1978*, Leiden: 1.409–37.
Grossardt, P. (2006) *Einführung, Übersetzung und Kommentar zum Heroikos von Flavius Philostrat*, 2 vols, Basel
Großlein, P. (1998) *Untersuchungen zum Juppiter confutatus Lukians*, Frankfurt-am-Main
Gual, C. García (1992) 'L'initiation de Daphnis et Chloé', in Moreau ed. (1992): 157–66
Guez, J.-P. (2001) 'Pourquoi Théron n'est-il pas amoureux?', in Pouderon *et al.* eds (2001): 101–10
Gumbrecht, H.U. (2006) 'The roads of the novel', in Moretti ed. (2006b): 611–46
Habrich, E. ed. (1960) *Iamblichi Babyloniacorum reliquiae*, Leipzig

Hägg, T. (1966) 'Die Ephesiaka des Xenophon Ephesios: original oder Epitome?', *CandM* 27: 118–61; trans. T. Hägg as 'The *Ephesiaca* of Xenophon Ephesius – original or epitome?' in Hägg (2004): 159–98
  (1971) *Narrative technique in ancient Greek romance: studies of Chariton, Xenophon Ephesius, and Achilles Tatius*, Stockholm
  (1983) *The novel in antiquity*, Oxford
  (2000) 'The black land of the sun: Meroe in Heliodoros's romantic fiction', *Graeco-Arabica* 7–8: 195–220; repr. in Hägg (2004): 345–78
  (2002) 'Epiphany in the Greek novels: the emplotment of a metaphor', *Eranos* 100: 51–61; repr. in Hägg (2004): 141–58
  (2004) *Parthenope: selected studies in ancient Greek fiction (1969–2004)*, L. Boje Mortensen and T. Eide eds, Copenhagen
Haines-Eitzen, K. (2000) *Guardians of letters: literacy, power, and the transmitters of early Christian literature*, Oxford and New York
Halfmann, H. (1979) *Die Senatoren aus dem östlichen Teil des Imperium romanum bis zum Ende des 2 Jh. n. Chr.*, Göttingen
Hall, E. (1995) 'The ass with double vision: politicising an ancient Greek novel', in D. Margolies and M. Jouannou eds, *Heart of a heartless world: essays in cultural resistance in honour of Margot Heinemann*, London: 47–59
Hall, E. and Wyles, R. eds (2008) *New directions in ancient pantomime*, Oxford
Halliwell, S. (1986) *The Poetics of Aristotle: translation and commentary*, London
  (2008) *Greek laughter: a study of cultural psychology from Homer to early Christianity*, Oxford
Halperin, D.M. (1992) 'Plato and the erotics of narrativity', in Hexter and Selden eds (1992): 95–126
Halperin, D.M. (1994) 'Historicizing the subject of desire: sexual preferences and erotic identities in the pseudo-Lucianic *Erôtes*', in J.M. Goldstein ed. *Foucault and the writing of history*, Oxford and Cambridge MA: 19–34
Halperin, D.M., Winkler, J.J. and Zeitlin, F.I. eds (1990) *Before sexuality: the construction of erotic experience in the ancient world*, Princeton
Hammerstaedt, J. (1988) *Die Orakelkritik des Kynikers Oenomaus*, Frankfurt-am-Main
  (1990) 'Der Kyniker Oenomaus von Gadara', *ANRW* 2.36.4: 2834–65
Hansen, W. 2003 'Strategies of authentication in ancient popular literature' in Panayotakis *et al.* eds (2003): 301–14
Hardie, P. (1997) 'Closure in Latin epic', in Roberts *et al.* eds (1997): 139–62
  (1998) 'A reading of Heliodorus, *Aithiopika* 3.4.1–5.2', in Hunter ed. (1998): 19–39
Harrison, S. (2003) 'Apuleius' *Metamorphoses*', in Schmeling ed. (2003): 491–516
Harrison, S.J. ed. (1999) *Oxford readings in the Roman novel*, Oxford
Harrison, S., Paschalis, M and Frangoulidis, S. eds (2005) *Metaphor and ancient narrative, Ancient Narrative Supplementum 3*, Groningen
Hartog, F. (1988) *The mirror of Herodotus: the representation of the other in the writing of history*, trans. J. Lloyd, Berkeley

(2001) *Memories of Odysseus: frontier tales from Ancient Greece*, trans. J. Lloyd, Edinburgh
Hawking, S. (2001) *The universe in a nutshell*, London
Haynes, K. (2003) *Fashioning the feminine in the Greek novel*, London and New York
Headlam, W. (1922) *Herodas: the mimes and fragments*, Cambridge
Heath, M. (1989) *Unity in Greek poetics*, Oxford
Heath, S. (2004) 'The politics of genre', in C. Prendergast ed., *Debating world literature*, London and New York: 163–74
Hedreen, G. (2004) 'The return of Hephaistos, Dionysiac processional ritual, and the creation of a visual narrative', *JHS* 124: 38–64
Hefti, V. (1950) *Zur Erzählungstechnik in Heliodors* Aithiopika, Vienna
Helm, R. (1906) *Lucian und Menipp*, Leipzig and Berlin
Helms, J. (1966) *Character portrayal in the romance of Chariton*, The Hague and Paris
Henderson, J. (1991) *The maculate muse: obscene language in Attic comedy*, 2nd edn, New York
Henne, H. (1936) 'La géographie d'Égypte dans les *Éphésiaques* de Xénophon d'Ephèse', *Revue d'histoire de la philosophie et d'histoire générale de la civilisation* 4: 97–106
Henrichs, A. (1972) *Die 'Phoinikika' des Lollianos, Papyrologische Texte und Abhandlungen 14*, Bonn
Herman, D. ed. (2007) *The Cambridge companion to narrative*, Cambridge
Herrmann, F.-G. (2007) 'Greek religion and philosophy: the god of the philosopher', in D. Ogden ed., *A companion to Greek religion*, Oxford: 385–97
Hexter, R. (1992) 'Sidonian Dido', in Hexter and Selden eds (1992): 332–84
Hexter, R. and Selden, D. eds (1992) *Innovations of antiquity*, New York
Hijmans, B.L. (1995) 'Curiositas', in B.L. Hijmans *et al.* eds, *Apuleius Madaurensis Metamorphoses Book IX*, Groningen: 362–79
Hill, T. (2004) *Ambitiosa mors: suicide and self in Roman thought and literature*, London
Hilton, J. (1998) *A commentary on books 3–4 of the Aithiopika of Heliodorus*, Diss. University of Natal
Hirschberger, M. (2001) 'Epos und Tragödie in Charitons Kallirhoe: ein Beitrag zur Intertextualität des griechischen Romans', *WJA* 25: 157–86.
Hock, R. (1997) 'An extraordinary friend in Chariton's *Callirhoe*: the importance of friendship in the Greek romances', in J.T. Fitgerald ed., *Greco-Roman perspectives on friendship*, Atlanta: 145–62
Holford-Strevens, L. (2003) *Aulus Gellius: an Antonine scholar and his achievement*, 2nd edn, Oxford
Holzberg, N. (1995) *The ancient novel: an introduction*, trans. C. Jackson-Holzberg, London and New York
  (2003) 'The genre: novels proper and the fringe', in Schmeling ed. (2003): 11–28
Hopkins, K. (1993) 'Novel evidence for roman slavery', *P&P* 138: 3–27

Hopwood, K. (1998) '"All that may become a man": the bandit in the ancient novel', in L. Foxhall and J. Salmon eds, *When men were men: masculinity, power and identity in classical antiquity*, London: 195–204
Höschele, R. (2006) *Verrückt nach Frauen: der Epigrammatiker Rufin*, Munich
Huet, P.D. (1670) *Zayde historie espagnole, par Monsieur de Segrais. Avec un traitté de l'origine des romans, par Monsieur Huet*, 2 vols, Paris; repr. (1966) with epilogue by H. Hinterhäuser, Stuttgart
Huizinga, J. (1949) *Homo ludens*, London
Humphrey, E.M. (2000) *Joseph and Aseneth*, Sheffield
Hunter, R. (1983) *A study of Daphnis and Chloë*, Cambridge
 (1985) *The new comedy of Greece and Rome*, Cambridge
 (1993) *The Argonautica of Apollonius: literary studies*, Cambridge
 (1994) 'History and historicity in the romance of Chariton', *ANRW* II.34.2: 1055–86
 (1998) 'The *Aithiopika* of Heliodorus: beyond interpretation?', in Hunter ed. (1998): 40–59; repr. in Hunter (2008b): 804–28
 (2005) '"Philip the philosopher" on the *Aithiopika* of Heliodorus', in Harrison *et al.* eds (2005): 123–38; repr. in Hunter (2008b): 829–44
 (2008a) 'Ancient readers', in Whitmarsh ed. (2008): 261–71
 (2008b) *On coming after: studies in post-classical Greek literature and its reception*, Berlin
 (2009a) *Critical moments in classical literature: studies in the ancient view of literature and its uses*, Cambridge
 (2009b) 'The curious incident... *polypragmosyne* and the ancient novel', in Paschalis *et al.* eds (2009): 51–63; repr. [*sic*] in Hunter (2008b): 884–96
Hunter, R. ed. (1998) *Studies in Heliodorus, PCPS supplement*, vol. 21, Cambridge
Hutchinson, G.O. (2008) *Talking books: readings in Hellenistic and Roman books of poetry*, Oxford
Hutton, W. (2005) 'The construction of religious space in Pausanias', in Elsner and Rutherford eds (2005): 291–317
Innes, D. and Winterbottom, M. (1988) *Sopatros the rhetor: studies in the text of the Διαίρεσις Ζητημάτων*, London
Imbert, C. (1980) 'Stoic logic and Alexandrian poetics', in M. Schofield, M. Burnyeat and J. Barnes eds, *Doubt and dogmatism*, Oxford: 182–216
Iser, W. (1978) *The act of reading: a theory of aesthetic response*, Baltimore
Jacquemain, A. (1991) 'Delphes au IIe siècle après J.-C.: un lieu de la mémoire grecque', in Saïd ed. (1991): 217–231
Janan, M. (1994) *When the lamp is shattered: desire and narrative in Catullus*, Carbondale
 (2001) *The politics of desire: Propertius IV*, Berkeley, Los Angeles and London
Jeanneret, M. (1991) *A feast of words: banquets and table-talk in the Renaissance*, trans. J. Whiteley and E. Hughes, Chicago
Johne, R. (1987) 'Dido und Charikleia: zur Gestaltung der Frau bei Vergil und im griechischen Liebesroman', *Eirene* 24: 21–33
 (2003) 'Women in the ancient novel', in Schmeling ed. (2003): 151–207

Johnstone, H.W. (1990) 'Pankoinon as a rhetorical figure in Greek tragedy', *Glotta* 58: 49–62
　(2000) 'Pankoinon as paradox', *Rhetoric Review* 19: 7–11
Joly, R. (1961) '*Curiositas*', *AC* 30: 33–44
Jones, C.P. (1966) 'Towards a chronology of Plutarch's works', *JRS* 56: 61–74
Jones, C.P. (1971) *Plutarch and Rome*, Oxford
　(1992) 'La personnalité de Chariton', in Baslez *et al.* eds (1992): 161–7
　(1999) *Kinship diplomacy in the ancient world*, Cambridge MA
　(2001) 'Pausanias and his guides', in Alcock, Cherry and Elsner eds (2001): 33–9
Kasprzyk, D. (2001) 'Théron, pirate, conteur et narrateur dans le roman de Chariton, Chairéas et Callirhoé', in Pouderon *et al.* eds (2001): 149–64
Kellman, S. (1980) *The self-begetting novel*, London
Kennedy, D.F. (1992) '"Augustan" and "anti-Augustan": reflections on terms of reference', in A. Powell ed., *Roman poetry and propaganda in the age of Augustus*, Bristol: 26–58
　(1993) *The arts of love: five studies in the discourse of Roman love elegy*, Cambridge
Kenny, N.J. (1998) *Curiosity in early-modern Europe: word histories*, Wiesbaden
　(2004) *The uses of curiosity in early modern France and Germany*, Oxford
Kerby, A.P. (1991) *Narrative and the self*, Bloomington
Kerényi, K. (1927) *Die griechisch-orientalische Romanliteratur in religionsgeschichtlicher Beleuchtung*, Tubingen
Kerferd, G.B. (1981) *The sophistic movement*, Cambridge
Kermode, F. (1967) *The sense of an ending: studies in the theory of fiction*, New York
Kestner, J. (1973) 'Ekphrasis as frame in Longus' *Daphnis and Chloe*', *CW* 67: 166–71
Keyes, C.W. (1922) 'The structure of Heliodorus' *Aethiopica*', *SPh* 19: 42–51
Kim, L. (2010) *Homer between history and fiction in imperial Greek literature*, Cambridge
Kindstrand, J.F. (1973) *Homer in der Zweiten Sophistik: studien zu der Homerlektüre und dem Homerbild bei Dion von Prusa, Maximos von Tyros und Ailios Aristeides*, Uppsala
Klein, R. (1983) *Die Romrede des Aelius Aristides: herausgegeben, übersetzt und mit Erläuterungen versehen*, Darmstadt
Kloss, G. (1994) *Untersuchungen zum Wortfeld 'Verlangen/Begehren' im frühgriechischen Epos*, Göttingen
Knibbe, D. (1998) *Ephesus-ΕΦΕΣΟΣ: Geschichte einer Bedeutenden antiken Stadt und Portrait einer modernen Grossgrabung*, Berlin
Knoles, J. (1980–1) 'The spurned doxy and the dead bride: some ramifications of ancient topoi', *CW* 74: 223–5
Koester, H. ed. (1995) *Ephesos: metropolis of Asia*, Cambridge MA
Konet R.J. (1976) 'The role of Tuche in Menander's *Aspis*', *CB* 52: 90–2
König, J. (2001) 'Favorinus' *Corinthian oration* in its Corinthian context', *PCPS* 47: 141–71
　(2005) *Athletics and literature in the Roman empire*, Cambridge

(2007) 'Orality and authority in Xenophon of Ephesus', in Rimell ed. (2007): 1–22

König, J. and Whitmarsh, T. (2007) 'Ordering knowledge', in König and Whitmarsh eds, *Ordering knowledge in the Roman empire*, Cambridge: 3–39

Konstan, D. (1994) *Sexual symmetry: love in the ancient novel and related genres*, Princeton

(2007) 'Love and murder: two textual problems in Xenophon's *Ephesiaca*', *AN* 5: 31–40

Konstan, D. and Rutter, K. eds (2003) *Envy, spite and jealousy: the rivalrous emotions in ancient Greece*, Edinburgh

Konstan, D. and Saïd, S. eds (2006) *Greeks and Greekness: the construction and uses of the Greek past among Greeks under the Roman empire*, Cambridge

Korenjak, M. (2000) *Publikum und Redner: ihre Interaktion in der sophistischen Rhetorik der Kaiserzeit*, Munich

Kost, K-H. (1971) *Musaios, Hero und Leander: Einleitung, Text, Übersetzung und Kommentar*, Borin

Koster, W.J.W. (1975) *Scholia in Aristophanem. Pars 1: Prolegomena de comoedia, Scholia in Acharnenses, Equites, Nubes. Fasc. 1A: Prolegomena de comoedia*, Groningen

Kövendi, D. (1966) 'Heliodors *Aithiopika*: eine literarische Würdigung', in Altheim and Stiel eds (1966): 136–97

Kselman, J.S. (2002) '"Wandering about" and depression: more examples', *Journal of Near Eastern Studies* 61: 275–7

Kuch, H. (1989) 'Die Herausbildung des antiken Romans als Literaturgattung', in Kuch ed. (1989): 11–51

(2003) 'A study on the margin of the ancient novel: "barbarians" and others', in Schmeling ed. (2003): 209–20

Kuch, H. ed. (1989) *Der antike Roman: Untersuchungen zur literarischen Kommunikation und Gattungsgeschichte*, Berlin

Kurke, L. (1991) *The traffic in praise: Pindar and the poetics of social economy*, Ithaca and London

Kytzler, B. (2003) 'Xenophon of Ephesus', in Schmeling ed. (2003): 336–59

Labhardt, A. (1960) '*Curiositas*: notes sur l'histoire d'un mot et d'une notion', *MH* 17: 206–24

Lacan, J. (1971) *Écrits II*, Paris

Lada-Richards, I. (2007) *Silent eloquence: Lucian and pantomime dancing*, London

Laird, A. (1990) 'Person, "persona" and representation in Apuleius's *Metamorphoses*', *MD* 25: 129–64

Lalanne, S. (1998) 'Récit d'un *télos éroticon*: réflexions sur le statut des jeunes dans le roman de Chariton d'Aphrodisias', *REG* 111: 518–550

(2006) *Une éducation grecque: rites de passage et construction des genres dans le roman grec ancien*, Paris

Lamberton, R. (1986) *Homer the theologian: neoplatonist allegorical reading and the growth of the epic tradition*, Berkeley, Los Angeles and London

Lang, M. (1972) 'War and the rape motif, or why did Cambyses invade Egypt?', *Proceedings of the American Philosophical Society* 116: 410–414
Lape, S. (2003) *Reproducing Athens: Menander's comedy, democratic Athens and the Hellenistic city*, Princeton
Laplace, M.M.J. (1983) 'Achilleus Tatios, Leucippé et Clitophon: P. Oxyrhynchos 1250', *ZPE* 53: 53–59
  (1991) 'Achille Tatius, Leucippé et Clitophon: des fables au roman de formation', *Groningen Colloquia on the Novel* 4: 35–59
  (1992) 'Les *Éthiopiques* d'Héliodore, ou la genèse d'un panégyrique de l'amour', *REA* 94: 199–230
  (1994) 'Récit d'une éducation amoreuse et discours panégyrique dans les *Éphesiaques* de Xenophon d'Ephèse: le romanesque anti-tragique et l'art de l'amour', *REG* 107: 440–79
  (2007) *Le roman d'Achille Tatios: 'discours panégyrique' et imaginaire romanesque*, Bern and Oxford
Lattimore, S. (1987) 'Scopas and the Pothos', *AJA* 91: 411–20
Lavagnini, B. (1922) 'Le origini del romanzo greco', *ASNP* 28: 9–104; repr. in Gärtner ed. (1984): 41–101
Lefteratou, A. (2010) 'Epic and tragic myth in the Greek novels', Diss. Oxford
Lehmann, W. (1910) 'De Achillis Tatii aetate: accedit corollarium de Achillis Tatii stadiis Lucianeis', Diss. Bratislava
Lesky, A. (1959) 'Aithiopika', *Hermes* 87: 27–38
  (1961) *Göttliche und menschliche Motivation im homerischen Epos*, Heidelberg
Lessing, G.E. (1985 (1766)) *Laocöon: an essay on the limits of painting and poetry*, trans. E.A. McCormick, Baltimore
Létoublon, F. (1993) *Les lieux communs du roman: stéréotypes grecs d'aventure et d'amour*, Leiden
Liatsi, M. (2004) 'Die Träume des Habrokomes bei Xenophon of Ephesus', *RhM* 147: 151–71
Lightfoot, J.L. (2003) *Lucian on the Syrian goddess: edited with introduction, translation and commentary*, Oxford
Liviabella Furiani, P. (1989) 'Di donna in donna: elementi "femministi" nel romanzo greco d'amore', in Liviabella Furiani and Scarcella eds (1989): 43–106
Liviabella Furiani, P. and Scarcella, A.M. eds (1989) *Piccolo mondo antico: le donne, gli amori, i costumi, il mondo reale nel romanzo antico*, Perugia
Llewellyn-Jones, L. (2003) *Aphrodite's tortoise: the veiled woman of ancient Greece*, Swansea
Long, A.A. (1991) 'Representation and the self in Stoicism', in S. Everson ed., *Companions to ancient thought 2: psychology*, Cambridge: 102–30; repr. in (1996) *Stoic studies*, Berkeley, Los Angeles and London: 264–85
  (2002) *Epictetus: a Stoic and Socratic guide to life*, Oxford
Lotman, Y.M. (1976) 'The modelling significance of the concepts "end" and "beginning" in artistic texts', trans. W. Rosslyn in, L.M. O'Toole and A. Shukman eds, *Russian poetics in translation: general semiotics*, vol. 3 Oxford: 7–11

Louden, B. (1993) 'Pivotal contrafactuals in Homeric epic', *ClAnt* 12: 181–98
Lowe, N. (2000) *The classical plot and the invention of Western narrative*, Cambridge
Lukinovich, A. (1990) 'The play of reflections between literary form and the sympotic theme in the Deipnosophistae of Athenaeus', in O. Murray ed., *Sympotica: a symposium on the symposium*, Oxford: 263–71
Lyne, O. (1987) *Further voices in Vergil's* Aeneid, Oxford
Ma, J. (1994) 'Black hunter variations', *PCPS* 40: 49–80
Maass, E. (1958) 2nd edn, *Commentariorum in Aratum reliquiae*, Berlin
MacAlister, S. (1996) *Dreams and suicides: the Greek novel from antiquity to the Byzantine empire*, London
Macintyre, A. (1984) *After virtue: a study in moral theory*, 2nd edn, Notre Dame
MacQueen, B.D. (1985) 'Longus and the myth of Chloe', *ICS* 10: 119–34
   (1990) *Myth, rhetoric and fiction: a reading of Longus's* Daphnis and Chloe, Lincoln NA
Maehler, H. (1976) 'Der *Metiochos-Parthenope* Roman', *ZPE* 23: 1–20
Malitz, J. (1983) *Die Historien des Poseidonios*, Munich
Malkin, I. (1998) *The returns of Odysseus: colonization and ethnicity*, Berkeley, Los Angeles and London
Manguel, A. (1997) *A history of reading*, London
Manuwald, G. (2000) 'Zitate als Mittel des Erzählens: zur Darstellungstechnik Charitons in seinem Roman Kallirhoe', *WJA* 24: 97–122
Marinčič, M. (2007) 'Advertising one's own story: text and speech in Achilles Tatius' *Leucippe and Clitophon*', in Rimell ed. (2007): 168–200
Marino, E. (1990) 'Il teatro nel romanzo: Eliodoro e il codice spettacolore', *MD* 25: 203–18
Marks, J. (2005) 'The ongoing *neikos*: Thersites, Odysseus and Achilleus', *AJP* 126: 1–31
Martindale, C. (1993) *Redeeming the text: Latin poetry and the hermeneutics of reception*, Cambridge
   (1997) 'Introduction: "the classic of all Europe"', in *id.* ed., *The Cambridge companion to Virgil*, Cambridge: 1–18
Mason, H.J. (1979) 'Longus and the topography of Lesbos', *TAPA* 109: 149–63
   (1994) 'Greek and Latin versions of the Ass-Story', ANRW II 34, 2: 1165–1707
Mazal, O. (1958) 'Die Satzstruktur in den *Aithiopika* des Heliodor von Emesa', *WS* 71: 116–31; repr. in Gärtner ed. (1984): 451–66
McGing, B.C. (1998) 'Bandits, real and imagined in Greco-Roman Egypt', *BASP* 35: 159–83
Merkelbach, R. (1962) *Roman und Mysterium in der Antike*, Munich
   (1988) *Die Hirten des Dionysos: die Dionysos-Mysterien in der römischen Kaiserzeit und der bukolische Roman des Longus*, Stuttgart
   (2001) *Isis regina – Zeus Sarapis*, Munich and Leipizig
Merkle, S. (1994) 'Telling the true story of the Trojan War', in Tatum ed. (1994): 183–96
Mestre, F. (2004) 'Refuting Homer in the *Heroikos* of Philostratus', in Aitken and Maclean eds (2004): 127–41

Mignogna, E. (1993) 'Europa o Selene? Achille Tazio e Mosco o il ritorno dell' "inversione"', *Maia* 45: 177–84
  (1996a) 'Narrativa greca e mimo: il romanzo di Achille Tazio', *SIFC* 14: 232–42
  (1996b) 'Il mimo Leucippe: un' ipotesi su PBerol inv. 13927 [Pack^2 2437]', *RCCM* 38: 161–6
  (1997) 'Leucippe in Tauride (Ach. Tat. 3, 15–22): mimo e "pantomimo" tra tragedia e romanzo', *MD* 38: 225–36
Millar, F. (1983) 'The Phoenician cities: a case-study in Hellenisation', *PCPS* 209: 54–71; repr. and cited from Millar, (2006) *Rome, the Greek world and the East: the Greek world, the Jews, and the East*, vol. 3 H.M. Cotton and G.M. Rogers eds, Chapel Hill: 32–50
  (1993) *The Roman near East, 31 BC–AD 337*, Cambridge MA
Miller, D.A. (1981) *Narrative and its discontents*, Princeton
Miller, T. (2005) *Making sense of motherhood: a narrative approach*, Cambridge
Milnor, K. (2005) *Gender, domesticity, and the age of Augustus*, Oxford
Mitchell-Boyask, R.N. (1996) '*Sine fine*: Vergil's masterplot', *AJP* 117: 289–307
Mittelstadt, M.C. (1967) 'Longus' *Daphnis and Chloe* and Roman narrative painting', *Latomus* 26: 752–61
Moles, J. (1978) 'The career and conversion of Dio Chrysostom', *JHS* 98: 96–100
Möllendorff, P. von (2009) 'Bild-Störung: das Gemälde von Europas Entführung in Achilleus Tatios' Roman *Leukippe und Kleitophon*', in A.-B. Renger and R.A. Ißler eds, *Europa: Stier und Sternenkranz*, Bonn: 145–64
Montague, H. (1992) 'Sweet and pleasant passion: female and male fantasy in ancient romance novels', in A. Richlin ed., *Pornography and representation in Greece and Rome*, New York and Oxford: 231–49
Montes Cala, J.G. (1992) 'En torno a la "impostura dramatica" en la novela griega: comentario a una ecfrasis de espectaculo en Heliodoro', *Habis* 23: 217–35
Montiglio, S. (2005) *Wandering in ancient Greek culture*, Chicago
  (2007) 'You can't go home again: Lucius' journey in Apuleius' *Metamorphoses* set against the background of the *Odyssey*', *MD* 58: 93–113
Morales, H. (2000) 'Sense and sententiousness in the Greek novels', in A. Sharrock and H. Morales eds, *Intratextuality: Greek and Roman textual relations*, Oxford: 67–88
  (2004) *Vision and narrative in Achilles Tatius' Leucippe and Clitophon*, Cambridge
  (2006) 'Marrying Mesopotamia: female sexuality and cultural resistance in Iamblichus' *Babylonian tales*', *Ramus* 35: 78–101
  (2008) 'The history of sexuality', in Whitmarsh ed. (2008): 39–55
Moreau, A. ed. (1992) *L'initiation: l'acquisition d'un savoir ou d'un pouvoir; le lieu initiatique; parodies et perspectives*, Montpellier
Moretti, F. ed. (2006a) *The novel: history, geography, and culture*, vol. 1, Princeton
Moretti, F. (2006b) *The novel, volume 2: forms and themes*, Princeton
Morgan, J.R. (1985) 'Lucian's *True Histories* and the *Wonders beyond Thule* of Antonius Diogenes' *CQ* 35: 475–90

(1989a) 'The story of Knemon in Heliodoros' *Aithiopika*', *JHS* 109: 99–113; repr. in Swain ed. (1999): 259–85
(1989b) 'A sense of the ending: the conclusion of Heliodoros' *Aithiopika*', *TAPA* 119: 299–320
(1991) 'Reader and audiences in the *Aithiopika* of Heliodoros', *Groningen Colloquia on the Novel* 4: 85–103
(1993) 'Make-believe and make believe: the fictionality of the Greek novels', in Gill and Wiseman eds (1993): 175–229
(1995) 'The Greek novel: towards a sociology of production and reception', in A. Powell ed. *The Greek world*, London: 130–52
(1996) '*Erotika mathemata*: Greek romance as sentimental education', in A.H. Sommerstein and C. Atherton eds, *Education in Greek fiction*, Bari: 163–89
(1997) 'Kleitophon and Encolpius: Achilles Tatius as hidden author', in Paschalis *et al.* eds (2007)
(1998) 'Narrative doublets in Heliodorus' *Aithopika*', in Hunter ed. (1998): 60–78
(2001) 'Apuleius and the prologues of Greek fiction', in A. Laird and A. Kahane eds, *A companion to the prologue of Apuleius' Metamorphoses*, Oxford: 152–62
(2003) 'Heliodorus', in Schmeling ed. (2003): 417–56
(2004a) *Longus, Daphnis and Chloe*, Warminster
(2004b) 'Chariton', in de Jong *et al.* eds (2004): 479–87
(2004c) 'Xenophon of Ephesus', in de Jong *et al.* eds (2004): 489–92
(2004d) 'Achilles Tatius', in de Jong *et al.* eds (2004): 493–506
(2004e) 'Heliodorus', in de Jong *et al.* eds (2004): 523–43
(2005) 'Le blanc et le noir: perspectives païennes et perspectives chrétiennes du l'Éthiopie d'Héliodore', in B. Pouderon ed., *Lieux, décors et paysages de l'ancien roman de ses origines à Byzance*, Lyons: 309–18
(2007a) 'Kleitophon and Encolpius: Achilleus Tatios as hidden author', in Paschalis *et al.* eds (2007): 105–20
(2007b) 'Chariton' in de Jong and Nünlist eds (2007): 433–51
(2007c) 'Xenophon of Ephesus' in de Jong and Nünlist eds (2007): 453–66
(2007d) 'Longus' in de Jong and Nünlist eds (2007): 467–82
(2007e) 'Heliodorus' in de Jong and Nünlist eds (2007): 483–504
Morgan, J.R. and Harrison, S.J. (2008) 'Intertextuality', in Whitmarsh ed. (2008): 218–36
Morgan, J.R. and Jones, M. eds (2007) *Philosophical presences in the ancient novel, Ancient Narrative Supplementum 10*, Groningen
Morgan, J.R. and Stoneman, R. eds (1994) *Greek fiction: the Greek novel in context*, London and New York
Morgan, T. (2007) *Popular morality in the Roman empire*, Cambridge
Morson, G.S. and Emerson, C. (1990) *Mikhail Bakhtin: creation of a prosaics*, Stanford
Mossman, H. (2010) 'Beyond the sea: narrative and cultural implications of multi-dimensional travel in Greek imperial fiction', Diss. Exeter

Most, G. (2007) 'Allegory and narrative in Heliodorus', in Swain *et al.* eds (2007): 160–7
Müller, C.W. (1976) 'Chariton von Aphrodisias und die Theorie des Romans in der Antike', *A&A* 23: 115–36
Murphy, T. (2004) *Pliny the elder's* Natural history: *the empire in the encyclopedia*, Oxford
Naber, S.A. (1901) 'Ad Charitonem', *Mnemosyne* 29: 92–9, 141–4
Naiden, F. (2006) '*Hiketai* and *theoroi* at Epidaurus', in Elsner and Rutherford eds (2005): 73–95
Nakatani, S. (2003) 'A re-examination of some structural problems in Achilles Tatius' *Leucippe and Clitophon*', *AN* 3: 63–81
Nesselrath, H.-G. (2007) 'Later Greek voices on the predicament of exile: from Teles to Plutarch and Favorinus', in Gaertner ed. (2007): 87–108
Newsom, R. (1988) *A likely story: probability and play in fiction*, London
ní Mheallaigh, K. (2008) 'Pseudo-documentarism and the limits of ancient fiction', *AJP* 109: 403–31
Nickau, K. (1966) '*Epeisodion* und Episode', *MH* 23: 155–71
Nimis, S. (1994) 'The prosaics of the ancient novel', *Arethusa* 27: 387–411
  (1998) 'Memory and description in the ancient novel', *Arethusa* 31: 99–122
  (1999) 'The sense of open-endedness in the ancient novel', *Arethusa* 32: 215–38
  (2001) 'Cycles and sequences in Longus', in J. Watson ed., *Speaking volumes: orality and literacy in the Greek and Roman world*, Leiden: 187–200
  (2003) '*In mediis rebus*: beginning again in the middle of the ancient novel', in Panayotakis *et al.* eds (2003): 255–69
  (2004) 'Egypt in Greco-Roman history and fiction', *Alif* 24: 34–67
Nünlist, R. (2009) *The ancient critic at work: terms and concepts of literary criticism in Greek scholia*, Cambridge
Nussbaum, M.C. (1994) *The therapy of desire: theory and practice in Hellenistic ethics*, Princeton
  (2002) 'The incomplete feminism of Musonius Rufus, Platonist, Stoic and Roman', in M.C. Nussbaum and J. Sihvola eds, *The sleep of reason: erotic experience and sexual ethics in Greece and Rome*, Chicago: 283–326
O'Sullivan, J.N. (1978) 'Notes on the text and interpretation of Achilles Tatius I', *CQ* 28: 312–29
  (1980) *A lexicon to Achilles Tatius*, Berlin
  (1995) *Xenophon of Ephesus: his compositional technique and the birth of the novel*, Berlin
  (2005) *Xenephon Ephesius, De Anthea et Habrocome Ephesiacorum libri* v, Munich
Obbink, D. (2006) '4762: narrative romance', in: N. Gonis, J.D. Thomas and R. Hatzilambrou eds, *The Oxyrhynchus Papyri* LXX, London: 22–9
Oliver (1953) *The ruling power: a study of the Roman empire in the second century after Christ through the* Roman oration *of Aelius Aristides, Transactions of the American Philosophical Society* 43: 871–1003
Oudot, E. (1992) 'Images d'Athènes dans les romans grecs', in Baslez *et al.* eds (1992): 101–11

Padilla, M. ed. (1999) *Rites of passage in ancient Greece: literature, religion, society*, London and Toronto
Panayotakis, S., Zimmerman, M. and Keulen, W. eds (2003) *The ancient novel and beyond*, Leiden
Pandiri, T. (1985) '*Daphnis and Chloe*: the art of pastoral play', *Ramus* 14: 116–41
Parker, G. (2008) *The making of Roman India*, Cambridge
Parker, P. (1979) *Inescapable romance: studies in the poetics of a mode*, Princeton
Parrinder, P. (2006) *Nation and novel: the English novel from its origins to the present day*, Oxford
Parry, A. (1963) 'The two voices of Virgil's *Aeneid*', *Arion* 2: 66–80
Paschalis, M. and Frangoulidis, S. eds (2002) *Space in the ancient novel, Ancient Narrative Supplementum 1*, Groningen
Paschalis, M., Frangoulidis, S., Harrison, S. and Zimmerman, M. eds (2007) *The Greek and the Roman novel: parallel readings, Ancient Narrative Supplementum 8*, Groningen
Paschalis, M., Panayotakis, S. and Schmeling, G. eds (2009) *Readers and writers in the ancient novel, Ancient Narrative Supplementum 12*, Groningen
Pattoni, M.P. (2004) 'I Pastoralia di Longo e la contaminazione dei generi: alcune proposte interpretative', *MD* 53: 83–123
Paulsen, T. (1992) *Inszenierung des Schiksals: Tragödie und Komödie im Roman des Heliodor*, Trier
Pavel, T.G. (2003) 'Literary genres as norms and good habits', *New Literary History* 34: 201–10
Pearcy, L.T. (1978) 'Achilles Tatius, *Leucippe and Clitophon* 1.14–15: an unnoticed lacuna?', *CPh* 73: 233–5
Peine, A. (1998) 'Agathe Tyche im Spiegel der griechischen und römischen Plastik: Untersuchungen Klassicher Statuentypen und ihre kaiserzeitliche Rezeption', Diss. Münster
Pelling, C.B.R. (1990) 'Childhood and personality in Greek biography', in Pelling ed. (1990): 213–44
Pelling, C.B.R. ed. (1990) *Characterization and individuality in Greek literature*, Oxford
 (2002) 'Speech and action: Herodotus' debate on the constitutions', *PCPS* 48: 123–58
Perkins, J. (1995) *The suffering self: pain and narrative representation in the early Christian era*, London
 (1999) 'An ancient 'passing' novel: Heliodorus' *Aithiopika*', *Arethusa* 32: 197–214
Pernot, L. (1997) *Éloges grecs de Rome: discours traduits et commentés*, Paris
Perrin-Saminadayar, É. (2004) 'L'éphébie attique de la crise mithridatique à Hadrien', in Follet, S. ed., *L'Hellénisme d'époque romaine: nouveaux documents, nouvelles approches (Ier s. a.C – IIIe s. p.C.)*, Paris: 87–103
Perry, B.E. (1967) *The ancient romances: a literary-historical account of their origins*, Berkeley and Los Angeles
Petri, R. (1963) *Über den Roman des Chariton*, Meisenheim-am-Glan

Petsalis-Diomidis, A. (2006) 'The body in space: visual dynamics in healing pilgrimage', in Elsner and Rutherford eds (2005): 183–218
Philippides, M. (1983) 'The proemium in Longus' *Lesbiaká*', *CB* 19: 32–5
Piccirilli L. (1984) 'Il filolaconismo, l'incesto e l'ostracismo di Cimone', *QS* 10: 171–77
Picone, M. and Zimmermann, B. eds (1997) *Der antike Roman und seine mittelalterliche Rezeption*, Basel, Boston and Berlin
Plazenet, L. (1995) 'Le Nil et son delta dans les romans grecs', *Phoenix* 49: 5–22
Plepelits, K. (1980) *Achilleus Tatios, Leukippe und Kleitophon*, Stuttgart
Polkinghorne, D.E. (1995) 'Narrative configuration in quantitative analysis', *Qualitative Studies in Education* 8: 5–23
Porter, J. (2003) 'Chariton and Lysias 1: further considerations', *Hermes* 131: 433–40
Porter, J.I and Buchan, M. eds (2004) *Before subjectivity? Lacan and the classics*, Lubbock = *Helios* 31
Postl, B. (1970) *Die Bedeutung des Nil in der römischen Literatur: mit besonderer Berücksichtigung der wichtigsten griechischen Autoren*, Diss. Vienna
Pouderon, B., Hunzinger, C. and Kasprzyk, D. eds (2001) *Les personnages du roman grec: actes du colloque de Tours, 18–20 novembre 1999*, Paris
Price, S.R.F. (1984) *Rituals and power: the Roman imperial cult in Asia minor*, Cambridge
Prince, G. (1992) *Narrative as theme: studies in French fiction*, Lincoln NA
Puech, B. (2002) *Orateurs et sophistes grecs dans les inscriptions de l'époque impériale*, Paris
Quint, D. (1993) *Epic and empire: politics and generic form from Vergil to Milton*, Princeton
Race, W.H. (1978) 'Panathenaicus 74–90: the rhetoric of Isocrates' digression on Agamemnon', *TAPA* 107: 175–86
Radway, J. (1987) *Reading the romance: women, patriarchy, and popular literature*, London
Ramelli, I. (2001) *I romanzi antichi e il Cristianesimo: contesto e contatti*, Madrid
Rattenbury, R.M. and Lumb, T.W. eds (1960) *Héliodore, Les Éthiopiques*, 2nd edn, Paris
Reardon, B.P. (1969) 'The Greek novel', *Phoenix* 23: 291–309; repr. in Gärtner ed. (1984): 218–36
  (1991) *The form of Greek romance*, Princeton
  (1994) 'Achilles Tatius and ego-narrative', in Morgan and Stoneman eds (1994): 80–96; repr. in Swain ed. (1999): 243–58
Reardon, B.P. ed. (1989) *Collected ancient Greek novels*, Berkeley, Los Angeles and London; repr. (2008) with a new foreword by J.R. Morgan
  (2004) *De Callirhoe narrationes amatoriae*, Munich and Leipzig
Reeve, M.D. (1989) 'Conceptions', *PCPS* 35: 81–112
  (1994) *Longus, Daphnis et Chloe*, ed. correctior, Stuttgart
Reeves, B.T. (2007) 'The role of the *ekphrasis* in plot development: the painting of Europa and the bull in Achilles Tatius' *Leucippe and Clitophon*', *Mnemosyne* 60: 87–101

Rehm, R. (1994) *Marriage to death: the conflation of wedding and funeral rituals in Greek tragedy*, Princeton
Reitzenstein, R. (1906) *Hellenistische Wundererzählungen*, Leipzig
Repath, I. (2005) 'Achilles Tatius' Leucippe and Clitophon: what happened next?', *CQ* 55: 250–65
Reynolds, J.M. (1982) *Aphrodisias and Rome*, JRS monograph 1, London
  (1986) 'Further information on imperial cult at Aphrodisias', *StudClas* 24: 109–17
Rhodes, P.J. (2003) 'Nothing to do with democracy: Athenian drama and the *polis*', *JHS* 123: 104–19
Richardson, N.J. (1974) *The Homeric Hymn to Demeter*, Oxford
Ricoeur, P. (1984–1988) *Time and narrative*, trans. K. McLaughlin and D. Pellauer, Chicago and London
Riedwieg, C. (1987) *Mysterienterminologie bei Plato, Philon und Klemens von Alexandria*, Berlin
Rijksbaron, A. (1984) 'Chariton 8, 1, 4 und Aristot., *Poet*. 1449b28', *Philologus* 128: 306–07
Rimell, V. ed. (2007) *Seeing tongues, hearing scripts: orality and representation in the ancient novel*, Ancient Narrative Supplementum 7, Groningen
Rissman, L. (1983) *Love as war: Homeric allusion in the poetry of Sappho*, Königstein
Roberts, D.H. (1997) 'Afterword: ending and aftermath, ancient and modern', in Roberts *et al.* eds (1997): 251–73
Roberts, D.H., Dunn, F. and Fowler, D. eds (1997) *Classical closure: reading the end in Greek and Latin literature*, Princeton
Robiano, P. (1984) 'La notion de *tyché* chez Chariton et chez Héliodore', *REG* 97: 543–49
  (2002) 'Lycénion, Mélité, ou la satisfaction du désir', *Pallas* 60: 363–73
Rogers, G.M. (1991) *The sacred identity of Ephesos: foundation myths of a Roman City*, London and New York
Rohde, E. (1914) *Der griechische Roman und seine Vorläufer 3*, rev. W. Schmid, Berlin; repr. (1960) Hildesheim
Rohde, G. (1937) 'Longus und die Bukolik', *RhM* 86: 23–49; repr. in Gärtner ed. (1984): 361–86
Roisman, H. (1990) '*Kerdion* in the *Iliad*: profit and trickiness', *TAPA* 120: 23–35
Romeo, I. (2002) 'The Panhellenion and ethnic identity in Hadrianic Greece', *CPh* 97: 21–40
Romm, J.S. (1994) *The edges of the earth in ancient thought: geography, exploration and fiction*, Princeton
Romm, J.S. (1998) *Herodotus*, New Haven and London
Rommel, H. (1923) *Die naturwissenschaftlich-paradoxographischen Exkurse bei Philostratos, Heliodoros und Achilleus Tatios*, Stuttgart
Rose, P.W. (1988) 'Thersites and the plural voices of Homer', *Arethusa* 21: 5–25
  (1992) *Sons of the gods, children of earth: ideology and literary form in ancient Greece*, Ithaca and London
Rouechè, C. (1993) *Performers and partisans at Aphrodisias in the Roman and late Roman periods*, JRS monograph 6, London

Ruiz Montero, C. (1988) *La estructura de la novela griega: análisis funcional*, Salamanca
  (1989) 'Caritón de Afrodisias y el mundo real', in Liviabella Furiani and Scarcella eds (1989): 107–49
  (2003) 'The rise of the novel', in Schmeling ed. (2003): 29–85
Russell, D. (1992) *Dio Chrysostom, Orations* VII, XII, XXXVI, Cambridge
Russell, D.A. and Wilson, N.J. (1981) *Menander rhetor*, Oxford
Rutherford, I. (2000) 'The genealogy of the *Boukoloi*: how Greek literature appropriated an Egyptian narrative-motif', *JHS* 120: 106–21
  (2001) 'Tourism and the sacred: Pausanias and the traditions of Greek pilgrimage', in Alcock, Cherry and Elsner eds (2001): 40–52
Rutherford, R.B. (1982) 'Tragic form and feeling in the *Iliad*', *JHS* 102: 145–60; repr. in D. Cairns ed., *Oxford readings in Homer's* Iliad, Oxford 2002: 262–93
Ryan, M.-L. (2007) 'Toward a definition of narrative', in Herman ed. (2007): 22–35
Said, E. (1975) *Beginnings: intention and method*, New York
  (1978) *Orientalism*, Harmondsworth
  (1983) *The world, the text and the critic*, London
Saïd, S. (1999) 'Rural society in the Greek novel, or the country seen from the town', in Swain ed. (1999): 83–107; trans. of S. Saïd (1987) 'La société rurale dans le roman grec, ou la campagne vue de la ville', in E. Frézouls ed., *Sociétés urbaines, sociétés rurales dans l'Asie Mineure et la Syrie hellénistiques et romaines: actes du colloque organisé à Strasbourg*, Strasburg: 149–71
  (2000) 'Dio's use of mythology', in Swain ed. (2000): 161–86
Saïd, S. ed. (1991) *ΕΛΛΗΝΙΣΜΟΣ: quelques jalons pour une histoire de l'identité grecque*, Leiden
Salmon, P. (1961) 'Chariton d'Aphrodisias et la révolte égyptienne de 360 avant J-C', *Chronique d'Égypte* 36: 365–76
Sandy, G.N. (1982) 'Characterization and philosophical decor in Heliodorus' Aethiopica', *TAPA* 112: 141–67
  (2001) 'A neoplatonic interpretation of Heliodorus' *Ethiopian Story*', in A. Billault ed., *ΟΠΩΡΑ: La belle saison de l'hellénisme*, Paris: 169–78
Sanz Morales, M. and Laguna Mariscal, G. (2003) 'The relationship between Achilles and Patroclus according to Chariton of Aphrodisias', *CQ* 53: 292–5
Sartori, L. (1989) 'L'Egitto di Senofonte Efesio', in L. Criscuolo and G. Geraci eds, *Egitto e storia antica dal'Ellenismo all' età Araba*, Bologna: 657–69
Schmeling, G. (1974) *Chariton*, Boston MA
  (2005) 'Callirhoe: god-like beauty and the making of a celebrity', in Harrison et al. eds (2005): 36–49
Schmeling, G. ed. (2003) *The novel in the ancient world*, 2nd edn, Leiden
Schmitz, T. (1997) *Bildung und Macht: Zur sozialen und politischen Funktion der zweiten Sophistik in der griechischen Welt der Kaizerzeit, Zetemata 97*, Munich
Schnepf, M. (1887) 'De imitationis ratione, quae intercedit inter Heliodorum et Xenophon Ephesium', Diss. Kempten
Schofield, M. (1991) *The Stoic idea of the city*, Cambridge

Schwartz, J. (1985) 'Remarques sur les *Éphésiaques*', *AC* 54: 200–3
Schwartz, S. (2003) 'Rome in the Greek novel? Images and ideas of empire in Chariton's Persia', *Arethusa* 36: 375–94
Scobie, A. (1973) *More essays on the ancient romance and its heritage*, Meisenheim am Glan
Scourfield, D. (2003) 'Anger and gender in Chariton's *Chaereas and Callirhoe*', in S.M. Braund and G.W. Most eds, *Ancient anger: perspectives from Homer to Galen*, Cambridge: 163–84.
Scullion, S. (2005) '"Pilgrimage" and Greek religion: sacred and secular in the pagan *polis*', in Elsner, J. and Rutherford, I. eds *Pilgrimage in Greco-Roman and early Christian antiquity: seeing the gods*, Oxford: 111–30
Seaford, R. (1987) 'The tragic wedding', *JHS* 107: 106–30
  (1994) *Reciprocity and ritual: Homer and tragedy in the developing city-state*, Oxford
  (2004) *Money and the early Greek mind: Homer, philosophy, tragedy*, Cambridge
Sedelmeier, D. (1959) 'Studien zu Achilleus Tatios', *WS* 72: 113–43; repr. in Gärtner ed. (1984): 330–60
Seeck, G.A. (1990) 'Dion Chrysostomos als Homerkritiker (*Or.* 11)', *RhM* 133: 97–107
Segal, C.P. (1962) 'The Phaeacians and the symbolism of Odysseus' return', *Arion* 1: 17–64; reworked as 'The Phaeacians and Odysseus' return' in Segal (1994): 12–64
  (1967) 'Transition and ritual in Odysseus' return', *PP* 116: 321–42; revised and repr. in Segal (1994): 65–84
  (1994) *Singers, heroes and gods in the Odyssey*, Ithaca
Seitel, P. (2003) 'Theorizing genres – interpreting works', *New Literary History* 24: 275–97
Selden, D. (1994) 'Genre of genre', in Tatum ed. (1994): 39–64
Sharples, R.W. (1983) *Alexander of Aphrodisias On Fate*, London
Shaw, B.D. (1996) 'Body/power/identity: passions of the martyrs', *Journal of Early Christian Studies* 4: 269–312
Silk, M. (2002) *Aristophanes and the definition of comedy*, Oxford
Sinko, T. (1906) 'De Homero Aegyptio', *Eos* 13: 12–20
Sipiora, P. and Baumlin, R.S. eds (2002) *Rhetoric and kairos: essays in history, theory, and praxis*, Albany
Sironen, E. (2003) 'Inscriptions in Greco-Roman novels', in Panayotakis *et al.* eds (2003): 289–300
Slater, N. (2005) 'And there's another country: translation as metaphor in Heliodorus', in Harrison *et al.* eds (2005): 106–22
Smith, B.H. (1968) *Poetic closure: a study of how poems end*, Chicago
Smith, R.R.R. (1988) '*Simulacra gentium*: the *ethne* from the Sebasteion at Aphrodisias', *JRS* 78: 50–77
  (2006) *Aphrodisias II: Roman portrait statuary from Aphrodisias*, Mainz am Rhein
Smith, S.D. (2007) *Greek identity and the Athenian past in Chariton: the romance of empire, Ancient Narrative Supplementum 9*, Groningen

Somers, M.R. (1994) 'The narrative constitution of identity: a relational and network approach', *Theory and Society* 23: 605–49
Sontag, S. (1971) 'Godard', in *Styles of radical will*, New York
Sperber, D. and Wilson, D. (1995) *Relevance: communication and cognition*, 2nd edn, Oxford
Speyer, W. (1970) *Bücherfunde in der Glaubenswerbung der Antike*, Göttingen
Spivak, G. (2004) 'Harlem', *Social Text* 22: 113–39
Stanzel, K.-H. (1991) 'Frühlingserwachen auf dem Lande: zur erotischen Entwicklung im Hirtenroman des Longos', *WJA* 17: 153–75
Starcky, J. (1975–1976) 'Stèle d'Elahagabal', *MUSJ* 49: 503–20
Stark, I. (1989) 'Religiöse Elemente im antiken Roman', in Kuch ed. (1989): 135–49
Stephens, S.A. (1994) 'Who read ancient novels?', in Tatum ed (1994): 405–18
  (2008) 'Cultural identity', in Whitmarsh ed. (2008): 56–71
Stephens, W. (1994) 'Tasso's Heliodorus and the world of romance', in Tatum ed. (1994): 67–87
Strawson, G. (2004) 'Against narrativity', *Ratio* 17: 428–52; abbreviated version 'A fallacy of our age: not every life is a narrative', *Times Literary Supplement* 15 October 2004: 13–15
Strohmaier, G. (1976) 'Übersehenes zur Biographie Lukians', *Philologus* 120: 117–22
Stroumsa, G. (1999) *Barbarian philosophy: the religious revolution of early Christianity*, Tübingen
Struck, P. (2004) *The birth of the symbol: ancient readers at the limits of their texts*, Princeton
Sturgess, P.J.M. (1992) *Narrativity: theory and practice*, Oxford
Swain, S.C.R. (1989) 'Character change in Plutarch', *Phoenix* 43: 62–8
  (1996) *Hellenism and empire: language, classicism, and power in the Greek world, AD 50–250*, Oxford
  (2007) 'Polemon's *Physiognomy*', in Swain ed., *Seeing the face, seeing the soul: Polemon's* Physiognomy *from classical antiquity to mediaeval Islam*, Oxford: 125–201
Swain, S.C.R. ed. (1999) *Oxford readings in the Greek novel*, Oxford
  (2000) *Dio Chrysostom: politics, letters, and philosophy*, Oxford
Swain, S.C.R., Harrison, S.J. and Elsner, J. eds (2007) *Severan culture*, Cambridge
Szepessy, T. (1957) 'Die *Aithiopika* des Heliodoros und der griechische sophistische Liebesroman', *AAAHung* 5: 241–59; repr. in Gärtner ed. (1984): 432–50
Szepessy, T. (1972) 'The story of the girl who died on the day of her wedding', *AAAHung* 20: 341–57
Taplin, O. (1999) 'Spreading the word through performance', in S. Goldhill and R. Osborne eds, *Performance culture and Athenian democracy*, Cambridge: 33–57
Tarán, L. (1992) 'The authorship of an allegorical interpretation of Heliodorus' *Aethiopica*', in M.-O. Goulet-Caze et al. eds, ΣΟΦΙΗΣ ΜΑΙΗΤΟΡΕΣ: *Chercheurs de sagesse: Hommage Jean Pépin*, Paris: 203–30
Tatum, J. (1997) 'Herodotus the fabulist', in Picone and Zimmermann eds (1997): 29–48

Tatum J. ed. (1994) *The search for the ancient novel*, Baltimore
Taylor, C. (1989) *Sources of the self: the making of the modern identity*, Cambridge
Teske, D. (1991) *Der Roman des Longos als Werk des Kunst*, Münster
Thomas, R. (2000) 'A trope by any other name: "polysemy", ambiguity and *significatio* in Virgil', *HSCP* 100: 381–407
  (2001) *Virgil and the Augustan reception*, Cambridge
Tilg, S. (2010) *Chariton of Aphrodisias and the invention of romance*, Oxford
Todorov, T. (1977) *The poetics of prose*, trans. R. Howard, Cornell
Tomashevsky, B. (1965) 'Thematics', in L.T. Lemon and M.J. Reis eds, *Russian formalist criticism: four essays*, Lincoln NA: 61–95
Toohey, P. (2004) *Melancholy, love, and time: boundaries of the self in ancient literature*, Ann Arbor
Tracy, S. (1994) '*IG*II^2 1195 and Agathe Tyche in Africa', *Hesperia* 63: 241–4
Trapp, M.B. (1990) 'Plato's *Phaedrus* in the second century', in D.A. Russell ed. *Antonine literature*, Oxford: 141–73
Trenkner, S. (1958) *The Greek novella in the classical period*, Cambridge
Trzaskoma, S. (2005) 'A novelist writing "history": Longus' Thucydides again', *GRBS* 45: 75–90
Tsagarakis, O. (1973) 'κατάχρησις of the Aristotelian term ἐπεισόδιον as applied to Homer', *REG* 86: 294–307
Tümpel, K. (1894) 'Ἀλκίνου ἀπόλογοι', *Philologus* 52: 523–33
Turcan, R. (1963) 'Le roman "initiatique": à propos d'un livre récent', *RHR* 163: 149–99
  (1992) 'L'élaboration des mystères dionysiaques à l'époque impériale: de l'orgiasme à l'initiation', in Moreau ed. (1992): 215–33
Turner, V. (1967) *The forest of symbols: aspects of Ndembu ritual*, Ithaca
  (1969) *The ritual process: structure and anti-structure*, London
Tzanetou, A. (2002) 'Something to do with Demeter: ritual and performance in Aristophanes' *Women at the Thesmophoria*', *AJP* 123.3: 329–67
Valley, G. (1926) *Über den Sprachgebrauch des Longus*, Uppsala
van Bremen, R. (1996) *The limits of participation: women and civic life in the Greek east in the Hellenistic and Roman periods*, Gieben
Van der Stockt, L. (1992) *Twinkling and twilight: Plutarch's reflections on literature*, Brussells
van Gennep, A. (1960) *The rites of passage*, trans. M.B. Vizedom and G.L. Caffee, London and Henley
Van Thiel, H. (1971) *Der Eselsroman I: Untersuchungen, Zetemata 54*, Munich
Vermeule, E. (1979) *Aspects of death in early Greek art and poetry*, Berkeley
Versnel, H.S. (1990) 'What's sauce for the goose is sauce for the gander: myth and ritual, old and new', in L. Edmunds ed., *Approaches to Greek myth*, Baltimore: 23–90
Veyne, P. (1978) 'La famille et l'amour sous le Haut-Empire romain', *Annales ESC* 33: 35–63; repr. (1991) as *La société romaine*, Paris: 88–130
Vidal-Naquet, P. (1986a) *The black hunter: forms of thought and forms of society in the Greek world*, trans. A. Szegedy-Maszak, Baltimore

(1986b) 'The black hunter revisited', *PCPS* 32: 126–44
Vilborg, E. (1955) *Achilles Tatius*, Leucippe and Clitophon, Stockholm
  (1962) *Achilles Tatius,* Leucippe and Clitophon: *a commentary*, Stockholm
Vizedom, M. (1976) *Rites and relationships: rites of passage and contemporary anthropology* = Sage Research Papers in the Social Sciences 4
Vogt-Spira, G. (1992) *Dramaturgie des Zufalls: Tyche und Handeln in der Komödie Menanders*, Munich
Vout, C. (2006) 'What's in a beard? Rethinking Hadrian's Hellenism', in S. Goldhill and R. Osborne eds, *Rethinking revolutions through ancient Greece*, Cambridge: 96–123
Walden, J.W.H. (1894) 'Stage terms in Heliodorus' *Aethiopica*', *HSCP* 5: 1–43
Walsh, G.B. (1984) *The varieties of enchantment: early Greek views of the nature and function of poetry*, Chapel Hill
Walsh, P.G. (1988) 'The rights and wrongs of curiosity (Plutarch to Augustine)', *G&R* 35: 73–85
Watanabe, A. (2003) 'The masculinity of Hippothous', *AN* 3: 1–42
Watson, G. (1988) *Phantasia in classical thought*, Galway
Webb, R. (2008) *Demons and dancers: performance in late antiquity*, Cambridge MA
  (2009) *Ekphrasis: imagination and performance in rhetorical theory and practice*, Farnham
Webber, A. (1989) 'The hero tells his name: formula and variation in the Phaeacian episode of the *Odyssey*', *TAPA* 119: 1–13
Weiss, M. (1998) '*Erotica*: on the prehistory of Greek desire', *HSCP* 98: 31–61
Weißenberger, M. (1997) 'Der "Götterapparat" im Roman des Chariton', in Picone and Zimmermann eds (1997): 49–73
West, M.L. (1966) *Hesiod*, Theogony, Oxford
West, M.L. (2003) *Greek epic fragments*, Cambridge MA
West, S. (2003) 'ΚΕΡΚΙΔΟΣ ΠΑΡΑΜΥΘΙΑ? For whom did Chariton write?', *ZPE* 143: 63–9
Whitehead, D. and Blyth, P.H. (2004) *Athenaeus mechanicus*, On machines, trans. with introduction and commentary, Stuttgart
Whitmarsh, T. (1998) 'The birth of a prodigy: Heliodorus and the genealogy of Hellenism', in Hunter ed. (1998): 93–124
  (1999) 'The writes of passage: cultural initiation in Heliodorus', in R.T. Miles ed. *Constructing identities in late antiquity*, London: 16–40
  (2001a) *Greek literature and the Roman empire: the politics of imitation*, Oxford
  (2001b) *Achilles Tatius,* Leucippe and Clitophon: *translated with notes*, Oxford
  (2002a) 'Alexander's Hellenism and Plutarch's textualism', *CQ* 52: 174–92
  (2002b) 'Written on the body: perception, deception and desire in Heliodorus' *Aethiopica*', *Ramus* 31: 111–24
  (2003) 'Reading for pleasure: narrative, irony, and erotics in Achilles Tatius', in Panayotakis *et al.* eds (2003): 191–205

(2004a) 'Philostratus,' in de Jong *et al.* eds (2004): 423–39
(2004b) 'The Cretan lyre paradox: Mesomedes, Hadrian and the poetics of patronage', in B.E. Borg ed., *Paideia: the world of the second sophistic*, Berlin: 377–402
(2005a) *The second sophistic, G&R New Surveys in the Classics*, Oxford
(2005b) 'The Greek novel: titles and genre', *AJP* 126: 587–611
(2005c) 'Quickening the classics: the politics of prose in Roman Greece', in J.I. Porter ed., *Classical pasts: the classical traditions of Greco-Roman antiquity*, Princeton: 353–74
(2005d) 'Dialogues in love: Bakhtin and his critics on the Greek novel', in Branham ed. (2005): 107–29
(2005e) 'Heliodorus smiles', in Harrison *et al.* eds (2005): 87–105
(2005f) 'The lexicon of love: Longus and Philetas grammatikos', *JHS* 125 (2005): 145–8
(2007a) 'Prose literature and the Severan dynasty', in Swain *et al.* eds (2007): 29–51
(2007b) 'Josephus, Joseph and the Greek novel', *Ramus* 36: 78–95
(2008) 'Class', in Whitmarsh ed. (2008): 72–87
(2009a) 'Performing heroics: language, landscape and identity in Philostratus' *Heroicus*', in E. Bowie and J. Elsner eds, *Philostratus*, Cambridge: 205–29
(2009b) 'Divide and rule: segmenting *Callirhoe* and related works', in M. Paschalis *et al.* eds, *Books and readers in the ancient novel*, Groningen: 36–50
(2010a) 'Roman Hellenism', in A. Barchiesi and W. Scheidel eds, *The Oxford handbook of Roman studies*, Oxford: 728–47
(2010b) 'Domestic poetics: Hippias' house in Achilles Tatius', *ClAnt* 29: 327–48
(2010c) 'Metamorphoses of the *Ass*', in F. Mestre ed., *Lucian of Samosata: Greek writer and Roman citizen*, Barcelona: 73–81
(2010d) 'Prose fiction', in M. Cuypers and J. Clauss eds, *A companion to Hellenistic literature*, Oxford: 395–411
Whitmarsh, T. ed. (2008) *The Cambridge companion to the Greek and Roman novel*, Cambridge
Whitmarsh, T. and Bartsch, S. (2008) 'Narrative', in Whitmarsh ed. (2008): 237–57
Wiersma, S. (1990) 'The ancient Greek novel and its heroines: a female paradox', *Mnemosyne* 43: 109–23
Willink, C.W. (1986) *Euripides, Orestes*, Oxford
Wills, L. (1995) *The Jewish novel in the ancient world*, Ithaca
Winkler, J.J. (1980) 'Lollianus and the desperadoes', *JHS* 155–81
  (1982) 'The mendacity of Kalasiris and the narrative strategy of Heliodorus' *Aithiopika*', *YCS* 27: 93–158; repr. in Swain ed. (1999): 286–350
  (1985) *Auctor and actor: a narratological reading of Apuleius*' The golden ass, Berkeley and Oxford
  (1990) *The constraints of desire: the anthropology of sex and gender in ancient Greece*, New York and London

Winter, I.J. (1995) 'Homer's Phoenicians: history, ethnography or literary trope? [A perspective on early orientalism]', in J.B. Carter and S.P. Morris eds, *The ages of Homer: a tribute to Emily Townsend Vermeule*, Austin: 247–71

Witt, R.E. (1971) *Isis in the Graeco-Roman World*, Ithaca; repr. (1997) as *Isis in the ancient world*, Baltimore

Wouters, A. (1989–90) 'The EIKONES in Longus' *Daphnis and Chloë* 4.39.2: Beglaubigungsapparat?', *SEJG* 31 (= M. Geerard ed., *Opes Atticae: miscellanea philologica et historica Raymondo Bogaert et Hermanno van Looy*, The Hague): 465–79

Wright, M. (2005) *Euripides' escape-tragedies*, Oxford

Wright, M. (2007) 'Comedy and the Trojan War', *CQ* 57: 412–31

Yatromanolakis, D. and Roilos, P. eds (2004) *Greek ritual poetics*, Washington DC

Yildirim, B. (2004) 'Identities and empire: local mythology and the self-representation of Aphrodisias', in B.E. Borg ed., *Paideia: the world of the second sophistic*, Berlin (2004): 23–52

Zanker, P. (1988) *The power of images in the age of Augustus*, trans. A. Shapiro, Ann Arbor

Zeitlin, F.I. (1990) 'The poetics of eros: nature, art and imitation in Longus' Daphnis and Chloe', in Halperin *et al.* eds (1990): 417–64

  (2001) 'Visions and revisions of Homer', in S. Goldhill ed., *Being Greek under Rome: cultural identity, the second sophistic, and the development of empire*, Cambridge: 195–266

  (2003) 'Living portraits and sculpted bodies in Chariton's theater of romance', in Panayotakis *et al.* eds (2003): 71–83

  (2008) 'Religion', in Whitmarsh ed. (2008): 91–108

Zhao, H.Y.H. (2006) 'Historiography and fiction in Chinese culture', in Moretti ed. (2006a): 69–93

Zimmermann, B. (1999) 'Zur Funktion der Bildbeschreibungen im griechischen Roman', *Poetica* 31: 61–79

Zimmermann, F. (1949/50) 'Die Ἐφεσιακά des sog. Xenophon von Ephesos: Untersuchungen zur Technik und Komposition', *WJA* 4: 252–86; repr. in Gärtner ed. (1984): 295–329

Zimmermann, F. (1961) 'Chariton und die Geschichte', in R. Günther and G. Schrot eds, *Sozialökonomische Verhältnisse im alten Orient und im klassischen Altertum*, Berlin: 329–45

Index

Figures in bold are references to ancient texts. Discussions of individual passages are only indexed where they are substantial.

Achilles Tatius: Alexandrian? 74–5; 'anti-closural' 107, 232; Calligone 163–4; Clinias 162–3, 207–10; cultural perspective 79–82; desire, representation of 149–50; digressions 238, 242–6; false death ('*Scheintod*') 162, 208–9; first-person (homodiegetic) narration 85–93, 161–2; *Leucippe and Clitophon* **1.1.1** 76–7; **1.1.2** 76, 77–8; **1.1.2–13** 79–80; **1.2.1** 78; **1.3.2** 198; **1.3.4** 163–4, 201; **1.6.6** 90; **1.7.1** 102–3; **1.8.4** 103; **1.9.1–2** 103; **1.9.7** 207–8; **1.10.1** 104; **1.11.2** 150, 151; **1.13.2** 162; **1.14.1** 162; **1.15.1** 90–1, 162; **1.16–18** 243–4, 246; **2.2** 81, 83; **2.13** 172; **2.14.6–10** 245–6; **2.35–8** 160; **2.38.1** 210; **3.15.5–6** 208; **4.1.3–8** 149, 150–5; **4.3.2–5** 244–5; **5.1** 83–5; **5.5.2–3** 81; **5.7** 208; **5.17** 215; **5.18.4–5** 165; **5.27.4** 104; **6.16.6** 216; **7.2.3** 187; **7.5.2** 208–9; **7.6.2** 209–10; **8.4–5** 91–3; **8.17.5** 105, 106; **8.19.2** 102, 150, 151; Melite 164–5; metamorphosis theme 106–7; mystery language 102–4, 207; prophecy 201; unreliable narration 90–3; *Varied history* 242–3

Acts of the pagan martyrs 31
Aelian, *On providence* 197
Agias of Troezen 14
Aidōs (shame/modesty) 63, 64–5
Alexander romance **3.18–23** 74
allegory 129–35, 195
Althusser, Louis 140, 141, 156
Alvares, Jean 54
Anaximenes 241
Andromeda 116–17, 124
anger 35, 60
Anonymus Crameri II = *On comedy* (anon.) 231
Anonymus Seguerianus **61** 238–9
Antoninus Liberalis 107

Antonius Diogenes: documentarism 87–8; Phoenician translation? 88; *Wonders beyond Thule* 69
Aphrodisias 26–8
Aphrodite 27–8, 55, 60
Apollo *see* Heliodorus, Apollo; Xenophon of Ephesus, Apollo
Apollodorus, *Library* 116
Apollonius of Rhodes 205
Apollonius of Tyana 72, 154 *see also* Philostratus, *Apollonius*
Apuleius, *Metamorphoses* 185, 215; **11.15** 249
Aristarchus 63
Aristides, Aelius: *Sacred tales* 196; *To Rome* **29** 259
Aristophanes 259; *Frogs* 142; *Lysistrata* 16, 59, 60; *Thesmophoriazusae* 116
Aristophanes of Byzantium 63
Aristotle: *Poetics* 205; **1450b** 40; **1451b** 236; **1452a** 231; **1452b–53a** 177; **1453a–54b** 61; **1455b** 236; *Politics* **1253a** 221; *Rhetoric* **1418a** 236
Aristoxenus 240
Arrian, *Anabasis* **1.3.5** 143
Artemidorus of Daldis 196
Artemis *see* Heliodorus, Artemis; Xenophon of Ephesus, Artemis
Artemis, Ephesian cult of 29–30
artworks, descriptions of 93–6, 172–6
Ass narratives 107, 215; *see also* Apuleius, *Metamorphoses*
Astarte/Ištar 79–80
Astrampsychus 196
Athenaeus, *Deipnosophists* 241
Athenaeus 'the mechanic' **4** 237
Augustine 78
Augustus 26

295

Bakhtin, Mikhail 17, 36, 40–1, 43, 46, 179, 180–2, 205
bandits 46, 158–9, 217
Barthes, Roland 173
Bartsch, Shadi 204, 239, 246
Beck, Roger 44
begging 221
Benjamin, Walter 11–12, 62
Bhabha, Homi 83–5
Bierl, Anton 46, 62
Billault, Alain 239–40
book divisions 129
Brahmans 124–5
Braun, Martin 74
Brooks, Peter 19, 36, 145, 154, 159, 182, 204, 218, 228
Burkert, Walter 101

CA Lyr. adesp. 34 250
Calligone 74
Callimachus 205; *Aetia* 240
Caracalla 71
Cave, Terence 16
Chariton, *Callirhoe*: Athens 53, 59; curiosity and rumour 186–91; desire 146–7; Dionysius 165–7; geography 51–2, 58; Ionia 52–3; naturalism of 38–9; opening scene 34–7; Persia 53–8; Polycharmus 206; privacy, association of Callirhoe with 188–90; recapitulations 59–60; Theron 217; **1.1** 38–9; **1.1.4** 35; **1.1.10** 159; **1.11.2–3** 146; **1.12.5** 224; **1.14.6–7** 146; **2.1.2** 166; **2.5** 187–8; **2.5.6–7** 215–16; **2.6.3** 157; **2.11.1–3** 166; **4.3.10** 165; **5.1.5–6** 51–2; **5.1.2** 59; **5.1.5** 222; **5.2.9** 189; **5.5.3** 189; **6.3.8** 57; **6.4.7** 173; **6.8.1** 247; **7.5.2–5** 146; **8.1.2** 182–4, 211, 246; **8.1.3** 28, 226; **8.1.4** 59, 60, 65, 140, 167, 182–3; **8.1.14–17** 63; **8.4.4** 67, 167; **8.5.15** 166; **8.7.2** 59; **8.7.3** 65; **8.7.4** 65, 66; **8.7.9–8.11** 63–4; **8.8.15–16** 67, 190–1
Christ, death and resurrection of 48
Christian asceticism 154; *see also* Martyr acts
Cicero, *On divination* 197
Clement of Alexandria, *Stromateis* **6.1.2.1** 240
Cleon 172
closure 59–68, 177–213
comic mode, in romances 230–2
commerce 217–20
Connors, Catherine 56
Constitutio Antoniniana 71
Cooper, Kate 153, 179
curiosity 185–91
Cynicism 197

Damis of Nineveh 72, 82
De Man, Paul 201

Demetrius of Phalerum, *On fortune* 250
depression 224
Derrida, Jacques 20, 87, 220
desire *see* Eros
despondency 223–32
Dictys of Crete 70, 85, 86, 88
digression (*parekbasis*) 235–40
Dio Chrysostom 233; *Orations* **1.9** 104; **7.81** 235, 238; **11** *passim* 85; **11.38** 86–7
Diogenes Laertius **1.3** 72
Diogenes of Oenoanda 197
Dionysius of Halicarnassus, *On imitation* 128; *Thucydides* **9** 237; ps.-Dionysius, *Art of rhetoric* **4.2** 253–4
Dionysius Scytobrachion 85
dreams 195–6

ecphrasis 171–6 *see also* artworks, descriptions of
Egypt, representation of 47–9
Einstein, Albert 209
Elagabalus 109, 110
Elahagabal 109, 110
Elsner, Jaś 174
Emesa 109–10
empire *see* Rome
Enargeia 171–6
encyclopedias 240–1
Ephesus 28–30, 216
Ephorus; and curiosity 187; digressiveness 237
Epictetus, *Diss.*: **1.1.7** 232; **3.24.17–18** 143–4
Epicureans: love and desire 143; predestination 197; prophecy 197
epiphany 193–5
episode (*epeisodion*) 235–40
Eros, as metanarrative plot stimulant 34–7, 38
Ethiopia, in Heliodorus 122–5
Eudaimonia 143
Euhemerus 85
Eupolemus 72
Euripides: *Andromeda* 116; *Iphigenia in Tauris* 123; *Orestes* **255–7** 172; *Phoenician women* 221
Europa, in Sidonian context 82
exegetes (religious interpreters) 99–100
exile 220–3

Favorinus 72
festivals 36
Fish, Stanley 61–2, 157, 159
fortune *see* Tukhē
Foucault, Michel 7, 160
Freud, Sigmund 20, 63, 116, 184–5, 192, 257–8
friendship (male) 206–10, 229
Frye, Northrop 17, 215
Fusillo, Massimo 240

Index

gaming metaphors 208–9, 227
Geertz, Clifford 44
Gellius, Aulus *Pref.* **2** 240
gender, complementarity in closure 59
Genette, Gérard 85
genre 12–14
Gill, Christopher 140, 257
Godard, Jean-Luc 40
gods, as figures for imperial power 32
Goldhill, Simon 170
Gorgias 180, 181

Hadrian 71
Hägg, Tomas 63, 242
Halperin, David 173–4
happy endings 61, 230–2
Hawking, Stephen 209
Hecataeus of Abdera 72
Hegesanax 85
Helen/Penelope dyad 190
Heliodorus: a Christian? 154; Emesa 109–10; *Charicleia and Theagenes*; Apollo 109, 110; art 127–8; Artemis 109, 110; desire 149, 150–5; digressions 238; intertextuality with Philostratus, *Apollonius* 120; intertextuality with Xenophon of Ephesus 117, 175; Isis and Osiris 131–2, 133–4; Nausicles 217–18; paternity theme 126–8; prophecy 201–4; religious elements 111–12; Selene 119, 124, 133, 134–5; tripartition of space and fatherhood 122; **1.1.1** 108; **1.1.8** 108; **1.2.1** 109; **1.8.6** 150, 151; **1.15.4** 173; **1.18.5** 170; **1.19.1** 170; **1.21–2** 216; **1.25.4** 152–3; **2.19.1** 221; **2.21.4–6** 25; **2.22.3–5** 233; **2.23.2** 126; **2.24.4** 234; **2.24.5** 234; **2.28.2–3** 120–1; **2.32.3** 121–2; **2.33.5** 151; **2.34.2–8** 125–6; **2.35.5** 201–3; **2.36.2** 119, 203; **3.1.2** 235; **3.4.7–9** 172–6; **3.12–15** 131; **3.14.2–4** 113–14; **4.4.2** 233; **4.10.6** 152; **4.18.2** 222; **4.19–21** 118; **5.4.5** 170–1; **5.4.6** 152; **5.6–7** 225–30; **5.12.1** 155; **5.15.1** 218; **6.7.9** 226; **6.9.4** 152; **6.11.3–4** 221; **6.15.4** 115; **7.6.4** 247–8; **7.14.5–6** 126–7; **7.21.5** 232; **8.1.1–2** 129–30; **8.8.91–5** 154; **9.9.3** 131; **9.9.4–9.10.1** 131–2; **9.22** 133, 134–5; **9.24.4** 230; **9.24.8** 127; **10.13** 16; **10.15.1** 127; **10.16.2** 127; **10.16.6** 115; **10.31.5** 123; **10.34.4** 126; **10.36.1** 118; **10.37.1** 118–19; **10.41.4** 115
Helios 49–50, 109, 110–11, 119, 124, 130, 133, 134–5, 194; *see also* individual novelists
Herodotus 124; **1.1–4** 90; **1.87.1–2** 47, 194; **2.35.1** 47; **3.80–2** 57; **6.105–6** 194–5
Himeros 141
Homer: criticism 205; as Egyptian 113–14; revisionism 85–9; *Iliad* 54, 55, 142, 179, 193, 218; **1.1** 35; **1.5** 148; **6.358** 190; **19.155–83** 233; **23.700–39** 123; *Odyssey* 14, 39, 52, 64, 88, 104, 112–13, 114–15, 142, 143–4, 168, 178, 186, 205, 215, 216, 221, 256; **8.161–4** 217; **9.14** 65; **11.328–84** 233; **14.508–9** 219; **17.286–7** 233; **23.310–41** 63; **23.321** 93
Homeric Hymns: *to Apollo* 194–5; *to Demeter* 15, 142; *to Dionysus* 194–5
Huet, Pierre-Daniel 6
Huizinga, Johan 252
human sacrifice 123
Hunter, Richard 133–4

Iamblichus: name and background 75; *Babyloniaca* 69, 74, 101
imperial cult, Roman 57
incest 163–4
initiation 101–6 *see also* passage rites
Iolaus 44–5
Isis *see* Heliodorus, Isis and Osiris; Xenophon of Ephesus, Isis and Osiris
Isocrates 125
Ištar/Astarte 79–80
iterative narration 34

Jakobson, Roman 204
Jewish narrative 31 *see also Joseph and Aseneth*
Joseph and Aseneth 25, 69, 129
Josephus 72
Julia Domna 109
Julian (emperor) 111

Kellman, Steven 62, 94
Kennedy, Duncan 171
Kerényi, Karl 15
Kermode, Frank 177
kingship 32, 55, 56–8, 251
König, Jason 62–3

Lacan, Jacques 139–40, 145, 146
Lalanne, Sophie 43–4
lamentation 208–9, 225–8
Lessing, Gotthold 95
liminality 214
Lollianus, *Phoenicica* 74, 88
'Longinus', *On the sublime* **15.1** 172
Longus: name 75; *Daphnis and Chloe*; desire, representation of 148; Lycaenion 165; metamorphosis theme 106–7; mystery language in 104–6; **1. pr.** 93–6; **1. pr. 2** 94, 95; **1. pr. 3** 210–11; **1. pr. 3–4** 97; **1.11.1** 148; **1.13.3** 148; **2.3.2** 104; **2.7** 104; **2.12.1** 96; **2.23.2** 148; **2.26–7** 194–5; **2.27.2** 148; **2.34.2–8** 125–6; **3.18** 170; **3.18.2** 105; **4.11.1** 96; **4.37.1** 73; **4.38.2** 106; **4.39.1** 73; **4.40.3** 105, 106
Lotman, Yuri 66

love rivals 155–67
Lowe, Nick 193, 212
Lucian 72; *Jupiter confutatus* 197; *Jupiter tragoedus* 197; *True stories* 85; **1.5** 185–6

Macintyre, Alasdair 4, 255
male passivity 224, 231–2
Marcellus, M. Claudius 237
marriage 37–8, 40, 101, 153, 253–4
Martin Guerre 16
martyr acts 31, 140, 156
Memnon 124
Menander: on Tukhē 249; *Shield* (**97–9** 193; **147–8** 248)
Merkelbach, Reinhold 27, 44
Meroe 110
metalepsis 85, 94, 99
metamorphosis narratives 106–7
Metiochus and Parthenope 31, 69, 241–2
Miller, D.A. 19, 61, 191
Mimēsis 128
miscellanies 240–1
money, and identity 218–19
Montiglio, Silvia 220
moon *see* Selene
Morales, Helen 157–8, 168–9, 171, 239, 246
Morgan, John 41, 42–5, 191–3, 196, 204, 225
Moschus, *Europa* 89

Nakatani, Saiichiro 239
narrative transmission 85–9
Neoplatonism; on predestination 197
Nergal and Ereshkigal 15
New Comedy 16; *see also* comic mode, in romances
Nile, representation of in Heliodorus 119–22, 130
Nimis, Steven 83, 129, 179–80, 183–4, 211
Ninus romance 30–1, 69
Nostos see return narrative
novels, cost and circulation of 215–20

obscenity 171
Oenomaus of Gadara 197
ogkhos 228
On comedy (anon.) = *Anonymus Crameri* II 231
oracles 195–204
Osiris 131–2, 133–4; *see also* Heliodorus, Isis and Osiris; Xenophon of Ephesus, Isis and Osiris
Ovid 135

Pamphila 240
Pan 194–5
Panhellenion 71

paradigmatic reading 204–11
Parker, Patricia 18
Parthia 53–8
passage rites 17, 41, 42–5
Paul and Thecla 140, 153
Pausanias 99, 196; **1.43.6** 141
pederasty 159–63; *see also* friendship (male)
Penelope *see* Helen/Penelope dyad
Peregrinus, Proteus 154
Periergia see curiosity
peripatetics, on predestination 197
Perry, Ben Edwin 6
Perseus 116–17, 124
Phantasia 171
Philip of Amphipolis, *Rhodiaka* 31
Philip the philosopher 132–3, 151
Philo, *On dreams* 197
Philodemus of Gadara 197
Philostratus, Flavius: *Apollonius* 72, 76, 77–8, 82, 120, 124–5, 154; **4.32.2** 218; *Heroicus* 73, 85; **53.3** 219; *Imagines* 174; *Lives of the sophists* 8
Phoenician 'translations' 88
Photius: *Library* **50a** 153; *AP* **9.203** 168–9
pilgrimage 99–100
Pindar 33, 50
pirates 158–9, 217
Plato: *Cratylus* **420a** 142; *Laws* **644d, 803c** 209; mystery language in 101, 111–12; *Phaedrus* 90; **264b** 236; **275d** 220; *Symposium* 104; **185d** 241; **199b** 242; *Timaeus* 72; *see also* Neoplatonism
Plutarch: *On curiosity* **516d, 517e–f** 187; **520c** 187; *Delphic dialogues* 196; *How a young man should listen to poetry* **25d** 205–6; *Isis and Osiris* **360e–f, 366a** 132; *Life of Themistocles* 107; *On divination* 196; *Political advice* 56
Polupragmosunē see curiosity
Polycrates of Samos 241
Pothos, meaning of 142
pragmatic linguistics 239
Prince, Gerald 184
prophecy 191–204
prostitution 217
Proteus (mythical god) 234
pseudo-documentarism 86–9
psychology, claimed absence in ancient romance 41

Quint, David 18

rape 157–9
Reardon, Bryon 32
reception, politics of 100
return narrative 14–15

Index

'return of Hephaestus' 15
Rhodes 29, 49
Ricoeur, Paul 4
ritual, as narrative articulation 36, 44
roads, metaphors of 207–8
Rohde, Erwin 6, 8
romance, definition of genre 12–14
Rome 31–2, 55–8, 251

Said, Edward 34, 70, 76, 109
Salutaris, C. Vibius 30
Samos 31
Schmeling, Gareth 189
Schwartz, Saundra 55, 56
sea 217
Seaford, Richard 218–19
second sophistic 8, 9–10
Selden, Daniel 79–80
Selene 49–50; *see also* individual novelists
selfhood, ancient concepts of 41
Semiramis 30–1
Sesonchosis 69
sexuality as paradigm for romance narrativity 40
Sidon, cultural background 82
singulative narration 34
Sinuhe 14
Smith, Barbara Herrnstein 177
Sopater 101
Spivak, Gayatri 124
statuschange 215
Stesichorus 15
Stoics: determinism 197; *to kathēkon peristatikon* 166; love and desire 143–4; *phantasia* 171; 'up to us' 231–2
suicide 228–9
Sulla 26, 29
sun *see* Helios
symposium 240–2
syntagmatic reading 204–11
Syracuse 55–6

Tale of the shipwrecked sailor 14
Taylor, Charles 4, 158, 255

Theon, Aelius 174
Theopompus: and curiosity 187; digressiveness 237
Thucydides 53, 237; **3.38.4** 172; **6.24.3** 143
Timaeus, digressiveness 237
Todorov, Tzvetan 18
Tomashevsky, Boris 34
traders 217–20
tragic mode, in romances 223–32
Tukhē 28, 183–4, 208–9, 211, 246–51
Turner, Victor 44, 214
Tyrtaeus **fr. 10.4** 221
Tzetzes, John 231

Van Gennep, Arnold 15, 41, 42–5, 214
Vergil, *Aeneid* 179
Veyne, Paul 7

wandering 225–6; in narrative 232–46
Winkler, John 172, 191–3, 196, 207, 219
women, trading of 217–20

Xenophon of Athens: *Anabasis* 54; (**4.7.24** 52); *Cyropaedia* **6.1.14** 104
Xenophon of Cyprus, *Cypriaca* 31
Xenophon of Ephesus *Anthia and Habrocomes*: Apollo 49–50; Artemis 49–50; desire, representation of 147; geography in 45–50; Hippothous and Hyperanthes 161, 207; intertextuality 194; Isis and Osiris 48–50; opening of 34–7; prophecy 198–201; **1.11.1** 148; **1.2.1** 35; **1.2–9** 33, 37–8; **1.6.2** 48, 198–9; **1.7.1** 200; **1.8.2–3** 38; **1.10.7** 179, 180–2, 225; **1.11.3–4** 147; **2.1.5** 147; **2.10.1** 147; **3.7.2** 200; **4.2** 47–8; **4.2.6** 194; **4.2.8–9** 200; **4.6.3–7** 48; **5.1.4–9** 1–4; **5.4.8–11** 48; **5.4.6** 48; **5.8.4** 147; **5.10.4** 147; **5.10.5** 224; **5.14.1** 226; **5.15.2** 48, 49, 62–3

Zeitlin, Froma 94

Printed in Great Britain
by Amazon